TEEN D... ...SHIP...
JONATHAN CANTERO'S
LIST OF ACTIVITIES FOR
OCTOBER 12, 1988*:

1. Go to school
2. Leave at 11:45
3. Pull up at Mom's house
4. Enter/greet Mom
5. Go to bathroom
6. Prepare knife and handkerchief
7. Go directly to Mom
8. When back is turned
9. Cover her mouth
10. Stab until dead
11. Cut off her left hand

(*Note discovered by Tampa police, buried along with a pile of bloody clothing—following the brutal slaying of Patricia Cantero)

MICHAEL NEWTON

Raising Hell

An Encylopedia of Devil Worship
and Satanic Crime

WARNER BOOKS

To Dave Frasier, for assistance above and beyond the call.

mn

A *Warner* Book

First published in the United States in 1993 by Avon Books

First published in Great Britain in 1994 by Warner Books

A CIP catalogue record for this book
is available from the British Library.

ISBN 0 7515 0673 7

Printed in England by Clays Ltd, St Ives plc

Warner Books
A Division of
Little, Brown and Company (UK) Limited
Brettenham House
Lancaster Place
London WC2E 7EN

Acknowledgments

Thanks are due to the following individuals and institutions for their valuable contributions to completion of this work:

Mary Allely, San Diego Public Library
Michael Aquino, Temple of Set
Yvetta Beeson, Dayton (OH) Newspapers, Inc.
Believe the Children, Manhattan Beach, CA
Nikki Bengal, *San Francisco Chronicle*
Lt. Ray Biondi, Sacramento County (CA) Sheriff's Department
The Blade library staff, Toledo, OH
Linda Blood
Shelly Brant, Washoe County (NV) Library
Cecelia Brown, Riverside (CA) City and County Public Library
Diane Brown, Greater Victoria (B.C.) Public Library
Capt. J.E. Burnett, Nebraska State Patrol
Charleston Newspapers Library, Charleston, WV
Connie Christensen, *Deseret News*
Joan Christianson
The Chronicle, Houston, TX
Dan Clark, San Bernadino County (CA) Sheriff's Department
John Clarke, Richmond (VA) Newspapers, Inc.
Jim Coppfer, *Rocky Mountain News*
Bob Corbin, Arizona State Attorney General
Kati Corsaut, California State Attorney General's office
The Courant, Hartford, CT
John Crewdson
Cult Awareness Network
Lynn Daniel, Seattle (WA) Public Library

Steve Daniels, Wisconsin Department of Corrections
Kate DeSnet, *The Detroit News*
Alyce Diamandis, *The Tampa (FL) Tribune*
Laurel Doud, Southnet, San Jose, CA
Larry Dunn, Clallam County (WA) Sheriff's Department
Donna Ekstrom, Tipton County (IN) Library
Kimberly Ellis, Maine Department of Corrections
Joan Emens, Chattahootchee Valley (GA) Regional Library
Susannah Farley, Richland County (SC) Public Library
Federal Bureau of Investigation
Col. C. Reid Franks, U.S. Army
Dave Frasier, Indiana University Library, Bloomington
Geraldine Frenette, Detroit Public Library
Claudette Gammon, *The Union Leader,* Manchester, NH
The Gazette, Charleston, SC
The Gazette, Montreal, Quebec
The Gazette, Worcester, MA
Col. Clifford Graviet, Delaware Department of Public Safety
Dr. Dale Griffis
Wanda Halsey, *Battle Creek Enquirer*
Harry Hatch, San Bernadino County (CA) Sheriff's Department
Ian Haworth
Bill Heidrick, grand treasurer general, Ordo Templi Orientis
Herald-Examiner library staff, Los Angeles
Mary Ann Herold
Lt. Lon Holbrook, Oregon Department of State Police
Nic Howell, Illinois Department of Corrections
The Houston Post library staff
Indianapolis *News* library staff
Ron Jones, Sullivan County (IN) Sheriff's Department
Sue Joyner, WATCH Network, El Paso, TX
Anita Kaschube, *The Sun,* San Bernadino, CA
Sandra Kellum
Paola Langford, Alachua County (FL) Library District
Misti Lange, Texas Department of Corrections
Michael Langone, American Family Foundation
Lonnie Lardner, KABC-TV, Los Angeles
Las Vegas Metropolitan Police Department
Sue-Ann Lewis, *The Toronto Star*
Sondra London

John Lynch, Montana Board of Pardons
Arthur Lyons
R.W. Macmaster, Florida Department of Corrections
V.L. Makings, librarian, *The Denver Post*
Kathleen Mann, Leon County (FL) Public Library
Gary Maynard, warden, Oklahoma state penitentiary
Michael McAteer, *The Toronto Star*
Dale McCulley
Maryhardy McElwain, Elizabeth Jones Library, Grenada, MS
Memphis/Shelby County (TN) Public Library
Patrick Metoyer, Los Angeles Police Department
Chief Henry Morris, New Orleans Police Department
Sgt. Bill Myer, Quincy (IL) Police Department
The *News-Sentinel*, Knoxville, TN
Oakland *Tribune* library staff
Teresa Osburn, San Diego County Library
Lisa Phillips, Georgia Department of Corrections
Jacqueline Smith Pierce
Ann Pieri, Minneapolis Public Library
Rod Poteete
The *Press-Herald*, Portland, ME
C.M. Price, San Bernadino (CA) Public Library
Dr. Carl Raschke, University of Denver
Debbie Reid, librarian, *The Chronicle-Herald*, Halifax, Nova Scotia
Billie Robinson, Spotswood (NJ) Public Library
Alan Rockoff, Middlesex County (NJ) prosecutor
Rocky Mountain News, Denver, CO
Salt Lake City (UT) Public Library
San Diego (CA) Police Department
San Diego Union library staff
Jack Sanders, *The Ridgefield* (CT) *Press*
Judy Savage, Santa Barbara (CA) Public Library
Pattie Scott, Richmond (VA) Public Library
Charles Sexson, Kansas Bureau of Investigation
Linda Shaw, Noblesville (IN) Southeastern Public Library
Al Sheppard, NYPD Intelligence Division
Maj. Jerry Shoemaker, Alabama Department of Public Safety
Lt. Col. Charles Shrader, U.S. Army
James Simon, Indianapolis-Marion County Public Library
Maj. Lewis Smith, Michigan Department of State Police

Star-Tribune library staff, Casper, WY

Susan Swanson, Morgantown (WV) Public Library

Sheriff David Swift, Brown County, IN

Maury Terry

Maj. Walter Tucker, Mississippi Department of Public Safety

J.E. Turner, Pacific Press Ltd., Vancouver, B.C.

Lt. David VanMeter, Kentucky State Police

Betty Wang, San Diego County (CA) Library

Lt. Raymond Watrous, Connecticut Department of Public Safety

Steve Watson, Tennessee Bureau of Investigation

Janet Williams, Scott County (MN) Library System

C. Daniel Wilson, City of New Orleans Public Library

Lesley Wimberly, president, VOCAL

Sgt. John Yarbrough, Los Angeles County (CA) Sheriff's Department

A belief in a supernatural source of evil is not necessary; men alone are quite capable of every wickedness.

JOSEPH CONRAD

Where true religion has prevented one crime, false religions have afforded the pretext for a thousand.

CHARLES CALEB COLTON

We may not pay Satan reverence, for that would be indiscreet, but we can at least respect his talents.

MARK TWAIN

Introduction

Something sinister is happening today in the United States, and all around the world. Reports of grisly animal—and human—sacrifice are on the rise. Police are inundated with accounts of child abuse involving weird, sadistic rituals. In some states, grave robbing and vandalism, including desecration of churches, has reached epidemic proportions. Authorities cite evidence of strange occult "religions" flourishing among purveyors of narcotics, prostitution, and pornography. From coast to coast, occult practitioners are seen to mingle with the membership of neo-Nazi groups involved in random, mindless acts of violence.

In recent years, concern with cult-related crime has graduated from the supermarket tabloid press to headlines in the *New York Times* and *Wall Street Journal.* Topics once monopolized by Pentecostal televangelists are now beamed nationwide by Oprah Winfrey, Sally Jesse Rafael, Phil Donahue, and Geraldo Rivera. "Satanism" has become the catchall label for a wide range of occult activities, in much the same way that "The Mafia" is still supposed, by some, to represent the ethnic melting pot of organized crime.

Of course, there *is* a Mafia, and some cults *are* satanic. Others practice ju-ju, santeria, voodoo, wicca, palo mayombe, abaqua, macumba, candomble, and a bewildering variety of other creeds. Despite a tendency to mix and match, each cult is separate and distinct in its beliefs, but there are two specific points they share in common.

First, regardless of their views on Satan as a deity or demon, all rely on magic rituals to shape the world around them, punish enemies, and gather personal rewards.

And second, representatives from each have lately stepped across the line from First-Amendment exercise of their religious freedom into violent criminal activity.

1

The heated controversy over cult-related crime has pushed the advocates of both sides to ridiculous extremes. On one hand, Christian fundamentalists circulate paranoid tales of satanic conspiracy, sometimes targeting national celebrities and corporations. In 1977, the McDonald's restaurant chain was accused of making a deal with the devil, donating profits to the Church of Satan in return for continued financial success. According to the rumor, McDonald's founder Ray Kroc had confessed the transaction on a May episode of the Phil Donahue show ... but the bubble burst when the relevant tape revealed no such remarks.

Three years later, Procter & Gamble was the target of a similar whispering campaign, this time alleging that the company's famous moon-and-stars trademark was a satanic logo, denoting a corporation run by devil worshipers. Remembering their lesson from the Kroc fiasco, rumormongers cited their source as an unspecified broadcast of "Donahue" or "60 Minutes." Flat denials from network spokesmen failed to throw the juggernaut off track. By mid-1982, Procter & Gamble was logging fifteen thousand calls per month from customers distressed by stories of satanic soap and lotion. Finally, the corporate trademark was discarded and the controversy died.

Renewed concern with the occult and cult-related crime has also given birth to instant "experts" who derive their daily bread from warning unbelievers of bizarre satanic plots. One such, British author Toyne Newton, suggests an ill-defined conspiracy involving Satanists in England, a Masonic lodge in Italy, and agents of the KGB. Canadian psychiatrist Will Gutowski was widely quoted on the peril of satanic child abuse—until British Columbia's Society of Physicians and Surgeons began investigating his use of exorcism as a therapeutic device. According to the *Vancouver Sun*, provincial coroners are also questioning Gutowski's role in the deaths of four patients. Closer to home, Dr. Rebecca Brown—stripped of her Indiana medical license for blaming leukemia and brain tumors on "demons"—has graced Geraldo Rivera's talk show with impassioned warnings against the satanic scourge.

The flip side of the coin, devoted to a stubborn game of see-no-evil, is composed of cult apologists who fervently reject all claims of cult-related crime. A few—like New York's Dr. Leo Martello, founder of the Witch's Antidefamation League—are cultists in their own right, but the vast majority are "liberal" academics, working overtime to counteract what they perceive as a revival of the Salem witch-hunt. Their basic arguments are sevenfold, designed to counter any opposition, and they run as follows:

(1) Accusations of occult/satanic crime are hysterical "urban legends," invariably spread by Christian fanatics, deranged mental patients, or small children incapable of separating truth from fantasy.

FACT: While anyone can launch malicious rumors, as described above, only police, district attorneys, or duly authorized grand juries can file the sorts of criminal charges that have landed cult criminals in various prisons across the nation and in several foreign countries.

(2) Malicious cops, psychologists, and prosecutors frequently exaggerate the "witchy angle" in sensational cases to promote their own careers or personal religious beliefs.

FACT: In case after case, authorities have deliberately ignored or suppressed cult-related evidence to avoid spooking judges and jurors. Crimes with clear occult involvement are too often advertised as "only" drug-related, "simple" child molestation, and so on.

(3) When criminal charges are filed, they invariably result in dismissal or acquittal of the accused. As FBI "cult expert" Ken Lanning declares, "There is not a shred of evidence. There are no bodies and there is not one conviction."

FACT: While some cult apologists may be forgiven their ignorance of current events, Agent Lanning—with access to nationwide police files—should know better. As this volume amply demonstrates, cult-related killers stand convicted of murder in twenty-three states and at least nine foreign countries. Numerous other occultists are now serving time for practicing their "faith" through acts of arson, rape, assault, cruelty to animals, and similar crimes. Courts in seven American states and in Canada have sustained charges of ritual child abuse in the years since 1984.

(4) When occult practitioners *are* convicted of criminal acts, they always prove to be psychotic loners, generally addicted to drugs.

FACT: Cases involving multiple defendants—"cults" by definition—have been successfully prosecuted in at least eleven states, with similar convictions recorded in Latin

America, Asia, and Africa. Charges range from vandalism and prostitution to first-degree murder, and drug abuse is clearly no defense, since many occult religions consider narcotics a "sacrament."

(5) Convictions are irrelevant in any case, since the accused are not "real Satanists." Satanism is an established religion, duly recognized by the U.S. military and Internal Revenue Service. True Satanists, despite their professed devotion to evil, are therefore law-abiding citizens by definition.

FACT: As demonstrated by Jim Bakker, Jimmy Swaggart, and others, official recognition of a church is clearly no proof against criminal acts by its leaders or membership. More to the point, "magick" religions are famous for their flexibility, defeating any effort to identify "authentic" worshipers. Author Carl Lyons, known for his friendly attitude toward organized Satanism, defines a genuine Satanist as "anyone who sincerely describes himself as a worshiper of the Christian Devil." The same litmus test, excluding Lucifer, should logically apply to followers of voodoo, santeria, wicca, and similar cults.

(6) If recognized occultists *do* commit criminal acts, the police, press, and public should ignore their defendant's religious beliefs, as they would if a Catholic or Presbyterian were charged with robbery. As Virginia criminologist Robert Hicks demands, "Law-enforcement investigators must remove the 'cult' from cult crime and do their jobs accordingly."

FACT: Motives are always critical to the investigation of unsolved cases, prosecution of defendants, and prevention of future crimes. A felon's personal beliefs *may* be irrelevant, depending on the case; not so, if his religion dictates or encourages commission of the crime. Where vandalism, sexual abuse, and homicide become integral parts of cult ritual, those rituals are clearly part of the problem. Police can no more divorce the "cult" from cult-related crimes than they can drop the "sex" from sexual assault or overlook the "race" in acts of racial violence.

(7) Finally, if there was *really* any kind of cult conspiracy, it would have been exposed by now. Somebody always talks. Case closed.

FACT: As the appended cases demonstrate, somebody *has* been talking since medieval times, and for at least a quarter century in the United States. There is no shortage of informants, witnesses, and testimony, much of it collected under oath in criminal proceedings. Even so, a brief review of history discloses how a secret order, pledged to violent crime, may flourish in the proper atmosphere.

In India, a cult devoted to the goddess Kali practiced brutal human sacrifice for some six hundred years before it was suppressed by British soldiers in the nineteenth century. The sect's membership and final body count remain uncertain, but 4,500 cultists were convicted of various crimes between 1830 and 1848, with at least 110 sentenced to death for murder. Colonial authorities estimated that 40,000 victims were butchered by the cult in 1812 alone; one member, Thuggee Buhram, single-handedly dispatched 931 victims before his arrest in 1840.

In the United States, a cult of sorts—complete with hoods and flowing robes, "religious" rituals, and oaths of secrecy—has been committing random acts of violence since the spring of 1866. The original Ku Klux Klan flogged, raped, murdered, and mutilated thousands of victims during Reconstruction, including a two-week orgy of mayhem that left eighteen hundred persons dead or wounded in Louisiana. Briefly suppressed by federal prosecution, the Klan returned with a vengeance in 1915 and has lingered ever since, murdering or brutalizing hundreds more. Its "secret" members have included governors, U.S. senators, at least one president of the United States . . . and still the endless string of crimes continues. Mississippi state authorities took a century to prosecute their first Klansman for killing a black; in North Carolina, jurors acquitted six Klansmen of multiple murder charges in 1980, despite videotapes of the crime. Today, fragmented into dozens of competing factions, openly cooperating with a swarm of neo-Nazi cells, the KKK continues to intimidate its chosen enemies. In several states, the Klansmen and their fascist allies have reorganized as "churches" to disguise their true intent.

Another oath-bound secret society, the Mafia or Cosa Nostra, invaded America in the late nineteenth century, putting down roots from New York to New Orleans, awaiting the bonanza of Prohibition in 1920. Since then, "made" members of the Mafia have mingled freely with criminals of all ethnic backgrounds to create a national—and international—crime cartel. Thousands of recognized syndicate "hits" have been logged in the past century, with only a handful of convictions. In recent years, the native mob has forged alliances with other ritualistic crime "families," including the Japanese Yakuza (featuring full-body tattoos and ceremonial finger cutting), the Chinese Triads (bound by a complex series of oaths dating from the twelfth century), and Latin American drug runners (deeply immersed in voodoo, santeria, and assorted variants).

This volume is designed to separate fact from fiction where the occult/satanic underground is concerned. The work in hand is not a "New Age" catalog or survey of the supernatural. Objective readers need not believe in a literal Satan, voodoo's Baron Samedi, or the Afro-Caribbean *orishas* to realize that others believe in them fervently, calling upon them for guidance and help in their daily affairs. Some rape and kill in that pursuit, convinced that they are acting in accordance with the wishes of their chosen deities. Thus, while the entries of the text include descriptions of some major cults, their leaders, historical background and general information on occult religions, the major emphasis remains on crimes recorded from around the world. With one exception noted in the text, no pseudonyms are used, no facts deleted or revised. It is unnecessary to embellish the reports of cult-related crime.

The truth is grim enough.

ABAQUA

A Cuban-based variant of the santeria religion, abaqua lends the name of its principal ceremony, *Las Matanzas*—literally "the massacre"—to a Cuban province and city fifty miles east of Havana. Worshipers deify most of the same *orishas* found in santeria, but their methods and motives vary. Chief among the differences is a flat rejection of black objects or animals for ritual sacrifice, whereas practicing santeros are less selective.

The aversion to black among followers of abaqua is ironic, considering the religion's pervasive reputation for evil. Texas journalist Jim Schutze describes abaqua as the "darkest" of all Afro-Caribbean sects, noting that members are widely accused by santeros of practicing torture, human sacrifice, and ritual cannibalism. Detective Jim Bradley, with the Metropolitan Police Department in Washington, D.C., agrees that abaqua is the "most dangerous" of santeria's fringe groups, surpassing even palo mayombe in its malignancy.

The cult proved its passion for secrecy in 1978, when a stage play titled *Abaqua* was produced in Havana, depicting various covert rituals for the public. Within two weeks of the performance, every member of the twenty-person cast had been tracked down and murdered by "persons unknown."

That pall of secrecy rules out a comprehensive census of the cult, but it is known that numerous disciples reached Miami in the 1980 Mariel boatlift. Their habit of posing as "Christian" santeros, or even the darker paleros, further confuses the issue. International authorities believe that elements of abaqua may have mingled with santeria and palo mayombe to produce Adolfo Constanzo's Mexican bloodbath in 1988 and 1989, but Constanzo's violent death precludes definitive proof. [See: Palo Mayombe; Santeria]

ABRAXAS FOUNDATION OF EVIL

Based in San Francisco and named for the ancient god of the Gnostics, the Abraxas Foundation of Evil was founded by Nikolas Schreck, an associate of Charles Manson who espouses the motto "Long live death!" In Schreck's credo, Abraxas represents a superior force of nature in which creation and destruction are "united and transcended." Typical humans, Schreck says, have rejected the natural "law of the strong," creating a "catastrophical situation which imperils this planet." To correct the problem, Schreck's foundation would eliminate the weak and undesirable, exalting dominant specimens to a hero's status in society.

On August 8, 1988, Schreck and company joined forces with white supremacist Boyd Rice to host a gathering at the Strand Theater, on San Francisco's Market Street. Described in local newspapers as a "satanic rally," the festival was advertised on posters as a nineteenth-anniversary celebration of Sharon Tate's "sacrifice" by the Charles Manson "family." Schreck and Rice shared the dais with Zeena LaVey, daughter of Anton, who read from her father's *Satanic Bible* while the crowd chanted "Hail Satan!" At this writing, the foundation remains a few million members short of its dominant goal.

ACREE, WILLIAM L.

In the summer of 1982, Denver police detectives Bill Wickersham and Cleotilde Wilson were assigned to investigate mounting reports of child prostitution in the city's Capitol Hill district. Surveillance identified various underage runaways as participants in the sex ring, most of them males between the ages of ten and seventeen. Investigators were struck by the prevalence of satanic tattoos and insignia among hard-core members of the group, including inverted crosses, pentagrams, and the numerals "666."

Interrogating several runaways, Wickersham and Wilson identified seventeen-year-old Donald Bradley as the leader of a seven-member "coven" involved in prostitution. Bradley, in turn, broke down under questioning and named his occult "master" as one William Acree, founder and executive director of a Denver halfway house, the respected Williams Street Center. Aside from pocketing his pimp's commission, Acree also used the boys for sex himself, while Bradley invoked satanic powers to keep the pack in line.

A background check on Acree identified him as a Vietnam combat veteran, wounded four times, who became addicted to heroin in Southeast Asia. The Veterans Administration helped him kick the habit in 1972, and Acree had founded a halfway house for returning veterans before he moved on to delinquents and ex-convicts in 1977. Arrested in September 1982 on two counts of prostituting children and one count of sexually assaulting a child, Acree was instantly fired from his post at the halfway house. A jury convicted him on all counts, in February 1983, and Judge John Sanchez sentenced Acree to ninety days in the county jail. A further five-year prison sentence was suspended, on condition that Acree undergo psychiatric counseling for a minimum of four years. [See: Prostitution]

ALAVE, HERMINIA

A native of Peru, residing near Lake Titicaca, Herminia Alave was the victim of a human sacrifice in 1965. Her infant daughter was killed in the same incident, both victims dismembered, their remains scattered along the lakeshore. The killer, an Indian *yatiri*—or shaman—disguised in American reports with the alias "Maximo Coa," confessed to the double sacrifice, stating that he wished to "pay the devil" in a bid for personal prosperity. Sentenced to six years in prison, Coa continued his career as a ritual killer for hire through the 1980s, with at least seven victims linked to his name.

ANIMAL SACRIFICE

From coast to coast—indeed, around the world—the grim, familiar signs are plain. Old churches, cemeteries, wooded glens, and green suburban lawns give up their dead. Decapitated goats and roosters. Cats eviscerated, some with broken necks, some set on fire. Dogs skinned alive and drained of blood. A silent, largely unprotested reign of terror.

Traditions of animal sacrifice are firmly rooted in history, from ancient Greece and Rome to the Old Testament. Bones and entrails helped divine the future. Blood, strategically applied, was thought to please the gods and ward off evil or disease. A living sacrifice might be a mark of celebration, an apology, a simple gesture of remembrance. Even Jesus was compared by his disciples to a sacrificial lamb. Medieval witch cults sacrificed to their "horned god" in Europe, with coven leaders donning the severed heads of goats, stags, and bulls. When blacks were shipped from Africa in chains, they carried with them rituals demanding blood, to satisfy a pantheon of gods.

Most "civilized," well-educated residents of North America and Europe take for granted that the days of such barbaric practices are well behind us now. If anyone still worships in the form of bloody sacrifice, the rituals would doubtless be attributed to superstitious "heathens" from the heart of Africa, perhaps the jungles of the Amazon. Some tiny, unwashed tribe of living fossils from the Stone Age.

Sadly, such is not the case.

Occult religions stand divided when it comes to sacrifice. Spokesmen for the larger, publicized satanic cults join members of the "wiccan" creed in denouncing blood sacrifice, suggesting alternatives like orgasm, while many of their followers ignore the plea to live and let live. Followers of the Afro-Caribbean cults, meanwhile, describe the act of mutilating helpless animals as an inalienable right of religious freedom, supposedly protected by the Bill of Rights. Jurists and legislators have debated the problem from Miami to Los Angeles without reaching a consensus . . . and while they argue, the slaughter goes on.

In Africa, where the religions of the Bantu and Yoruba tribes provide the roots for New World sects like voodoo, santeria, and palo mayombe, blood sacrifice remains a cornerstone of religious ceremony. Initiations in the ju-ju cult demand an orchestrated list of animals for slaughter, including pigeons, tortoises, hyenas, jackals, snakes, and dogs. On special holidays, a hapless goat is executed by a method known as "the 200 cuts," skinned alive in a protracted ritual of pain before a slash across the throat—the 201st cut—finally releases it from agony. In ju-ju rituals, consumption of the blood and viscera is commonplace, celebrants smearing each other with gore once the sacrifice is complete.

In the New World, blood sacrifice remains an integral part of the various Afro-Caribbean religions, whether it be voodoo in Haiti, macumba in Brazil, or santeria, abaqua, and palo mayombe in Cuba. All these cults, and several more besides, have been transplanted into the United States, with voodoo easily the oldest of the lot. Successive waves of immigration, much of it from Cuba and Haiti, have spread such cults across the continent, their membership most numerous in areas where new arrivals congregate.

In santeria, cultists base their sacrifice upon the preferences of different gods. Thus, Chango—easily pleased—is satisfied with the slaughter of a lamb, goat, rodent, or red rooster. Oshun and Obatala are more selective, demanding white birds or female goats as their due, while Yemaya gets by on ducks and turtles. So numerous are the *orishas*, in fact, that wise santeros like to keep a fair supply of stock on hand. In June 1980, Bronx raiders rescued 138 barnyard animals from three cramped apartments, finding ten more dead at a fourth santero residence. In July 1985, similar raids were staged in Miami and Atlantic City, New Jersey. Police in Washington, D.C., cleaned out an urban santero "holding pen" in October 1987. Dozens of chickens, pigs, dogs, and goats were saved from a filthy Chicago apartment in August 1988 . . . and the list goes on.

Raids aside, practitioners of voodoo, santeria, and related cults succeed in a majority of their attempted rituals. By June 1981, within a year of the infamous Mariel boatlift, Miami River cleanup crews were netting an average of one hundred mutilated carcasses per week. Ron Petty, spokesman for the Dade County Department of Animal Services, told reporters: "Often we'll find sacks of animal parts or little displays set up on intersections, with a goat's head on top. There's no way to stop it." In Orange County, California, during February 1986, decapitated chickens and burned corncobs were found at the base of a tree festooned with severed cow's tongues. Seven months later, in nearby Wildwood Park, three decapitated chickens and a piece of raw coconut were left by santeros. In Newark, New Jersey, sixteen dead animals were found in a public park on September 1, 1988; the list included chickens, dogs, and a decapitated goat whose head was never found. Over the past decade, police in Miami and

San Francisco have also found mutilated animal remains beside the corpses of ritual murder victims.

Pure religion aside, priests of the Afro-Caribbean religions are not above turning a profit on bloodshed if there is money to be made. Petitioners can make arrangements for a special sacrifice to benefit their health, employment, love life— anything at all. Mexico's Adolfo Constanzo preferred human sacrifice as a rule, but he was also glad to torture animals if someone else picked up the tab. His menu listed roosters for $6, goats for $30, boa constrictors for $450, adult zebras for $1,100 each, and lion cubs for $3,100 apiece.

In *The Satanic Bible,* Anton LaVey proclaims that "Under NO circumstance would a Satanist sacrifice any animal or baby." Michael Aquino is quick to echo that sentiment for his Temple of Set, but there is a grim world of difference between theory and practice. LaVey and Aquino claim to speak for all "true Satanists"—that is to say, loyal followers of one man or the other—but the fact remains that their disciples constitute a small minority of modern demonologists. Satanic orders like New York's Asmodeus Society and Michigan's Shrine of the Little Mother have both sacrificed fowl, with the latter group advertising its rituals ahead of time. In Poland, during February 1987, members of the Worshippers of Satan went to jail for torturing a dog to death on Lammas Day. The satanic Process Church of Final Judgment idolized German shepherds, keeping numerous dogs around cult headquarters, but later spin-offs like the "Four P Movement" chose to skin the shepherds, draining them of blood.

Charles Manson's homicidal "family" had contact with the Process, "Four P" cultists, the Kirke Order of Dog Blood, and various other death cults in the latter 1960s. "Family" insiders have related tales of animal sacrifice and blood drinking, supported in part by discovery of numerous animal bones when police dug up the Spahn movie ranch in search of murder victims. At least two such rituals were allegedly filmed by Mansonoids, later described by witnesses for author Ed Sanders.

    It was like a nighttime thing. It started out with people, you know, everybody was sitting around— and they just, uh, one of the cats came, and uh, it was about eleven o'clock at night and uh, they started their trip, right—and, uh, type thing. Just sitting around and a guy brought out a thing of blood and everybody took a hit. Then the guy was, you know, poured it over everybody.

They cut up a dog. Then they brought in a girl in there—two girls. They took their clothes off and poured the blood of the dog on top of the girls. They just held the dog. And they took the girls and they put the blood—and the bodies—all over both of them. And everybody balled the two girls.

In 1979, confessed New York serial killer and Satanist David Berkowitz described an incident from 1976, in which leaders of his coven ordered him to take a job with the Yonkers Animal Shelter. Berkowitz was supposed to steal dogs for the cult—preferably German shepherds—to be used in sacrificial rites. The job fell through, but cult investigators suspect the same group of planting "moles" inside other New York animal shelters. Between October and December of 1980, for example, three German shepherds vanished from a Mt. Vernon shelter in what police called an obvious "inside job," with no signs of forced entry.

A sampling of other cases linked by authorities to Satanworship would include:

August 1964—Guilford, England: Evidence of a black mass held inside a ruined church consists of melted candles, satanic graffiti, and two sheep hearts pierced with wooden stakes.

May 1968—Warwickshire, England: Police seek those responsible for sacrificial rites held in Malvern Park. Evidence includes black candles, an inverted cross, and two animal hearts skewered on an altar improvised from park benches.

February 1975—San Antonio, Texas: A dog is found hanging by its hind legs from a barbed wire fence, skinned and drained of blood, its genitals carved out.

1976–1977—Minot, North Dakota: Several mutilated dogs are found behind the Falcon's Nest, a tavern frequented by known Satanists. Cult member John Carr, suspected in New York's "Son of Sam" murders, admits participation in animal sacrifices around Minot.

1976–1982—Conejo Valley, California: At least two hundred cats are killed and mutilated, many of them disemboweled, by persons unknown.

December 1976—New York City: Three German shepherds are found shot and strangled to death near a satanic ritual site in Untermyer Park.

1977—Nashville, Tennessee: Satanists using an old church as their base of operations sacrifice several dogs and cats, cutting the throats and draining off the blood.

October 1977—Walden, New York: Animal control officers announce the discovery of eighty-five skinned, bloodless dogs over the past twelve months. All the animals were German shepherds or Doberman pinschers.

December 1984—Union County, Ohio: Authorities report at least seventy-six chickens, plus thirty-two dogs and cats, killed in ritual style over several months. In one case, twenty-four cats with broken necks are "stacked very neatly" in the driveway of a Plain City home. Most of the animals are found during cycles of the full moon.

February 1985—Las Vegas, Nevada: Police find a dog decapitated in ritual fashion.

July 1985—Provo, Utah: A teenage Satanist describes the rituals of his coven for police: "Initially we killed cats and stuff—not such a bad deal because there's cats all over the place, you know. We slit their throats across and then cut down to get lots of blood so everyone could drink it. It was salty and sort of scary, but I went for it anyway. You sorta don't think about anything else."

August 1985—St. Clair County, Michigan: Four boys, aged twelve to fourteen, are arrested for torturing animals to death in an old barn. Carcasses recovered from the site include eight cats, a dog, a fox, and a squirrel. The twelve-year-old says he and his friends were "making sacrifices to Satan." The father of one juvenile blames the incident on a twenty-one-year-old man who "got neighborhood kids involved in devil worship a couple of years ago."

November 1985—San Diego, California: The morning after Halloween, a dead cat is found hanging from a basketball hoop at Wilson Junior High School, with ritual candles on the ground below. Another cat, this one with its heart cut out, is found at Pershing Junior High School, in suburban San Carlos.

October 1985—Las Vegas, Nevada: Cult vandals strike at the home of resident Jim Hill, clubbing one of his cats, shaving another and setting it on fire. A pentagram is burned in the front lawn, with "Satin"[sic] painted on the driveway.

1986—Delhi, Ontario: Three teenagers are caught sacrificing animals in a rural barn. The structure is later destroyed by arsonists.

May 1986—Orange County, California: Three dead goats, all hog-tied, are found discarded in plastic bags.

November 1986—Orange County, California: Satanist Ronald Shostrom is jailed for vandalizing an ex-friend's home with occult graffiti, hanging a dead cat on the fence, and smearing blood on the garage door.

1987—Oakland, California: Police receive tips on alleged plans for the satanic sacrifice of a child. Nearing the described ritual site, they hear screams and rush the building, catching several men and women in the act of butchering a cat.

January 1987—Monroe County, Indiana: A resident finds two severed cat legs in his yard. Two months later, a disemboweled, dismembered cat is dumped at the same house.

February 1987—Orange County, California: Six dead cats are found, heads crushed by repeated blows against a brick wall, bodies mutilated in death. The bloodstained wall is decorated with satanic and "ninja" graffiti.

April 1987—Allen County, Indiana: Police find three headless dogs and two adult deer with their heads and legs sawed off.

August 1987—Waikiki, Hawaii: Twelve cats are butchered at Magic Island Park, in Ala Moana.

Autumn 1987—Joplin, Missouri: Teenage Satanists warm up for the ritual murder of classmate Steve Newberry by torturing animals to death, cutting off legs and gouging out eyes. One dog is burned to death in a clothes dryer. As a participant recalls the experience: "I was fascinated to see the guts. It was a momentous thing to look back on and talk about."

October 1987—Geneva, Alabama: Authorities report forty animals killed and mutilated over two months, all with their sex organs removed.

March 1988—Bedford, Indiana: Police suspect cultists in the disappearance of 250 dogs and cats over a span of five months.

Authorities typically investigate such cases under statutes dealing with cruelty to animals, with mixed results. Some self-proclaimed Satanists have been convicted, in America and Poland, but the major thrust of prosecution is directed toward Afro-Caribbean cults that freely admit to animal sacrifice. In July 1985, fifteen santeros were jailed for abusing animals in Miami; another nineteen were arrested the same month in Atlantic City, New Jersey. Florida's state attorney general banned animal sacrifice in July 1987, backing down a month later with pronouncements that the butchery should be "humane." The Los Angeles City Council, meanwhile, outlawed animal sacrifice in October 1990, imposing penalties of six months in jail and a $1,000 fine. Most jurisdictions have adopted a "wait-and-see" attitude, apparently hoping the problem will disappear on its own. [See: Livestock Mutilations]

AQUINO, MICHAEL

Born in Santa Barbara, California, where he ranked tenth in his 1964 high school graduating class, Michael Aquino is also a former national commander of the Eagle Scouts Honor Society. A volunteer soldier in uneasy times, he served nine months in Vietnam as a lieutenant with the army's 82d Airborne unit. Stateside, looking forward to a San Francisco wedding in 1968, Aquino noted an advertisement for Anton LaVey's Church of Satan in the *Berkeley Barb*. Intrigued, he wound up visiting LaVey's home on a whim, taking his fiancée and several friends along for the ride.

Aquino was instantly impressed with the Black Pope, comparing LaVey to "a grizzly bear on its hind legs." They became fast friends, and Aquino was ordained as a satanic priest in 1970, heading up a small "grotto" in Kentucky, where he was then stationed with the army. On the side, he lectured on Satanism at the University of Louisville, an estimated dozen followers—including military personnel—convening at his home for rituals aimed, in Aquino's words, at "destroying the influence of conventional religion in human affairs." (Satanism, in Aquino's view, qualified as an "unreligion.") In August 1973, Aquino was elevated to the rank of Magister Templi, the only Church of Satan member besides LaVey to wear that exalted title.

All was not well in the Black Pope's dominion, however. Aquino came to see the Church of Satan as increasingly corrupt, while LaVey was put off by Aquino's egotism and intellectual snobbery. Perhaps the best-educated devil worshiper of modern times, Aquino had earned his Master of Public Administration from George Washington University, and would later earn a Ph.D. in political science from UC Santa Barbara, submitting a dissertation on tactical deployment of the neutron bomb in Europe. By mid-1975, dissension had reached the point where Aquino decided to jump ship, followed by wife-to-be Lilith Sinclair and several members of her "Lilith Grotto" in Spotswood, New Jersey.

On the night of June 21, 1975, Aquino performed a magical "working" that produced a manuscript, *The Book of Coming Forth by Night.* As spelled out in the book, Aquino had a visitor—none other than Set, the Egyptian god of the dead. In the course of their chat, Set formally terminated LaVey's "Age of Satan," anointing Aquino as "Magus V of the Age of Set." Aquino would also henceforth be known as "the second beast"—the first being Aleister Crowley, who claimed a visit from Set's mouthpiece, "Aiwass," in 1904. To spruce himself up for the role, Aquino plucked his eyebrows, cut his hair in a severe widow's peak, and had the numbers "666" tattooed on his scalp. Adopting Crowley's vacant title of "Ipsissimus," he christened his wife as "Magistra" in the new Temple of Set.

Church and military duties competed for Aquino's time throughout the latter 1970s. In 1979, he stepped down as high priest of the temple, resuming the office three years later in a dispute with his replacement, whose "restrictive policies" interfered with the "free dialogue of ideas." In the meantime, Aquino had received a Top Secret clearance from the army in June 1981, and began reporting directly to the Joint Chiefs of Staff the same year, with the rank of lieutenant colonel.

Aquino's public statements stress his devotion to the constitutional separation of church and state, but there is reason to suspect that his satanic—or "Setian"—philosophies have influenced Aquino's performance in uniform. A glance at the official Temple of Set Reading List reveals Aquino's fascination with ESP—dubbed "Metamind" in Setian jargon—and the application of mind-control techniques—christened "lesser black magic" or "LBM"—in what Aquino vaguely calls "appropriate situations." The military uses of LBM are explored in an article coauthored by Aquino for the army's *Military Review,* titled "From PSYOP to MindWar: The Psychology of Victory." America lost the Vietnam war, Aquino writes, "not because we were out-fought, but because we were out-PSYOPed." In future conflicts, he suggests, we can avoid defeat by utilizing the "national will to victory" as a kind of ESP superweapon against our enemies.

Copies of the MindWar article distributed within the Temple of Set came complete with a cover sheet identifying the source as "HEADQUARTERS IMPERIAL STORMTROOP FORCE/Office of the Chief of Staff/MindWar Center/Hub Four." A joke, perhaps, but during 1985 the U.S. Army commissioned a two-year, $425,000 study by the National Research Council on military applications of biofeedback, psychokinesis, ESP, and "remote viewing." The December 1987 NRC report dismissed such techniques as "scientifically unsupportable," but the army continues to spend an annual 200,000 tax dollars in the pursuit of "MindWar."

Another pet topic of Aquino's is Nazi Germany, specifically the occult delusions of Heinrich Himmler and other ranking fascists. As Aquino describes Nazi magic: "Many of the techniques perfected by the Nazis continue to be used/abused—generally in a superficial and ignorant fashion—by every country of the world in one guise or another. The magician who can recognize and identify these techniques and the principles behind them can thus control or avoid their influence as desired."

To that end, Aquino interrupted an October 1984 tour of NATO bases in Europe with a stop at Himmler's Wewelsburg castle, in Westphalia. There, in the "Hall of the Dead" where Himmler and his SS cronies once performed their own black magic rituals, Aquino devoted ninety minutes to a "working" of his own. As he later described the experience for his disciples: "The reality of this chamber rushed in upon me. This was no Hollywood set, no ordinary room painted and decorated to titillate the senses. Twelve hundred thirty-five inmates of the Niederhagen concentration camp died during the reconstruction of the Wewelsburg for the SS. If the Marble Hall and the Walhalla were memorials to a certain unique quality in mankind, they also serve as grisly reminders of the penalty mankind pays for that quality."

A year later, Aquino's fascination with the "unique quality" of Nazism was cited as a major complaint by defectors who left his church to form the competing Temple of Nepthys. Published denials notwithstanding, Aquino's deliberately ambiguous treatment of Nazism, tinged with open admiration for "a state based on magical rather than conventional principles," remains a major bone of contention with his critics.

Aquino was virtually unknown to the public before January 1986, when a *Penthouse* article on Satanism described his role in the Temple of Set and named him (falsely) as an instructor at the army's War College. My query to the army, fourteen months later, brought a curious response from Lt. Col. Charles Shrader, which read:

> I did some checking on the mysterious Dr. Michael Aquino. He certainly has never taught anything at the U.S. Army War College and there is no one by that name in the Army Register (the official list of officers in all components of the Army). I suspect he may be a figment of the *Penthouse* author's imagination.

A few months later, when Lieutenant Colonel Aquino surfaced in California news reports, I sent the clippings on to Shrader, and received this response from his replacement, Col. C. Reid Franks, in December 1987.

> Unfortunately the information [Shrader] provided you was not correct. Lt. Col. Aquino does exist. He is a reserve officer who has been serving on active duty for about the past six years. Maybe [Shrader] checked the wrong section of the Army Register, but I am sorry that we gave you false information.

By that time, the army's motive for wishing Aquino out of existence was obvious. A three-year-old girl, reportedly molested at the army's Presidio day-care center in San Francisco, had fingered Aquino as the same "Mikey" who photographed her in the nude and sexually abused her in a black-painted room with a cross on the ceiling. On August 14, 1987, Aquino's home was raided by police detectives, FBI agents, and members of the army's Criminal Investigation Division. Several carloads of "evidence" were seized in what Aquino called a "modern witch-hunt in the most classical sense," but no charges were ever filed against Aquino or any member of his church. In April 1989, Aquino filed formal complaints against two SFPD detectives involved in the raid, and police commissioners sustained the complaints in November 1990. Detective Sandi Gallant was "counseled" to avoid derogatory comments on Aquino's church or lifestyle, while Detective Glen Pamfiloff got a written reprimand for his conduct on the 1987 raid.

Aside from bookings on the Oprah Winfrey and Geraldo Rivera TV talk shows, Aquino's brush with the police provided him with an excuse for endless, windy editorials bemoaning the cruel persecution of innocent Satanists by hysterical Christians—a penchant for correspondence described by author Art Lyons as "computer diarrhea." The net result appears to be a gradual decline in the Temple of Set's already-small membership, with no recovery in sight. [See: Nazism; Temple of Nepthys; Temple of Set]

ARYAN BROTHERHOOD

Spawned by California's prison system in the early 1960s, this violent gang was to white convicts what groups like the Mexican Mafia and Black Guerrilla Family were to Hispanic and black inmates: a combination of armed self-defense, racial pride, and an opportunity to continue criminal activities inside "the joint." Early initiates were required to kill a black as the price of admission, and resignations were unheard of, hence the group's motto: "Kill to get in. Die to get out." The blood initiation was reportedly discarded around 1967, when eager recruits began to outnumber prospective targets.

Today, the Aryan Brotherhood has spread from coast to coast, dealing in drugs, weapons, and contract murders on both sides of prison walls. One of the first politically conscious crime syndicates, the brotherhood remains virulently racist and anti-Semitic, frequently participating in prison racial violence. Hard-core racist groups like the Idaho-based Aryan Nations and the Ku Klux Klan actively recruit from the brotherhood to fill out their slim ranks, and the gang has also displayed a strong affinity for satanic causes. Display of a "666" tattoo apparently began with members of the brotherhood in California's Folsom Prison, and the numerals—arranged in a pyramid configuration or within the leaves of a stylized shamrock—are now widely recognized as the gang's "official" brand.

Gang affiliation with satanic elements apparently dates from 1971, when a merger of sorts was effected between the

Aryan Brotherhood and the Charles Manson "family." By that time, Manson and three of his ladies were sentenced to die for mass murder, but "down" and "out" are two distinctly separate concepts in the underworld of·cults and drugs. As lawmen reconstruct the action, Manson was afraid of blacks in prison, based upon recorded testimony of his racist motives in the Tate-LaBianca murders, and he formed a loose alliance with the brotherhood in self-defense. To pay for his protection, Manson would arrange for his disciples still at large—most of them young and willing women—to cohabit with members of the brotherhood and lend a hand on any minor jobs that came along. With luck and some audacity, both groups might finally achieve their basic goal of freedom for their leaders serving time.

Manson's original link with the Aryan Brotherhood was thirty-three-year-old Kenneth Como, a.k.a. "Jesse James," who finessed the tentative union of fascists and family. Setting a pattern for the future, Manson called Como as a defense witness in his upcoming trial for the murders of Gary Hinman and Shorty Shea. Como was ignorant of the case, but it scarcely mattered, since he was never really meant to take the stand. In July 1971, as planned, Como escaped from the L.A. Hall of Records and promptly disappeared into the Manson maze.

He surfaced again on August 21, leading five Mansonites into a Los Angeles gunshop, where the gang held staff and customers at gunpoint, preparing to flee with a cache of 143 stolen rifles. Silent alarms brought police to the scene, and a ten-minute shootout erupted, climaxed by the capture of five would-be robbers. Arrested with Como were: Mary Brunner, 27 (Manson's first recruit from 1967); Catherine Share, 29; Dennis Rice, 32; and Lawrence Bailey, 23. Another Masonoid, nineteen-year-old Charles Lovett, escaped in the confusion of the firefight, but was later taken·by police. According to authorities, the gang had also robbed a local beer distributor on August 16, making off with $2,600 in cash. Their master plan involved a courthouse raid to liberate Charles Manson—then appearing as a witness in the murder trial of disciple Steve Grogan—followed by an airline hijack scheme to take them who-knows-where.

On October 21, 1971, Como escaped from custody once more, sawing through bars on the window of his thirteenth-floor cell, descending five stories on a rope of bed sheets and crashing into the very courtroom where Manson and friends were tried for the Tate-LaBianca massacre. Fleeing to the street, he was met by Mansonite Sandra Good, but she crashed their getaway van and was caught at the scene. Como remained at large for seven hours before he was bagged and returned to maximum security.

When the L.A. shootout came to trial in February 1973, Dennis Rice filed a guilty plea and was packed off to state prison without delay. His five cohorts pleaded innocent by reason of insanity, but all in vain. Convicted on two counts each of armed robbery, they were sentenced on March 21: fifteen years to life for Como; twenty to life for Brunner and Bailey; ten to life for Share; two consecutive terms of five years to life for Lovett. Sandra Good was tried for helping Como flee captivity, and the court chuckled at her claim that she was kidnapped for the mission, giving her six months in jail to work on new material.

Meanwhile, the link between Manson's disciples and the brotherhood continued. AB member Billy Gaucher was met by one of Charlie's girls when he emerged from prison, and they lived together for a while, before a murder rap put Billy back inside. In San Francisco, members of the brotherhood were linked with several petty robberies, one of them arrested with ID cards belonging to James Willett, a cult groupie who met several Mansonoids during the first Los Angeles trial, later moving his wife Lauren and infant daughter Heidi to a cabin near Guerneville, north of San Francisco, where they shared quarters with brotherhood thugs. Regarding Willett as a potential weak link, the ABers beheaded him on October 20, 1972, and planted him beside the Russian River. Lauren and Heidi remained with the gang, moving to a "safe" house in Stockton. A hiker discovered Willett's body on November 8, and police spotted his car outside the Stockton house three days later, staging a surprise raid that bagged two prison escapees—AB members Michael Monfort and James Craig—along with Mansonites Nancy Pitman and Priscilla Cooper. All were charged with possession of marijuana and a sawed-off shotgun, with the ante raised when officers discovered Lauren Willett's body buried in the cellar. On April 2, 1973, Monfort pleaded guilty to Lauren's murder and received a sentence of seven years to life; the other three pleaded guilty as accessories after the fact and were handed shorter prison terms.

Meanwhile, Manson's relationship with the Aryans had soured in prison, ironically based on the fact that Charlie wasn't racist enough to suit the AB. Words came to blows that summer, with Manson reportedly clobbering Como, and "persons unknown" responded by spiking Charlie's Tang with a strong dose of rat poison. The grizzled doper shrugged it off, describing his near-miss with death as "a new experience," but the AB-Manson alliance was finished, ex-groupies like Pitman and Share defecting to the Como camp, while fading remnants of the family stood fast.

Even without Manson's input, however, the AB continues to walk a fine line between mercenary racism and the occult. In Kenton, Delaware, a member of the brotherhood, condemned to die for murdering a local woman, sports the tattooed name of Abaddon, an angel from the bottomless pit described in Manson's favorite section of the Bible—Revelations, Chapter 9. [See: Ku Klux Klan; Nazism]

ASMODEUS SOCIETY

In 1976 and 1977, Westchester County, New York, was noted for a sudden rash of bizarre, violent crimes, including fourteen attacks by a serial rapist, the wounding of twenty-three women by an elusive "Dartman," and mutilation of numerous dogs in apparent satanic ceremonies. Investigation of the latter incidents unearthed apparent links with New York City's brutal "Son of Sam" attacks during the same period.

Four years prior to the eruption of violence in Westchester County, author John Godwin described the local activities of a satanic cult with Afro-Caribbean overtones. Members were barred from speaking Satan's "sacred name," invoking him with synonyms from the Greek, Persian, Arabic, Syrian, and other languages. One meeting observed by Godwin was held at the luxurious home of a dental surgeon, with eleven cultists in attendance. All consumed drugs during the course of a chaotic ritual, climaxed when a nude black woman lay down on the floor, on top of a Brazilian flag. A naked man wearing a horned goat's head entered the room at that moment, bearing a child-sized white casket in his arms. Removing a straight razor and a live chicken from the casket, he proceeded to decapitate the bird, sprinkling blood over the woman's prostrate body. Following the sacrifice, cult members crowded around the human "altar," smearing blood over the woman and themselves.

At this writing, continued operations of the Asmodeus Society are impossible to confirm or deny. Likewise, no solid evidence has been revealed to link the group with Westchester County's reign of terror, but it strains credulity to imagine two or more bloodletting cults on the prowl in the same neighborhood, working independently of one another.

ATLANTA "CHILD MURDERS"

The curious and controversial string of deaths that sparked a two-year reign of terror in Atlanta, Georgia, have been labeled "children's" murders even though a suspect, ultimately blamed for twenty-three of thirty homicides, was finally convicted only in the deaths of two adult ex-convicts. Today, more than a decade after that suspect's arrest, the case remains, in many minds, an unsolved mystery.

Investigation of the case began, officially, on July 28, 1979. That afternoon, a woman hunting empty cans and bottles in Atlanta stumbled on a pair of corpses, carelessly concealed in roadside undergrowth. One victim, shot with a .22-caliber pistol, was identified as Edward Smith, fourteen, reported missing on July 21. The other was thirteen-year-old Alfred Evans, last seen alive on July 25. The coroner ascribed his death to "probable" asphyxiation. Both dead boys, like all of those to come, were black.

On September 4, Milton Harvey, age fourteen, vanished during a neighborhood bike ride. His body was recovered three weeks later, but the cause of death remains officially unknown. Yusef Bell, a nine-year-old, was last seen alive when his mother sent him to the store on October 21. Found dead in an abandoned school November 8, he had been strangled manually by a powerful assailant.

Angel Lenair, age twelve, was the first recognized victim of 1980. Reported missing on March 4, she was found six days later, tied to a tree with her hands bound behind her. The first female victim, she had been sexually abused and strangled with an electric cord; someone else's panties were extracted from her throat.

On March 11, Jeffrey Mathis vanished on an errand to the store. Eleven months would pass before recovery of his skeletal remains, advanced decomposition ruling out a declaration on the cause of death. On May 18, fourteen-year-old Eric Middlebrooks left home after receiving a telephone call from persons unknown. Found the next day, his death was ascribed to head injuries, inflicted with a blunt instrument.

The terror escalated into summer. On June 9, Christopher Richardson, twelve, vanished en route to a neighborhood swimming pool. Latonya Wilson was abducted from her home on June 22, the night of her seventh birthday, bringing federal agents into the case. The following day, ten-year-old Aaron Wyche was reported missing by his family. Searchers found his body on June 24, lying beneath a railroad trestle, his neck broken. Originally dubbed an accident, Aaron's death was subsequently added to the growing list of dead and missing blacks.

Anthony Carter, age eight, disappeared while playing near his home on July 6, 1980; recovered the following day, he was dead from multiple stab wounds. Earl Terrell joined the list on July 30, when he vanished from a public swimming pool. Skeletal remains discovered on January 9, 1981, would yield no clues about the cause of death.

Next up on the list was twelve-year-old Clifford Jones, snatched off the street and strangled on August 20. With the recovery of his body in October, homicide detectives interviewed five witnesses who named his killer as one Jamie Brooks, a white man jailed in 1981 on charges of attempted rape and aggravated sodomy. These witnesses provided details of the crime consistent with the placement and condition of the victim's body, but detectives chose to file their affidavits, listing Jones with other victims of the "unknown" murderer.

Darron Glass, an eleven-year-old, vanished near his home on September 14, 1980. Never found, he joins the list because authorities don't know what else to do about his case. October's victim was Charles Stephens, reported missing on the ninth and discovered the next day, his life extinguished by asphyxiation. Capping off the month, authorities discovered skeletal remains of Latonya Wilson on October 18, but they could not determine how she died.

On November 1, nine-year-old Aaron Jackson's disappearance was reported to police by frantic parents. The boy was found on November 2, another victim of asphyxiation. Patrick Rogers, fifteen, followed on November 10. His pitiful remains, skull crushed by heavy blows, were not unearthed until February 1981.

Two days after New Year's, the elusive slayer picked off Lubie Geter, strangling the fourteen-year-old and dumping his body where it would not be found until February 5. Terry Pue, fifteen, went missing on January 22 and was found the next day, strangled with a cord or piece of rope. This time, detectives said that special chemicals enabled them to lift a suspect's fingerprints from Terry's corpse. Unfortunately, they were not on file with any law-enforcement agency.

Patrick Baltazar, age twelve, disappeared on February 6. His body was found a week later, marked by ligature strangulation, and the skeletal remains of Jeffrey Mathis were found nearby. A thirteen-year-old, Curtis Walker, was strangled on February 19 and found the same day. Joseph Bell, sixteen, was asphyxiated on March 2; Timothy Hill, on March 11, was recorded as a drowning victim.

On March 30, police added their first adult victim to the list of murdered children. He was Larry Rogers, twenty, linked with younger victims by the fact that he was suffocated. No cause of death was determined for the second adult victim, twenty-one-year-old Eddie Duncan, when his body was found on March 31. On April 1, ex-convict Michael McIntosh, age twenty-three, was added to the roster on grounds that he had also been asphyxiated.

By April 1981, it seemed apparent that the "children's murder" case was getting out of hand. Community critics denounced the official victims list as incomplete and arbitrary, citing cases like the January 1981 murder of Faye Yearby to prove their point. Like "official" victim Angel Lenair, Yearby was bound to a tree by her killer, hands tied behind her back; she had been stabbed to death, like four acknowledged victims on the list. Despite these similarities, police rejected Yearby's case on grounds that (a) she was female—as were Wilson and Lenair—and (b) at twenty-two, she as "too old"—although the last acknowledged victim had been twenty-three. (Chet Dettlinger, examining police malfeasance in *The List,* suggests that sixty-three "pattern" victims were capriciously omitted from the "official" roster, twenty-five of them killed after a suspect's arrest supposedly ended the murders.)

During April, spokesmen for the FBI declared that several of the crimes had been "substantially solved," outraging blacks with suggestions that some of the dead had been slain by their own parents. On April 22, Jimmy Paine, a twenty-one-year-old ex-convict, was reported missing in Atlanta. Six days later, when his body was recovered, death was publicly ascribed to suffocation and his name was added to the list of murdered "children." William Barrett, seventeen, went missing May 11; he was found the next day, another victim of asphyxiation.

Several bodies had, by now, been pulled from local rivers, and police were staking out the waterways by night. In the predawn hours of May 22, a rookie officer stationed under a bridge on the Chattahoochee River reported hearing a "splash" in the water nearby. Above him, a car rumbled past and officers manning the bridge were alerted. Police and FBI agents halted a vehicle driven by Wayne Bertram Williams, a black man, and spent two hours grilling him, poking through the car, before they let him go. On May 24, the corpse of Nathaniel Cater, a twenty-seven-year-old convicted felon, was fished from the river downstream, authorities putting two and two together as they focused their probe on Wayne Williams.

From the start, he made a most unlikely suspect. The only child of two Atlanta schoolteachers, Williams still lived with his parents at age twenty-three. A college dropout, he cherished ambitions of earning fame and fortune as a music promoter. In younger days, he had constructed a working radio station in the basement of the family home.

On June 21, Williams was arrested and charged with the murder of Nathaniel Cater, despite testimony from four witnesses who reported seeing the victim alive on May 22 and 23, *after* the infamous "splash." On July 17, Williams was indicted for killing two adults—Cater and Payne—while newspapers trumpeted the capture of Atlanta's "child killer."

At his trial, beginning in December 1981, the prosecution painted Williams as a violent homosexual and bigot, so disgusted with his race that he hoped to wipe out future generations by killing black children before they could breed. One witness testified that he saw Williams holding hands with Cater on the night of May 21, a few hours before "the splash." Another, fifteen years old, told the court that Williams had paid him two dollars for the privilege of fondling his genitals. Along the way, authorities announced the late addition of a final victim, twenty-eight-year-old John Porter, to The List.

Defense attorneys tried to balance the scales with testimony from a woman who admitted having "normal sex" with Williams, but the prosecution won a crucial point when the presiding judge admitted testimony on ten other deaths from The List, designed to prove a pattern in the case. One of those admitted was the case of Terry Pue, but neither side had anything to say about the fingerprints allegedly recovered from his corpse in January 1981. If they had matched those of Wayne Williams, it is reasonable to assume the prosecutors would have made it known in court.

The most impressive evidence of guilt was offered by a team of scientific experts dealing with assorted hairs and fibers found on certain victims. Testimony indicated that some fibers from a brand of carpet found inside the Williams' home had been identified on several bodies. Further, victims Middlebrooks, Wyche, Cater, Terrell, Jones, and Stephens all bore fibers from the trunk liner of a 1979 Ford automobile owned by the Williams family. The clothes of victim Stephens *also* yielded fibers from a second car—a 1970 Chevrolet—owned by the family. Jurors were *not* informed of eyewitness testimony naming Jamie Brooks as Jones's killer, nor were they advised of a critical gap in the prosecution's fiber evidence.

Specifically, Wayne Williams had no access to the vehicles in question at the times when three of the six "fiber" victims were killed. Wayne's father took the Ford in for repairs at 9:00 A.M. on July 30, 1980, nearly five hours *before* Earl Terrell vanished that afternoon. Terrell was long dead before Williams got the car back on August 7, and it was returned to the shop next morning, still refusing to start. A new estimate of repair costs was so expensive that Wayne's father refused to pay, and the family never again had access to the car. Meanwhile, Clifford Jones was abducted on August 20 and Charles Stephens on October 9, 1980. The defendant's family did not purchase the 1970 Chevrolet until October 21, twelve days after Stephens's death.

On February 27, 1982, Wayne Williams was convicted on two counts of murder and sentenced to a double term of life imprisonment. On March 1, the Atlanta "child murders" task force officially disbanded, announcing that twenty-three of thirty "List" cases were considered solved with Wayne's conviction. The other seven cases, still open, reverted to the normal homicide detail. Police and agents of the FBI were satisfied with their "solution" to the case. And yet . . .

Persistent rumors of cult involvement in the murder series had been dogging homicide detectives since the early days of 1981. That January, an anonymous phone call led searchers to an abandoned house in southwest Atlanta, where neighbors reported strange comings and goings at all hours of the day and night. Inside, manhunters were sickened by a strong smell "like decaying flesh," though no bodies were found. They *did* find two Bibles nailed to the walls, open to passages dealing with human sacrifice, and the old house was littered with cast-off items including an ax, a hatchet, and articles of children's clothing.

Meanwhile, the Congress of Racial Equality was conducting its own investigation of the murders, urged on by local blacks who mistrusted police and the feds. The cornerstone of CORE's efforts was Shirley McGill, a Miami cocktail waitress who described her own participation in a drug-dealing devil-worship cult reportedly active in Florida and Georgia. One of the ringleaders was named as Parnell Traham, a Vietnam veteran and McGill's part-time lover, who sent her to work in Atlanta as the cult's bookkeeper. In Georgia, McGill reportedly worked with a man named Ted Shaw and a woman known only as Joanne; her observations and perusal of financial records indicated a total cult membership of forty or fifty, with most members using code numbers in place of names. Invited to join a cult ritual in March 1980, McGill declined further involvement after her first exposure to drugs and group sex. Assigned to the role of a perimeter guard at subsequent gatherings, she allegedly witnessed animal and human sacrifices, with celebrants slitting their victim's throats and drinking the blood from a chalice. The group was interracial, but ceremonies were led by a naked white man in a goat's-head mask, who materialized in the magic circle "from a puff of smoke." In addition to human sacrifice, McGill also linked the cult with several "business" murders—including that of the woman Joanne, caught embezzling from the treasury. Three other victims were young black boys, one strangled with rope, two others suffocated with plastic bags shoved down their throats. McGill identified Wayne Williams as a member of the cult who sometimes filmed ceremonies but never killed anyone in her presence.

CORE's Roy Innis sketched McGill's story for the press in April 1981, producing immediate demands for her name from the FBI and Atlanta police. With twenty-four hours of the "classified" information changing hands, newspapers headlined McGill's identity, the *Miami Herald* falsely describing her as a drug addict, prostitute, and accused murderer. Police spokesmen were content to dismiss her as a "crackpot" and "pathological liar," prompting CORE to commission a battery of tests. In short order, McGill passed two polygraph examinations, repeated her story in detail while hypnotized and was declared sane by New York psychiatrists. McGill also led private investigators to outlying ritual sites where, among other curious items, they found pornographic magazines, a ten-foot wooden cross, and a squirrel with its throat slit. Ted Shaw, meanwhile, admits knowing Shriley McGill but denies any criminal activity, while Parnel Traham remains unavailable for comment.

Another bizarre twist, first aired in November 1985, involves the possible involvement of Ku Klux Klansmen in the Atlanta "child murders." In that month, attorneys for Wayne Williams, pursuing new evidence for his appeal, uncovered the FBI's classified "8100" file, dealing with covert investigations of the Georgia Klan. Informants told G-men that the KKK "was killing the children" in Atlanta to provoke black rioting, and suspicion focused primarily on brothers Charles, Don, and Ted Sanders. Agents learned that victim Lubie Geter once scraped Charles's car with a go-cart, whereupon Sanders declared: "See that little black bastard? I'm gonna kill him. I'm gonna choke that black bastard to death." When Geter was kidnapped and strangled three weeks later, Klansmen took Sanders as a man of his word. Later, a wiretap caught Ted Sanders telling brother Don to "Find you another little kid." Don's reply: "Yeah, scope out some places. We'll see you later." In early 1981, informants advised that "after twenty black-child killings, they, the Klan, were going to start killing black women." And, in fact, the murders of twenty-seven black women went unsolved by Atlanta police in 1980 and 1981. In May 1982, less than three months after Wayne Williams's murder conviction, a new task force was organized to solve the crimes—a goal which eludes them to the present day. [See: Ku Klux Klan]

AX MURDERS—LOUISIANA AND TEXAS

Between January 1911 and April 1912, an unidentified killer (or killers) slaughtered forty-nine victims in the states of Louisiana and Texas, leaving police baffled. In each case, the dead were mulattoes or black members of families with mulatto children. The killers were supposed, by blacks and law-enforcement officers alike, to be dark-skinned Negroes, selecting victims on the basis of their mixed—or "tainted"—blood, eliminating chosen targets with all the grim efficiency of a fanatic's ritual.

The first attack took place in early January 1911, at Rayne, Louisiana, when a mother and her three children were hacked to death in their beds. The following month, at Crowley, Louisiana—ten miles from Rayne—three members of the Byers family were dispatched in identical fashion. Two weeks later, the scene shifted to Lafayette, where a family of four was massacred in the small hours of the morning.

Texas endured the killer's first visit in April 1911, when five members of the Cassaway family were axed to death at their home in San Antonio. As in preceding cases, the victims died in their sleep, with no evidence of robbery or any other "rational" motive.

On the last Sunday of November 1911, the action shifted back to Lafayette, Louisiana. Six members of the Norbert Randall family were butchered in their beds, each killed with a single blow behind the right ear. This time, police arrested a black woman, Clementine Bernabet, on suspicion of involvement in the crime. She would be held in custody through the spring of 1912, but her incarceration would not halt the carnage. On January 19, 1912, a woman and her three children were hacked to death as they slept in Crowley, Louisiana. Two days later, at Lake Charles, Felix Broussard, his wife and three children were killed in their beds, each with a single blow near the right ear. This time, the killer left a note behind. It read: "When He maketh the Inquisition for Blood, He forgetteth not the cry of the humble—human five."

Stirred by the quasi-Biblical implications, police made several arrests, including two ministers of the miniscule "Sacrifice Church." Rev. King Harris, leader of the sect, had addressed a meeting in Lafayette on the night of the Randall massacre, and informants reported links between the "Sacrifice Church" and certain voodoo cults in New Orleans. Try as they might, police could find no evidence against their several suspects, and all were soon released.

On February 19, 1912, a mulatto woman and her three children were axed in their sleep at Beaumont, Texas. Seven weeks later, on March 27, another mulatto mother, her four children, and a male overnight guest were slaughtered in Glidden, Texas.

Police began to note a geographical pattern in the crimes. Since November 1911, the killer(s) had been moving west, striking at stops on the Southern Pacific Railroad line. The next murders, likewise, would occur further westward on that line, in San Antonio.

Meanwhile, in April 1912, Clementine Bernabet surprised authorities with a confession to the early crimes. While she admitted sitting in on meetings of the "Sacrifice Church," Bernabet insisted that the slayings were related to a voodoo charm, called *candja,* purchased from a local witch doctor. The charm reportedly assured Bernabet and her friends that "we could do as we pleased and we would never be detected." For no apparent reason, they had chosen to test the magic by committing a series of ax murders. Police were ultimately dubious, and Bernabet was never sent to trial.

On the night of April 11–12, five members of the William Burton family were hacked to death in their beds, in San Antonio. Two nights later, the ax-wielding prowlers claimed three more mulatto victims, thereafter lapsing into a four-month hiatus.

The lull was broken in San Antonio, at 4:00 A.M. on August 16, 1912, when the wife of mulatto James Dashiell woke to the pain of an ax shearing through her arm. The killer had missed his target for the first time, and he took to his heels as anguished screams roused the sleeping family. His shaken victim glimpsed only one prowler, but she could offer no coherent description to police.

The bungled raid in San Antonio wrote *finis* to the murder spree, and left police without a single solid piece of evidence. Defectors from the "Sacrifice Church" referred authorities to a text from the New Testament Book of Matthew—"Every tree that bringeth not forth good fruit is hewn down, and cast into the fire"—but detectives never managed to identify a valid suspect in the case. Persistent rumors of a voodoo link in the murders cast further doubt on the theory of ritual slayings by a bizarre Christian splinter group. [See: Voodoo]

BACKWARD MASKING

Defined as the process of recording words or music backward on audiotapes and records, "backward masking" has become a topic of heated controversy in recent years, with some evangelists, politicians, and private groups like the Parents Music Resource Center alleging deliberate attempts to "brainwash" young people with hidden advertisements for sex, drugs, and Satan. Arguments range from flat denials of any backward masking to bizarre allegations of a worldwide conspiracy involving thousands of executives, performers, and technicians in the music industry. The truth, as usual, lies somewhere in between.

It is a demonstrated fact that backward masking *does* exist, and has for many years. In 1969, the Beatles planted backward lyrics on their *Abbey Road* album, hinting at guitarist Paul McCartney's death as a morbid publicity stunt. Popular singers like David Bowie and Marvin Lee Aday—a.k.a. "Meat Loaf"—have acknowledged use of backward masking on their albums, while specifically denying any sinister intent. In 1990, Rob Halford—lead singer for the heavy metal band Judas Priest—told newsmen that backward masking "has been going on for thirty or forty years."

The question, then, must be: To what effect is backward masking used? Musicians who acknowledge use of the technique defend backward masking as an enhancement of their musical range—or, more practically, as a sales gimmick to help move recordings in a glutted market. Fundamentalist spokesmen like Jacob Aranza, on the other hand, cite "expert sources" in defense of their contention that subliminal persuasion is the goal, converting fans of rock 'n' roll to the occult without their conscious knowledge.

In support of that contention, backward masking's enemies produce a list of songs containing "hidden messages" that sometimes strain the ear—and the imagination—of the listener. Led Zepplin's "Stairway to Heaven" played backward, presents a rather garbled "Hail to my sweet Satan." "Snowblind," by Styx, allegedly contains the imprecation: "Satan, move in our voices." Black Oak Arkansas takes a knock for their song "When Electricity Came to Arkansas," reportedly hiding the message: "Satan, Satan, Satan. He is God, he is God, he is God." In April 1986, evangelist Jim Brown convinced Ohio teenagers to burn their records of television's "Mr. Ed" theme song, somehow persuading them that reversal of "A Horse is a Horse" yields "Someone sung this song for Satan."

And so it goes.

Some "hidden" messages are less garbled than others, but how many are deliberate, much less demonic? Is there *any* proof of a conspiracy to brainwash fans of modern music? In the absence of conclusive scientific proof, we must rely upon decisions made in court.

In December 1985, two Sparks, Nevada, "stoners"—eighteen-year-old Raymond Belknap and twenty-year-old Jay Vance—climaxed an epic beer-and-marijuana binge by shooting themselves with a shotgun. Vance survived his disfiguring wound, but died two years later from a drug overdose. In the wake of his passing, product liability lawsuits were filed against CBS Records and the rock band Judas Priest, alleging that the group's 1978 *Stained Glass* album contains a subliminal message—"Do it"—which drove the young men to suicide. A Washoe County judge acknowledged that the words were audible, but expert witnesses identified the sounds as a coincidental overlap of a guitar riff and the singer's breathing. CBS and Judas Priest were cleared in August 1990, but sworn testimony on the subject of backward masking left the door open for future litigation. At this writing, singer Ozzy Osbourne faces charges that one of his songs, "Suicide Solution," was responsible for two teenage deaths in Georgia.

As with any public controversy, image-conscious politicians have scrambled to board the bandwagon. In 1982, the U.S. House of Representatives debated a resolution demanding labels on albums suspected of bearing hidden messages, and the Arkansas State Senate passed a similar bill the following year, with some legislators delivering their arguments backward. It remains to be seen how such legislation will be enforced—or who will decide which recordings are "suspect." [See: Heavy Metal Music]

BAKER, STANLEY DEAN

On July 13, 1970, California Highway Patrol officers received reports of a hit-and-run accident at Big Sur. Three persons had been injured in one car, while two long-haired males sped away in another, fleeing the scene of the crash. Patrolmen found two long-hairs walking down a nearby road and noted similarities in the descriptions. Under questioning, one suspect readily confessed involvement in the accident, startling police when he added, "I have a problem. I'm a cannibal."

To prove his point, twenty-two-year-old Stan Baker turned his pockets out, producing a copy of *The Satanic Bible* and a human finger bone—the latter object removed, he said, from his latest victim in Montana. Baker's sidekick, twenty-year-old Harry Allen Stroup, was also carrying a bony digit, and the pair were taken into custody on suspicion of homicide. A stolen car was found nearby, registered to Montana resident James Schlosser, and detectives in the Treasure State followed Baker's directions to a lonely site on the Yellowstone River, where Schlosser's body was buried, his heart and several fingers missing from the scene.

The case was grim enough, but Baker had not finished talking, yet. According to his statement, he had been recruited by satanic cultists from a college campus in his home state of Wyoming. As a member of the homicidal "Four P Movement," Baker had sworn allegiance to the cult's master—known to initiates as the "Grand Chingon"—and had murdered other persons on the cult's behalf. There had been human sacrifices, he reported, in the Santa Ana Mountains, south of Los Angeles. Displaying cult tattoos, Baker also confessed participation in the April 20, 1970 murder of Robert Salem, a forty-year-old lighting designer in San Francisco. Salem had been slaughtered in his apartment, stabbed twenty-seven times and nearly decapitated, his left ear severed and carried away in a crime that Baker attributed to orders from the Grand Chingon. Slogans painted on the walls in Salem's blood—including "Zodiac" and "Satan Saves"—were meant to stir up panic in an atmosphere already tense from revelations in the Manson murder trial. Bloody fingerprints found in Salem's apartment were matched to Baker's, but San Francisco prosecutors gave Montana first crack at the cannibal killer, losing their man forever when a California court ruled that the delay violated Baker's right to a speedy trial.

Returned to Montana on July 20, Baker and Stroup were convicted of murder and sentenced to prison, where Stanley continued his efforts on behalf of the cult. Authorities report that he actively solicited other inmates to join a satanic coven, and full moons seemed to bring out the worst in Baker, prompting him to crouch in his cell and howl like a wolf. He also threatened prison guards, and was relieved of homemade weapons on eleven separate occasions before he was finally moved to a maximum-security prison in Illinois, for stricter discipline. There, Baker suddenly became a model inmate, counseling fellow prisoners on the fine points of transactional analysis, but he remained devoted to Lucifer. In 1976, the San Francisco—based Church of Satan rejected Baker's application for membership.

Harry Stroup discharged his sentence and was released from prison in 1979. Stanley Baker was paroled in 1985, requesting that his whereabouts remain confidential, but journalists traced him to a Minneapolis suburb six years later. In a televised interview, Baker denied any knowledge of the Salem murder, lapsing into Indian dialect to describe himself as "a good man." In retrospect, he blamed John Schlosser's death on drug abuse and "that outfit in California" which, Baker said, "used powerful prayers in an incorrect manner." [See: "Four P Movement"]

BAKERSFIELD, CA—CHILD ABUSE

A fast-growing town at the southern tip of California's San Joaquin Valley, Bakersfield is best known for agriculture, oil, and country-western music. Singers Merle Haggard and Buck ("Hee Haw") Owens have called Bakersfield their home, but in the 1980s, something twisted poked its head above the placid surface, creeping into headlines that would sicken and embarrass local residents, making their town notorious from coast to coast.

Overnight, it seemed, conservative Bakersfield had become the state capital of child-sex rings, with perverted adults—frequently related by blood or marriage—swapping young victims as if they were baseball cards. In April 1982, two married couples—Alvin and Deborah McCuan, Scott and Brenda Kniffen—were jailed on charges of abusing their own and each other's children over several years. If they ran short of prey, Deborah McCuan was also a Bluebird troop leader, who operated a licensed day-care center in her home. Deborah's parents, Rodney and Linda Phelps, were also charged with thirty-three counts of child molesting, but they skipped bail and disappeared prior to trial. The four remaining defendants were convicted in 1984, collecting aggregate prison terms of over one thousand years. There had been ritualistic elements present in the McCuan-Kniffen case, but prosecutors were willing to dismiss them as signs of "normal" perversion ... until June 1984.

On the twenty-sixth of that month, a young girl complained that she and a neighbor's child had been repeatedly molested by several adults, including the victim's father. Gerardo Gonzales, 31, was arrested the same day on the strength of his daughter's accusation, and the ripples quickly spread, exposing what authorities described as three more child-sex rings in Bakersfield. The "Gonzales-Thomas ring" was said to include at least nine participants, all arrested and charged with multiple counts of child-molesting by February 4, 1985. They included: Gerardo Gonzales (88 counts); his wife Cheryl, 31 (43 counts); Rev. Willard Thomas, 31 (45 counts); Bradford Nokes, 27, and his 30-year-old wife Mary (133 counts); Kathy Scott, 26 (15 counts); Robert Sabovich, 32 (10 counts); Jerry Radford, 34 (5 counts); and Leroy Stowe III (16 counts).

A second group, the "Cox-Taylor ring," was said to include another eight molesters, named by detectives as: Richard Cox, 47 (14 counts); Ruth Ann Taylor, 31 (14 counts); Anthony Cox, 25 (7 counts); George Cox, 24 (7 counts); Theresa Cox, 21 (3 counts); Jeffrey Modahl, 30 (26 counts); Billy Mossman, 31, and 32-year-old Cathy Cox (one count each). Apparently unrelated to the Gonzales-Thomas ring and the furor that followed, most members of the Cox-Taylor ring had been tried by July 1985. Ruth Taylor and four members of the Cox family were convicted on all counts, drawing prison terms that ranged from ten to forty-one years; charges against Cathy Cox and Billy Mossman were dismissed.

Yet another group of pedophiles, the "Pitts-Dill ring," included seven local defendants, identified as: Ricky Pitts, 31; his wife Marcella, 29; Colleen Dill Forsythe, 26; Colleen's husband Wayne Forsythe, 28; Wayne Dill, 26; Grace Dill, 50 (mother of Colleen and Wayne Dill); and Gina Miller. On August 2, 1985, all seven defendants were convicted on multiple counts of molestation, child endangerment, assault with a deadly weapon, and producing child pornography. Wayne Forsythe was found guilty on forty-four counts, with the other six molesters tagged on a minimum of fifty counts each, facing cumulative sentences of some twenty-one hundred years in prison.

Meanwhile, though, the Gonzales-Thomas ring was causing problems for authorities. Suspect Leroy Stowe was convicted on March 6, 1985, and sentenced to thirty years, but the case took a surprising turn nine days later, when victims of the ring began expanding their allegations, incorporating tales of pornography, satanic rituals, blood drinking, urination and defecation, crucifixion on inverted crosses, infant sacrifice, and cannibalism. It was suddenly a whole new game.

·By March 1985, twenty-one alleged victims of the Gonzales-Thomas ring had been sequestered in protective custody. At least nine of those children wound up in group therapy with counselor Carolyn Heim, at a local child-guidance clinic, and it was there that stories of satanic abuse began to unfold for the first time. Sheriff Larry Kleier created a special task force to investigate the case on March 15, and ten detectives began working overtime to collect evidence in a case that had suddenly broadened to include allegations of serial murder. By mid-July, when journalists first learned of the satanic allegations, Sheriff Kleier reported that sixty children and eighty-five adults were involved in the case, with accusations including some twenty-two separate murders.

Sheriff Kleier told the press he was "absolutely convinced" that at least nine children had witnessed—or had been forced to participate in—the ritual sacrifice of infants. Victims spoke of being drugged for rituals, carried to a "bad church" where ceremonies were conducted, later watching corpses burned or buried, sometimes dumped in lakes near Bakersfield. Statements concerning black robes and bondage, defecation, blood drinking and other bizarre rites precisely matched reports from other alleged victims in California and at least a dozen more states.

Critics of the investigation instantly began denouncing the sheriff's "witch-hunt," claiming the children had concocted their stories during group therapy sessions, perhaps with the help of malicious adults. An aunt of one defendant organized the Bakersfield chapter of VOCAL—"Victims of Child Abuse Laws"—and mounted demonstrations at the jail, while accused molesters launched a hunger strike, demanding polygraph tests (inadmissible as evidence in California courts). A rash of death threats and attempted break-ins at the child-guidance clinic cost Carolyn Heim her job in May 1985, but she stood fast in her support of the young victims.

"I believe that all of this occurred," Heim told the media, "meaning the satanic stuff, the molest, the pornography. Those are things that I have heard over and over again in vivid detail and descriptions. I believe there were parents involved. I believe there were families involved, that it was a family kind of activity."

Indeed, Heim reported that some of the alleged crimes dated back at least five years, suggesting the tip of a morbid, insidious iceberg. A thirty-one-year-old Bakersfield woman, identified only as "Ann," told newsmen that she had been subjected to identical tortures around age seven, suppressing the memories for nearly two decades, until they surfaced during psychotherapy. It is also worth noting that I personally interviewed a Bakersfield resident, in 1978, who claimed his sister was part of a child-killing "witches' coven" in Taft, twenty miles southwest of Bakersfield. The sheriff's office was informed, but the results of their investigation—if any—remain classified.

Sheriff Kleier's task force soon ran into difficulties with their search for evidence. Backyards were excavated in vain, and divers plumbed the depths of two nearby lakes in a fruitless search for corpses. Bloodstains were found in one suspect's home, but laboratory tests could never determine if they were animal or human. Worse yet, from the standpoint of witness credibility, several alleged murder victims—all young children—were found alive and well. On the plus side of Kleier's investigation, six children identified a four-by-three-foot board, removed from one defendant's home, as the "rack" they were bound to while being molested. Detectives also flew to Oklahoma, where a seven-year-old former Bakersfield girl told them identical tales of satanic abuse, without prior exposure to counselors or group therapy.

Supporters of the sheriff's case point out that it is easy to confuse a five-year-old, especially one who is already terrified or drugged. In fact, some experts say, deliberate lies are frequently employed by pedophiles to help discredit minor victims, just in case one cracks and spills the sordid story to police. If five-year-old Jane Doe observes a murder, and is told the victim's name is Johnny Smith, she logically believes that Johnny Smith is dead—no matter that the victim's *real* name may be Eddie Jones. When homicide detectives search for Johnny Smith and find him sitting in his first-grade class some afternoon, Jane Doe becomes "a liar," and the case goes up in smoke.

Bizarre as it may seem, allegations of such mind games are typical in ritual abuse cases, a "get-out-of-jail-free" card for accused molesters. Children in Bakersfield and several other jurisdictions recalled incidents of "magical surgery," convinced that bombs were planted in their bodies, primed to detonate the first time they revealed their secret shame. Others were told that hang-ups or wrong numbers on the family telephone were really cultists "checking in" to make sure nasty secrets were safe. Still others were taught to fear men in uniform (like police) or black robes (like judges) as disciples of the cult.

On August 1, a Bakersfield grand jury asked California Attorney General John Van de Kamp to examine the controversial case and report his findings. The probe consumed nine months, and Van de Kamp's report was not released until September 1986. The sheriff's office was criticized for lack of training in child abuse cases and poor coordination that resulted in lost opportunities. Several alleged victims had never been tested for drugs or symptoms of abuse, and haphazard search techniques further hampered the quest for evidence. Likewise, nineteen children had been subjected to 134 interviews—35 for one girl alone—thus producing chaos, contradictions, and accusations of "coaching." Van de Kamp took no position on the satanic allegations, beyond the fact that they had not been proven yet.

As a sideshow to the main event in Bakersfield, victims of the McCuan-Kniffen child-sex ring added satanic allegations to their list of complaints in August 1985. Police in Atascadero dug up the backyard of fugitives Rodney and Linda Phelps, searching for bodies, but nothing was found. The accused molesters are still at large.

With Van de Kamp's report on the record, prosecutors were forced into an unsavory plea bargain. On January 23, 1987, Gerardo Gonzales and Willard Thomas each pleaded "no contest" to one count of child endangerment; Thomas also admitted the unrelated statutory rape of a seventeen-year-old girl. In return for those pleas, pending charges were dismissed against Cheryl Gonzales, Brad and Mary Nokes, and Kathy Scott. (Charges against suspects Robert Sabovich and Jerry Radford were dropped earlier because alleged victims "were not ready to testify.") The "no contest" pleas, while equivalent to a plea of guilty, may not be cited as an admission of guilt in any other court proceeding—such as lawsuits by a victim's family.

Deputy District Attorney Stephen Tauzer was unhappy with the bargain, but he had no choice. "I don't feel good about ending the case this way," he told reporters, "but it is ended." His superiors had judged the case would be "difficult if not impossible to put on" while public doubt surrounded the credibility of youthful witnesses. [See: Child Abuse]

BALDWIN, RICHARD

On July 13, 1982, a San Francisco tugboat operator found a human body floating in the shallows near Two Sister Island, off San Rafael's McNear Beach. Wrapped in a bizarre cocoon of clear plastic and bamboo, the bloated corpse was anchored to an outboard motor lying on the bottom, six feet down. Hitching a line to the bundle, the captain towed it behind his tug to the Mare Island Naval Shipyard, where it was handed over to authorities.

Detectives cautiously opened the reeking parcel, cutting away rope, duct tape, and coaxial television cable before they could unwrap layers of plastic, a bamboo window shade, and a beige corduroy slipcover. Inside, a man's rotting corpse was similarly bound in silver tape, a heavy two-inch rope connecting wrists and ankles, with a towel stuffed in his mouth. The corpse was tied to its makeshift anchor with a six-foot length of bungee cord.

A Vallejo pathologist, Dr. Harold Brazil, performed an autopsy on July 14, discovering two stab wounds in the victim's heart and a star-shaped wound on the left temple, the skull crushed underneath. Decomposition ruled out precise findings, but Dr. Brazil estimated his subject had been dead from five to fifteen days. No identification was found on the corpse, but the fingers were peeled and photographed for prints, identifying the victim as one Richard Baldwin.

The owner of a San Rafael custom auto shop, Baldwin was reported missing by a relative on July 5. Eight days later—the same day his body was found in San Francisco Bay—some unknown person had charged $868 worth of merchandise on Baldwin's Montgomery Ward credit card. Also missing from the body were Baldwin's wallet and the large roll of cash he always carried.

A search of the victim's auto shop on July 15 revealed copious bloodstains, along with a cracked and bloodied baseball bat. Detectives also came away from the shop with duct tape, rope, and bungee cord that matched the corpse's bindings. At Baldwin's Venetia Meadows home, neighbors recalled a young man carelessly backing a pickup truck into the victim's fence on July 6. A contractor's crew had begun remodeling Baldwin's home that morning, but they left at the end of the day and never returned. Inside the house, a safe was missing from the bedroom closet.

The remodeling crew, police learned, had been led by twenty-eight-year-old Mark Richards. Grilling his employees, detectives heard that Richards had been boasting of a robbery and murder that had netted $1,400 cash, a safe filled with jewelry, firearms, and the registration slips for several cars. A coworker nicknamed "Crossy" was involved in the crime, and teenaged Harry Templar had been talking up his own minor role. Richards's girlfriend was sporting flashy new baubles, while informants reported new stereo equipment and an unfamiliar safe in the prime suspect's home. One employee had received a Ruger .44 Magnum revolver in lieu of his last paycheck, and the serial number traced its ownership to Richard Baldwin.

Police had enough for their warrant, swooping down on Richards's home in San Rafael. Arrested at the scene were Richards, Templar, and nineteen-year-old Crossan "Crossy" Hoover. Searchers confiscated more duct tape, a roll of coaxial cable and a bloodstained boat seat, two more of Baldwin's guns, his safe and stereo, plus various keys to the victim's shop, home, and car. Additional evidence seized at the house included objects of medieval appearance and literature for a cult called "Pendragon."

Facing murder charges, young Harry Templar bargained with authorities to save himself. He had helped Richards distract Baldwin with idle talk, Templar said, while "Crossy" Hoover clubbed their victim with a bat and cracked his skull. Afterward, Crossan hammered a screwdriver into Baldwin's chest and temple to make sure he was dead. The motive was far from simple robbery, however, with Richards claiming he needed the proceeds for "Pendragon," to establish a pipe dream kingdom called "Imperial Marin." In Richards's vi-

sion, Marin County would be isolated from the outside world
by blocking Highways 1 and 101, dynamiting the Richmond
and Golden Gate bridges. A nonexistant laser gun would be
mounted atop Mr. Tamalpais to repel air attacks, while Richards's handful of disciples ruled the roost with titles like
"Lord of Nature," "Lord of the Land," and "Lord of Angel
Island." A confiscated list of cultists named victim Baldwin
as "Lord of Transportation," while Richards saved the ultimate rank of "Pendragon" for himself.

With physical evidence in hand and Harry Templar testifying for the state, prosecutors had an airtight case against
Richards and Hoover. Convicted of first-degree murder on
June 4, 1984, Mark Richards was sentenced to life imprisonment without parole. Crossan Hoover got off "easy" with a
term of twenty-five years to life, while Templar was granted
immunity in return for his testimony.

BAPHOMET

A catchall symbol of evil for modern Satanists, the character of Baphomet is traceable to twelfth century occult rituals
practiced by the crusading Knights Templar. Descriptions of
the original Baphomet vary, including a jewel-studded skull
and a pale human head with curly black hair; some accounts
describe a beard, variously portrayed as that of a man or a
goat. Some reports even describe Baphomet as the preserved
head of the original Templar grand master, but the secret was
lost forever in the early 1300s, when the knights were put on
trial for witchcraft and subsequently executed.

The origins of Baphomet's name remain obscure. Joseph
von Hammer-Purgstall, a nineteenth century Austrian occultist, considered the title a merger of two Greek words, whose
conjunction spelled "wisdom," but a review of classical and
modern Greek dictionaries fails to support his theory. Author
Richard Cavendish, in *The Black Arts,* recalls time spent by
the Templars in the Holy Land, and considers Baphomet
"possibly a corruption of Mahomet" . . . but the fact is, no
one really knows.

The face of Baphomet, as with the meaning of its name, remains a controversial subject with occultists. In the late nineteenth century, magician Eliphas Levi sketched the "classic"
Baphomet, depicting a bare-breasted, goat-headed woman

with wings, a pentagram stamped on her forehead, with a torch sprouting between her horns. Aleister Crowley, meanwhile, after tagging himself as Baphomet in 1912, produced drawings of a composite creature including portions of a rooster, ram, elephant, and human being. In 1966, Anton LaVey came up with a new Baphomet, stylized as a goat's head superimposed on a satanic pentagram, which became the Church of Satan's official logo. LaVey's copyright has not prevented the symbol—or Baphomet's name—from appearing in graffiti at ritual sites and crime scenes across the United States.

BATTLE CREEK, MI—UNSOLVED MURDERS

Between August 1982 and March 1983, residents of Battle Creek, Michigan, were stunned by the murders of three young women. Authorities suggested possible satanic motives in the case, and while no link with devil-worship cults was ever proved, the mere suggestion was enough to spread a pall of fear throughout the town.

The first to die was twenty-year-old Margaret Hume, an ex-cheerleader and National Honor Society member found strangled in a closet of her own apartment on August 18, 1982, her body hidden by a pile of clothes and bedding. She had been living on her own for just three months before she died.

Patricia Rosansky, age seventeen, was walking to school on February 3, 1983, when she disappeared within two blocks of campus. She was found outside of town on April 6, her skull crushed, body concealed by leaves and branches in a shallow ravine. "Street talk" linked her murder to a local Satan cult and, while no charges have been filed, police admit their leading suspect is a self-styled Satanist who boasts of leading black masses around Kalamazoo.

On March 13, seventeen-year-old Karry Evans disappeared from rural Bellevue, thirteen miles from Battle Creek. Last seen walking near her grandparents' home, she was found by mushroom hunters on May 10, strangled to death, her body concealed by brush in a swampy area south of town. Once again, there were rumors of demonic involvement, with Evans describing her own occult beliefs in letters to friends, allegedly sporting a jacket with the satanic emblem "666."

To date, no suspects have been named or prosecuted for the crimes in Battle Creek. With passing time, it seems unlikely that the case will now be solved, but homicide detectives still invite new leads, in hopes that someone, somewhere, may provide a crucial piece of evidence to break the stalemate.

BEESON, JOSEPH and BENNETT, EDWARD

Before they pledged themselves to Satan's service, Utah teenagers Joseph Beeson and Edward Bennett were as different as night and day. The only thing they seemed to share in common was a separation from society that made the young men view themselves as outcasts, set apart.

Ideal for Lucifer.

Joe Beeson's "difference" was a matter of rebellion that began in 1981, at age eleven, with his first arrest for shoplifting. By age seventeen, Beeson had run away from home three times, collecting multiple convictions for shoplifting, burglary, theft, forgery, and escape. Court and juvenile homes left little time for high school, and Joseph dropped out during his junior year. Classmates and teachers recall his penchant for paramilitary garb, Nazi salutes, and "white power" slogans. His various tattoos included a swastika, a dragon, and a skull festooned with snakes.

A year older than Beeson, Ed Bennett seemed to be the opposite of Joe in every way. A Boy Scout, Little Leaguer, and devout Mormon, he did well at everything but schoolwork. The difficulty was diagnosed as dyslexia when Bennett was fourteen, and he was enrolled at an experimental facility, without much success. Budget cuts closed the program in Bennett's junior year, and while he dropped out of school, the youth still appeared "normal" to friends and family. Working briefly at a mink farm outside Lehi, Utah, Edward was fired when he refused to help slaughter and skin the animals. "He couldn't do it," Edward's father told the press. "He would never harm anything, animal or human being."

That began to change in 1987, when Bennett was introduced to Joe Beeson by eighteen-year-old Lewis Ivey, a mutual friend in American Fork. In short order, Bennett began his slide into Beeson's world of Satanism and white supremacy, drugs and heavy metal music. Bennett began calling himself "Eddie the Rotting Corpse," venting a new fascination with death when he joined Beeson and Ivey in a short-lived rock band, christened "Rigor Mortis." One of Bennett's songs was later confiscated by police. The lyrics read:

> *Death is rising through the air as thunderbolts strike. Blood is dripping from the walls, someone's going to die. You hear screams of pain and agony as children are nailed on crosses. Kill 'em, let's kill 'em dead. I cry to the depths of Hell. I'm crying to you, oh Lord. I need to kill somebody or tear someone apart. I got to satisfy my need. Cure this thirst for blood. So as I make this sacrifice, I'm doing it just for you and kill this child for it is a first.*

As it turned out, Bennett's lyrics were not strictly metaphorical. By the time Rigor Mortis was organized, Beeson, Bennett, and a dozen other young Satanists were conducting regular rituals in Provo, meeting in condemned buildings that once housed Brigham Young University. Here they sprayed obscene graffiti and satanic emblems in deserted classrooms, labeling a basement as the "Devil's boiler room." Police searches, conducted in 1987, found blood smears on the floor and walls, along with the remains of butchered animals.

Ed Bennett was learning.

The young Satanists combined occultism with Nazi doctrines, calling themselves "skinheads," experimenting with heroin and LSD when they weren't torturing helpless animals or harassing blacks. Unknown to Beeson and Bennett, one of the cultists, eighteen-year-old Jeff Chidester, also doubled as a police informant, keeping detectives up-to-date on local demonology. On January 30, 1988, Chidester set up a drug bust in Salt Lake City, where police confiscated LSD and narcotics paraphernalia, arresting Beeson, Bennett, and three other "skins."

Reluctant to face their day in court, Beeson and Bennett fled westward in Joseph's car, winding up in Las Vegas, Nevada, on February 9. That night, twenty-one-year-old Michelle Moore was shot and killed in the robbery of a local convenience store; a teenage customer, Derrick Franklin, escaped from the store with a .45-caliber bullet in his leg.

Police were stymied for the best part of a month, until Jeff Chidester started talking again, in Utah. This time, he described a March 5 meeting in Pleasant Grove, midway between Orem and Lehi, at which Edward Bennett had boasted of murdering Moore. Joe Beeson was named as the gunman who wounded Derrick Franklin, and Franklin identified both suspects after they were arrested on March 7. On conviction, in June 1988, Bennett was sentenced to die. Joe Beeson pleaded guilty and drew a double term of life imprisonment. In August 1990, Beeson was stabbed and strangled to death by inmates in the state prison at Ely. Ed Bennett awaits execution.

BERKOWITZ, DAVID RICHARD

New Yorkers are accustomed to reports of violent death in every form, from the mundane to the bizarre. They take it all in stride, accepting civic carnage as a price of living in the largest, richest city in America. But residents were unprepared for the commencement of an all-out reign of terror in July 1976. For thirteen months, New York would be a city under siege, its female residents afraid to venture out at night while an apparent homicidal maniac was waiting, seeking prey.

The terror came with darkness, on July 29, 1976. Two young women, Donna Lauria and Jody Valenti, had parked their car on Buhre Avenue, remaining in the vehicle and passing time in conversation. If they saw the solitary male pedestrian at all, he didn't register. In any case, they never saw the pistol that he raised to pump five shots directly through the windshield. Donna Lauria was killed immediately; her companion got off "easy," with a bullet in the thigh.

The shooting was a tragic incident, but in itself was not unusual for New York City. There was scattered sympathy, but no alarm among the residents of New York's urban combat zone . . . until the next attack.

On October 23, Carl Denaro and Rosemary Keenan parked outside a bar in Flushing, Queens. Again, the gunman went unnoticed as he crouched to fire through the windows at close range. Wounded, Carl Denaro would survive. A .44-caliber bullet was found on the floor of the car, and detectives traced it to a Charter Arms Bulldog revolver, but the slug was too damaged for precise ballistics comparison.

Just over one month later, on November 26, Donna DeMasi and Joanne Lomino were sitting together on the stoop of a house in the Floral Park section of Queens. A man approached them from the sidewalk, asking for directions, but before he could complete the question he had drawn a pistol, blasting at the startled women. Both were wounded, Donna paralyzed forever with a bullet in her spine.

Again, the slugs were identified as .44-caliber, without a specific match to earlier shootings. Even so, the Bulldog was comparatively rare in New York's shooting gallery, and detectives suspected they had a random killer on their hands. The gunman seemed to favor girls with long, dark hair, and there was speculation that the shooting of Denaro in October may have been an "accident." The young man's hair was dark and shoulder-length; a gunman closing on him from behind might have mistaken Carl Denaro for a woman in the darkness.

Christmas season passed without another shooting, but the gunman had not given up his hunt. On January 30, 1977, John Diel and Christine Freund were parked and necking in the Ridgewood section of New York, when bullets hammered out their windshield. Freund was killed on impact, while her date was physically unscathed.

March 8th. Virginia Voskerichian, an Armenian exchange student, was walking toward her home in Forest Hills when a man approached and shot her in the face, killing her instantly. Detectives noted that she had been slain within three hundred yards of the January murder scene, and this time they had a positive ballistics match, linking Voskerichian's death with the murder of Donna Lauria.

On April 17, Alexander Esau and his date, Valentina Suriani, were parked in the Bronx, a few blocks from the site of the Lauria-Valenti shooting. Caught up in each other, they may not have seen the gunman coming; certainly they never heard the fusillade of shots that killed them both immediately, fired from point-blank range.

Detectives found a crudely printed letter in the street, near Esau's car. Addressed to the captain in charge of New York's hottest manhunt, the note contained a chilling message.

I am deeply hurt by your calling me a wemon-hater [*sic*]. I am not. But I am a monster. I am the Son of Sam ... I love to hunt. Prowling the streets looking for fair game—tasty meat. The wemon of Queens are prettyist [*sic*] of all ... I live for the hunt—my life. Blood for Papa.

The note described "Sam" as a drunken brute who beat the members of his family, drank blood, and sent his son out hunting "tasty meat," compelling him to kill. The author also called himself "Beelzebub" and the "Chubby Behemoth," occult references that were largely ignored by police. There would be other letters from the gunman, some addressed to newsman Jimmy Breslin, hinting at more crimes to come and fueling the hysteria that had already gripped New York. The writer was apparently irrational—or else he had a message for the city, which detectives were unable to interpret.

On June 26, Salvatore Lupo and girlfriend Judy Placido were parked outside the Elephas disco, in Bayside, Queens, when four shots pierced the windshield of their car. Both were wounded; both survived.

On July 31, Robert Violante and Stacy Moskowitz went parking near the Brooklyn shore. The killer found them there and squeezed off four shots at their huddled silhouettes, striking both young people in the head. Stacy Moskowitz died instantly; her date survived, but damage from his wounds left Robert Violante blind for life. Confused eyewitness reports seemed to describe at least two participants in the shooting, driving separate cars.

It was the last attack, but homicide detectives didn't know that yet. A woman walking near the final murder scene recalled two traffic officers writing a ticket for a car parked close beside a hydrant; moments later, she had seen a man approach the car, climb in, and pull away with squealing tires. A check of parking ticket records traced an old Ford Galaxy belonging to one David Richard Berkowitz, of Pine Street, Yonkers. Staking out the address, officers discovered that the car was parked outside; a semiautomatic rifle lay in plain view on the seat, together with a note in "Son of Sam's" distinctive, awkward style. When Berkowitz emerged from his apartment, he was instantly arrested and confessed his role in the murders, asking police, "What took you so long?"

The story told by Berkowitz seemed tailor-made for an insanity defense in court. The "Sam" referred to in his letters was a neighbor, one Sam Carr, whose Labrador retriever was allegedly possessed by ancient demons, beaming out commands for Berkowitz to kill and kill again. On one occasion, he had tried to kill the dog, but it was useless; demons spoiled his aim, and when the dog recovered from its wounds, the nightly torment had redoubled its intensity. A number of psychiatrists described the subject as a paranoid schizophrenic, suffering from delusions and, therefore, incompetent to stand trial. The lone exception was Dr. David Abrahamson, who found that Berkowitz was sane and capable of understanding that his actions had been criminal. The court agreed with Abrahamson and ordered Berkowitz to trial. The gunman filed a plea of guilty at his court appearance and was sentenced to 365 years in prison.

Ironically, Berkowitz seemed grateful to Dr. Abrahamson for his sanity ruling, and later agreed to a series of interviews that Abrahamson published in a book, *Confessions of Son of Sam*. The interviews revealed that Berkowitz had tried to kill two women during 1975, attacking them with knives, but he turned squeamish when they screamed and tried to fight him off. ("I didn't want to hurt them," he explained. "I only wanted to kill them.") A virgin at the time of his arrest, Berkowitz was prone to fabricate elaborate lies about his bedroom prowess, all the while intent upon revenge against the women who habitually rejected him. When not engaged in stalking female victims, Berkowitz reportedly was an accomplished arsonist; a secret journal listed details of three hundred fires he allegedly set throughout New York. In his conclusion, Dr. Abrahamson describes his subject as a homicidal exhibitionist with fantasies of "dying for a cause."

There is another side to David Berkowitz, however, and it surfaced shortly after his arrest, with allegations of his membership in a satanic cult. In letters mailed from prison, Berkowitz described participation in a New York cult affiliated with the lethal "Four P Movement," based in California. He revealed persuasive inside knowledge of a California homicide, unsolved since 1974, and wrote that "There are other Sons out there—God help the world."

According to the story told by Berkowitz, two of neighbor Sam Carr's sons were also members of the killer cult that specialized in skinning dogs alive and gunning victims down on darkened streets. One suspect, John Charles Carr, was said to be the same "John Wheaties" mentioned in a letter penned by Berkowitz, containing other clues that point to cult involvement in the random murders. Calling themselves "The Children," the cultists operated from a base in Untermyer Park, where mutilated dogs were found from time to time. Cult members represented the "Twenty-Two Disciples of

Hell," mentioned in one "Son of Sam" letter. Suspect John Carr fled New York, in February 1979, and "committed suicide" in Minot, North Dakota, two days later. Brother Michael died in an October 1979 car crash, and New York authorities officially reopened the "Sam" case after his death.

Newsman Maury Terry, after six years on the case, believes there were at least five different gunners in the "Son of Sam" attacks, including Berkowitz, John Carr, and several suspects—one a woman—who have yet to be indicted. Terry also notes that six of the seven shootings fell in close proximity to recognized satanic holidays, the March 8 Voskerichian attack emerging as the sole exception to the pattern. In the journalist's opinion, Berkowitz was chosen as a scapegoat by the other members of his cult, who then set out to "decorate" his flat with weird graffiti, whipping up a bogus "arson ledger"—which includes peculiar out-of-order entries—to support a plea of innocent by reason of insanity.

Berkowitz himself confirmed the occult connection in conversations with fellow inmates and letters mailed out of prison. One such, posted in October 1979, reads:

> I really don't know how to begin this letter, but at one time I was a member of an occult group. Being sworn to secrecy or face death I cannot reveal the name of the group, nor do I wish to. This group contained a mixture of satanic practices which included the teachings of Aleister Crowley and Eliphaz [sic] Levi. It was (still is) totally blood oriented and I am certain you know just what I mean. The Coven's doctrines are a blend of Druidism, the teachings of the Secret Order of the Golden Dawn, Black Magick and a host of other unlawful and obnoxious practices.
>
> As I said, I have no interest in revealing the Coven, especially because I have almost met sudden death on several occasions (once by half an inch) and several others have already perished under mysterious circumstances. These people will stop at nothing, including murder. They have no fear of man-made laws or the Ten Commandments.

The latest near-death experience for Berkowitz had been a July 10 prison assault that left his throat slashed, requiring fifty-six stitches to close the wound. Less talkative following his narrow escape, Berkowitz still agreed to a January 1982 meeting with attorney Harry Lipsig. In that conversation, he referred to the killer cult as follows:

Q: You had some connection with the Church of Scientology, did you not?

A: It wasn't exactly that. But I can't go into it. I really can't.

Q: Were you connected in any way or an adherent or convert of the Church of Scientology?

A: No, not that way. It was an offshoot, fringe-type thing.

Q: Were John and Michael [Carr] with the Church of Scientology?

A: Well, not really that church. But something along that line. A very devious group.

Q: Did this devious group have a name?

A: I can't disclose it.

Q: Roughly, how large would you say its membership was?

A: Twenty.

Q: Were they all residents of the New York metropolitan area?

A: No.

Q: Were they spread across the nation?

A: Yes.

Q: Did they meet on occasion?

A: Yes, but I really can't say more without legal counsel.

As Maury Terry noted, both the satanic Process Church of Final Judgment and its spin-off successor, the "Four P" cult, were "offshoot, fringe-type" movements spawned by Scientology. Both groups were also linked to the Charles Manson "family" in California—as was a convicted killer William Mentzer—named by Berkowitz prison contacts as the triggerman in the January 1977 shooting of John Diel and Christine Freund. Investigation of the bizarre case continues today. [See: Carr, John; Carr, Michael; Cowan, Frederick; "Four P Movement"; Mentzer, William; Perry, Arlis]

BLACK CROSS

Exposed by journalist Maury Terry in 1986, the Black Cross is described by informants as an East Coast satanic cult, closely allied with the national "Four P Movement" and other demonic groups involved with narcotics, prostitution, and pornography. The group reportedly serves its affiliates as a kind of elite, professional "hit squad"—a satanic Murder Incorporated—that eliminates would-be defectors, informers, inconvenient witnesses, and other human prey across the country. Closer to home, Black Cross members are suspected of involvement in New York City's "Son of Sam" serial killings and other, more recent homicides. A reputed triggerman for the group, William Mentzer, stands convicted of a high-profile contract murder in Los Angeles, but authorities have failed to build a solid case against the cult at large. [See: Berkowitz, David; "Four P Movement"; Mentzer, William; Radin, Roy]

"BLACK MAGIC CULT"

A group of teenage Satanists drawn from two Denver, Colorado, high schools, this cult was exposed in 1972, following police investigation of the theft of thirteen choir robes from a church in suburban Northglenn. As it turned out, the robes had been stolen for use in nocturnal rituals that included drug abuse, animal sacrifice, and blood drinking. The case was disposed of in juvenile court.

BLACK MASS

The central feature of satanic worship, popularly known as the Black Mass, apparently began as a gesture of rebellion by European witches during the Inquisition. From relatively benign worship of a pagan "horned god," the early witch cults progressed to active Satanism in the face of clerical persecution, incorporating mockery of the Catholic Mass and desecration of Christian symbols as part of the quarterly sabbat revels. In such fashion, accusations of peasant Satanism soon became a self-fulfilling prophecy.

Descriptions of the Black Mass vary widely from place to

place and one era to the next, but certain common elements
prevail. In most "black" ceremonies, the Catholic missal was
either read backward, or with selective word substitutions—
"Satan" for "God," "evil" for "good," and so on. Defrocked
or renegade priests were sometimes chosen to preside, especially where wealthy Satanists convened. A nude woman was
preferred as an altar, but in the absence of willing females, a
casket might suffice. Sacramental wine was sometimes replaced with plain water, more often with a noxious mixture of
blood, semen, and urine; in some documented cases, infants
were sacrificed, their blood employed as "wine." The sacred
host was either stolen from a church, or else replaced by
items ranging from moldy turnips to human feces, either
eaten by celebrants or rubbed on their faces. Most Black
Masses were said to climax in a sexual orgy, including all
manner of blasphemy and perversion.

In fact, the Black Mass seems to have developed along par-
allel lines, among several different constituencies. While
peasant witch cults mocked the Catholic Mass as a form of
religious protest, heretical sects like the Gnostics, Cathari,
and Luciferians treated the dark rituals as a solemn form of
worship in the thirteenth century. In the early 1300s, members
of the crusading Knights Templar were tried and condemned
for perverting the Catholic Mass in their worship of Baphomet. Gilles de Rais, the original Bluebeard, was executed in
1440 for slaughtering scores of children during Black Mass
rituals in France.

A change of sorts came over the satanic scene in the mid–
sixteenth century, thanks to Catherine de Médicis (1519–89).
The wife of French King Henry II and instigator of the St.
Bartholemew's Day massacre of more than three thousand
Huguenots in 1572, Catherine was known as a woman of "li-
centious and depraved tastes," with a strong affinity for the
occult. Following her husband's death in 1589, she gathered
a personal entourage of cultists and set about refining the
Black Mass into a spectacle of debauchery, initiating royal associates as a means of extending her own influence throughout France and Europe at large.

For the next three centuries, common practitioners aside,
the stylized Black Mass became a tool or pastime of the European rich and famous. France remained a center of satanic
activity, climaxed by the scandalous "Chambre Ardente affair" of the 1670s, linking a mistress of King Louis XIV to

mass murder in the name of Lucifer. Sixty years later, blood sacrifice was conspicuously missing from the rites of England's several "Hell-Fire Clubs," composed of wealthy brigands using Satanism as front for kinky sex. The newspaper *Le Matin* described a French Black Mass in 1889, and six years later, Italian authorities discovered a satanic chapel concealed within the walls of Rome's Borghese Palace.

The twentieth century Black Mass retains its traditional decadence, but many of the modern celebrants are deadly serious in their devotion to the Prince of Darkness. Author William Seabrook, writing in 1940, claimed to have witnessed Black Masses in London, Paris, Lyons, and New York City. In 1942, four men and three women met on a farm in the Spanish Basque country, feasting before they stripped naked, boiled a cat in soup and drank the potion, afterward celebrating a Black Mass with sliced sausage in place of the host. Fresh reports emerged from Italy in the 1950s, and Great Britain suffered a rash of incidents through the early 1960s. In March 1963, six graves were desecrated at Clophill, in Bedfordshire, England, with the bones of one woman arranged on the altar at St. Mary's Church; a rooster was also sacrificed on the altar, while inverted crosses were chalked on the walls. Similar church invasions were reported from Sussex, England, and Ayrshire, Scotland, in 1964. Two years later, in Switzerland, a young girl was beaten to death during a Black Mass conducted by the ironically named "Seekers of Mercy." In 1968, the action shifted back to England, with reports of animal sacrifice in Warwickshire and a violent church desecration in Sussex. Satanists brawled with church elders in the latter incident, before fleeing a twelfth century chapel and leaving their ritual candles behind.

On our side of the Atlantic, Herb Sloane's Our Lady of Endor Coven began practicing Black Masses in Toledo, Ohio, in 1948. Anton LaVey's Church of Satan brought such rituals out of the closet in 1966, inspiring all manner of imitators from coast to coast. While not technically a Satanist, Adolfo Constanzo likewise presided over stylized Black Masses in Mexico City through the mid-1980s, before he shifted his attention to drug smuggling and human sacrifice in the name of palo mayombe. From the admissions of "legitimate" Satanists and evidence recovered at countless crime scenes, there is no doubt whatsoever that Black Masses continue on a regular, if clandestine, basis throughout the United States and Canada.

[See: "Chambre Ardente Affair"; Grave Robbing; Hell-Fire Clubs; Witch Cults]

BLOOD RITUALS

Rejected by prominent American Satanists as Hollywood hokum or the product of Christian paranoia, blood rites remain a standard feature of many occult religions. Whether the donors are human or animal, voluntary or otherwise, the extraction and ritual use (or consumption) of blood is typically viewed as a means of unleashing personal energy, channeling its power toward some predetermined goal.

In the Yoruban ju-ju religion and most of its Afro-Caribbean offshoots, animal blood is freely spilled, splashed, and swallowed in a wide variety of ceremonies ranging from initiations to fertility rites and harvest festivals. African infants selected as future priests of the ju-ju cult are ritually circumcised soon after birth, their bodies smeared with blood from a fresh-killed baby goat. Human sacrifice is also performed by ju-ju practitioners on occasion, for profit or personal reasons, with the blood and flesh of victims serving as ingredients for "magic" powders, soaps, and potions.

In parts of Latin America and the United States, Bantu tribal witchcraft has taken root in the form of palo mayombe, a necrophilic cult that uses a cauldron of blood—the *nganga*—to communicate with ghosts and gods beyond the earthly pale. A stark example of palero magic was revealed at Matamoros, Mexico, in 1989, when authorities broke up a cult responsible for at least twenty-three ritual murders. Fifteen of those victims were tortured to death on a desert ranch, their hearts devoured by cultists, blood and brains stirred into the *nganga* to enhance communications with the spirit world.

Practitioners of "wicca"—pagan witchcraft—typically strive to distance themselves from voodoo and Satanism, claiming devotion to "white magic" and Mother nature. All the same, we know that early European witch cults practiced bloody sacrifice of animals—and, some say, human beings—adding mockery of Christian Masses to their sabbats as the Inquisition gathered steam. Even today, Ann Grammary's *Witch's Workbook* calls for human blood—albeit voluntarily obtained—in certain mystic recipes. If a witch desires to keep a wandering lover, he or she must first obtain a drop of the fickle one's blood. Practitioners tap their own veins for a spell "to make a virgin desire you ardently," while menstrual blood may suffice for conjuring a demon.

While spokesmen for the Church of Satan and Temple of Set publicly denounce blood sacrifice, it still remains a common practice among "black" magicians, especially young, self-styled Satanists who adapt traditional texts and rituals to meet their own needs. Groups like the Asmodeus Society and the Shrine of the Little Mother have publicly advertised bloodletting ceremonies, while other cults prefer clandestine rituals. Defectors from the sinister "Four P Movement" describe bouts of ritual blood drinking—both human and animal—from California, North Dakota, and New York. In the late 1960s, southern California harbored the Kirke Order of Dog Blood, and Charles Manson's disciples enjoyed a hit of blood from time to time. A decade later, L.A.'s "Skid Row Stabber" drew cups of blood from his indigent victims, celebrating in the name of Lucifer. More recently, in Philadelphia, addiction counselors at the St. Francis Medical Center report teenage Satanists guzzling the blood of dogs, cats, chickens, goats, and pigs. Across the country, since the 1970s, police and journalists have logged reports of mutilated livestock, often drained of blood without a drop left at the scene.

In the 1980s, ritual bloodletting was a standard allegation in far-flung cases of satanic child abuse. From Miami and New York to El Paso, Los Angeles, San Francisco, and Washington state, across the border into Canada, scores of children described identical ceremonies, including the sacrifice of animals and infants, with the blood consumed from bowls or chalices. In Bakersfield, California, bloodstains were discovered in one suspect's home, but lab tests failed to determine whether their source was human or animal blood. Across the country, in Maplewood, New Jersey, Margaret Kelly Michaels stands convicted of molesting several youngsters at the Wee Care Day Nursery; one of her proven perversions involved forcing children to swallow her menstrual blood.

Aside from the obvious risk of criminal prosecution, ritual bloodletting may have exposed practitioners to a new hazard within the past decade. Isaiah Oke, a former ju-ju priest in Nigeria, blames ceremonial blood drinking for the rapid spread of AIDS among Africans and voodoo-prone Haitians, neither group known for a high rate of homosexuality or intravenous drug use. While scientists have not addressed the problem, similar concerns have lately filtered down to southern California, where health clinics report increasing numbers of teenagers asking whether AIDS is transmitted by drinking blood. [See: Animal Sacrifice; Human Sacrifice; Livestock Mutilations]

BOILED ANGEL

Described by editor-publisher Mike Diana as a collection of "satanic filth," *Boiled Angel* is a bizarre periodical, issued irregularly—cash permitting—from a post office box in Largo, Florida. Diana addresses his audience as "all you Sick Fucks," catering to that sickness with cartoons and grainy photographs of mutilation, deformity, pustulent genitals, incest, and pedophilia. Typical filler items include photos of surgical implements or Xeroxed news clippings on teenage suicides and priests arrested for molesting children.

In fact, it is the strong "religious" slant that sets *Boiled Angel* apart from the septic mainstream of sadomasochistic pornography. Throughout the magazine, Diana inserts countless pentagrams and goat's heads, inverted crosses, prayers to Satan, and sketches of Christ with a huge, protruding phallus or the caption "Asshole." Crucifixion images repeat obsessively throughout the magazine, including one of Jesus writhing on a giant phallic cross. A collateral fascination with child sacrifice appears in Diana's oft-repeated motto: "Fuck Her and Kill Her." The message becomes explicit in one drawing of a small girl crucified, the cross decorated with pentagrams and the numerals "666," while her frilly pinafore bears the legend "Kill Me!" In case Diana's target audience should miss the point, a sample pact with Lucifer appears wherever space permits, reading as follows:

My Lord and master Satan
I acknowledge you as my God and Prince and promise to serve and obey you while I live. And I renounce the other god and Jesus Christ, the saints and the Church and its sacraments, and I promise to do whatever evil I can and I renounce all the merits of Jesus Christ, and if I fail to serve and adore you, paying homage to you daily, I give you my life as your own. This pact was made the th day of   , 19   , signed

Considering *Boiled Angel*'s preoccupation with the murder and sexual abuse of infants, it is ironic—and, perhaps, coincidental—that the magazine emanates from a town boasting two organizations dedicated to the location of missing children.

BRAKEL, SYLVIA

On May 31, 1982, Düsseldorf police were summoned to a squalid two-room apartment on Metzer Street, pursuing a report of violent death. Discovered by a coworker, Spanish immigrant Jose Luis Mato Fernandez was seated on his couch, completely nude, the fingers of his right hand wrapped around the handle of a butcher knife protruding from his chest. The blade had pierced his heart in one deep thrust, and blood had soaked the cushions where he sat.

Mato Fernandez had been dead over twenty-four hours when police arrived and while the case initially resembled suicide, detectives searched the flat as a matter of routine. Amid heaps of trash and dirty clothes, they found a woman's diary, its first page marked with inverted crosses and a warning that "He who reads this book shall be damned for all eternity." Subsequent entries confirmed the author's obsession with Satanism. "Lucifer, Lord of Darkness," she wrote on one page, "I would sell you my soul; I would bring with you evil into the world. I wait your sign." On April 30—Walpurgisnacht—the diary's owner wrote: "Lucifer. Lord of Darkness. Give me a sign. I believe in you. I want to belong to you wholly. Come to me when Mato is sleeping."

Suspecting that the Spaniard's "suicide" was staged, detectives probed his background, learning that Mato Fernandez had lived with twenty-two-year-old Sylvia Brakel since August 1981. At that, the relationship was a strange one, Mato Fernandez sharing his bed with numerous other women, while Brakel sometimes slept over with a teenage lesbian who called Sylvia "my wife." Aside from kinky sex, Brakel was widely known for her interest in Satanism and witchcraft, frequently serving as the nude human "altar" for orgiastic black masses.

A closer look turned up Brakel's police record, including an August 1981 suspended sentence for stabbing her ex-lover, a baker's apprentice with whom she had lived for three years.

A file assembled at the time named Brakel as a victim of childhood sexual abuse, molested by her grandfather at age eight, gang raped by nine youths at sixteen. A few weeks after the rape, she was arrested for shoplifting and confined to a juvenile "education center" until her eighteenth birthday. Upon release, she moved in with the baker's apprentice, a bisexual Satanist who introduced her to magic ... and other things.

A survey of Düsseldorf's underground soon revealed other Satanists, including Brakel's lesbian "husband," who named Sylvia as the killer of Mato Fernandez. One cultist, a twenty-nine-year-old truck driver, had listened to Brakel's account of the stabbing four hours after it happened. According to Sylvia, Mato Fernandez had hypocritically accused her of infidelity, and a knife thrust ended the raging argument.

Confronted with formal charges and the testimony of her "friends," Sylvia Brakel confessed the murder to police. After four days of deliberation, a German court convicted her of intentional homicide without extenuating circumstances. On March 25, 1983, Brakel was sentenced to life imprisonment.

BROTHERHOOD OF THE RAM

Organized by huckster Don Blythe in the early 1960s, this satanic cult held weekly meetings in its seedy, second-floor quarters fronting Hollywood Boulevard. Income was derived from a Los Angeles bookstore and a campy disco christened Satan's A Go-Go. When not engaged on cult business, Blythe punched the clock at an L.A. pathology lab, pilfering "decorative" relics that included a mummified corpse and various appendages for the sect's ritual chamber.

A typical ceremony, attended by author Art Lyons around 1969, drew twenty celebrants, chiefly long-haired "doper" types. The meeting opened with a reading of Baudelaire's "Litany to Satan," followed by a ritual invocation of Lucifer. Four recruits were initiated that evening, reciting prayers to Satan before each pricked a finger and smeared blood on a scrap of paper bearing his or her signature. The ceremony also featured luminescent "floating eyes" and other cheapjack carnie tricks, climaxing when Blythe commanded a fifteen-year-old disciple to bear her breasts for the mummy.

Apparently geared more toward fraud and cheap sex than assaultive behavior, Blythe's cult lingered into the late 1970s, dissolving from sheer lack of interest near the turn of the decade. At this writing, no visible trace of the Brotherhood remains.

BRUJERIA

Drawing its name from the Spanish word for witchcraft, *brujeria* is an amalgam of the Aztec pagan religion and Roman Catholicism imposed on native tribesmen by Spanish *conquistadores* in the sixteenth century. Primarily concerned with folk magic—including herbal medicine, astrology, magic spells, and divination of the future with tarot cards—*brujeria* claims a goddess, Our Lady of Guadalupe, as its principal deity. As with other forms of witchcraft, *brujeria* is an amoral religion, flexible enough to work for good or evil as the individual practitioner requires.

Today, *brujeria* is found throughout Mexico, and in parts of the United States—especially the Southwest—where Mexican-Americans or immigrants from Mexico have settled in large numbers. As with santeria, some disciples of the cult are known to use their faith in the defense of outlaw enterprises, notably narcotics smuggling. The Aztec bent toward human sacrifice, with hearts removed from slaughtered victims, may explain a rash of unsolved mutilation-murders seen in Mexico throughout the 1970s and 1980s. It has been suggested that Adolfo de Jesus Constanzo may have borrowed elements from *brujeria* to conduct a string of homicides at Matamoros, and authorities in Mexico admit that there are more "religious" killers still at large. [See: Constanzo, Adolfo; Santeria]

BUGH, RANDOLPH S.

Sioux City, Iowa, lies 150 miles from the geographical center of America's heartland, a bedrock of agriculture, political conservatism, and old-time religion in the great Midwest. Famous natives of the Hawkeye State include Buffalo Bill Cody, Herbert Hoover, Billy Sunday, and John Wayne. It is the last place on earth where anyone should logically expect to find the stain of violent satanic crime.

And yet . . .

On March 21, 1991—the spring equinox—a fifteen-year-old runaway from eastern Iowa met three male party crashers at the Sioux City home where she was staying. Around midnight, she joined the trio on a foray to a local all-night market, stealing cigarettes. Instead of returning to the party, though, her new acquaintances drove the girl to a nearby Catholic cemetery, punching her and dragging her behind them when she started to resist.

Inside the cemetery, she was raped repeatedly by two of her assailants, while the third stood by and helped to hold her down. In addition to the sexual assault, she was beaten and kicked, showered with urine, and her head slammed against a gravestone. When she found the strength to question her attackers' motive, one of them replied: "The devil is making us do this to you." Later, in a statement to police, the girl would also recall continuous chanting throughout her ordeal.

Following the rape, her three assailants drove the girl back to the same all-night market, sending her inside to steal more smokes. Instead, she told her tearful story to the manager, and uniformed police arrived in time to bag her rapists in the parking lot.

The three, all known for their devotion to black magic, were identified as twenty-one-year-old Randolph Bugh, twenty-year-old Jayme Mohr, and Jason B. Darrah, age seventeen. In the course of their booking, when routinely asked about religious preferences, one of the rapists answered: "Satanism. I just want to kill somebody."

Justice moves more swiftly in Iowa than in some other states, and all three defendants were convicted at trial in April 1981. Bugh and Darrah, identified as the actual rapists, were each sentenced to seventy-five years in prison. Their accomplice, Mohr, got off "easy," with a sentence of thirty-five years. [See: Rape]

BURKE, FRED KENNETH, Jr.

A thirty-one-year-old Satanist, residing in the Fort Worth suburb of Arlington, Texas, Fred Burke made headlines in May 1989, when he was charged with the abduction of his seven-year-old daughter. Guinevere Burke had become the prize in a custodial tug-of-war between Fred and his estranged wife, Agnes, with Burke's ex branding him an unfit father, citing his occult obsession to support her claim. On May 13, Tarrant County deputies called on Burke at the trailer home he shared with his mother; they had a warrant granting them possession of the child, but the officers left empty-handed, accepting Burke's promise to show up on time for a May 15 custodial hearing in court.

To no one's great surprise, the big day came and went without a sign of Fred or Guinevere. Returning to the trailer, deputies found Burke and his daughter long gone. Their search turned up stockpiles of occult literature, along with a cache of weapons including various knives, swords, and a blowgun. Other items seized included child pornography and a chart with instructions for dismembering a human body. Burke's mother, Coylene Weaver, identified herself to police as a practicing witch, and the search for her son exposed a twenty-member coven in Fort Worth.

Authorities, meanwhile, were understandably concerned for Guinevere's safety, alarmed by Fred's kiddie porn collection and his apparent interest in butchering humans. Agnes Burke hired a private detective to recover her daughter, but the case was broken two months later by standard police work, before the PI could pick up Fred's trail.

On Thursday, July 13, Nebraska conservation officers stopped a stolen car driven by Brad Allen Kovar, of Wilbur, Nebraska. Kovar's passengers were Fred and Guinevere Burke, the girl apparently unharmed. Kovar was booked on auto theft charges, and Guinevere was delivered to a Texas foster home, pending disposition of her case. Fred Burke was held in lieu of $50,000 bond on a Texas kidnapping warrant, later tried and convicted on the charge. In the absence of identifiable accomplices, his links with cult activity in Texas and Nebraska were not pursued.

CANTERO, JONATHAN ERIC

Known to classmates as a "brainy loner" and a wizard with computers, Jonathan Cantero would have passed inspection as a basic "nerd" before he entered high school, in Tampa, Florida. There, around age fifteen, he developed an obsessive fascination with the game "Dungeons & Dragons," pursuing the game's occult motif into serious study of black magic, collecting satanic literature and heavy metal albums by the score. Within a few short months, he was a practicing Satanist, scrawling weird symbols on his body and jotting homicidal daydreams in a journal, focusing around a new desire to kill his mother.

Patricia Ann Cantero, for her part, was not cut out to tolerate a devil worshiper beneath her roof. A Bible-quoting fundamentalist, she tried repeatedly to "free" her son through intercession by the church. She took Jon in for counseling on more than one occasion—to her pastor, rather than a trained psychologist—and finally, in 1986, she swept his bedroom clean of "evil" books and albums, torching the offensive items in a backyard bonfire. The cookout failed to make her point, and a few days later, Patricia slit her wrists, scrawling "GO HELL SATAN" across a vanity mirror before she set the room on fire. A note explained that Jonathan had put a curse on her, and she could no longer live with his blatant Satanism.

Patricia Cantero survived the suicide attempt, and things seemed better for a while, until she started telling coworkers at a local diner that she feared for her life.

With good reason.

On October 12, 1988, Patricia's younger son found her dead in the hallway of the family's Tampa apartment. Her throat had been cut, and she was stabbed forty times in the chest, abdomen, and back. Deep slashes on her hands told homicide detectives she had struggled to defend herself.

The following day, Jon Cantero dropped by police headquarters to make a routine statement. Now a nursing student at a local junior college, he claimed to have last seen his mother three days before she died. Cantero was sporting a bandage on his left hand, and he informed detectives he had fallen on some broken glass. The young man's doctor told a different story, describing the gash as a definite knife wound. When Jonathan dropped by the station house again on October 25, police confronted him with the lie and he broke down on the spot, confessing to the homicide.

Cantero led police to the site where he had buried bloody clothing and some chilling documents, neatly printed in his own hand. One item was a list of "Equipment & Material," including:

1. Knife and sheath
2. Vial and lid for blood
3. Plastic bag for left hand
4. Small bag for money
5. Handkerchief to cover mouth
6. Jeans
7. T-shirt
8. A book of shadows

Another document, dated October 11, was a list of things to do. It read:

Summary
1. Go to school
2. Leave at 11:45
3. Pull up at Mom's house
4. Enter/greet Mom
5. Go to bathroom
6. Prepare knife and handkerchief
7. Go directly to Mom
8. When back is turned
9. Cover her mouth
10. Stab until dead
11. Cut off her left hand

In fact, Jonathan had accidentally slashed his own hand in the struggle, his crime so unnerving him that he refrained from collecting his mother's hand and blood, as planned. He *did* retain enough control to stand above the butchered corpse and read a "poem," found by homicide detectives with his lists and bloody clothes. It ran: "Lord Satan thou I had stricken this woman from the earth, I have slain the womb from which I was born. I have ended her reign of desecration of my mind. She is no longer of me, yet only a simple serpent on a lower plane."

On March 17, 1989, Jon Cantero pleaded guilty to first-degree murder in Tampa. He was sentenced to a term of life imprisonment, required to serve a minimum of twenty-five years before parole. [See: Dungeons & Dragons]

CAROZZA, JOSEPH

Journalist Maury Terry, during his marathon investigation of New York's "Son of Sam" murders, established communications with prison sources close to gunman David Berkowitz, receiving some uncanny predictions of future cult-related crimes in the process. On November 27, 1981, an informant identified as "Vinny" sent a letter out of Attica state prison, including this passage:

Crimes continue. On October 31 was "something." I have details. I sent them out prior to then as insurance. But December 31 is the next date to watch out for. Publicity now would be rash, foolish, and lose a greater good. I want no publicity. *None.* And no "deals" with authorities. Is that enough to show you where I stand? My hope is to prevent any December 31 harm.

In fact, the warning was too vague to prevent more violence on New Year's Eve. Between six and seven o'clock that evening, forty-seven-year-old Joseph Carozza was shot and killed on board his yacht, the *Sarc,* berthed at the Five Slip Yacht Club in New Rochelle, New York. One bullet missed Carozza when the gunman opened fire with a .38-caliber revolver, but two more hit the mark, inflicting fatal wounds to the victim's head and back.

New Rochelle police were "mystified completely" by the slaying, which appeared to have no motive, but Terry had already logged several links between New Rochelle's Westchester County and a satanic cult suspected in the "Son of Sam" serial murders. Furthermore, Terry's investigation exposed business links between Carozza and an unindicted suspect in the "Sam" case. And, while police were stumped for a motive in Carozza's death, acquaintances of the victim did not seem surprised. When news of the shooting broke into a country club New Year's party, some two hours after Carozza's death, a female friend burst into tears, shouting: "I knew they were going to get him."

Terry's information was placed at the disposal of New Rochelle police in early 1982, but the rest is silence. At this writing, the murder of Joseph Carozza remains unsolved. [See: Berkowitz, David]

CARR, JOHN CHARLES

Posthumously named as a suspect in the brutal "Son of Sam" murders, John Carr was born in New York on October 12, 1946, sharing a birthday with premier Satanist Aleister Crowley. He dropped out of college to join the air force, serving in several foreign countries before his transfer to the Strategic Air Command near Minot, North Dakota. Briefly married in 1974, Carr was discharged from the military two years later, in response to charges of drug abuse and disciplinary problems. By that time, New York City was embroiled in "Son of Sam" hysteria, and Carr—by various reliable accounts—was deeply involved in the crimes.

Even before the arrest of triggerman David Berkowitz, in August 1977, there were clues pointing toward Carr as a participant in the serial murders that terrorized New York. Carr was, in fact, a "son of Sam"—Sam Carr, that is—and references to both men abound in the letters that Berkowitz mailed to the press during 1976 and 1977: "Papa Sam," "Sam the Terrible," and "John 'Wheaties'—Rapist and Suffocater of Young Girls." The latter nickname fell into place when journalists discovered Carr had once been listed in a New York phone directory as John *Wheat* Carr—his sister's given name, in fact, was Wheat—and John was often known as "Wheaties" to his friends. The rape-and-murder corresponds to statements given by acquaintances of Carr, who linked him with a murderous satanic cult that practiced rape and human sacrifice.

In North Dakota, undercover officers knew Carr as "a cultie" who was "up to his neck in drugs" as both a dealer and a user. Shortly after his October 1976 air force discharge, Carr was picked up on the streets of Minot, suffering from symptoms of an overdose and injuries related to ejection from a moving vehicle. Under questioning by sheriff's detective Glenn Gietzen, Carr admitted membership in a satanic cult, whose members showed obedience by guzzling their leader's urine from a silver chalice. The group was heavily drug-oriented, and practiced canine sacrifice among other mystic rituals. Cultists were said to hang out around a Minot coffee shop, the Falcon's Nest, where butchered dogs were found from time to time.

Phil Falcon, an associate of Carr's and owner of the Falcon's Nest, confirmed the description of Carr as a cultist. "He kept a list of the demons of hell on him," Falcon said. "And to gain power over people, to put a curse on them, he'd go out and bury [dog] shit on their lawns. He thought this was some black magic curse. He was a Satanist." In fact, Falcon told journalist Maury Terry, Carr was involved with *two* cults—or two branches of the same cult—in Minot and Westchester County, New York. The New York group was described as "very violent, large and underground. They were really into the occult. Their sacrifices went all the way."

On one occasion, Falcon came home unexpectedly to find Carr and another Satanist—Donny Boone, since deceased— slaughtering an animal in Falcon's kitchen, drinking the blood while they stood in a magic circle drawn on the floor. Furious, Falcon threw them out of the apartment, recalling that the blood made "an unbelievable mess to clean up."

If further confirmation of Carr's satanic bent is needed, it comes from his own sister, Wheat, who told police: "John's involvement in the occult I'm not going to deny. There's no way I could deny it. I'd be stupid to deny it."

By the same token, there seems to be no doubt about Carr's link with David Berkowitz. Phil Falcon recalls that Carr often spoke of his "friend Berkie in Yonkers," and Carr's psychiatrist watched him draw pictures of Berkowitz—and floor plans of the gunman's apartment— during therapy sessions. Air force roommate Jeffrey Sloat remembers Carr discussing his friendship with Berkowitz, along with "strange behavior" that included Carr devouring ten-dollar bills smeared with mayonnaise. Carr's brother Michael, another suspect in the New York murders, said that John had been in Houston, Texas, on the day when Berkowitz purchased his .44 Bulldog revolver there. Even Berkowitz himself confirmed the link, in prison interviews. In October 1979, questioned by attorney Felix Gilroy, Berkowitz participated in the following exchange:

Q: Who was John Wheaties?
A: I'd rather not say.
Q: Isn't it true that John Wheaties is John Carr?
A: It is a strong possibility.
Q: You deliberately used his name in a letter, didn't you?
A: Yes.

By that time, however, John Carr was beyond the law's reach. Through the summer of 1977, Carr had begun to travel back and forth, erratically, between New York and North Dakota. Watching television with some friends in Minot on the night that Berkowitz was jailed, Carr saw the bulletin and blurted out, "Oh shit!" On January 31, 1979, he started driving toward New York, intent on staying several months with members of his family, but something changed Carr's mind. Arriving February 4 in New York City, he remained a mere ten days before abruptly flying back to North Dakota, thus abandoning his car.

And two days later, he was dead.

Carr's luck ran out while he was staying with a girlfriend, on the Minot Air Force Base. His friend was out the night of February 16, when a bullet from a .30–30 rifle smashed Carr's skull, his death initially described as an "apparent suicide." As Detective Gietzen told the press, "New York told us Carr was wanted for questioning. I viewed him as a devil worshiper who blew himself away rather than get caught."

Still, there was much that disputed the suicide theory. The day before he died, Carr rented a new post office box, opened a checking account, and spoke with the air force to assure continued delivery of his disability checks—hardly typical behavior for a man who expected to die within twenty-four hours. Carr's girlfriend remembers lifting some money from his wallet as she left the apartment, leaving more cash than she took, but Carr's wallet was empty when police found his body; also missing were a picture of his daughter and a Buddha amulet Carr wore around his neck. More pertinently, blood smears on the wall beside his body contradicted reconstructions of a suicide, suggesting that the body had been moved. The numbers "666" were scratched in blood on Carr's right hand, obviously *after* he was shot, and someone used his blood to write "NY SS" on the baseboard, a cryptic message Maury Terry interprets to mean "New York Son of Sam."

If this was not sufficient proof of homicide, police lieutenant Terry Gardner also received a series of anonymous phone calls after Carr's death, accurately describing the body as found, threatening to "get" Gardner the same way if he pressed his investigation of the case.

Subsequent digging by Maury Terry revealed that John Carr was present in New York City for at least four of

"Sam's" shootings, and he closely resembled eyewitness descriptions of the gunman who wounded Joanne Lomino and Donna DeMasi on November 7, 1976. His subsequent flight from New York was linked by friends to Carr's description of "a chain of safe houses for Satanists on the run in the United States and Canada." Lieutenant Gardner recalls: "We checked with the Canadian authorities, and we were told that some kind of network existed up there for bikers, and that they heard Satanists also sometimes used the same facilities."

It is appropriate for David Berkowitz to have the final word on John Carr's death, in this exchange from a January 1982 interview with lawyer Harry Lipsig.

Q: I take it very frankly that since we have clothed this group in anonymity, that included in the group were Michael and John Carr?
A: Yes.
Q: Do you have any thought that either John or Michael Carr lost their life through the activities of a member of this group?
A: Yes, definitely.
Q: What motive could the members have? Knowledge of your activities?
A: Yes. Violence, fear and rage.
Q: Desire to accomplish their silence?
A: Yes. And just plain sickness—moral sickness.
Q: Were they dedicated to violence?
A: Yes, and depravity and everything else.

[See: Berkowitz, David; Carr, Michael]

CARR, MICHAEL VAIL III

An associate of serial killer David Berkowitz and younger brother of a Satanist linked to the "Son of Sam" murders, Michael Carr was a free-lance photographer and advertising stylist in New York City through the 1970s, doubling as a counselor for L. Ron Hubbard's Church of Scientology. According to reports from close acquaintances, Carr first met Berkowitz in 1975, befriending the chubby loner and inviting Berkowitz to "a floating coven party" in the Bronx. From that association grew a reign of terror that came close to paralyzing social life in parts of New York City for a solid year.

For his part, Berkowitz prefers to hedge about his first encounter with the real-life "son of Sam." An excerpt from the killer's prison interview with lawyer Felix Gilroy indicates his strange relationship with Carr.

Q: When did you meet Michael Carr for the first time?
A: I don't remember.
Q: Was he a nice fellow?
A: No.
Q: Can you distinguish between a person who is—as you would say Michael Carr is—not a nice fellow and an ordinary person?
A: I'd say anybody who worships the devil is not a nice person.
Q: Are you telling me that Michael Carr worshiped the devil?
A: I believe he did.
Q: What was the basis of that belief?
A: I'd rather not say.

At that, the two men got along well enough to go barhopping in October 1976, three months after the "Son of Sam" shootings began. On October 16, an employee of Westchester's Candlelight Inn ejected Carr, Berkowitz, and a companion named Bobby from the tavern on a complaint of boisterous behavior. Moments later, two shots were fired into the bar, one wounding a female patron in the leg. Because no one witnessed the shooting, however, no charges were filed.

Aside from his interest in Satanism and Scientology, Michael Carr also collected fraudulent credit cards, including several in the name of "Baron De Czarnkowski." Indeed, he seemed to fantasize himself as a Russian nobleman, once taking time to sketch a nonexistent family coat of arms. Carr's fascination with nobility leads newsman Maury Terry to suggest that Carr may be the "Duke of Death" referred to in a letter penned to the police by Berkowitz, during the "Sam" murder spree.

In fact, police were anxious to question both Carr brothers in 1979, but they never got the chance. John's North Dakota "suicide" is described elsewhere; his younger brother survived him by less than eight months.

On October 4, 1979, Michael Carr rammed his auto into a streetlight stanchion on New York's West Side Highway, impaling himself on the steering column. Police estimate he was approaching speeds of 75 mph when he crashed, and autopsy results show a blood-alcohol level of .15, though relatives insist he had abstained from all liquor the past three years. In prison, Berkowitz blamed cultists for the "accident," and some detectives were inclined to agree, but no suspects have been identified at this writing. [See: Berkowitz, David; Carr, John]

CARTEGENA, NILDA
and MARRERO, HERIBERTO

On June 9, 1989, thirteen-year-old Nilda Cartegena and fifteen-year-old Heriberto Marrero were driven to school in the Bronx by their uncle. When they failed to come home on time, inquiries were made, but the teenagers had vanished, as if into thin air. Police were summoned, but they had no relevant reports of accidents, arrests, or injuries. Friends and neighbors scoured the Bronx in a desperate search, passing out flyers with photographs of the two teens, and they were still hoping eleven days later, when the case broke.

The cousins were dead, stripped naked, wrapped in plastic garbage bags and dumped near the Whitestone Bridge. A mutilated chicken and a coconut were found nearby, prompting some investigators to describe the murders as ritualistic in nature. Boosting the odds, the double slaying came barely a week after the murder of a Bronx man, his dismembered remains also found in garbage bags.

As yet, no suspects or "rational" motive are apparent in the case.

CARTER, LEROY

Shortly after noon on February 8, 1981, San Francisco police received complaints of a transient sleeping near Alvord Lake, in Golden Gate Park. The report was not unusual, by any means. A verbal warning would suffice, perhaps a trip downtown in handcuffs if the subject was disorderly or drunk. Patrolmen answering the call were not prepared for an excursion through the Twilight Zone of cults and human sacrifice, and yet . . .

Arriving at the scene, two officers were met by a complaining witness, who led them to a clump of bushes where a sleeping bag was partially concealed. A nightstick drew the top flap of the sleeping bag aside, revealing a decapitated human body with a chicken wing and two kernels of corn where the missing head should be. Detectives were summoned, and a search of the area turned up several mutilated chickens in a cardboard box, some fifty yards distant from the corpse. No trace of the victim's head could be found.

Fingerprints identified the dead man as one Leroy Carter, twenty-nine, a black petty criminal whose record included arrests for trespassing, auto theft, assault, and battery. A canvass of his known associates produced no motive for the slaying, but Coroner Boyd Stevens publicly described the murder as a ritual homicide.

With that in mind, the case was referred to SFPD's resident "cult expert," Detective Sandi Gallant. She, in turn, placed a call to Charles Wetli, coroner of Dade County, Florida, and the nation's top expert on santeria. Wetli noted that chickens are routinely sacrificed to various *orishas* in the Afro-Caribbean religion, but corn is specifically sacred to the god Eleggua, ruler of gates and crossroads. Based on evidence from cases in Miami, Wetli advised that the missing head would be buried for twenty-one days, then unearthed by the killers and kept for another three weeks to extract psychic powers, before it was discarded back at the murder scene.

Gallant relayed Wetli's information to homicide detectives, facing ridicule for her efforts, becoming the subject of countless "chicken jokes" around the squadroom. The laughter stopped abruptly when a new report came in from Golden Gate Park on March 22. A black man's severed head had been discovered close to Alvord Lake . . . exactly forty-two days from the date Carter's body was found.

Unfortunately, proof of santeria cult involvement in the case would bring police no closer to a suspect. At this writing, more than a decade after the fact, the murder of Leroy Carter remains unsolved. [See: Santeria]

CASTELLANO, MARIANNA

A native of Naples, Italy, born in 1880, Marianna Castellano was a practicing witch from late adolescence, throughout her adult life. She supported herself by dispensing to her neighbors for a price, spells, charms, and "magic" potions concocted from herbs, animal skulls and bones, the beaks and feathers of birds. Business was good in a land where the evil eye was considered a serious threat, with Marianna able to apply or break a curse, depending on her client's needs.

In 1937, Castellano was hired by a female acquaintance to cast a spell on some of her customer's relatives. Marianna's fee for the job was one dollar a month, for the rest of her life. The payoff seemed modest enough, until the end of World War II and the collapse of Mussolini's government required adjustments for postwar inflation. Even so, the client kept up her payments until 1957, when she decided enough was enough. Informed that no more cash would be forthcoming, Marianna went to call on her customer, armed with a pan full of flaming gasoline. A brief struggle ensued, and Marianna's magic must have slipped that day, for it was she who burned to death. The client was excused on grounds of self-defense.

CATHEDRAL OF THE FALLEN ANGEL

Claiming affiliation with a Los Angeles congregation of the same title, this cult was founded in Cincinnati, Ohio, during November 1970. "High Priest" James Guthrie, twenty-two, claimed forty members in a December interview, confusing matters when he used the alternate title "Church of Satan" for his sect, all the while disavowing connections with Anton LaVey's group of the same name. Unlike the San Francisco Church of Satan, Guthrie said, his group allowed no sexual activity as part of worship, although animal sacrifice was featured during initiations at a thrice-yearly "high mass." Regular "Black Mass" ceremonies were performed each Sunday night, with Tuesday evenings devoted to the study of astrology, ritual magic, and demonology.

Cincinnati proved itself inhospitable to fledgling sorcerers that winter, and Guthrie announced his withdrawal from the city on January 2, 1971. Cutting his members adrift in the absence of a qualified high priest, Guthrie looked forward to a

six-week "missionary-type thing" as he made his way back to
L.A. The confusion of titles was finally resolved when
Guthrie announced his plans to replace mentor Don Blythe as
leader in California's Brotherhood of the Ram. Blythe would
henceforth be semiretired, managing a new "weird museum"
next door to Brotherhood headquarters, on Hollywood Boulevard. [See: Brotherhood of the Ram]

CATRILAF, JUANA

A member of Chile's Mapuche Indian tribe, twenty-seven-
year-old Juana Catrilaf was charged with murdering her
grandmother in 1953. In her confession, Catrilaf described
the victim as a *machi*—sorceress—believed responsible for
both the death of Juana's infant child and the persistent epi-
lepsy which had troubled the defendant over several years.
Finally acting on her superstition, Juana clubbed her grandmother to death, slashing the old woman's forehead, and
sucked some of her blood from the wound, whereupon she
felt "a spirit like a fiery devil" leave her body. Following the
murder, as described by transcripts from her trial, Catrilaf
"felt much better and all the Indians were content." At trial,
Juana was acquitted in the first application of Chile's peculiar
"irresistible force" doctrine applying to cases of human sacrifice.

"CHAMBRE ARDENTE AFFAIR"

In the latter part of the seventeenth century, with the Inquisition already fading, France experienced a sudden rash of
cases linking Satanism to the upper crust of affluent society.
Between 1673 and 1680, at least fifty French priests were executed for performing Black Masses, with additional clerics
imprisoned, but none of those cases matched the scandal that
eventually touched the very court of "Sun King" Louis XIV
himself.

Exposure to the labyrinthine plot began one night in Paris,
near the end of 1678. A wealthy socialite named Madame
Bosse was hosting a banquet for friends, enjoying the wine a
bit too much, regaling her guests with her exploits as a well-
paid fortune-teller for the cream of high society. Along the

way, she let slip a curious comment: "Only three more poisonings, and I shall be able to retire with a fine fortune!" All her guests were amused, except for a young lawyer named Perrin, who filed the remark away and soon carried his tale to a friend on the Parisian police force.

Detectives in Paris were no strangers to murder by poison. Two years earlier, the infamous Marquise de Brinvilliers had been executed for a series of aristocratic poisonings, and rumor had it that she was not the only practitioner in town. A quiet investigation was mounted, with the wife of a detective sent to purchase poison from the talkative Madame Bosse. In custody, Madame Bosse began singing to save herself, painting her operation as strictly small-time, compared with the business conducted by one Catherine Deshayes, a.k.a. La Voisin.

Another fortune-teller to the rich and famous, Deshayes often handled abortions and disposed of unwanted infants for affluent clients. She also dealt in poison, for a price, and rounded off her busy schedule as an occult adviser to some of the wealthiest people in France. Arrested in 1679, she freely confessed to the murders of some twenty-five hundred babies, most of them buried in her garden or cremated in a furnace at her home. No final body count for poison victims was established, but excavation of several thousand bones bore out her story where the children were concerned, and La Voisin was executed on February 20, 1680.

At that, Deshayes was dead and buried before police uncovered the most bizarre aspect of her crimes. Returning for a final search of her home in the spring of 1680, detectives found a hidden ritual chamber, done all in black, with candles and a black drape covering a mattress on the altar. By July, Marguerite Deshayes was describing her mother's participation in satanic rituals, alternately led by a trio of Catholic priests identified as Abbe Guibourg, Abbe Lesage, and Abbe Mariette. Black Masses were performed at the Deshayes mansion on a regular basis, invoking this or that demon on behalf of paying clients.

Chief among La Voisin's customers, in fact, had been Madame de Montespan, chief mistress of Louis XIV. Her specialty was the perverse "Amatory Mass," initially designed to win the king's love, later—after she had borne him several children—aimed at holding his affections when they went astray. Montespan herself had served as the nude "altar" for ritual sacrifice of infants, provided by Deshayes, with Abbe Guibourg invoking Astaroth and Asmodeus, the demons of love and lust. On more than one occasion, Montespan had smuggled renegade priests into the Royal Palace at Versailles, where they performed dark rituals. King Louis had been the unsuspecting recipient of "unholy wafers," concocted out of flour and the blood of murdered babies, but his wandering eye defied common magic. At last, a jealous Montespan planned to kill the king, but La Voisin's arrest had scuttled the conspiracy.

With the exposure of a royal connection, King Louis established a special investigative commission. The group met in a black-draped room, lighted with candles—hence its nickname as the *chambre ardente,* or "burning chamber." Some 367 persons were arrested, including numerous priests, but only 74 were finally sentenced. King Louis ultimately quashed the probe to spare himself from scandal, and Madame Montespan went free, remaining with the royal court for another decade. Abbe Guibourg, then age sixty-seven, was sentenced to prison, where he survived for three years chained to the wall of his gloomy cell. [See: Black Mass]

CHAPMAN, MARK DAVID

Once a fervent fundamentalist and board member of the Decatur, Georgia, YMCA, Mark Chapman abandoned his Christian faith in 1977. Moving to Hawaii with a tropic suicide in mind, Chapman tried to gas himself with carbon monoxide in a rented car, but the attempt failed when heat from the exhaust pipe melted a length of garden hose, leaving Chapman nauseous but alive. He took the failure as "a sign," and began directing his new prayers for guidance to Satan.

As Chapman later described his satanic prayer sessions in a 1987 interview, "I said, 'Just make me crazy. I want to be psycho. I don't want to have to take this.' I wanted to be totally mad, out of touch with the world."

By all accounts, his prayers were answered. Chapman soon became obsessed with murdering celebrities, choosing targets for his death list on the basis of their popularity. Finalists included President Ronald Reagan, actor George C. Scott, and TV host Johnny Carson, but Chapman's real focus—like that of Charles Manson before him—remained with the Beatles.

First intending to kill Paul McCartney, Chapman switched to John Lennon when he decided Lennon was "more accessible." On the side, psychiatrists later testified, Chapman had begun to think he *was* John Lennon, charting "similarities" in their lives that included marriage to women of Japanese descent and Chapman's attempt to "retire"—albeit without Lennon's millions—at age twenty-five.

On the night of December 8, 1980, Chapman ambushed Lennon outside the Dakota Apartments, in New York City, pumping four bullets into the forty-year-old singer and killing him on the spot. Chapman pleaded guilty to the murder, and in August 1981 he was sentenced to a prison term of twenty years to life. New York law requires him to complete the minimum twenty-year sentence before he is considered for parole.

CHILD ABUSE

Beginning in 1983, the American public was introduced to a "new" kind of crime, so shocking in its details and its implications for society that battle lines were swiftly drawn between the skeptics and believers. Almost overnight, from coast to coast, scores of young children were pouring out tales of sexual abuse in homes and churches, preschools and day-care centers, naming parents, teachers, even clergymen as their molesters. Worse, the sexual assaults allegedly had been accompanied by bizarre religious rituals, sometimes including sacrifice of animals and human beings. From a state of blissful ignorance, society at large had been propelled into a confrontation with the murky underworld of ritual abuse.

In their book *Nursery Crimes,* authors David Finkelhor and Linda Williams define ritual child abuse as "abuse that occurs in a context linked to some symbols or group activity that have a religious, magical, or supernatural connotation, and where the invocation of these symbols or activities, repeated over time, is used to frighten and intimidate the children." Thus, the trappings of occult/satanic ritual reported by so many children in America, in Canada, and England, may suggest a cult at work, or else a conscious effort by some devious adults to frighten and deceive their victims with a ceremonial display.

The first publicized investigation of ritual child abuse surfaced in August 1983, with charges filed against teachers at the McMartin Preschool, in Manhattan Beach, California. Before the month was out, similar stories were heard from children in nearby communities, swiftly covering the Los Angeles basin and spreading north. By 1986, a total of sixty-four preschools were embroiled in satanic allegations in the L.A. area alone, but the ripples had spread far and wide.

Perhaps predictably, given its "weird" reputation and surfeit of wacky cults, California generated the majority of ritual abuse reports. In Concord, a mechanic was named by his stepdaughter as part of a cult that forced her to eat feces and murder a baby, his case ending with a hung jury. Nearby, in Antelope Valley, three children horrified their foster mother with tales of ritual murder and cannibalism; no bodies were found, but the accused father was convicted of felony child abuse. Several children at a fundamentalist preschool in Mendocino reported being raped and tied to crosses, forced to chant "Baby Jesus is dead." In Pico Rivera, ten-year-old David Tackett broke the story of six adult neighbors involved in orgies, urine drinking, and the sacrifice of infants; nine other children supported the story, fingering neighborhood molesters, but no charges were filed. Similar investigations in Torrance, Whittier, and Covina failed to produce hard evidence for trial. In Fremont, a five-year-old boy complained of being removed from his preschool by strangers, taken to a church where he was injected with drugs, sexually abused, forced to watch the candlelit mutilation of humans and animals. At Fort Bragg, five children from a church day-care center spoke of drugs and pornography, black candles and pentagrams, drinking urine and blood while pets were sacrificed. In Redwood City, two victims described similar black robes and candles, injection of drugs, and the cremation of a sacrificed infant, whose burned body "really stunk." In Atherton, a seventeen-year-old girl outlined identical abusive rituals performed by her stepfather and ten strangers; after speaking to police, she found a dead cat in her school locker.

In San Francisco, northern seat of weirdness for the Golden State, Detective Sandi Gallant was contacted by a frightened mother in May 1984. The woman had been watching television with her eight-year-old daughter when they saw a news report about a missing child. The girl remarked, "My daddy and I picked up a little boy named Kevin the other day, and he looks like him." As it happened, the caller's ex-husband already had a child abuse charge on file, but he retained visitation rights. The woman had already noted her daughter's "spacey" behavior after visits with her father; in therapy, the girl refused to speak, but constantly drew swastikas, pentagrams, and pictures of robed figures tossing infants into blazing fires. Now, the mother listened, stunned, as her child began to tell a graphic tale of ritual abuse. As summarized in an excerpt from the police report—

> Rhonda describes rituals in great detail and recalls one Halloween when they all dressed up in costumes and went to the [stepmother's house] where members of the group were dressed up in their blue robes. There were candles lit, and they all stood in a circle and called upon Satan. There were swastikas on the wall, and they would say Hail, Hail to the swastika. She recalls a picture of a dark haired man with a mustache on the wall. She says this particular night no one was hurt, but she described other rituals in which animals are killed and dismembered. She says these animals were dogs, sheep and goats. Knives were used in most rituals, and sometimes the children were threatened with them.

In nearby Contra Costa County, a nine-year-old girl told her story of satanic abuse to a child psychologist who accepts the report as truthful. "This happened in her father's home," the therapist recalled. "She was able to recite for me what she called their Egyptian names, to sing for me the chants and songs they sang. She described every conceivable sex act you can imagine. She described their playing with live snakes. She talked about how young women in their teens were sacrificed. Her description of how guts pop out when you slit open a live abdomen does justice to a Vietnam war veteran."

A county prosecutor blamed the sensational charges for a hung jury that left the girl's father at liberty. "They were as detailed as they were, I hesitate to use the word 'unbelievable'," he said, "because to at least some degree I believed them, although I had questions about some of it. I question how much of it was exaggeration or misunderstanding, and how much of it was fact. There's no doubt in my mind that she was a participant in satanic worship, but she also described at one point how her father put his hand around her hand holding a knife and how the two of them plunged the knife into the chest of an infant. There was some question in my mind about whether that was an actual sacrifice or possibly a simulated sacrifice, and that's what I said to the jury. I argued that this case wasn't about devil worship, and that whether they believed or disbelieved the child about the satanic stuff, there should be no question that she was a victim of child molest."

In the state capital at Sacramento, during January 1985, five men were jailed on 150 counts of child molestation. The alleged ringleader, thirty-three-year-old Arthur Dill, was accused by nine children—including four of his own—of ritual abuse that included sexual assault, murder of infants, and the production of "snuff" films. Incidents reportedly dated from 1982, surfacing only in June 1984, when Dill's children entered therapy for aberrant behavior, resulting from their parents' divorce. Authorities followed numerous leads in a search for physical evidence, while Dill blamed his ex-wife and former mother-in-law for "brainwashing" the children with false accusations. Prosecutors initially felt they had a strong case, but charges were finally dismissed, without trial, in September 1985.

Meanwhile, allegations of ritual abuse spread far beyond the borders of California. A December 1986 survey found thirty-six ritual cases awaiting trial in sixteen states, and others have surfaced since that time. In Parker, Arizona, four children regaled police with stories of satanic sex and drug abuse, but no charges were filed. A Denver pediatrician told the press: "The only thing I know about [ritual abuse] is that it exists. We've seen at least two families here where there was an enormous amount of acting out of satanic activities and where the children were also sexually abused. How widespread it is, I don't know. I think that whatever's going on has been going on underground, and that every now and then something bubbles up."

In Memphis, Tennessee, a routine pediatric checkup exposed charges of ritual abuse when a three-year-old girl told her doctor that a preschool teacher had fondled her genitals. The girl named three other victims for police, and those children in turn named others, all from the church-run Georgian Hills Early Childhood Center. Prosecutors ultimately charged a fifty-four-year-old female staff member, the woman's son, and Rev. Paul Shell with sexually abusing twenty-six children, torturing some, and baptizing others "in the devil's name." Reports from the children included now-familiar descriptions of black robes and masks, burning candles, plus mutilation of gerbils, hamsters, and a human infant. Bewildered jurors deadlocked on the case in 1987, producing a mistrial.

In July 1984, the wife of an army sergeant stationed at West Point, New York, noted her three-year-old daughter bleeding from the vagina after her second day at the West Point Child Development Center. At the hospital, doctors found her vaginal canal lacerated with small punctures, and the girl described a teacher probing her genitals with a pen. By September, when the case began making news, eleven children had complained of being fondled or "hurt down there" by two of their teachers, one of whom fled the state after being suspended. One girl reported being driven to a nearby high school, where she was allegedly photographed nude in the school's darkroom. Photos of the darkroom and other sites on the high school campus—including a charred tree, inexplicably wrapped with heavy cables—were snapped by investigators and shown to the other complaining children without comment. Several of the kids reacted violently, spilling out their own traumatic experiences at the school, describing other children bound to the tree while they were abused. A West Point physician, Dr. Walter Grote, turned down a scheduled promotion after learning that his own daughter had been abused in the day-care center. In an open letter to the secretary of the army, Grote said: "By the time I left West Point, I knew of approximately three dozen children who were ritually abused there."

Indeed, there seemed to be an established history of sexual abuse at West Point. In 1984, a senior commissioned officer at the post—later implicated in ritual abuse charges—was convicted of enticing two children to pose for pornographic photos. A year later, a civilian employee at the West Point officer's club was also convicted of sexually abusing several boys on the academy grounds. The U.S. attorney probing the latest charges told newsmen "there isn't much question" that children were molested at the day-care center, with staff members "probably responsible" . . . but no indictments were ever returned in the case.

Around the same time, in Chicago, multiple charges of child molesting were filed against Deloartic Parks, a janitor at the Rogers Park Jewish Community Center, where several children complained of sexual abuse in a day-care setting. The allegations included satanic rituals and pornography, with two teachers named as participants and two more suspended by administrators for failure to report ongoing abuse. Of eighty-eight children in the day-care program, doctors listed thirty-two as showing symptoms of molestation. In October 1984, state investigators decided that "most" of the Rogers Park allegations were unsupported by "credible evidence." Defendant Parks was subsequently acquitted at his nonjury trial on charges of raping a seven-year-old girl. In an ironic footnote, it was discovered that Allen Friedman, an "expert" leader of the state's investigation, had grossly falsified his résumé to claim expertise in the field of child abuse. Friedman's work experience, various college credits and graduate courses, professional affiliations, all were proven false upon examination ... but his committee's verdict was allowed to stand.

Another bizarre case, reported from Evansville, Indiana, featured a two-year investigation of ritual abuse charges which prosecutor Steve Levco called "inherently unbelievable." The probe folded without indictments in July 1991, with critics calling Levco's retreat "a political decision" catering to public apathy. As a sideshow to the main event, an elderly Evansville couple filed suit against the tabloid TV program "A Current Affair," after their house was featured in a broadcast on satanic cults.

Outside the United States, authorities in Ontario, Canada, reportedly investigated ten separate cases of ritual abuse in 1988 alone. Two years later, in Roachdale, England, similar claims placed twenty children in foster homes while their stories were checked by police. Again, there were reports of drugs, slaughtered sheep, and murdered infants. News reports mentioned hundreds of children in surrounding towns with similar stores. At nearby Manchester, young victims led detectives through a maze of limestone tunnels at a local cemetery, pointing out crude altars, crosses etched in the walls, and puddles of black candle wax. The director of Roachdale's society service agency declared: "The abuse the children describe is real and not the product of their imaginations." All the same, no charges were filed, and one town official later described the whole affair as "a horrendous mistake."

Professors Finkelhor and Williams list three kinds of ritual abuse, based on their study of some 270 child abuse cases, with 1,659 victims. In *true cult-based rituals,* an elaborate belief system is involved, with the ultimate goal of abuse transcending sex, aimed more at producing a mystical experience for the offenders and corrupting a new generation of cultists. Investigators in such cases note that many reported acts are geared toward indoctrination of young victims, discrediting traditional heroes or deities, debasing their own self-esteem, and making them accomplices through forced participation in violent or perverted acts. *Pseudoritualistic abuse* may closely resemble the cult-based variety, but it occurs without a developed belief system, borrowing symbols and slogans to intimidate children, thereby coercing submission and silence. Finally, *psychopathological ritualism* stems entirely from the abuser's private obsessions or compulsions, coincidentally resembling cult activities in certain cases, but without any conscious link to real or feigned occult beliefs.

Motives for ritual abuse, as described by the experts, fall into two general categories. One, aimed at "mortification of the child's sexuality," stems from a pedophile's own background of early abuse and humiliation, driving the offender to resent and envy the innocence of uncorrupted children. Such an offender may adopt religious systems like Satanism to justify his own perversity, in the same way that some serial killers are drawn to the occult. On the other hand, some offenders are seemingly driven by an "identification with evil," adopting physical or sexual abuse of children as a twisted kind of "sacrament." Yet another motive for ritual abuse, proposed in 1988 by a special task force of the Women's Commission of the Los Angeles County Board of Supervisors, involves the deliberate infliction of trauma so bizarre that its very revelation automatically discredits complaining victims in the eyes of "rational" adults.

Most of the ritual cases examined by Professors Finkelhor and Williams involved both multiple abusers and multiple victims, the latter ranging from four months to seven years of age. Younger children were typically preferred as easy to intimidate, incapable of verbal complaints, and simple to discredit or confuse in the event a charge is leveled. Forty percent of the day-care offenders were female, a much higher percentage than average in child abuse cases, but males still held a 60% majority, though they accounted for barely 5% of the national day-care staff. A full 75% of reported cases involved men and women acting together, and 34% of the cases involved abusers related by blood or marriage. Solitary abusers were normally male, but there are still exceptions to the rule, as with New Jersey's Margaret Michaels, who, among other perversions, forced numerous children to eat her feces and drink her menstrual blood.

As previously noted, ritual allegations from unrelated witnesses and far-flung locations have been remarkably consistent. Of the children involved in 36 ritual cases pending trial in 1987—

92% reported sexual abuse by multiple offenders, male and female

78% described sex acts being filmed or photographed

76% named items of clearly identified ritual paraphernalia, including robes (27%), candles (22%), knives and swords (22%), religious icons or symbols (17%), and bones or skeletons (17%)

75% said they were removed from the primary care facility and taken to private homes (50%), churches (25%), or cemeteries (23%)

74% reported abuse in a preschool or day-care center

64% described specific ritual acts, including mutilation of animals or humans (36%), songs and chanting (25%), and specific reference to Satan (15%)

59% claimed they were drugged during cultlike ceremonies

46% said they were forced to consume the flesh and blood of butchered animals and human beings

42% were allegedly forced to eat feces or drink urine

36% were locked in cramped spaces like closets or coffins

Adult coercion was reported by children in every case, though it took various forms. A full 56% of alleged victims reported being threatened with supernatural powers, while 10% claimed to have undergone "magical surgery," with bombs or other lethal objects planted in their bodies. As coercion takes many shapes, so it may have varied motives. In some cases it effects compliance, as when drugs are used, or in the Eagle's Nest preschool case, where abusers pretended to phone home and ask parental "permission" for sex acts with selected children. Coercive action also insures future silence, with many children reporting the slaughter of pets and direct death threats against their parents or siblings in the event they carry tales out of school. Finally, some abusers clearly receive a sadistic thrill from violent abuse, as in the case of several Bakersfield, California, molesters—all convicted—who suspended their victims from hooks on the ceiling. Use of drugs, documented by police in Miami and elsewhere, also has the fringe benefit of confusing young victims, rendering their testimony less credible at a later date.

A 1991 survey of ninety-seven ritual abuse victims, conducted by physicians at the UCLA Medical Center, reported the following symptoms as common:

87% displayed irritability and unexplained outbursts of anger
83% showed symptoms of posttraumatic stress disorder
80% experienced recurring nightmares
80% had intrusive recollections of abuse
79% had difficulty sleeping
73% evidenced hypervigilance (extreme lack of trust)
70% suffered problems with poor concentration
59% showed evidence of emotional detachment from family

Skeptics predictably deny the occurrence of *any* ritual abuse, describing the widespread reports as "mass hysteria," "urban legends," or "another Salem witch-hunt." (Ironically, they fail to note that voodoo played a role in the initial Salem allegations and a known occult society—the Osirian Order—was active in Salem throughout the witch scare.) Critics point to the 1980 publication of *Michelle Remembers,* the biography of an alleged ritual abuse survivor, with implications that child psychologists and counselors around the world are somehow caught up in a plot to "brainwash" dozens of children and "frame" innocent adults for no apparent motive. On balance, though, when such claims are considered, it is easier to believe in small, secretive bands of child-abusing cultists than an international conspiracy of mental health professionals hell-bent on embarrassing themselves with unfounded charges.

Critics point out that in most cases, accusations of ritual abuse are slow to surface, lagging weeks or months behind initial claims of "normal" sexual abuse. The delay, skeptics insist, proves that counselors and therapists are coaching the children, feeding them slanderous lies which the victims later regurgitate as sworn testimony. In fact, as Professors Finkelhor and Williams explain, such delayed revelations are perfectly natural in cases where children are systematically terrorized, requiring long-term therapy to make them feel secure and help them trust adults once more.

If we believe the skeptics, charges of ritual abuse are typically filed by right wing fundamentalist detectives and corrupt district attorneys trying to profit from a windfall of publicity. Ironically, the evidence is overwhelming that police and prosecutors actively attempt to bury cult-related claims in many cases, fearful that bizarre allegations will scuttle their case with a jury. In Hamilton, Ontario, detectives openly ridiculed children who spoke of pornographic films and ritual activities during a 1985 child abuse investigation, refusing to pursue the allegations, and similar reactions are common in the United States. In Chicago, recalling the Rogers Park case, Detective Scott Keenan recalls: "This was not our finest moment. We had one simple case with one offender, and we felt uncomfortable with the nature of [ritual] allegations. To be honest with you, I didn't want to hear this. This was going to destroy our case."

Federal agents are especially reluctant to tackle cases of ritual abuse, with the FBI adopting an expressed attitude of "it doesn't happen, so we aren't going to investigate." At West Point, in 1984, FBI agents refused to believe an accused teacher would molest children, because she didn't look "butch" enough. G-men insisted that a complaining girl had been abused by other children; when she refused to agree, they demanded that her parents submit to polygraph tests as possible suspects in the crime. In the same year, Detective Sandi Gallant approached the feds with a satanic abuse case from San Francisco. She explains: "We had tried to get the Department of Justice to look at it, but if it's got anything to do with religion they don't want anything to do with it. At least to your face, they tell you they don't want to know anything about it."

That "see-no-evil" approach is manifest in the statements of FBI "cult expert" Ken Lanning, who writes that "Ritualistic crime may fulfill the cultural, spiritual, sexual and psychological needs of the offender." Lanning warns police that while child molesting "may be criminal [sic] if performed for sexual gratification," they enter a whole new ball game when "the ritualistic activity and child abuse may be integral parts of some spiritual belief system." More to the point, Lanning cautions that once "acts of ritualistic abuse are performed for spiritual indoctrination, potential prosecution may be jeopardized." In short, give up.

Dr. Roland Summit, an expert in ritual abuse and professor of clinical psychiatry at UCLA, described the typical response to such cases in a 1985 report to the U.S. Attorney General's Commission on Pornography.

> The appropriate defenses against charges of sexual misconduct are "aging the case" and "discrediting the victim." By the time a case is argued through pretrial motions, depositions, preliminary hearings and delayed adjudications, both the children and the public have tried to put the crime away. If child, parent and clinical interviewer can survive the public exposure, leering, scapegoating and assault of endless adversarial examinations, the only lesson for future planning is avoidance. It is little wonder that families avoid reporting. Considering the normal immaturity and confusion of the victims, the typically trustworthy style of child molesters, and the predictable adultism and ambivalence of jurors (and judges), the reasonable doubt of one adult will cancel the testimony of dozens of children.

> The rejection of cases and the in-camera bargaining of pleas create an illusion of unfounded or trivial offenses. Focus on only the chargeable offenses diverts attention from the real dimensions of crimes still only dimly understood. Even if convicted, the narrowly contrived charges of sexual molestation avoid hearsay allegations of studio cameras, drugging, group prostitution, conspiracy and bizarre ritual.

> The ultimate obscenity, mutilating and killing a child for the titillation of viewers, has been described by numerous children throughout the country. Descriptions of drinking blood or urine and eating feces are almost routine. The suspicion that such atrocities might be staged in a trusted neighborhood preschool is simply intolerable to anyone. The continuing voices

of alarm come mainly from the parents of those who hear these accounts from their three- and four-year-old children.

Such reports, while remarkably consistent from one outcropping to another have yet to be confirmed by a credible adult eye-witness or by recovery of the photos, movies and videos or the bodies and ritual paraphernalia that the children insist they have seen. Yet the descriptions are so graphic and the scenes so strikingly similar and the implications of any such reality so massive that some kind of adult conceptualization is urgent.

In my informal and scattered overview of some 25 investigations involving reports of blood ritual, each has become hopelessly confused and deadlocked. Investigations are suspended. Charges are contrived to avoid the issue. Witnesses who talk of ritual are dropped from consideration. Many cases are simply never filed because of the inflammatory effects of the unprovable rumors. And those that go to trial may be dropped in midcourse, acquitted or reversed on appeal. Each failed attempt at prosecution buttresses the logical and welcome argument that such charges are obviously ridiculous, and that adults who choose to believe them should be viewed with suspicion.

In their review of 270 day-care abuse cases, Professors Finkelhor and Williams note that 10% were dismissed without even a pretense of police investigation. Of the 90% investigated by authorities, another 12% were dropped as "unfounded"—that is, police disbelieved the accusations, most often in cases with only one complaining victim. Of the "founded" cases, only 68% resulted in arrests or charges being filed against a suspect. Of *those* cases, 44% were dropped by prosecutors prior to trial based on legal technicalities, "incompetent" witnesses, and so forth. Fifteen percent of the alleged abusers brought to trial were acquitted, and 12% of those found guilty escaped with the wrist slap of probation. At the end of a process lasting months or years, barely 23% of the original suspects wound up serving prison time.

Even so, these figures give the lie to skeptics' claims that "no one has ever been found guilty" in a case of ritual abuse. In fact, prosecutors have won convictions on such cases in California, Florida, Iowa, Massachusetts, Nevada, Texas, and Virginia (with the Texas verdict reversed on a technical appeal). The fact that most of the defendants were convicted on "ordinary" sex charges indicates a deliberate blindness on the part of legislators, prosecutors, and police which must be overcome before this type of heinous crime can be eradicated from society. [See: Bakersfield, CA; Childress, Joy; Christianson, Joan; Felix, Martha; Fuster, Francisco; Jordan, MN; Kellum, George; McMartin Preschool; Multiple Personality Disorder; Noble, Michelle; Pornography; Smith, Michelle; "Snuff" Films; Underwager, Ralph; Wells, Gordon; Wilkins, Robert]

CHILDREN OF WRATH

Nestled in the wooded, rolling hills of southern Indiana, tiny Nashville—population 750, give or take—has had its share of cult-related rumors, "witchy" sightings, and reported torchlight ceremonies in the past two decades, but the harsh reality of teenagers preoccupied with the occult did not hit home until February 1987. On February 18, police were summoned to Brown County High School by reports of a "slight stabbing," and they found a fifteen-year-old sophomore wounded in the abdomen. His assailant—also fifteen, and thus unnamed in media reports—was booked for assault with a deadly weapon and held for a week without bond.

Authorities determined that six or seven heavy metal "stoners" in the school had lately joined ranks as the "Children of Wrath," boasting of their dedication to Satan. Threatening notes were delivered to various enemies of the group, marked with inverted crosses and the numerals "666." When the sophomore victim refused invitations to an after-school fight, he was assaulted and stabbed near the high school gymnasium, sustaining a superficial wound. The clumsy attacker also slashed himself in the process, requiring ten stitches in his knife hand.

As Deputy Marshal Donnie Allender explained the incident: "The members of the group said they believe in the devil. They think they are a satanic group, but I just think they're stupid. It's just kid stuff, but someone happened to get hurt."

Facing a potential eight years in prison and a $10,000 fine if tried as an adult, the fifteen-year-old delinquent got off with expulsion from school and a sentence of three years' probation with mandatory counseling, his parents shelling out $1,000 to cover the victim's medical expenses. At Brown County High, the Children of Wrath went up in smoke with members required to submit written resignations from the short-lived "cult" or face expulsion themselves.

CHILDRESS, JOY

A veteran high school teacher in Tucson, Arizona, Joy Childress was forty-eight years old when memories of child-hood ritual abuse began to surface during psychotherapy sessions, in early 1986. After twenty years of therapy, dating from the collapse of her marriage in the 1960s, she was stunned by sudden, graphic images of sexual abuse by men dressed in black robes and hoods. Childress named her older brother as a participant in the abuse, though he staunchly denies it. As Childress pieced her story together for author Larry Kahaner, in his book *Cults That Kill:*

I was in a satanic cult from birth until I was twenty-one years old. My whole family was in the cult. It was generational, as my grandfather on my mother's side also participated. My experience deals with ritualistic rape, ritualistic sacrificing of children and dogs, mainly German shepherds, ritualistic eating of flesh, feces, vomit, and urine, and ritualistic drinking of animal or human blood.

In the cult I grew up with, the men usually wore black robes with black hoods, similar to the Ku Klux Klan, and it was the men who usually took charge of the ceremonies. We had a high priest who was the father of us all. It was a family cult, made up of entire families. At one time, the high priest was an ordained Baptist minister of a prominent church in Denver, Colorado. The cult didn't have a name, as far as I know.

Childress describes "sexual purification" ceremonies involving the gang rape of young girls, along with the murder and mutilation of numerous children, their bodies burned after bones and other relics were removed for ceremonial uses. In her description, some of the ritual murders were "staged" for dramatic effect, while others were all too real. The sacrifice of German shepherds matches information on satanic cults in California, North Dakota, and New York, reported from the 1960s to the present day.

Childress allegedly fled her family and the cult at age twenty-one, with the help of a sympathetic aunt. Somehow, within the next few months or years, her frightful memories were buried and suppressed, though she continued suffering emotional and psychiatric problems until therapy revived the gruesome images a quarter century later.

Skeptics dismiss the Childress revelations as paranoid fantasies or worse, noting her appearance on various TV talk shows in the 1980s, calling for prosecution of identified ritual killers if her story is true. In response, Childress describes her public statements as a warning to law-enforcement officers and potential victims, sounding the alarm on a pervasive threat. Meanwhile, with the passage of time, most identified cult members are deceased, and ashes of their alleged victims impossible to locate or identify. [See: Child Abuse]

CHIPANA UCHARIO, NIEVES

A resident of Peru's Unicachi village, on an isolated inlet of Lake Titicaca, Nieves Chipana was living with convicted drug smuggler Kalisto Ramos when he fell victim to human sacrifice in 1980. The whole Ramos family was suspect at first, since Peruvian dealers are known to support their profession with magic, but suspicion soon shifted to another quarter. Villagers recalled a black Dodge automobile with six occupants, seen in Unicachi on the day Chipana vanished, and police traced the vehicle's ownership to one Victor Ceballos, a wealthy local. Detectives identified Ceballos's five companions as his wife, sister, brother-in-law, and his wife's parents. Despite persistent threats from one Conejo Rocha, Yunguyo district's richest drug dealer, police finally arrested the *yatiri* responsible for Chipana's sacrifice. Identified in American reports by the alias "Maximo Coa," the hired killer and his six sponsors—all from the Dodge—were convicted of murder in 1981. Each defendant received a twenty-year sentence, but Coa's sons bribed authorities to have their father released, his record expunged, leaving him free to pursue his trade as a mercenary assassin.

CHRIST FAMILY

In 1980, word of a new satanic cult reached Detective Sandi Gallant at San Francisco police headquarters. Undercover officers working the narco beat had stumbled on a group that billed itself as the Christ Family, led by a zany character dubbed "Brother Jesus Christ Lightning Amen"— but the thrust of the sect was far from Christian. As described by the officers:

> Reliable sources state that in the past year or so the trend of this group has gone from relative passivity to one responsible for numerous bizarre happenings. Christ Family members are known to be heavily into drugs such as LSD and PCP.
>
> Numerous sources now indicate that Christ Family members have taken the usual progression of a cult, from a quasi-religious group to a bizarre, satanic movement. There is also speculation that members may be involved in ritualistic killings of animals and human beings. The following information is being included in this report, due to this speculation, however, it must be noted that there is no evidence directly connecting these incidents to the Christ Family at this time.

The appended police reports dealt with suicides and apparent murders in Colorado, Florida, and Illinois. It was also reported that the Christ Family claimed an estimated two thousand members nationwide, scattered from Hawaii to the East Coast. Disciples traveled the countryside dressed in white robes, driving "brown or dark green vans, trucks and cars, usually with the Star of David emblem." More than a decade after the fact, the San Francisco investigation remains inconclusive, with no charges filed against members of the "bizarre" cult.

CHRISTIANSON, JOAN

A self-described survivor of ritual child abuse, Joan Christianson claims that she was born into a multi-generational satanic cult. Her parents were members, she says, and they participated in years of sadistic sexual abuse that began when Christianson was seven years old. Her earliest childhood memories involve being dragged from bed in the middle of the night, transported to basements, crypts, and mortuaries where the dark rites were conducted by a coven of thirteen members.

As luck would have it, Christianson recalls, she was selected as a "breeder" by the cult, bearing four children over a period of years. Impregnation ceremonies were conducted in a casket, timed to coincide with holy days on the satanic calendar. Each of the four infants, delivered at home without benefit of birth certificates or hospital records, was reportedly sacrificed to Lucifer.

Aside from serving the cult as a sexual object, Christianson says she was also forced to pose for numerous pornographic films and photos. She was frequently kept home from school, once for a period of sixty-seven consecutive days, and the injuries from parental beatings or other forms of abuse were tended by a local physician involved with the cult. Aside from being shut in crypts and coffins with rotting corpses, Christianson also recalls being tied to her bed on occasion, left for hours or days with plates of food placed just beyond her reach. On one occasion, following a five-hour gang rape by thirteen men, she was "thrown away" in a trash dumpster to emphasize her personal worthlessness.

Christianson finally ran away from home in her teens, supporting herself through prostitution until she met her future husband—"coincidentally" another Satanist. "I didn't know any better," she explains. "I thought all men were like my father." Ten years and three children later, disgusted with her husband's chronic drug abuse, ritual activities, and life in general, Christianson filed for divorce in Contra Costa County, California. In court, her husband admitted his satanic activities, but still received initial custody of all three children on the grounds that Joan had been a prostitute. The custody ruling was later reversed in a bitter lawsuit, and Christianson sought therapy to turn her life around.

"I found I couldn't take enough drugs, couldn't drink

enough booze, and I couldn't run away from the problems any more," she says. "In order to make it better, I had to go out and talk about it."

To that end, she has been lecturing national audiences on the perils of ritual child abuse since 1982. Skeptics describe Christianson as "paranoid," "delusional"—even "dangerous"—pointing to the lack of physical evidence to support her story, but she takes such criticism in stride. "Right now," she says, "with ritual abuse, we're where we were ten years ago with incest. People say it doesn't happen. Satanists get away with this because it's so unbelievable. That's their strength." [See: Child Abuse; Childress, Joy]

CHURCH OF SATAN

Founded on Walpurgisnacht (April 30), in 1966, the Church of Satan grew out of weekly "Magic Circle" meetings at the San Francisco home of Anton LaVey. Participants in the original gathering and founding members of the church included filmmaker Kenneth Anger and novelist Steven Schneck. LaVey christened himself high priest of the cult, with his wife Diane installed as high priestess to keep things in the family. LaVey's group was initially called the "First Church of Satan," but Herb Sloane's Toledo coven had a twelve-year lead, and the self-styled "Black Pope" of San Francisco soon settled on the cult's present title.

National publicity eluded the church for several months, but LaVey began reaping headlines in January 1967, with the satanic marriage of journalist John Raymond to socialite Judith Case. Five months later, the cameras were back to cover the baptism of LaVey's three-year-old daughter, Zeena, and Anton finished out the year with a December funeral service for a seaman in the U.S. Navy, complete with color guard.

Publicity brought new members, many of them drawn from the decadent world of Tinseltown. Celebrities like Keenan Wynn, Jayne Mansfield, Barbara McNair, and Sammy Davis, Jr., forged ties with LaVey, as the church began to spread nationwide. Charters for independent "grottoes" were issued to disciples in Los Angeles, Phoenix, Denver, Seattle, Las Vegas, Chicago, Indianapolis, Detroit, Dayton, Louisville, Boston, New York, and St. Petersburg. Across the Canadian border, satanic outposts were established in Vancouver and

Edmonton. LaVey boasted of members in Africa, forging definite ties with a group in the Netherlands, but ex-members insist that his 1970 claim of ten thousand followers was close to double the actual number of dues-paying Satanists.

At that, the membership was clearly inflated by LaVey's practice of charging journalists a $20 membership fee before they could cover his rituals. Many other recruits dropped out in the early days, mostly young men disappointed by the lack of eagerly anticipated orgies, but all remain technical "members" under LaVey's system requiring a one-time payment of fees. On the side, Satanists wishing to attend weekly rites were charged $2.50 a head, at the door.

By the early 1970s, LaVey had overextended himself, and the Church of Satan experienced a problem familiar to other fringe groups, with ambitious would-be leaders spinning off to form competing bodies of their own. Wayne West, a defrocked British priest in charge of Detroit's Babylon Grotto, was excommunicated by LaVey when members complained of his aggressive homosexuality and taste for bondage; undismayed, West led his faithful followers into a new Universal Church of Man, described as "Satanism without Satan." Other Detroit rejects soon founded the Shrine of the Little Mother and the Order of the Black Ram. Dayton's Stygian Grotto lost its charter in February 1973, with LaVey charging "violations of the law," but its leaders simply set up shop with new titles like the Church of Satanic Brotherhood and the Ordo Templi Satanas. The greatest rift occurred in 1975, when Michael Aquino and New Jersey "witch" Lilith Sinclair led a mass defection to form the new Temple of Set, officially declaring LaVey's "Age of Satan" at an end.

One problem for the Church of Satan was clearly the indiscriminate acceptance of new members, cash up front, with little or no attempt to bar the unstable. In 1970, Arthur Lyons described an elaborate screening process for new recruits, including indoctrination lectures, complex written tests, and personal interviews with the cult's inner council, but such defensive measures were ignored outside San Francisco, with individuals and whole "grottoes" welcomed into the fold by mail order. In a group that champions self-indulgence above all else, dissension and eventual disintegration were inevitable.

In essence, the Church of Satan closely follows the beliefs of Aleister Crowley, laid down in his *Book of the Law*. LaVey has subtly altered and refined Crowley's doctrines in publications like *The Satanic Bible* and *The Satanic Rituals,* adding a cynical twist of his own, but the heart of cult philosophy is contained in the "Nine Satanic Statements." To wit:

1. Satan represents indulgence instead of abstinence.
2. Satan represents vital existence instead of spiritual pipe dreams.
3. Satan represents undefiled wisdom instead of hypocritical self-deceit.
4. Satan represents kindness to those who deserve it instead of love wasted on ingrates.
5. Satan represents vengeance instead of turning the other cheek.
6. Satan represents responsibility to the responsible instead of concern for psychic vampires.
7. Satan represents man as just another animal—sometimes better, more often worse than those that walk on all-fours—who, because of his "divine spiritual and intellectual development" has become the most vicious animal of all.
8. Satan represents all of the so-called sins, as they will lead to physical, mental, or emotional gratification.
9. Satan has been the best friend the Church has ever had, as he has kept it in business all these years.

At that, Satan is not a literal deity for LaVey's faithful, but rather a symbol of enlightened selfishness. Use of drugs during rituals is prohibited in theory, and "official" satanic rites include no sexual activity, despite the presence of a nude woman as the "altar." (All the same, Art Lyons has reported the ceremonial flogging of masochistic members as a form of self-indulgence). The stylized Enochian language is used for many rituals, at least by those cultists able to pronounce the words. Group charters are no longer issued, but individuals are still welcome to join LaVey's "alien elite" at a price of $100 per head.

Much of the cult's activity is thinly veiled playacting, or "psychodrama," including rituals gleaned by LaVey and Michael Aquino from the horror fiction of author H.P. Lovecraft. To date, despite LaVey's publicized affiliation with mass killers Susan Atkins and Richard Ramirez, no documented member of the church has been convicted of a criminal offense. At the same time, killer cultists from coast to coast—including Steven Hurd, Philip Galimanis, Lloyd Gamble, Bunny Dixon, Scott Waterhouse and others—have proclaimed their adoration for LaVey, drawing inspiration for their bloody actions from LaVey's *Satanic Bible*. LaVey, for his part, consistently repudiates such followers as renegades and "crazies" who have "misinterpreted" his message of indulgence over abstinence. *Anyone* should understand, LaVey insists, that his published outline for selection of a human sacrifice was only meant to be "symbolic." If homicidal misfits take him literally, LaVey—like Pilate before him—is prepared to wash his hands of all responsibility. [See: LaVey, Anton]

CHURCH OF SATANIC BROTHERHOOD

In the early 1970s, Anton LaVey's Church of Satan was rocked by dissension, with much of the controversy centered in Midwestern states. Practitioners Wayne West, of Detroit, and John De Haven, from Dayton, Ohio, were among the loudest critics of LaVey's "commercialized" religion, blasting San Francisco headquarters for prostituting "pure" Satanism in the name of profit. De Haven's Stygian Grotto announced its disbandment on February 11, 1973, and La Vey responded by yanking the group's charter, accusing his erstwhile disciples of "acting in violation of the law."

A few weeks later, in March, the new Church of Satanic Brotherhood was organized by some two dozen defectors from Ohio, Michigan, and Indiana. Public leaders were named as De Haven, Harry L. Booth, Joseph M. Daniels, and a three-hundred-pound biker named Ronald Lanting. Wayne West, meanwhile, set up shop on his own, billing his new Universal Church of Man as a vehicle for promoting "Satanism without Satan."

The Church of Satanic Brotherhood still followed LaVey's basic dream, while eschewing the "butchered" *Satanic Rituals*. Once started, the new sect spread rapidly, putting down roots in New York City, Indianapolis, Louisville, St. Petersburg, plus Columbus and Dayton-Centerville in Ohio. Individual grottoes were led by "magisters," while priests ranked slightly higher, at the third degree. A satanic Council of Churches was organized, composed of fourth-degree bishops, but their recruiting efforts faltered over time, and the church disappeared during 1976.

CHURCH OF SATANIC LIBERATION

New Haven, Connecticut, English teacher Paul Douglas Valentine was a fifteen-year veteran of occult studies when he picked up a copy of *The Satanic Bible* in late 1985. It was, by all accounts, a moving experience, with Valentine finally seeing the light—or the darkness—deciding that "Satanism is a viable religion quite unlike what the movies and the Christers made it out to be."

That decided, Valentine announced formation of his own satanic church on January 8, 1986. New members are recruited via tabloid advertisements, or through the Magickal Childe occult shop in New York City, where Valentine maintains useful connections. Most of Valentine's identified recruits appear to be well-educated, affluent females, promoting the church's strong emphasis on sex magic. Proud of his legendary libido, Valentine bills himself as the "Roman Polanski of the satanic world," disinterested in the age of his sex partners "as long as they coincide with any individual state's 'age of consent.'"

Sex aside, Valentine cultivates a peculiar love-hate relationship with Anton LaVey and the Church of Satan. On one hand, he blasts LaVey for letting the parent church "become a halfway house for misanthropes and social pariahs"; on the other, Valentine has adopted LaVey's satanic calendar and "Baphomet" trademark, borrowing freely from *The Satanic Bible* and *Satanic Rituals*. If anything, Valentine seems to view himself as the Black Pope's successor, "taking up where LaVey's Church of Satan seems to be slacking off—educating those people of like mind who realize there is something better, something more honest, than what the major religions are offering."

And if he turns a profit in the meantime . . . well, so much the better. Two years after its foundation, the Church of Satanic Liberation claimed corresponding members from coast to coast, with particular concentrations noted in California, Nevada, Texas, Pennsylvania, New York, New Hampshire, and Maine. No hard numbers are available, and there have been no charges of illegal actions by the cult to date.

CLAWSON, EUGENE A.

One of the most bizarre, confusing cases in modern police history began on January 18, 1970, when nineteen-year-old coeds Karen Ferrell and Mared Malarik vanished from a state university campus in Morgantown, West Virginia. Neither young woman fit the typical runaway profile, and foul play was immediately suspected. Police and FBI agents were mobilized to solve the mystery, but massive publicity and a $3,500 reward failed to generate any leads as the days turned into weeks and months.

In April, the case took a sharp turn from traditional criminology into the Twilight Zone. In LaVale, Maryland—eighty miles east of Morgantown—resident Fred Schanning had followed the fruitless search with rapt attention. Finally, on April 3, he decided to solve the riddle himself, consulting his "psychic counselor," Rev. R. Warren Hoover. The Reverend Hoover, in turn, put himself into a trance and began to converse with Schanning in the voice of his "spiritual guide," a nineteenth-century London physician known as "Dr. Spencer." With a tape recorder running, "Dr. Spencer" said the missing women had been sacrificed by Satanists, their bodies planted twenty-five miles south of Morgantown in two "sloppy, triangular gravesites."

Anxious to help with the investigation, Schanning persuaded his niece, Annabelle Young, to write the police in Morgantown on April 6. The letter read;

Gentlemen,

I have some information on the whereabouts of the bodies of the two missing West Virginia University coeds, Mared Malarik and Karen Ferrell.

Follow directions very carefully—to the nth degree and you cannot fail to find them.

Proceed 25 miles *directly south,* from the southern line of Morgantown. This will bring you to a wooded forest land. Enter into the forest exactly one mile. There are the bodies.
25 + 1 = 26 miles total
Will reveal myself when the bodies are located.

Sincerely,
Δ

Newspapers published the letter on April 10, but police showed no inclination to launch a search, so Annabelle Young composed a second note. The same basic directions were repeated, along with a rough diagram of the scene. Young added that the bodies were concealed by brush and had been gnawed by forest scavengers.

On April 14, Governor Arch Moore ordered state police and national guardsmen to begin a search of the area described in the letters. Two days later, troopers saw a foot protruding from a shallow grave, hidden by loose brush and nearly stripped of flesh by animals. Two headless bodies were recovered, but the missing skulls were nowhere to be found. The county coroner reported that seven slabs of stone had been moved thirty feet from a creek bed to construct the grave.

By this time, "Dr. Spencer" had described the murders as a grim initiation ceremony, conducted by two satanic recruits in the presence of their high priest. On April 21, the Reverend Hoover mailed another letter to police in Morgantown.

Gentlemen:

I have delayed writing another letter in hope you would conclude more information by this time, concerning the finding of the bodies. Since this has not substantially happened, I will send along another clue while your men are still in the area.

The heads can be found from the position of the bodies by striking out 10 degrees S.W. for the first head and approximately 10 degrees S.E. for the second roughly one mile. You are already 7/10 of that mile. They are within the mine entrance—if you can call it an entrance considering its condition. They are buried not over 1 ft. in depth.

The ones responsible for the murders scattered some of the girls' personal effects over the general area creating a pattern of confusion making it difficult for you to pinpoint any exact location.

My first two letters triggered your intensive search. Don't give up now!

Sincerely,

△

Publication of the latest note touched off a bitter controversy among investigators. Morgantown authorities denied the letters had been any help at all, while FBI agent Ian McLennon told newsmen, "It is my understanding that the letter aided the police in locating the bodies." The Reverend Hoover and Fred Schanning finally revealed their identities, playing their tapes of "Dr. Spencer" for bemused detectives, and while both were initially suspected of murder, a July 24 press release declared both men "absolved of all involvement in the case."

There the matter rested until January 1976, when prison inmate Eugene Clawson suddenly confessed to the double slaying. A longtime mental patient with a history of numerous false confessions in criminal cases, Clawson seemed an unlikely suspect. A policeman who had known him since high school told the press "there is nothing on the record which makes it appear that he was capable of something like this." More to the point, his thirty-five-page confession was rife with factual errors. At one point, Clawson stated he had handcuffed one victim and raped the other, actions flatly refuted by autopsy reports. He also gave directions to a site where he supposedly buried the missing heads, but nothing was found.

Even so, a lame suspect was better than none at all. County prosecutors brought Clawson to trial in October 1976, and he was convicted on the basis of his own shaky confession, with no supporting physical evidence. Immediately following pronouncement of his life sentence, Clawson tearfully recanted his admission of guilt, claiming he picked his few accurate statements from an article in a detective magazine.

The Reverend Hoover, meanwhile, remains convinced of Clawson's innocence. As he told the press: "Regardless of what the police or anyone else says, Mr. Clawson did not commit the murders. I know what I receive psychically is valid, and the vibrations indicate that he is not the one responsible, because there were two men involved who were members of a ritualistic cult. One was black, five feet seven inches tall, and from West Virginia. The other was white and had blond hair, cold, steel blue eyes, and an expressionless face." At this writing, authorities stand by their solution to the case. The missing heads have not been found.

CODAY, DONALD

A resident of Fullerton, California, sixteen-year-old Donald Coday was the product of a severely abusive home. Between 1982 and 1984, the teenager's parents were investigated three times on allegations of child abuse, but no charges were ever filed. Police scrutiny notwithstanding, forty-seven-year-old Rex Coday continued to brutalize his son, beating Don with rubber hoses and a dog leash on occasion, constantly humiliating him, and making his life miserable at every turn. Finally, in desperation, Donald turned to Satan and black magic in a bid to save himself. As psychologist William Heard later told authorities, "He said he prayed to Satan to help him kill his father because he knew God would not help him."

On March 23, 1985, Rex Coday pushed his luck too far, slamming Donald across the back with a piece of lumber for "taking too long" in the bathroom. Acting on advice from Satan, Donald said, he fetched a gun and sat down in the living room, waiting for his father to return from jogging. Nine bullets later, one part of his problem was solved; another part was just beginning, in the courts.

"I think if his mother had been there," Dr. Heard testified, "he would have killed her, too."

Perhaps. In any case, the young defendant's age and family background led to disposition of his case in juvenile court, where therapy and healing theoretically take precedence over punishment. With any luck, he may find something better than a hope of hellfire to sustain him in the years ahead.

"COLE, TOBY"

On September 18, 1989, a disheveled teenage girl wandered into the office of William B. Jack Elementary School in Portland, Maine. She did not speak, but rapid, urgent gestures prompted Judi Fox, a teacher's aide, to summon a staff member proficient in sign language. As it turned out, the girl was pleading for help, but the message was confused, disoriented. She was coaxed into a car and driven to the Governor Baxter School for the Deaf, in nearby Falmouth, where authorities began unraveling her eerie tale.

For openers, the deaf girl identified herself as Toby Cole, but she suspected that the name might not be hers. She had been kidnapped several years ago, in California, and the name she used had been supplied by her abductors. Toby thought that she was fifteen years of age, perhaps born on Christmas Day 1974, and yet . . .

It took several weeks for police and FBI agents to unravel the story, and still they had no satisfactory conclusion. Toby believed her kidnappers had snatched her from a foster home, but she could not recall a town or address, dates or names. She had been moved across the country, possibly from coast to coast and back again, but the authorities got nowhere trying to determine her itinerary.

Then, she started sketching for the FBI and opened up a whole new angle on the case. As Agent Paul Cavanagh, from the FBI's Boston field office, explained: "From some of the drawings she was able to provide, it is believed that some of the people she was with since her abduction may have been tied to the occult." In fact, the symbols drawn by Toby Cole were starkly and specifically satanic.

Police speculate that Toby was kidnapped at random on the West Coast, shuttled across country by stages, perhaps used in rituals, child pornography, or prostitution. Rumors of satanic slave-trading cults suddenly seemed more credible . . . but, sadly, Toby's story has no ending. She was never able to provide specific information leading to arrests, no further clues to her identity were ever found, and with her placement in a foster home, the trail went cold. As for her current whereabouts, authorities will only say: "She's in a safe place in the state. She's comfortable. She's been taken care of." [See: Slavery]

CONSTANZO, ADOLFO DE JESUS

Miami-born on November 1, 1962, Adolfo Constanzo was the son of a teenaged Cuban immigrant. He was still an infant when his widowed mother moved to Puerto Rico and acquired a second husband. There, Adolfo was baptized a Catholic and served the church as an altar boy, appearing to accept the standard tenets of the Roman faith. He was ten years old when the family moved back to Miami, and his stepfather died a year later, leaving Adolfo and his mother financially well-off.

By that time, neighbors in Little Havana had begun to notice something odd about Aurora Constanzo and her son. Some said the woman was a witch, and those who angered her were likely to discover headless goats or chickens on their doorsteps in the morning. Adolfo's mother had introduced him to the santeria cult around age nine, with side trips from Puerto Rico to Haiti for instruction in voodoo, but there were still more secrets to be learned, and in 1976 he was apprenticed to a practitioner of palo mayombe. His occult "godfather" was already rich from working with local drug dealers, and he imparted a philosophy that would follow Adolfo to his grave: "Let the nonbelievers kill themselves with drugs. We will profit from their foolishness."

Around the same time, Constanzo's mother recalls that her oldest son began displaying psychic powers, scanning the future to predict such events as the 1981 shooting of President Ronald Reagan. Be that as it may, Adolfo had problems foretelling his own future, including two 1981 arrests for shoplifting—one involving the theft of a chainsaw. On the side, he had also begun to display bisexual inclinations, with a strong preference for male lovers.

A modeling assignment took the handsome young sorcerer to Mexico City in 1983, and he spent his free time telling fortunes with tarot cards in the city's infamous "Zona Rosa." Before returning to Miami, Adolfo collected his first Mexican disciples, including Martin Quintana, homosexual "psychic" Jorge Montes, and Omar Orea, obsessed with the occult from age fifteen. In short order, Constanzo seduced both Rodriquez and Orea, claiming one as his "man" and the other as his "woman," depending on Adolfo's romantic whim.

In mid-1984, Constanzo moved to Mexico City full-time, seeking what his mother called "new horizons." He shared quarters with Quintana and Orea, in a strange *ménage à trois*, collecting other followers as his "magic" reputation spread throughout the city. It was said that Constanzo could read the future, and also offered *limpias*—ritual "cleansings"—for those who felt they had been cursed by enemies. Of course, it all cost money, and Constanzo's journals—recovered after his death—document thirty-one regular customers, some paying up to $4,500 for a single ceremony. Adolfo established a menu for sacrificial beasts, with roosters going for $6 a head, goats for $30, boa constrictors at $450, adult zebras for $1,100, and African lion cubs listed at $3,100 each.

True to the teachings of his Florida mentor, Constanzo went out of his way to charm wealthy·drug dealers, helping them schedule shipments and meetings on the basis of his predictions. For a price, he offered magic that would make dealers and their hit men invisible to police, bulletproof against their enemies. It was all nonsense, of course, but smugglers drawn from Mexican peasant stock, with a background in *brujeria,* were strongly inclined to believe. According to Constanzo's ledgers, one dealer in Mexico City paid him $40,000 for magical services rendered over three years time.

At those rates, the customers demanded a show, and Constanzo recognized the folly of disappointing men who carried Uzi submachine guns in their armor-plated limousines. Strong medicine required first-rate ingredients, and Adolfo was rolling by mid-1985, when he and three of his disciples raided a Mexico City graveyard for human bones to start his own *nganga*—the traditional cauldron of blood employed by practitioners of palo mayombe. The rituals and air of mystery surrounding Constanzo were powerful enough·to lure a cross section of Mexican society, with his clique of disciples including a physician, a real estate speculator, fashion models, and several tranvestite nightclub performers.

At first glance, the most peculiar aspect of Constanzo's new career was the appeal he seemed to have for ranking law-enforcement officers. At least four members of the Federal Judicial Police joined Constanzo's cult in Mexico City: one of them, Salvador Garcia, was a commander in charge of narcotics investigations; another, Florentino Ventura, retired from the *federales* to lead the Mexican branch of Interpol. In a country where bribery—*mordida*—permeates all levels of law enforcement and federal officers sometimes serve as triggermen for drug smugglers, corruption is not unusual, but the devotion of Constanzo's followers ran deeper than cash on the line. In or out of uniform, they worshiped Adolfo as a minor god in his own right, their living conduit to the spirit world.

In 1986, Florentino Ventura introduced Constanzo to the drug-dealing Calzada family, then one of Mexico's dominant narcotics cartels. Constanzo won the hard-nosed dealers over with his charm and mumbo jumbo, profiting immensely from his contacts with the gang. By early 1987, he was able to pay $60,000 cash for a condominium in Mexico City, buying himself a fleet of luxury cars that included an $80,000 Mercedes Benz. When not working magic for the Calzadas or other clients, Adolfo staged scams of his own, once posing as a DEA agent to rip off a coke dealer in Guadalajara, selling the stash through his police contacts for a cool $100,000.

At some point in his odyssey from juvenile psychic to high-society witch, Constanzo began to feed his *nganga* with the offerings of human sacrifice. No final tally for his victims is available, but twenty-three ritual murders are well documented, and Mexican authorities point to a rash of unsolved mutilation-slayings around Mexico City and elsewhere, suggesting that Constanzo's known victims may only represent the tip of a malignant iceberg. In any case, his willingness to torture and kill total strangers—along with close friends—duly impressed the ruthless drug dealers who remained his foremost clients.

In the course of a year's association, Constanzo came to believe that his magical powers alone were responsible for the Calzada family's continued success and survival. In April 1987, he demanded a full partnership in the syndicate and was curtly refused. On the surface, Constanzo seemed to take the rejection in stride, but his devious mind was working overtime, plotting revenge.

On April 30, Guillermo Calzada and six members of his household vanished under mysterious circumstances. They were reported missing on May 1, police noting melted candles and other evidence of a strange religious ceremony at Calzada's office. Six more days elapsed before officers began fishing mutilated remains from the Zumpango River. Seven corpses were recovered in the course of a week, all bearing signs of sadistic torture—fingers, toes, and ears removed, hearts and sex organs excised, part of the spine ripped from one body, two others missing their brains.

The vanished parts, as it turned out, had gone to feed Constanzo's cauldron of blood, building up his strength for greater conquests yet to come.

In July 1987, Salvador Garcia introduced Constanzo to another drug-running family, this one led by brothers Elio and Ovidio Hernandez. At the end of that month, in Matamoros,

Constanzo also met twenty-two-year-old Sara Aldrete, a Mexican national with resident alien status in the United States, where she attended college in Brownsville, Texas. Adolfo charmed Sara with his line of patter, noting with arch significance that her birthday—September 6—was the same as his mother's. Sara was dating Brownsville drug smuggler Gilberto Sosa at the time, but she soon wound up in Constanzo's bed, Adolfo scuttling the old relationship with an anonymous call to Sosa, revealing Sara's infidelity. With nowhere else to turn, Sara plunged full tilt into Constanzo's world, emerging as the *madrina*—godmother or "head witch"—of his cult, adding her own twists to the torture of sacrificial victims.

Constanzo's rituals became more elaborate and sadistic after he moved his headquarters to a plot of desert called Rancho Santa Elena, twenty miles from Matamoros. There, on May 28, 1988, drug dealer Hector de la Fuente and farmer Moises Castillo were executed by gunfire, but the sacrifice was a disappointment to Constanzo. Back in Mexico City, he directed his drones to dismember a transvestite, Ramon Esquivel, and dump the grisly remains on a public street corner. His luck was holding, and Constanzo narrowly escaped when Houston police raided a drug house in June 1988, seizing numerous items of occult paraphernalia and the city's largest-ever shipment of cocaine.

On August 12, Ovidio Hernandez and his two-year-old son were kidnapped by rival narcotics dealers, the family turning to Constanzo for help. That night, another human sacrifice was staged at Rancho Santa Elena, and the hostages were released unharmed on August 13, Adolfo claiming full credit for their safe return. His star was rising, and Constanzo barely noticed when Florentino Ventura committed suicide in Mexico City on September 17, taking his wife and a friend with him in the same burst of gunfire.

In November 1988, Constanzo sacrificed disciple Jorge Gomez, accused of snorting cocaine in direct violation of *el padrino*'s ban on drug use. A month later, Adolfo's ties to the Hernandez family were cemented with the initiation of Ovidio Hernandez as a full-fledged cultist, complete with ritual bloodletting and prayers to the *nganga*.

Human sacrifice can also have its practical side, as when competing smuggler Ezequiel Luna was tortured to death at Rancho Santa Elena, on February 14, 1989; two other dealers—Ruben Garza and Ernesto Diaz—wandered into the ceremony uninvited, and promptly wound up on the menu. Conversely, Adolfo sometimes demanded a sacrifice on the spur of the moment, without rhyme or reason. When he called for fresh meat on February 25, Ovidio Hernandez gladly joined the hunting party, picking off his own fourteen-year-old cousin, Jose Garcia, in the heat of the moment.

On March 13, 1989, Constanzo sacrificed yet another victim at the ranch, gravely disappointed when his prey did not scream and plead for mercy in the approved style. Disgruntled, he ordered an Anglo for the next ritual, and his minions fanned out with their noses to the ground, abducting twenty-one-year-old Mark Kilroy outside a Matamoros saloon. The sacrifice went well enough, followed two weeks later by the butchery of Sara Aldrete's old boyfriend, Gilberto Sosa, but Kilroy's disappearance marked the beginning of the end for Constanzo's homicidal family.

A popular premed student from Texas, Mark Kilroy was not some peasant, transvestite, or small-time pusher who could disappear without a trace or an investigation into his fate. With family members and Texas politicians turning up the heat, the search for Kilroy rapidly assumed the trappings of an international incident ... but it would be Constanzo's own disciples who destroyed him in the end.

By late March 1989, Mexican authorities were busy with one of their periodic antidrug campaigns, erecting roadblocks on a whim and sweeping the border districts for unwary smugglers. On April 1, Victor Sauceda, an ex-cop turned gangster, was sacrificed at the ranch, and the "spirit message" Constanzo received was optimistic enough for his troops to move a half ton of marijuana across the border seven nights later.

And then, the magic started to unravel.

On April 9, returning from a Brownsville, Texas, meeting with Constanzo, cultist Serafin Hernandez drove past a police roadblock without stopping, ignoring the cars that set off in hot pursuit. Hernandez believed *el padrino*'s line about invisibility, and he seemed surprised when officers trailed him to his destination in Matamoros. Even so, the smuggler was arrogant, inviting police to shoot him, since the bullets would merely bounce off.

They arrested him instead, along with cult member David Martinez, and drove the pair back to Rancho Santa Elena, where a preliminary search turned up marijuana and firearms. Disciples Elio Hernandez and Sergio Martinez stumbled into the net while police were on hand, and all four were interrogated through the evening, revealing their tales of black magic, torture, and human sacrifice with a perverse kind of pride.

Next morning, police returned to the ranch in force, discovering the malodorous shed where Constanzo kept his *nganga*, brimming with blood, spiders, scorpions, a dead black cat, a turtle shell, bones, deer antlers ... and a human brain. Captive cult members directed searchers to Constanzo's private cemetery, and excavation began, revealing fifteen mutilated corpses by April 16. In addition to Mark Kilroy and other victims already named, the body count included two renegade federal narcotics officers—Joaquin Manzo and Miguel Garcia—along with three men who were never identified.

The hunt for Constanzo was on, and police raided his luxury home at Atizapan, outside Mexico City, on April 17, discovering stockpiles of gay pornography and a hidden ritual chamber. The discoveries at Rancho Santa Elena made international headlines, and sightings of Constanzo were reported as far away as Chicago, but in fact, he had already returned to Mexico City, hiding out in a small apartment with Sara Aldrete and three other disciples. On May 2, thinking to save herself, Sara tossed a note out the window. It read:

Please call the judicial police and tell them that in this building are those that they are seeking. Give them the address, fourth floor. Tell them that a woman is being held hostage. I beg for this, because what I want most is to talk—or they're going to kill the girl.

A passerby found the note, read it, and kept it to himself, believing it was someone's lame attempt at humor. On May 6, neighbors called police to complain of a loud, vulgar argument in Constanzo's apartment—some say, accompanied by gunshots. As patrolmen arrived on the scene, Constanzo spotted them and opened fire with an Uzi, touching off a forty-five minute battle in which, miraculously, only one policeman was wounded.

When Constanzo realized that escape was impossible, he handed his weapon to cultist Alvaro de Leon Valdez—a professional hit man nicknamed "El Duby"—with bizarre new orders. As El Duby recalls the scene: "He told me to kill him and Martin [Quintana]. I told him I couldn't do it, but he hit me in the face and threatened me that everything would go bad for me in hell. Then he hugged Martin, and I just stood in front of them and shot them with a machine gun."

Constanzo and Quintana were dead when police stormed the apartment, arresting El Duby and Sara Aldrete. In the aftermath of the raid, fourteen cultists were indicted on various charges, including multiple murder, weapons and narcotics violations, conspiracy, and obstruction of justice. In August 1990, El Duby was convicted of killing Constanzo and Quintana, drawing a thirty-year prison term. Cultists Juan Fragosa and Jorge Montes were both convicted in the Ramon Esquivel murder and sentenced to thirty-five years each; Omar Orea, convicted in the same case, died of AIDS before he could be sentenced. Sara Aldrete was acquitted of Constanzo's murder but sentenced to a six-year term on conviction for criminal association. At this writing, her long-delayed trial on thirteen other homicides is pending. To this day, Constanzo's *madrina* insists that she never practiced any religion but "Christian santeria." Televised reports of the murders at Rancho Santa Elena, she says, took her by complete surprise.

Police in Mexico are still uncertain of Constanzo's final body count, some officers trying to clear every ritualistic murder on the books by posthumously blaming Constanzo. On the other hand, in June 1989, Martin Quintana's sister told police that Adolfo's first *madrina* was still at large, practicing her blood magic in Guadalajara. And from jail, before he died, Omar Orea said, "I don't think that the religion will end with us, because it has a lot of people in it. They have found a temple in Monterrey that isn't even related to us. It will continue." [See: Palo Mayombe; Santeria]

CONTINENTAL ASSOCIATION OF SATAN'S HOPE

A mail order "cult" based in Montreal, Canada, the Continental Association of Satan's Hope claims a preposterous worldwide membership of forty-five thousand disciples.

Founder Eric McAllister advertises widely in pulp magazines, encouraging readers to "turn your fantasies into reality and discover for yourself the infernal power of mighty Satan!" For a three-dollar fee, "members" receive a newsletter, *The Rage*, that purports to cure illness, conjure wealth, and guarantee success with women. McAllister's ads promise to disclose "rituals by which you can conjure up the infernal powers of the Mighty Satan and hold them in servitude. Find out how good it feels to have security in life, to know if anything goes wrong in your life you will always have someone to turn to in order to help you out of the toughest jams!" The huckster's bottom line is spelled out in his group's initials: CASH.

COPA, ROLANDO ADOLFO

A fourteen-year-old resident of Tacapisi, Peru, Copa left home on November 20, 1987, and never returned. His stone-battered corpse was discovered the following day, at an Indian ritual site on a nearby mountain. Police found a black dog killed at the same spot, conforming with tribal beliefs that such animals accompany souls into the afterlife. A teenage friend of the victim, Mario Gregorio Cotipu, was jailed for the murder and promptly confessed. According to Cotipu's statement, he and two other youths had studied magic with Copa's father, self-professed *yatiri* Marciano Victor Copa. The sacrifice of Copa's son was planned and carried out in accordance with rituals drawn from magic books supplied by Marciano Copa himself.

COVEY, DAVID and PAMELA

In late March 1980, David and Pamela Covey, both in their twenties, drove 145 miles from their home in Lakewood, Colorado, to a remote mountain area, where David shot his wife and then himself, in an apparent murder-suicide pact. A snowplow operator found their bodies on March 31, near the small town of Walden. Police determined that the couple shared a marijuana joint before David shot Pamela with an old-fashioned .45-caliber cap-and-ball revolver, afterward turning the gun on himself. Both victims wore rings and medallions bearing satanic insignia, and a search of their home turned up numerous books on witchcraft and ritual magic. No specific motive for the murder-suicide was found, but police describe the crime as "occultic" and "satanic."

COWAN, FREDERICK W.

A 250-pound bodybuilder who dropped out of college in his freshman year, Fred Cowan was subsequently discharged from the army after two courts-martial for going AWOL and leaving the scene of an auto accident. Back home in New Rochelle, New York, he found menial employment with the Neptune Worldwide Moving Company, devoting his free time to the study of Nazi history and philosophy.

No piker when it came to racism, Cowan decorated his attic apartment with portraits of Adolf Hitler and Heinrich Himmler, Wermacht helmets, vintage German weapons, and a Nazi battle flag. He joined the fanatical, Georgia-based National States Rights Party and stocked up on anti-Semitic literature, but friends still thought he was joking when Cowan spoke about the possibility of "shooting up a synagogue." In Cowan's view of life, "Nothing is lower than blacks or Jews except the police who protect them."

Big Fred's attitude caused problems on the job, where supervisor Norman Bing—a Jew—was not inclined to stand for insubordination from a neo-Nazi thug. In early February 1977, Cowan drew two weeks' suspension for refusing to move a refrigerator, and he spent his time off brooding over the injustices of life, as dominated by the Jewish world conspiracy.

His first day back at work, February 14, Cowan showed up at 7:45 A.M., lugging a fifty-pound arsenal of weapons. Bing saw him coming and slipped under a desk to hide, while Cowan unloaded his hardware. Deprived of his primary target, Fred opened fire on minority coworkers, killing three blacks and an Indian immigrant before police arrived. Cutting loose on the squad cars, he killed one patrolman and wounded five more victims—one of whom would die months later—before his rampage ran out of steam.

With SWAT officers surrounding the Neptune warehouse, Cowan phoned police headquarters at 12:13 P.M., ordering potato salad and hot cocoa to go. He also apologized to New

Rochelle's mayor, in absentia, for "causing the city so much trouble." At 2:40, a single shot rang out, and officers crept inside to find Cowan dead by his own hand, still wearing a black beret with a skull-and-crossbones insignia. In the parking lot, his car bore a prophetic bumper sticker: I WILL GIVE UP MY GUN WHEN THEY PRY MY COLD, DEAD FINGERS FROM AROUND IT.

In the massacre's aftermath, NSRP chairman J.B. Stoner convened a hasty news conference, telling journalists, "The FBI caused niggers to start harassing Cowan on the job. Apparently the FBI's to blame for the whole incident." Media reports dubbed Cowan a "Nazi cultist," but there was more to his sickness than met the eye.

In New York City, gathering material on the "Son of Sam" murders, Maury Terry learned that suspect David Berkowitz had rented rooms from one of Cowan's coworkers in early 1976. More to the point, Berkowitz had kept a file of news clippings on Cowan after the shootout, several times referring to Cowan as "one of the Sons." In October 1978, Terry helped arrange a prison interview between Berkowitz and lawyer Felix Gilroy, which included the following exchange:

> Q: Do the words "witches' coven" mean anything to you?
> A: I have heard it before.
> Q: Were some of these people involved in the witches' coven?
> A: I believe they were. Yes.
> Q: Were you in the same coven?
> A: Yes.
> Q: Did you meet regularly?
> A: Well, I can't really say. I don't want to say.
> Q: Was Mr. Cowan involved in that?
> A: I don't want to talk about it.

At that point, Berkowitz digressed to explain that some cultists were more "spirit" than flesh, frustrating mundane administration of justice, but Gilroy persevered.

> Q: Was Fred Cowan a real person when you knew him?
> A: Yes.

While difficult—if not impossible—to verify, the Berkowitz report on Cowan dovetails perfectly with independent descriptions of neo-Nazi leanings in the sinister "Four P Movement" both allegedly belonged to . . . and in other modern satanic cults, as well. [See: Berkowitz, David; "Four P Movement"; Nazism]

"CROWD, THE"

A near-legendary occult society based in Joplin, Missouri, "The Crowd" reportedly takes its name from the army base at Camp Crowder, near Neosho in neighboring Newton County. The group has been well-known to Midwestern occultists for years, maintaining reputed links with several thriving covens in Missouri and Kansas. Despite local notoriety, however, national exposure was delayed until 1988, with the Joplin murder of victim Steve Newberry by members of a teenage satanic cult. When police examined the telephone records of killer Jim Hardy, they noted numerous calls to Neosho and various towns in Kansas, but Hardy refused to discuss the matter, and their significance remains unclear.

A self-professed member of The Crowd was interviewed by author Carl Raschke in 1989, describing his initiation to the group by older friends who promised him "exotic travel" in the form of LSD, cocaine, and mescaline. Indoctrination into Satanism was gradual, with free-flowing drugs to sweeten the journey. In time, the informant deduced that The Crowd functioned primarily as "a purchasing service for the occult," moving dope and other contraband throughout the Midwest, virtually monopolizing drug traffic in southwestern Missouri. Prominent residents of Joplin and Neosho were allegedly involved, but their names have not been publicized and no prosecutions have resulted to date. Joplin police confirm that Raschke's informant was at least peripherally involved with the group responsible for Steve Newberry's ritual murder in 1988. [See: Newberry, Steven]

CROWLEY, ALEISTER

The premier Satanist of modern times was born Edward Alexander Crowley, in England, on October 12, 1875. His parents were ardent members of the fundamentalist Plymouth Brethren, and Crowley's strict upbringing taught him to despise Christianity at an early age. In adolescence, Crowley—by his own account—began to experience "psychic" flashes, including one that predicted his father's death from cancer of the tongue when Crowley was eleven years old.

Without paternal restraint, Crowley grew increasingly rebellious, showing off a strong sadistic streak. Around age twelve, as outlined in his later memoirs, he devised a cruel experiment to test the maxim that cats have nine lives. According to Crowley:

> I caught a cat, and having administered a large dose of arsenic, I chloroformed it, hanged it above the gas jet, stabbed it, cut its throat, smashed its skull, and, when it had been pretty thoroughly burnt, drowned it and threw it out of the window that the fall might remove the ninth life. The operation was successful. I was genuinely sorry for the animal; I simply forced myself to carry out the experiment in the interests of pure science.

Such "experiments" became routine, and Crowley also showed an increasing preoccupation with sex of all kinds, culminating in his expulsion from a Plymouth Brethren school for "corrupting" another boy. Emily Crowley was moved to denounce her son as the "Great Beast" from the biblical Book of Revelation, an honor which Crowley repaid by dubbing his mother "a brainless bigot of the most narrow, logical and inhuman type."

Forced to continue his education over strenuous objections, Crowley—now calling himself "Aleister"—finally wound up at Cambridge, where he began his occult studies in earnest. On one occasion, Crowley built a wax effigy of a professor who had scolded him, performed a "black" ritual in the company of several classmates, and stabbed the figurine's leg with a needle. If we believe Crowley's publicity, largely self-generated, the professor tumbled down a flight of stairs the next day and broke his leg.

Aside from sex and "magick," Crowley had a fierce passion for mountain climbing, but it was safest for all concerned when he climbed alone. Over the years, he earned an unsavory reputation for injuring his climbing partners—

deliberately or otherwise—with several deaths resulting. For the egocentric Crowley, there was no such thing as *bad* publicity, and he took the incidents in stride. It was all part of the cosmic game.

In November 1898, Crowley joined a prominent ritual magic society, the Hermetic Order of the Golden Dawn. He enjoyed the ceremonial trappings, but Crowley was frustrated by the OGD's aversion to drugs and sex magic. He also developed an instant personality conflict with the OGD's dominant magician, Samuel Lidell MacGregor Mathers, which would blossom into a "magic war" of sorts over time. Denied initiation into the OGD's second level because of his flagrant bisexuality, Crowley took the magic name Perdurabo—Latin for "I will endure to the end"—and settled in for the long haul. (Mathers, for his part, regarded Crowley as "an unspeakably mad person.")

Meanwhile, ever the con man, Crowley was living in London as "Count Svareff," an alleged Russian nobleman. In 1900, maintaining a lifelong fondness for royal pseudonyms, he moved to Boleskine House, near Foyers, in Inverness, Scotland, and christened himself "Laird of Boleskine." A total lack of Scottish blood meant nothing when Crowley's fertile imagination was on a roll.

In 1903, Crowley married Rose Kelly, sister of prominent artist Sir Gerald Kelly, and embarked on a globe-hopping honeymoon—described by Aleister himself as "an uninterrupted sexual debauch"—that finally landed them in Cairo. As befit his Egyptian surroundings, Crowley renamed himself "Prince Chioa Khan" and dubbed his wife a princess, insisting that everyone—her parents included—address them by their fabricated titles.

It was in Cairo that Crowley recorded his visits from "Aiwass," an ephemeral mouthpiece for the Egyptian god Horus. Quoting Aiwass at length, Crowley produced his *Book of the Law,* which remains a classic text among believers in ritual magic. Selected excerpts make it clear that Aiwass had found a kindred spirit in his ghost writer.

To worship me take wine and strange drugs whereof I will tell my prophet, & be drunk thereof.

There is no law beyond Do what thou wilt.

Be strong, O man! lust, enjoy all things of sense and rapture:
fear not that any God shall deny thee for this.

Now ye shall know that the chosen priest and apostle of infi-
nite space is the prince-priest the Beast.

In case there were any doubts about the identity of said
"prince-priest," Crowley began calling himself "the Great
Beast 666," proclaiming the onset of a demonic "Aeon of
Horus." In 1904, he fired off a letter to MacGregor Mathers,
claiming that a group of occult "secret chiefs" had named
Crowley head of the OGD, with a new magical policy he
dubbed "thelema"—Greek for "will." Mathers was predictably unimpressed with the order to vacate his throne, hitting
back with a series of "magical attacks" on Crowley. The
Great Beast, for his part, summoned up "the 49 servants of
Beelzebub" and sent them after Mathers. It was a prolonged
war of nerves, ending only with Mathers' death in 1918 . . .
an event for which Crowley predictably claimed credit
through means of a "death curse."

On the home front, Rose was pregnant with Crowley's first
child, and he sent her back to England for the duration, while
he embarked on a rambling trek through the Far East. In
1905, a disastrous climbing expedition furthered his odious
reputation, with reports of Crowley beating porters and leaving two companions to die after they were buried by an av-
alanche. Returning to England in 1906, he found that his
young daughter had died, and blamed his wife's supposed
negligence for the loss. Rose later bore him a son, but the
damage was done, and Crowley divorced her in 1909. An alcoholic nervous wreck by that time, Rose retired to an asylum, where she later died.

Denied the fellowship of the OGD while Mathers held the
reins, Crowley scored an end run in 1907, with his creation
of a new society, the Astrum Argentium, or "Silver Star."
Based on a line from his *Book of the Law* proclaiming that
"Every man and woman is a star," Crowley's new cult had
the added benefit, so he said, of outranking Mathers and the
OGD. In fact, according to Crowley's alleged communication
with spirits from beyond, his A.A. was actually the "Inner
Order of the Great White Brotherhood," a group vastly superior to the Golden Dawn.

Self-proclaimed divinity is still a lonely place without followers, and Crowley went shopping for an established cult in 1912. A visit to German occultist Theodor Reuss introduced Crowley to the ten-year-old Ordo Templi Orientis, claiming direct lineal descent from the Knights Templar, and Crowley soon emerged as leader of the OTO in Britain. Better yet, considering his childish obsession with royal titles, he was also proclaimed "the Supreme and Holy King of Ireland, Iona, and all the Britains that are in the Sanctuary of the Gnosis." On the side, Crowley took to calling himself "Ipsissimus."

It was a mouthful, and then some, but Crowley took his duties seriously . . . and one of those duties was evangelism. In 1915, he traveled to North America for an extended stay, planting OTO chapters in Canada before he finally settled in New York City. There, he took up painting and advertised in newspapers for models of a unique sort.

WANTED

Dwarfs, Hunchbacks, Tattooed Women, Harrison Fisher Girls, Freaks of All Sorts, Coloured Women, only if exceptionally ugly or deformed, to pose for artist. Apply by letter with a photograph.

On the side, he churned out several books which sold poorly, and tried to inaugurate a new satanic age in a ceremony that featured the baptism and crucifixion of a toad. In daily life, Crowley was better known for his published words of pro-German propaganda, later dismissed by the portly magician as an attempt "to wreck the German propaganda on the roof of Reductio ad Absurdum." In either case, his bizarre life-style was too much for traditional OTO leaders, and the German-based society severed its connections with Crowley's British realm in 1916.

Back in England two years later, calling himself "Baphomet" and anything else that came to mind, Crowley found himself a prophet without honor in his own country. Following his personal inclinations and the sage advice of Aiwass, he was deeply immersed in narcotics by this time, with his daily dosage of heroin sometimes exceeding ten grains—when *one* can be fatal. In 1920, tired of living hand-to-mouth, Crowley packed up his magic kit and his mistress—"Scarlet Woman" Leah Hirsig—and struck off for Sicily, where he rented a villa at Cefalu and christened it the "Abbey of

Thelema." Over the next three years, Crowley collected a motley crew of disciples at Cefalu, making the rituals up as he went along and working on his memoirs, aptly titled *The Diary of a Dope Fiend*. As Crowley described himself in print:

I am myself a physical coward, but I have exposed myself to every form of disease, accident, and violence; I am dainty and delicate, but I have driven myself to delight in dirty and disgusting debauches, and to devour human excrements and human flesh. I am at this moment defying the power of drugs to disturb my destiny and divert my body from its duty. I am also a mental and moral weakling, whose boyhood training was so horrible that its result was that my will wholly summed up in hatred of all restraint, whose early manhood, untrained, left my mind and animal soul like an elephant in rut broken out of the stockade. Yet I have mastered every mode of my mind, and made myself a morality more severe than any other in the world if only by virtue of its absolute freedom from any code of conduct.

Crowley's "severe morality" was typified by a 1921 ritual at Cefalu, where he induced a goat to copulate with Leah Hirsig, Crowley slitting the animal's throat at the moment of orgasm. In fact, satanic rites and animal sacrifice were routine at the abbey, climaxed in 1923 when one of his disciples died from drinking the blood of a distempered cat. Expelled from Sicily following a government investigation of his cult, Crowley wandered Europe and North Africa, his reputation growing with each new report of personal debauchery. At home, the British press dubbed him "the wickedest man alive," "the king of depravity," and "a cannibal at large."

In Germany, Theodor Reuss retired from leadership of the OTO in 1923, naming Crowley as his chosen successor. It took the society's leaders a year to make up their minds, but Crowley was finally confirmed in 1924. One of his first acts as chief of the order was the creation of a homosexual "11th degree" to dominate the other levels of OTO membership.

At home in London, Crowley cultivated his reputation as a dark and terrible figure. It was rumored that he drove servants to suicide, sacrificed children and dumped their bodies in the Thames, and caused a rude butcher to sever his own artery by means of a magic incantation. The apex—or nadir—of his magical career came with the death of his own son MacAleister, during a locked-room ceremony to invoke a nameless demon. Disciples waiting outside were startled by loud noises at the climax of the ceremony, breaking down the door to find Crowley huddled nude in a corner, his black robe in tatters, while MacAleister lay dead of an apparent heart attack.

Crowley spent four months in a sanitarium following MacAleister's death, and he emerged a broken man, largely forgotten by newsmen who had found a greater devil in the person of Adolf Hitler. Crowley eked out a marginal existence, variously pimping for his prostitute wife, laying plans for a Black Magick Restaurant, and hawking "Elixir of Life" pills that included his semen as a prime ingredient. Nearly destitute, scarred by years of needles and self-mutilation, he retired to a small Hastings rooming house in January 1947, and died there on December 1. On his death bed, Crowley is said to have cursed the physician who refused him a final dose of morphine, the doctor dropping dead with eighteen hours of Crowley's demise. The seventy-two-year-old magician was embalmed in the Egyptian style, then cremated in accordance with his last wishes.

A half century after his death, Aleister Crowley exerts greater influence on the world of black magic than he ever did in life. Leaders of competing OTO factions quarrel endlessly over their claims to "spiritual descent" from the master, and rock musicians from the Beatles to Hall and Oates have proclaimed their admiration for Crowley in print. Crowley's philosophy pervades Anton LaVey's Church of Satan and its various spin-offs, legitimate and otherwise. A notorious snapshot from the late 1960s shows Bobby Beausoleil, later a triggerman for the homicidal Manson "family," posing in nineteenth century dress on the steps of an abandoned San Francisco church. Behind him, painted on the door, we see the motto of contemporary Satanism: DO WHAT THOU WILT. [See: Order of the Golden Dawn; Ordo Templi Orientis]

DANIEL, ST. CLAIR

At 7:22 A.M. on March 2, 1988, police on St. Thomas, Virgin Islands, were summoned to Vessup Bay Beach, where callers reported a naked man with a machete "hacking away at a body." On arrival, patrolmen found *two* corpses, some five hundred feet apart. Each had been decapitated, dismembered, and brutally disemboweled.

There were at least a dozen witnesses to the crime, including residents of beachfront homes and several passengers of boats offshore. Some bystanders had even photographed the attack in progress, but a search of the surrounding jungle nailed a suspect before the snapshots were developed. Cornered in a clump of undergrowth, still nude, the hacker pleaded with arresting officers to "Take it easy on me."

By the time of his arrest on double murder charges, St. Clair Daniel was familiar to police around the island. At age thirty-four, he had lived on St. Thomas since 1982, logging several arrests. Long-standing mental illness worsened after Daniel's wife abandoned him for the father of her illegitimate child in 1984, and a year later he was wounded in a clash with police while trying to board an aircraft without a ticket. His record showed two more arrests since New Year's, the latest for a pickax assault against an unarmed man. Blood tests on that occasion showed that he was high on PCP.

With Daniel safe in jail, police set about identifying his victims. One, fifty-three-year-old Genevieve Lewis, had known her killer, reporting several confrontations with Daniel in recent months. Ten days before the double slaying, he had been forcibly removed from an office where she worked. The second victim, twenty-nine-year-old Steve Cornish, was a dedicated windsurfer and apparent stranger to the killer, butchered for being in the wrong place at the wrong time.

As witnesses described the scene, Daniel had approached victim Lewis on her regular morning walk, slashing her with his machete and disemboweling her corpse in a "careful, methodical manner" before he "took a big piece of cement and started smashing what was left of the torso." That done, Daniel stripped off his clothes and was bathing in the surf when Steven Cornish happened along, his presence prompting a second attack.

Family members recalled Daniel's erratic behavior prior to the crimes, along with his devotion to an odd mix of voodoo and Satanism. "I'm Lucifer," he told one relative. "I'm the one who has been tossed down from heaven." Another relative was told that Daniel's missing front teeth constituted the "mark of the beast." "He told me if I didn't believe him, I must read Revelations."

On January 12, 1989, Daniel entered a plea of not guilty by reason of insanity. A state psychiatrist countered the claim by describing his mutilation of victims as "pure voodooism"—a "cultural belief," rather than proof of insanity. As explained by the doctor, "voodoo followers fear becoming zombies" if their victims remain intact and are allowed to rise from the dead in search of revenge. Decapitation and dismemberment are thus insurance that the dead will rest in pieces—and in peace.

Jurors reached a split decision on January 19, convicting Daniel of first-degree murder in the Lewis case, finding him insane where victim Cornish was concerned. The killer's prior relationship with Lewis and the evidence that he was stalking her made all the difference, while his fierce assault on Cornish was considered totally irrational. A single count of Murder One would do the job, however, and the trial judge sentenced Daniel to a term of life imprisonment without parole.

"DARTMAN"—NEW YORK CITY

Between February 28, 1975 and May 13, 1976, at least twenty-three female residents of New York's Westchester County were wounded by one-inch steel darts, fired by an unknown assailant armed with an air gun. All the victims lived in ground-floor apartments, and each was wounded in the head, neck, or chest by the projectiles fired through windows. No suspect was identified in the case, and police lost interest two months after the final attack in Nanuet, New York, when a gunman calling himself the "Son of Sam" brought terror to Manhattan after dark. The "Westchester Dartman" remained at large.

Journalist Maury Terry, investigating satanic connections in the "Sam" case, discovered that the dartman was a symbol of death in fifteenth century Europe. It made a tantalizing lead, combined with reports of cult gatherings, canine sacrifice, and ritual gang rapes in Westchester County, but without a suspect or a solid lead, the trail went cold.

By June 1990, New York had a new random gunman on the prowl, this one dubbing himself "Zodiac," selecting victims by their birth signs ... and, perhaps coincidentally, there was another dartman in the neighborhood, as well. The new practitioner used homemade darts, a pin or needle fitted with a paper stabilizer, and he found his targets on the street, in broad daylight. He was also more prolific than his predecessor, tagging at least fifty-three women with shots to the buttocks between June 26 and July 4. Victims ranged in age from twenty-one to forty-four, but all were dressed in business clothing, stung while walking to and from their jobs.

On July 5, police released eyewitness descriptions of their suspect, a black man with a mustache and neatly trimmed beard, early thirties, sometimes carrying a satchel. Tips led them to thirty-three-year-old Jerome Wright on July 11, and three dart victims picked him from a lineup the same evening. A messenger whose duties kept him active on the street most days, Wright was still on probation from a previous drug conviction. On July 13, he reportedly confessed the attacks, changing his tune two days later. As police explained: "Mr. Wright has made numerous statements to us, none of which has given us real insight into why he is doing this."

Whatever his motive, no one has suggested a connection with the "Zodiac," the "Son of Sam," or the earlier dart attacks in Westchester County (committed when Wright was eighteen years old). Speculation abounds in the puzzling case, with potential solutions relegated to the vague realm of theory and "coincidence." [See: Berkowitz, David; "Zodiac" Killer–New York]

DIAZ, MARIA

A ten-year-old resident of Figueras, Spain, Maria Diaz disappeared without a trace from her neighborhood on May 21, 1963. In the predawn hours of May 22, a shepherd watching his flock on the Holy Mountain of San Salvador heard chanting and wild shouts on the summit above him, where a leaping bonfire lighted up the darkness. At daybreak, the shepherd ventured to investigate, climbing to the summit where monks had long ago constructed a roofed-over worship site. On this occasion, though, a rather different ceremony had apparently been carried out, with black candles left at the scene, strange symbols scratched on the earthen floor, embers of a large fire still smoldering, and a pungent smell of incense in the air. Among the ashes of the fire, a piece of cloth was found, its pink checkered pattern still visible, identified by grieving relatives as a scrap from Maria's dress.

Police in Figueras discovered that Maria Diaz was last seen climbing into a big, shiny car, occupied by two men in bright-colored shirts. Aside from the piece of her skirt, no trace of the missing child has been found to this day, and the mystery of her abduction remains unsolved. With the evidence in hand, it comes as no surprise that local authorities consider Maria a victim of satanic ritual murder.

DICKSON, ANTHONY

Authorities in Caddo Parish, Louisiana, officially describe twenty-two-year-old Anthony Dickson as a victim of "ritualistic cult murder," but they still have no idea who killed him, or why. Found by motorists outside of Shreveport on June 4, 1990, Dickson was lying on the ground beside his car, the vehicle in flames. His head, still missing, had been "cleanly removed with a sharp instrument." In the absence of viable suspects, police note vague similarities with an earlier California slaying linked to santeria. [See: Carter, Leroy]

DIXON, BUNNY NICOLE:
See NGOC VAN DANG

DOWNS, DAMON HENRY

Described by all who knew him as a teenage "electronics genius" and "computer wizard," Damon Downs provides a classic illustration of the fine line between brilliance and madness. A child of divorce and an ardent Satanist, Downs was repeatedly committed to Texas juvenile facilities and mental institutions, spending less than a year at liberty between the ages of twelve and eighteen. Recaptured shortly af-

ter his escape from one "juvey" lockup in 1984, he was
described by his keepers as "disturbed."

A year later, during a brief stint of freedom, Downs set an
estimated fifteen arson fires in Houston, entering headlines as
the "Fondra Firebug," after his neighborhood of preference.
Arrested that November and held in lieu of $200,000 bond,
Downs told authorities that he was planning his last fire—
intended to be suicidal—at the time of his arrest. In February
1986, Downs began mailing threatening letters from jail to
the judge in charge of his case, but his mood had apparently
changed by March 13, when he pleaded guilty on twelve
counts of arson, keeping his fingers crossed for leniency.
Instead, he was sentenced to a fifty-year prison term on
April 7, briefly escaping from a courthouse holding cell eight
days later, recaptured by police in short order.

A new round of threatening letters ensued, bringing Downs
back to court on October 8, 1986. In that appearance, he
pleaded guilty to escape and retribution charges, receiving
two concurrent ten-year sentences, for a total of sixty years in
prison. Additional harassment charges, linked to threats
against a second judge, were dismissed as part of the plea
bargain, leaving Downs eligible for parole around age forty.

Media exposure of the teenage arsonist's devout Satanism
created a furor in Houston, amplified two months later by the
arrest of five young cultists in an unrelated murder case.
Downs, meanwhile, has offered to leave the United States
forever, in return for commutation of his sentence, but Texas
authorities are disinclined to oblige. [See: Smith, Harold]

DREW, CARL

The town of Fall River, Massachusetts, is best known as
the home of Lizzie Borden, tried and acquitted on charges of
hacking her parents to death in 1892, but an even more grisly
case emerged from the town almost ninety years later. This
time around, there were three victims instead of two, and the
killers were self-professed members of a satanic cult.

On October 13, 1979, joggers found the corpse of
seventeen-year-old Doreen Levesque underneath some
bleachers at a Fall River high school. Doreen's wrists and
ankles were bound, her skull crushed with stones, and
an autopsy found stab wounds in the back of her head. A

background check revealed the girl's troubled history, with drinking and drug abuse dating from age twelve, interspersed with several juvenile arrests. Most recently, she had been working as a prostitute, but police had no immediate suspects in the case.

Three months later, on January 26, 1980, a local hunter stumbled on the battered, decomposing corpse of Barbara Raposa, reported missing in November. Like Doreen Levesque, the latest victim's wrists were bound, her face and skull demolished by heavy blows that suggested deliberate stoning. The missing person report on Raposa had been filed by one Andre Maltais, age forty-three, familiar to state police from an October 1979 call claiming knowledge of the Levesque murder. When he met with detectives on that occasion, Maltais brought along two prostitutes, twenty-year-old Karen Marsden and seventeen-year-old Robin Murphy, whom he named as his sources of information. Murphy was reluctant to speak with police, but Marsden had named Doreen's killer as Carl Drew, a local pimp and die-hard Satanist.

By this time, Fall River authorities were already well acquainted with the local occult scene. Undercover officers attended cult gatherings at the apartment of prostitute Maureen Sparda, noting the appeal that Satanism seemed to have for pimps and hookers. Stories of gruesome animal sacrifices were recorded, along with hints that humans might be on the menu now and then.

Carl Drew, for his part, took to Satanism like a duck to water. His criminal record included three armed robbery charges between December 1974 and February 1975. Pimping required less work, but Drew continued to display a violent temper, keeping his women in line with frequent threats of death or mutilation. In February 1978, Drew was arrested for beating a "john"; he escaped from the Fall River jail and fled through a blizzard, recaptured near the Canadian border by New Hampshire state troopers, but Massachusetts detectives neglected to question his victim before the man died, and their case fell apart. Now, it seemed, Drew had turned to the occult with a passion, wearing tattoos of the devil on his chest and left arm, the latter sporting a caption that read "Satan Avengers."

Police still had no evidence to support a murder charge against Drew, and Karen Marsden had stopped talking to detectives in late September, citing her fears that Drew—whom

she called "the Devil"—planned to kill her for saying as
much as she already had. On January 30, another prostitute
told lawmen that Marsden knew details of Barbara Raposa's
death, but Marsden refused to discuss it, repeating her story
of threats from Carl Drew.

The case took a bizarre turn on February 5, when Andre
Maltais approached detectives with news of a "psychic vision" which had briefed him on the details of Barbara
Raposa's murder. By the time he finished leading officers on
a tour of the crime scene, Maltais found himself charged as
a suspect, Robin Murphy stepping forward on February 9 to
say that she had watched Maltais beat Raposa to death in November. On the same day, Karen Marsden was reported missing by her grandmother, the woman confirming repeated
threats from Carl Drew. Questioned by police on February
10, Drew, age twenty-six, proudly admitted his worship of
Satan, denying any role in any local homicides or disappear-
ances. His satanic tattoos were photographed for the record,
and Drew was released for lack of solid evidence.

On February 16, 1980, police found a crude altar in the
woods near Fall River. Nearby, they discovered the burned-
out hulk of a car stolen on February 6, two days before Karen
Marsden was last seen alive. Bone chips were found in the
trunk, but their size and condition made them useless as fo-
rensic evidence. Meanwhile, rumors continued to surface
about Carl Drew's cult involvement, with stories describing
the ritual murders of several women and at least one unidentified man, allegedly tortured to death with a baseball bat
shoved up his rectum. Another member of the cult, some
said, was twenty-four-year-old pimp Carl Davis.

On April 13, a partial human skull was found in the woods
near Fall River. New searches of the area turned up scalp
fragments with hair still attached, articles of women's clothing, and the rotting carcasses of three dead cats. In time, the
partial skull was identified as Karen Marsden's, using X-rays
taken during 1978, when she was treated for a sinus ailment.

Meanwhile, on April 14, Robin Murphy confessed her role
in Marsden's murder to a girlfriend. Grilled by police, she
named other participants in the crime as Carl Drew and Carl
Davis, both cited as members of the "Satan Avengers." She
had also witnessed the murder of Doreen Levesque, Murphy
said, committed by Drew and "a black man named Willie"—
identified by police as thirty-one-year-old William Smith.

On May 9, 1980, Drew, Davis, and Murphy were indicted for the murder of Karen Marsden. The formal charge stated that Carl Drew "participated with others in the prearranged, ritualistic slaying of the victim and the dismemberment of the victim's body." Carl Davis was already in jail, serving thirty days for assault and battery, when the indictments were handed down, and all three defendants were held without bail.

In January 1981, Robin Murphy turned state's evidence against Andre Maltais, pleading guilty to second-degree murder in the Raposa case and drawing a life prison term, with eligibility for parole in fifteen years. Maltais's courtroom display of Bibles and portraits of Jesus failed to persuade jurors of his piety, and he was convicted of first-degree murder, earning a sentence of life without parole. He served six years, still proclaiming his innocence, before a series of strokes claimed his life in 1987.

Carl Drew's trial for the murder of Karen Marsden convened on March 2, 1981. Prosecutors did their best to sidestep the satanic issue, viewing it as too imflammatory for a court of law, while Fall River detectives objected that occult ritual was the very heart of the case. At that, Robin Murphy's testimony for the state was grim enough, describing how Marsden was stoned by her killers, tortured by having her hair and fingernails ripped out, beaten and slashed with a knife before Drew manually snapped her neck. (In the process, with Marsden still alive, Drew also ordered Murphy to perform oral sex on the victim as a sign of obedience to his will.) Unsatisfied, the killer pimp had Murphy slash Marsden's throat, after which he severed her head and kicked it around like a football. Marsden's fingers were lopped off in an effort to steal her rings, and Drew finished by raping the headless corpse, carving an "X" on the chest, and smearing Marsden's blood on Murphy's forehead as a symbol of cult membership.

Carl Drew was his own defense witness, blandly denying any occult ties or involvement in criminal activity. By the time of his trial, Drew had removed a portion of the tattoo from his arm, so that it merely read "Avengers," but his makeshift plastic surgery failed to cancel Murphy's eyewitness report. Convicted of first-degree murder on Friday, March 13, Drew was sentenced to the mandatory term of life without parole, while Murphy walked off with another life sentence for second-degree murder.

Indictments for the murder of Donna Levesque were returned in March 1981, with Drew's trial still in progress, naming the killers as Drew, Robin Murphy, William Smith, and the late Karen Marsden. In May 1982, on the eve of Smith's murder trial, Murphy recanted her story of watching the murder take place, and Smith was discharged for lack of evidence. That November, prosecutors announced their plan to postpone Drew's trial as "an exercise in futility," and the charges were dropped in January 1983, a judge ruling that Drew's right to a speedy trial had been violated. Carl Davis was never tried for murder in Fall River, but he was convicted in 1982 of assaulting Satanist/prostitute Maureen Sparda with a deadly weapon, drawing a prison term of seven to ten years. Davis was released after serving the minimum possible time, and he is currently at large.

DRUGS

Throughout recorded history, narcotics and hallucinogenic drugs have played a major role in the occult experience. From medieval times to the present, drugs have helped practitioners of witchcraft, Satanism, and related creeds achieve a state of "mystic consciousness," experience "possession" by the god or demon of their choice, and conjure spirits from the "astral plane." More recently, within the past three decades, traffic in narcotics has provided cultists with a source of ready cash beyond their wildest pipe dreams, effecting a merger of sorts between occult religions and the established structure of organized crime.

In medieval Europe, witches ran the full gamut from pagan pantheists to hard-core Satanists, but all apparently shared a fondness for what a later generation would call "tripping out." Today, it is known that the widespread reports of witches flying to their quarterly sabbat gatherings were generated by use of various "flying ointments"—commonly rubbed into a witch's genital membranes—which included such hallucinogenic ingredients as belladonna, henbane, hemlock, aconite, and ergot (a natural source of LSD). Meanwhile, African practitioners of ju-ju—later transported to the New World as voodoo, santeria, macumba, and a host of variants—celebrated their seven-day *ikunle* ceremony with "sacraments" including liquor and marijuana (adding cocaine in more recent times). One of the ju-ju worshipers' favorite drugs is a narcotic derived from the *iboga* plant, common in Nigeria and surrounding territory.

Aleister Crowley, the premier Satanist of modern times, built a twisted religion of sorts around his personal penchant for drug abuse. In his "classic" *Book of the Law,* Crowley— speaking for the demon "Aiwass"—counseled his followers to "take wine and strange drugs whereof I will tell my prophet [i.e., Crowley], & be drunk thereof." A few years later, in his autobiographical *Diary of a Dope Fiend,* Crowley maintained that "The taking of a drug should be a carefully thought out and purposeful religious act. Experience alone can teach you the right conditions when it assists your will." This from a hopeless drug addict who mainlined at least ten grains of heroin per day throughout the declining years of his life.

Satanists have been taking Crowley's advice ever since, although established religious bodies like the Church of Satan and the Temple of Set are careful to avoid public connections with the drug scene. From coast to coast, drugs are cited by police as a causal factor in most of the crimes committed by recognized Satanists, ranging from vandalism and malicious mischief to murder. In many cases, police and prosecutors actually choose to describe such crimes as "drug-related" rather than satanic, thus avoiding "inflammatory" issues that often confuse jurors, resulting in mistrials or acquittals in otherwise solid cases. Such squeamishness is the norm in cases of alleged ritual child abuse, where young victims routinely complain of being drugged by cultists prior to weird, sado-sexual ceremonies. Drugging potential victims, especially children, has the dual benefit of forcing compliance and rendering future testimony "inherently unbelievable." In such cases, even where drugs are seized by police, the charges are rarely pursued and defendants are typically allowed to bargain for reduced sentences.

To some extent, except where violent crimes result, it may be said that cultists who indulge in drugs harm no one but themselves. The picture changes, though, when cults begin to deal in drugs for profit, joining hands with organized crime to participate in the international narcotics trade. According to narcotics officers from coast to coast, the transition from religion to criminal enterprise is an accomplished fact, with cultists giving the old-line Mafia and cocaine cowboys a serious run for their money.

Ex-Satanist Mike Warnke, himself a former heroin addict, reports that a satanic cult he calls "the Brotherhood" was already smuggling narcotics from Mexico to the United States when he joined the group in the mid-1960s. Around the same time, Charles Manson's "family" was heavily immersed in dealing LSD, marijuana, hashish, and cocaine in Los Angeles. On one occasion, flush with $30,000 cash from a drug sale, the Mansonoids spent every dime of their loot on musical instruments, trashing them all the same day in a drug-crazed jam session at their Spahn Ranch hideaway. Indeed, from the recorded testimony of "family" members and outsiders alike, it would seem that most of the murders linked to Manson's cult had their roots in the drug trade. In June 1969, Manson shot and wounded a drug dealer named Bernard Crowe, when Crowe turned up at the ranch to complain of a recent dope rip-off. Victim Gary Hinman, likewise, was butchered as the result of a drug deal gone sour. In August 1969, investigation of the Tate-LaBianca massacre revealed that several of the victims were involved in the sale or manufacture of illicit drugs. Victims Abigail Folger and Vojtek Frykowski were both recognized dealers, and both were high on the drug MDA when they died. Other sources report that Rosemary LaBianca was involved with LSD sales, and stories persist that the Manson bloodbath had more to do with contract killings for an established drug syndicate than any dreams of "Helter Skelter."

Across the country, outlaw motorcycle gangs—many of them linked to satanic cults from the 1960s to the present day—monopolize production and sale of methamphetamines, popularly known as "speed" and "crank." Chicago cultists, led by Robin Gecht in the early 1980s, took time from their ritual murder and cannibalizing of young women to gun down a local drug dealer when he tried to rip them off. In August 1985, raiders in Weld County, Colorado, arrested three men in an outlaw drug lab, surrounded by barbed wire fences and gun towers; weapons were seized in the raid, along with a cache of "Satan-worship material." According to sworn testimony, the cult-gang's leader had been running his operation from prison, passing orders to his loyal disciples outside. Narcotics traffic in southwestern Missouri is reportedly dominated by a satanic cult calling itself "The Crowd." In Minot and Bismarck, North Dakota, narcotics officers have traced heavy drug use and sales to another satanic cult linked with the sinister "Four P Movement." One of the North Dakota members, John Carr, was also a suspect in New York's "Son of Sam" serial killings in 1976 and 1977. And from New York itself, convicted "Sam" triggerman David Berkowitz has told newsman Maury Terry, through prison contacts, that "Drugs are involved. I feel the real key to exposing the group is through drug and porn connections." Some of the last decade's most sensational drug murders, including those of New York's Ronald Sisman and entertainment mogul Roy Radin, have been linked as much to Satanism as cocaine.

It should not be supposed, however, that Satanists have the modern drug trade all to themselves. Within the past decade, devotees of such Afro-Caribbean cults as santeria, abaqua, and palo mayombe have invaded the narcotics traffic with a vengeance, rising to dominance in parts of the United States and Latin America. The most notorious case in recent memory involved Adolfo Constanzo and his clique of palo mayombe cultists in Matamoros, Mexico, blamed for at least twenty-three ritual murders in the span of two years. It would be comforting to dismiss Constanzo and his disciples as a grim aberration, spawned by a "backward" society, but the drug-dealing Hernandez brothers—who first employed Constanzo, then joined his cult as ardent followers—have been named as major narcotics supplies for Chicago's dominant Mafia "family," and evidence suggests that Afro-Caribbean witchcraft has become the leading religion of choice for Hispanic pushers.

Along the Mexican border, local residents are well acquainted with the *narcosatanistos* who drive armored limousines and kill without a vestige of compassion. Detective Jaime Escalante, assigned to the Houston Police Department's narcotics detail, says of black magic, "It's just like guns are a part of the drug trade. Cocaine dealers carry weapons—it's part of the business. These cults have evolved as part of the drug traffic world, too." Escalante cites five drug-related murders in Houston during 1989 alone, with evidence of palo mayombe rituals involved. Elsewhere in Harris County, he recalls a team of Colombian hit men who killed two rivals, then chanted over the corpses before dumping them in the woods.

"They did the ritual so that the evil spirit of their victims couldn't harm them," Escalante says. "These same people have been linked with eleven drug-related murders in the Houston area. They are absolutely ruthless."

Indeed, between 1985 and 1989, Texas authorities recorded 226 incidents of cult-related crime, the vast majority involving drugs. In San Antonio, DEA chief Vernon Parker sees a strong Cuban and Colombian influence in the cult-drug scene. "They are heavily involved in black magic religion," Parker told newsmen. "They believe it protects them from police and rival gangs. Mixing drug dealers with black magic gives you an organization that is more loyal and willing to do whatever the cult leader says. For them, moving drugs is a spiritual act, not just a business." And from Brownsville, Texas—just across the border from the Matamoros killing ground—DEA agent Armando Ramirez reports, "Every arrest we make on the border, the suspect has some kind of black magic pouch on his person. It's about as common as driver's licenses."

On one raid in Brownsville, conducted in October 1989, FBI agents found a secret ritual chamber inside a drug dealer's home. The walls and ceiling were painted red, while an altar sported votive candles, voodoo dolls, mutilated photographs of Mexican narcotics officers, and a strip of paper reading "Law Be Gone." A nearby refrigerator contained vials of blood and other noxious fluids, each labeled with the name of enemies the dealer sought to curse through ritual magic.

Miami, Florida, with an estimated 100,00 santeria cultists and at least two thousand priests of the palo mayombe sect, is another hotbed of drug-cult activity. Narcotics officers have been reporting discovery of cult paraphernalia, including human remains and the classic *nganga*—palo mayombe's cauldron of blood—since the local "war on drugs" was launched in 1979. A year later, the Mariel boatlift brought thousands of Cuban ex-convicts to southern Florida, and the rate of cult-related crimes exploded overnight. Cautious Miami narcotics officers now make it a regular practice to check their suspect's religious background before launching a raid, and some detectives wear santeria beads themselves, since the dealers have no fear of badges or guns.

In 1986, DEA agents raided the home of a Colombian smuggler, finding their man in a living room chair, unarmed. Ordered to raise his hands, the suspect bolted into a back room and slammed the door. When he emerged moments later, the smuggler had a gun in each hand, several beaded necklaces and a golden amulet dangling around his neck to ward off bullets. The charms failed to save his life, but one of the raiders was shot in the face and blinded before his companions finished off their adversary.

Three years later, two Miami drug gangs declared war on each other, using palo mayombe as a weapon before they turned to conventional firearms. The leader of one gang, crack addict and murderous rip-off artist Juan Vera, touched off the gang war when he kidnapped a leader of the rival clique, burning his hostage alive in an effort to locate four kilos of cocaine. Both sides hired palero priests for the ensuing battle, but Vera's choice, a witch doctor named Inelio, turned out to be a close friend of Vera's rivals. It was no surprise, therefore, when Vera's invisible bulletproof screen let him down and his body, drilled by nine slugs, was found in the trunk of an abandoned Cadillac on March 7, 1989. Homicide detectives uncovered Vera's own ritual chamber, and the list of enemies he planned to curse led police to his killers. Following their arrest, Sgt. Ken Singleton told reporters, "We see this kind of thing every day now. We have murder cases pending all the time in which black magic plays a role."

Nor are Texas and Florida the only states where Afro-Caribbean drug cults have a foothold. Since the mid-1980s, ritual altars, *ngangas,* and human remains have been found in drug raids in New York City, Sacramento, Los Angeles, and San Francisco. In San Mateo County, California, federal raiders bagged six narcotics dealers, ages twenty-six to fifty-three, in a house where animal organs, human skulls and spinal columns, an altar and *nganga* were found. DEA spokesmen linked the gang to a widespread syndicate controlled by Colombian and Cuban immigrants. And in March 1989—a month before the Constanzo cult was exposed at Matamoros—two Americans and three Mexican nationals were found shot to death in Agua Prieta, a border town 120 miles southeast of Tucson, Arizona. Two days later, police pulled twelve more bodies from a nearby septic tank, all bearing marks of ritual torture and mutilation. Several suspects were arrested, police seizing 225 pounds of marijuana, 100 grams of cocaine, twelve guns, and eleven vehicles equipped with state-of-the-art communications gear.

Throughout Latin America, the story is the same. When

Panamanian dictator Manuel Noriega was captured by U.S. forces in December 1989, and returned to America for trial on drug-running charges, troops found an occult ritual chamber in the presidential palace. In Chile and Peru, incidents of human sacrifice by well-known narcotics dealers have been documented for at least the past two decades. Cocaine smugglers on the Peruvian border routinely consult *yatiris*—native shamans—before moving their shipments. The *yatiri* prepares a concoction of coca leaves to reach his decision: if the leaves are whole, the trip proceeds; if not, it is postponed. Successful seers take credit for the safe arrival of narcotics shipments throughout South America, and they are rewarded accordingly. Some infamous smugglers, like Peru's Uriarti family, cherish traditions of human sacrifice spanning several generations, with servant girls or peasant kidnap victims offered to the *orishas* in return for financial success. [See: Carr, John; Child Abuse; Chipana, Nieves; Constanzo, Adolfo; "Crowd, The"; Crowley, Aleister; Limachi, Clemente; Manson "Family"; Mentzer, William; Motorcycle Gangs; Radin, Roy; Sisman, Ronald; Santeria; Palo Mayombe; Uriarti, Juan]

"DUNGEONS & DRAGONS"

Created by Gary Gygax in 1974 and marketed by TSR Inc., of Geneva, Wisconsin, "Dungeons & Dragons" (D&D) is a fantasy role-playing game that transports its players to a medieval fantasy world of swords and sorcery, demons and damsels in distress. Launched with an initial investment of $2,000, the game reaped profits of $4 million in 1979, with no end in sight. By 1986, TSR's official rule books, packaged "campaigns," and monthly magazines had been translated into six languages, for marketing in fifteen countries. Financial success inevitably gave rise to look-alike competition, with similar games produced under titles like "Top Secret," "Mazes & Monsters," "Villains & Vigilantes," or "The Aztec Circle of Destiny."

Since 1979, when D&D first began making headlines, a growing backlash has developed among concerned parents, educators, psychologists, and clergymen (the latter frequently accused—with some justification—of attacking a popular game on TV to fatten their own church coffers). In simple terms, critics of D&D cite the game and its imitators as sex-ist, racist, amoral, cult-oriented and proviolence. Players are urged to collect treasure by means fair or foul, and some are apt to lose themselves in the game, critics say, lapsing from D&D into the study of witchcraft and Satanism, even turning violent when afflicted by competitors with the curse of "homicidal or suicidal mania." Gygax responds—inaccurately—that his game contains "no mention whatsoever" of rape or torture, dismissing complaints with reminders that D&D is, after all, a mere exercise of the imagination.

While thousands—perhaps millions—of fantasy gamers enjoy D&D or its clones with no apparent side effects, there have also been numerous cases of violent behavior linked to the game. Some examples include:

Aug. 15, 1979: James Egbert III, age sixteen, disappeared from Michigan State University in the midst of a D&D marathon game. Located after a month, he wrote: "I'll give Satan my mind and power." A year and a day later, Egbert shot himself to death, the two incidents boosting D&D sales with massive free publicity.

May 19, 1981: Avid D&D player Michael Dempsey, sixteen, shot himself to death moments after relatives saw him mumbling incantations, trying to conjure demons in his bedroom.

April 23, 1982: Mitchel Rupe shot and killed two bank tellers in Bremerton, Washington. At his trial in 1985, resulting in a murder conviction, psychologists testified that Rupe's obsession with D&D had caused him to lose touch with reality.

June 9, 1982: Irving "Bink" Pulling, sixteen, shot himself in the heart hours after receiving a curse of "suicidal mania" from a D&D "dungeon master" at school.

Oct. 14, 1982: Steven Loyacano, sixteen, gassed himself to death in the family garage, in Castle Rock, Colorado. Police found satanic scribblings and a suicide note linking the death to a passion for D&D.

Jan. 17, 1983: D&D fanatic Timothy Grice, twenty-one, shot and killed himself in Lafayette, Colorado. Handwritten manuscripts on out-of-body travel led detectives to report: "Apparently, D&D became reality."

April 30, 1983: Harold Collins, eighteen, hung himself during an auto-erotic experiment, leaving copious D&D paraphernalia behind. Relatives say he talked as if he were living the game.

Oct. 23, 1983: Charles Tyberg, seventeen, dressed in his father's police uniform and shot a patrolman to death at a San Diego, California, cemetery. Close friends describe Tyberg's immersion in D&D as "a catalyst for disaster."

Jan. 1984: John Witte, a fifteen-year-old D&D fan, killed his grandmother with a crossbow in LaPorte, Indiana, first putting himself in the "neutral" moral state advised for fantasy gaming.

March 1984: Darrell Molitor, nineteen, strangled a fellow D&D player, eighteen-year-old Mary Towey, in St. Louis, Missouri. Molitor signed his confession with the names of his two favorite D&D characters.

Sept. 8, 1984: Kurt McFall, seventeen, was found at the foot of a cliff near Concord, California, beaten to death, with mystic designs carved on his back. Friends recall his involvement in D&D, plus fraternization with a satanic cult.

Nov. 1984: Daniel Babineau, eleven, and his sister Monique, age nine, were murdered in Orangeville, Ontario. Their thirteen-year-old killer was acquitted on grounds of insanity after psychiatrists described his obsession with D&D.

Nov. 2, 1984: Steven Erwin, twelve, shot and killed his sixteen-year-old brother, Daniel, before turning the gun on himself. Fantasy gaming was an obsession for both boys, with police declaring: "D&D cost them their lives."

Jan. 1, 1985: Juan Kimbrough, fourteen, of Oakland, California, asked his brother to shoot him with a pistol, declaring that his powers as a dungeon master would deflect the bullet. He was wrong.

Jan. 18, 1985: Paul Sargent, seventeen, fatally stabbed a neighbor, forty-three-year-old Bonnie Brown, in Kansas City, Missouri. In custody, Sargent explained that D&D "teaches you to become a thief and to kill."

Jan. 23, 1985: D&D gamers Daniel Dower and Eric Nelson, both sixteen, ambushed and killed Dower's foster father, Joseph Vite, in Kenosha, Wisconsin. Psychiatric testimony linked their actions to the game.

Feb. 8, 1985: Jeffrey Jacklovich, fourteen, shot himself to death in Topeka, Kansas, leaving a suicide note that read: "I want to go to the world of elves and fantasy and leave the world of conflict. I love D&D and that's where I'm going."

Feb. 13, 1985: D&D gamers Danny Remeta, twenty-seven, and Mark Walter, eighteen, went on a murder rampage in northwestern Kansas, killing three men before Walter was shot by police and Remeta was captured. Remeta claims two other murders in Michigan, with victims still missing, and credits D&D as the inspiration for his crimes.

March 5, 1985: Teen cultist Sean Sellers murdered his mother and stepfather in a ritual "sacrifice to Satan." Sellers traced his interest in the occult and Satanism to D&D.

May 26, 1985: Cayce Moore, seventeen, a D&D dungeon master with a genius-level IQ, led two other gamers in the robbery of a Ragland, Alabama, convenience store, linked to a game of "Top Secret." Clerk Missy Macon, twenty-six, was shot and killed before the trio fled to Florida with $700, living out their fantasy as "thieves and assassins."

June 1985: Fantasy gamer Patrick Beach, fifteen, fatally shot sixteen-year-old Larry Brock and fifteen-year-old Amy Boyle in the San Juan Mountains of Colorado. Paraphernalia for "Villains & Vigilantes" was scattered around the murder site.

Nov. 1985: David Ventiquattro, fifteen, shot and killed eleven-year-old Martin Howland as part of his current D&D assignment to "extinguish evil."

Nov. 19, 1985: Leif Boyd, age twelve, leaped to his death from a fifteenth-floor hotel room in Austin, Texas. Friends and family report that Boyd was obsessed with D&D, talking about the game constantly.

Dec. 17, 1985: Jonathan Wiggins, sixteen, was shot and killed in a running gun battle with police, while driving a stolen car. Officers found him wearing towels under his clothes and a stocking on his head. The youth's father stated: "Everything points to the fact that it was a game and this was part of his assignment."

Feb. 24, 1986: Maurice Huish, a twenty-one-year-old D&D player in Hobart, Australia, dressed as a woman to infiltrate the apartment of gaming competitor Leigh Turner, stabbing his fantasy opponent to death.

Dec. 2, 1986: Soldiers Jeffrey Meyer, twenty, and Mark Thompson, seventeen, dressed in ninja costumes when they invaded the Fort Bragg, North Carolina, home of Paul and Janie Kutz. Both elderly victims were knifed to death, throats cut, their jewelry stolen. Police found a D&D "Oriental Adventures" game book in Meyer's truck.

Dec. 13, 1986: Wyley Gates, seventeen, an honors student

in East Chatham, New York, murdered his father, brother, cousin, and his father's girlfriend to experience the "thrill" of murder promised by a D&D clone, "Infierno."

Critics of D&D, led by Patricia Pulling, link the game with at least ninety murders and suicides between 1976 and 1987, claiming that "D&D deaths equal all other toy deaths combined." While some of the cases are shaky at best, enough bizarre incidents remain to warrant concern, especially where unstable players with histories of mental illness, drug abuse, or occult involvement are drawn to the game.

ENRIQUETA, MARTI

A Barcelona witch who made her living through the sale of charms and potions, Marti Enriqueta was arrested by Spanish police in March 1912, on charges of kidnapping local children. Her latest victim, a young girl named Angelita, was rescued alive from the witch's lair, chilling police with a tale of ritual murder and cannibalism. According to the girl, she had been forced by Enriqueta to partake of human flesh. Her "meal" had been the pitiful remains of yet another child, abducted by the murderess a short time earlier.

According to the story ultimately pieced together by authorities, the witch had claimed at least six local victims. After murdering the children, Enriqueta boiled their bodies down for use as prime ingredients in her expensive "love potions." Convicted on the basis of her own confession, coupled with the testimony of her sole surviving victim, Enriqueta was condemned to death and executed for her crimes.

EVANGELISTA, BENJAMINO

A native Italian who immigrated to the United States near the turn of the century, "Benny" Evangelista settled first in Philadelphia, finding work on a railroad crew. Although a practicing Catholic, Evangelista was also fascinated—some said obsessed—with the occult "sciences," a passion he shared with coworker Aurelius Angelino. Both men apparently participated in mystic rituals, joined by Evangelista's wife, but their studies were disrupted in 1919, when Angelino went berserk and killed two of his own children with an ax, winding up in a state asylum for the criminally insane.

Shaken by the grim turn of events, Evangelista moved his family to Detroit, where he invested his savings in real estate, soon emerging as a prosperous landlord and realtor. On the side, he earned a supplemental, tax-free income from the sale of hexes, herbs, and "spiritual remedies" in Little Italy, often performing chants, dances, and chicken sacrifices to "cure" his ailing customers. The basement of Evangelista's home, on St. Aubin Avenue, contained an occult ritual chamber, complete with a crude altar, "evil eye," and "divine" figurines dangling on strings from the ceiling. In his spare time, Benny authored an unpublished manuscript, titled *The Oldest History of the World, Discovered by Occult Science in Detroit Michigan,* which detailed workings of an imaginary cult, the Great Union Federation of America.

On the morning of July 3, 1929, a fellow realtor dropped in to visit Benny in his office, attached to the house. The caller was stunned to find Evangelista slumped behind his desk, his severed head reposing on the floor beside his chair. Police were summoned, and they found Evangelista's wife in bed, her own head nearly severed. All four of Evangelista's children had been brutally dismembered while they slept. The only clue, a single bloody thumbprint from the back door of the house, would never be identified.

Police briefly suspected one of Evangelista's tenants, posthumously accused of the murders by a vengeful ex-wife, but the dead man's thumbprint did not match. Another possible solution lay with Aurelius Angelino, who escaped from the Pennsylvania asylum in 1923, on his third attempt, and was never seen again. Since Angelino's fingerprints were not on file, he cannot be eliminated as a suspect, and the gruesome case remains unsolved.

"FEAST OF THE BEAST"

Curiously missing from the standard texts on black magic and witchcraft, this alleged satanic ceremony was first publicized in 1980, in the memoirs of Michelle Smith, a self-described survivor of ritual child abuse in British Columbia. Smith's gruesome childhood memories surfaced during therapy with Dr. Lawrence Pazder, a Canadian psychiatrist and coauthor of the book *Michelle Remembers*. As described therein, Dr. Pazder related Smith's disjointed recollections to a Catholic priest, Father Guy Merveille, and it was Father Merveille's research that pinpointed a specific occult ritual, dubbed the "Feast of the Beast."

According to Pazder and Merveille, this ceremony is a special black Mass, celebrated once every twenty-seven years and preceded by eighty-one days of ritual preparation—sex orgies, visits to graveyards, animal sacrifices, and so forth. In the climactic rite, worshipers proceed through several stages of a symbolic procession—the "Horns of Death"—including chants and incantations, sacrifices, and initiation of new priests (with each recruit severing the middle finger of his left hand as a sign of allegiance to Lucifer). If done correctly, the ritual is said to produce Satan in the flesh, complete with greetings to his disciples and specific details of his "master plan" for the next twenty-seven years.

Dr. Pazder calculated that Michelle Smith's "Feast of the Beast" ran from September 7 to November 27, 1955, climaxing on the last day of the Catholic liturgical year. Assuming that the ritual exists, its next performance would have fallen near the end of 1982—eight months before the sudden rash of satanic child abuse charges surfaced from southern California to Minnesota. Meanwhile, the only corroboration of Smith's story comes from another occult survivor, Joan Christianson, who alludes to the "Feast of the Beast" in her lectures on Satanism. In Christianson's version, the ceremony may occur "every twenty-six or twenty-seven years, depending on your cult." No mention of nine-fingered priests is made in the latter account. [See: Child Abuse; Christianson, Joan; Smith, Michelle]

FELIX, MARTHA
and ONTIVEROS, FRANCISCO

A resident of Carson City, Nevada, Martha Felix operated an unlicensed baby-sitting service in her home between 1981 and 1984. Her nephew, Francisco Ontiveros, lived with Felix during most of that time and often "helped out" with the children. Parents who took advantage of the service trusted Felix implicitly, never suspecting the nightmare to come.

In fact, the awful truth did not emerge until 1985, several months after Felix closed up shop. One afternoon, a seven-year-old girl who stayed with Felix frequently in 1981 and 1982 spontaneously told her mother that she "really hated it" when she was left in Martha's care. The child refused to elaborate, but later, while her family watched a television special dealing with *Sports Illustrated* swimsuit models, she began to ask questions about nude photography, explaining that *she* had been photographed naked on several occasions, at Felix's home. Aside from pornographic snapshots, she described how "Paco" Ontiveros sat on her, "pulled her eyebrows," and occasionally "stuck his penis in her."

News of the allegations spread quickly, and other apprehensive parents started questioning their children, unearthing more tales of sexual abuse. Three reputed victims had since moved to California, where they poured out their stories for a child psychologist. Eleven other children were identified as victims by police in Carson City, winding up in therapy with Dr. Samantha Payne. Some were only a few months old when the crimes occurred, and none had been older than five at the time. Still, most recalled their ordeals in graphic detail—and those details went far beyond "normal" molestation.

In addition to fondling, intercourse, and pornographic sessions, the children described incidents of torture with spoons, knitting needles, scissors, and an electric cattle prod. Cats and chickens were allegedly slaughtered at Felix's house, along with a horse and cow, the blood pumped into jars and bottles while Felix and Ontiveros chanted prayers to Satan. The children were threatened with death if they talked, their tormentors brandishing pistols and knives to drive home the point. As the stories emerged, distraught parents began to recognize physical and psychological signs of abuse in their children. Three toddlers from the day-care center had been treated for vaginal infections over the years, while a fourth suffered from unexplained rectal bleeding. Others threw hysterical tantrums at bath time, suffered from nightmares, or indulged in compulsive masturbation. One girl slashed her wrists and repeatedly bit herself to the point of drawing blood. Another, who later described having scissors thrust underneath her fingernails, came home one afternoon and slashed her mattress with a pair of scissors.

Carson City detectives raided the Felix home in August 1985, digging up the back yard in a search for animal remains, but only small chips of bone were found, possibly buried by Felix's dog. The raiders did find a pump, as described by the children, confiscating a number of guns, knives, and glass jars for good measure. Felix and Ontiveros were arrested on the spot, jailed on charges of child molestation.

At their 1985 preliminary hearing, the defendants were bound over for trial on forty-two counts of alleged sexual and child abuse, lewdness and pornography involving fourteen victims. As time went on, the case was ultimately pared down to twenty-four felony counts: nineteen against Felix for sexual assault, child abuse, and lewdness with a child; five against Ontiveros for sexual assault and lewdness with a child. Of nine victims remaining on the "official" list, at least five displayed physical symptoms of sexual abuse.

Heading off defense complaints of pretrial publicity, Judge Michael Griffin imposed a gag order on the case in 1986, but the actual trial would not convene until September 1987. Defense attorney Ben Walker warned jurors to expect "the most bizarre case you will ever hear," adding: "But what's bizarre about it, in my way of thinking, is how the children were interviewed, how this case was investigated, how it got this far." Taking his cue from attorneys in similar cases around the country, Walker stressed the "fantastic" and "unbelievable" nature of the children's allegations, dismissing the case as a witch-hunt.

"There's going to be example after example," Walker said, "of things the therapists will twist to make you think they were abused. We have children in this case saying things happened that could not possibly have happened." Walker dismissed the symptoms of psychological trauma out of hand, insisting, "It isn't strange behavior. It's what all kids go through." In fact, he maintained, the children were repeating vicious lies that had been planted in their minds by counselors who "put therapy first, the truth of the allegations second."

District Attorney Noel Waters spent the trial's early days laying groundwork with a series of expert witnesses, including psychologists who specialized in child abuse cases. Eight of the complaining children were ruled competent to testify, either in person or by means of videotape, and despite minor inconsistencies under cross-examination, their testimony clearly impressed the jury. One girl described a rape at the hands of Ontiveros, recounting how Felix had also abused her, once forcing the child to have sex with a boy six years older than herself. A male victim described Martha Felix shocking him with the cattle prod, coercing him to fondle his two younger sisters. Felix was also pictured "laughing her head off" as she stabbed a calf to death and pumped its blood into bottles, invoking Satan's name while children were forced to sample the blood.

In all, jurors listened to seventy-two witnesses over five months' time, setting a record for the longest criminal trial in Carson City's history. On February 11, 1988, Martha Felix was convicted on three counts of child sexual abuse, with Ontiveros found guilty on one count. Six weeks later, on March 28, Judge Griffin sentenced Felix to three consecutive life terms, requiring that she serve a minimum of thirty years before parole. Francisco Ontiveros was also sentenced to life, with a minimum ten years behind bars.

Both defendants were held for eleven months without bail, pending appeal, before the Nevada Supreme Court set bond at $25,000 each in December 1988. At this writing, nearly four years after their conviction, Felix and Ontiveros are still at liberty, awaiting a decision on their case.

FLANAGAN, DALE:
See GORDON, CARL and COLLEEN

"FOUR P MOVEMENT"

In 1969, while gathering material for a book on the Charles Manson case, journalist Ed Sanders encountered reports of a sinister satanic cult alleged to practice human sacrifice in several parts of California, luring youthful members from college campuses throughout the western half of the United States. Calling itself the "Four P Movement," or "Four Pi" for short, the cult originally boasted fifty-five members, of whom fifteen were middle-aged, the rest consisting of young men and women in their early twenties. The group's leader—dubbed the "Grand Chingon" or "Head Devil"—was said to be a wealthy California businessman of middle years, who exercised his power by compelling younger members of the cult to act as slaves and murder random targets on command. The central object of the cult was to promote "the total worship of evil."

Organized in northern California during 1967, the "Four P Movement" evolved from a rift in the satanic Process Church of Final Judgment, drawing its cryptic name from the parent organization's stylized "power sign."

The new cult held its early secret gatherings in the Santa Cruz Mountains, south of San Francisco. Rituals were conducted on the basis of a stellar timetable, including the sacrifice of Doberman and German shepherd dogs. Beginning in June 1968, authorities in San Jose, Santa Cruz, and Los Gatos began recording the discovery of butchered canines, skinned and drained of blood without apparent motive. As the director of the Santa Cruz animal shelter told Sanders, "Whoever is doing this is a real expert with a knife. The skin is cut away without even marking the flesh. The really strange thing is that these dogs have been drained of blood."

If we accept the word of several alleged eyewitnesses, the missing blood was drunk by cultists in their ceremonies. So, according to reports, was human blood, obtained from sacrificial victims murdered on a dragon-festooned altar. Death was the result of stabbing with a custom-made six-bladed knife, designed with blades of varied length to penetrate a victim's stomach first, before the heart was skewered, bringing merciful release. Each sacrifice allegedly was climaxed by removal of the heart, which cultists then divided up among themselves to eat. The evidence of murder was incinerated in a portable crematorium, mounted in the back of a truck.

According to reports from self-styled members of the "Four P" cult, its victims were mostly hitchhikers, drifters, and runaways, with an occasional volunteer from the ranks. One such, a young woman, reportedly went to her death with a·smile in November 1968, near Boulder Creek, but even sacrifice of willing victims is a risky business, and the cult was said to mount patrols around its rural meeting places, using guards with automatic weapons and attack-trained dogs to guarantee privacy.

In 1969, the cult reportedly moved southward, shifting operations to the O'Neil Park region of the Santa Ana Mountains, near Los Angeles. The move produced—or was occasioned by—a factional dispute within the group, one segment striving to deemphasize satanic ritual and concentrate wholeheartedly on kinky sex, while more traditional adherents clung to Lucifer and human sacrifice. The group apparently survived its schism and expanded nationwide, author Maury Terry citing evidence of a thousand or more members across the country by 1979. One hotbed of activity appears to be New York, where eighty-five German shepherds and Dobermans were found skinned in the year between October 1976 and October 1977. Back in Los Angeles, the cult reportedly purchased a small private college in 1989, maintaining a normal front despite reports of occult rituals flourishing on campus.

Along the way, the "Four P Movement" has apparently rubbed shoulders with a number of notorious killers, feeding—or, perhaps, inspiring—their sadistic fantasies. Serial slayer Stanley Baker, jailed in Montana for eating the heart of one victim, confessed to other murders perpetrated on orders from the Grand Chingon. Recruited from a college campus in Wyoming, Baker remained unrepentant in confinement, organizing fellow inmates into a satanic coven of his own, but his testimony brought lawmen no closer to cracking the cult.

Charles Manson and his "family" reportedly had contact with the "Four P Movement" prior to making headlines in Los Angeles. Ed Sanders reports that some of Manson's followers referred to him—in Sanders's presence—as the "Grand Chingon," distinguished from the original article by his age and the fact that Manson was jailed while the real "Head Devil" remained at large. Likewise, family hacker Susan Atkins has described the sacrifice of dogs by Manson's group, and searchers digging for the last remains of Manson victim Shorty Shea reported finding large numbers of chicken and animal bones at the family's campsite—a peculiar form of refuse for a group reputedly composed of vegetarians.

Convicted killer David Berkowitz—more famous as the "Son of Sam" who terrorized New York in 1976 and 1977—has also professed membership in the "Four P" cult, backing his claim with inside information on an unsolved California homicide allegedly committed by the group. Aside from participation in human and canine sacrifice, with the occasional gang rape of teenage girls, "Four P" cultists also reportedly share a fascination with Nazi racist doctrines. Berkowitz named mass murderer Fred Cowan as a member in good standing, and Maury Terry has also linked cult activity with the unsolved case of the "Westchester Dartman," who wounded twenty-three women in New York's Westchester and Rockland Counties between February 1975 and May 1976.

Despite the testimony of reputed "Four P" members, authorities have yet to build a case against the cult. Some suspects, named by witnesses, have died in "accidents" or "suicides" before they could be questioned by police. Another obstacle appears to be the use of code names, which prevent the cultists from identifying one another under questioning. The group itself relies on different names from place to place, with New York members meeting as "The Children," while reports from Alabama refer to "The Children of the Light." Berkowitz has also described active covens in Texas and North Dakota, with hired killers on call from one region to another. A hard-core faction called the "Black Cross" is said to operate as a kind of satanic Murder Incorporated, fielding anonymous hit teams for cultists nationwide, disposing of defectors and offering tips on the fine points of human sacrifice. If law-enforcement spokesmen are correct, the cult is also deeply involved in white slavery, child pornography, and the international narcotics trade. [See: Baker, Stanley; Berkowitz, David; Cowan, Frederick; "Dartman"; Manson "Family"; Perry, Arlis; Process Church of Final Judgment]

FRANCIS, SAGE TAYLOR

Cocaine and Satanism were the trademarks of rebellion for Sage Francis, a fifteen-year-old student at Valley High School in Las Vegas, Nevada. On June 4, 1984, while freebasing coke with nineteen-year-old Deron Knepp, Francis began to expound on his worship of Satan, expressing a desire to visit San Francisco and meet "head devil" Anton LaVey. The diatribe was interrupted by a phone call, and Knepp was speaking to a friend when Francis crept up behind him, drawing a razor-edged box cutter, slashing Knepp's throat in an effort to kill him and cut out Knepp's tongue.

The plan, as Francis later told police, had been to steal Knepp's money, drugs, and guns before he left for California. Francis blew it, in the words of Detective Dan Newman, when he "stayed too long at the scene of the crime and became fascinated with the victim's blood." In fact, the teenage Satanist was covered with it when he started thumbing out of town. The motorist who picked him up believed that he was injured, and promptly telephoned the police.

Knepp managed to survive his wounds, and Francis readily confessed the crime. A guilty plea was filed on August 10, and Francis drew a fifteen-year prison sentence on September 19, with the court's recommendation that he serve his time in Arizona's Rincon program, housed with other juveniles. His lawyer, Susan Roske, said that Francis had been "born again" in jail, but she acknowledged his psychological and drug-dependency problems, telling the court that "Worshiping Satan was a way to lash out at his parents and seek attention."

FRYMAN, JOHN LEE

On February 14, 1987, members of a wedding party found a pair of severed human legs near the Little Cedar Baptist Church, in Franklin County, Indiana. The legs lay thirty feet apart, still clad in blue jeans, boots, and red-and-white striped socks. Each had been severed eight inches above the knee, and a coroner reported they were dumped two days before discovery.

Three days later and fifty miles away, residents of Cincinnati, Ohio, identified the pitiful remains of Monica Lemen, age twenty-one, reported missing by her father on February 10. Police investigation of her background turned up Lemen's interest in Satanism, complete with occult paraphernalia at her home, and detectives started working their way through a list of known acquaintances.

One of their first stops, on February 18, was a trailer home in suburban Fairfield, north of Cincinnati. Resident John Fryman, twenty-four, was another dedicated occultist, one room of his trailer painted black, decorated with satanic trappings which included "a gravestone that appears to be an altar." After some preliminary questions, Fryman was booked by police on charges of aggravated murder and desecrating a corpse. A female companion, twenty-year-old Beverly Cox, was held as an accomplice to the crime.

As detectives pieced the story together, Fryman—a convicted robber—had begun to correspond with Lemen while he served his prison sentence in Ohio. They grew closer after his parole, in May 1986, and police believed the relationship had ended with ritual murder. In fact, they announced on February 24, Fryman had freely confessed to the crime. Additional charges were filed against Fryman in the February 11 robbery of a Fairfield gas station, where clerk Tammy Rose was shot and wounded.

Fryman, for his part, dismissed the confession as a product of third-degree tactics. "I'm involved with the occult," he told newsmen. "I think everybody knows that. You don't have a room like that in your trailer if you're not. But I wasn't involved in it to the extent they're saying."

As the trial date approached, prosecutors traded Beverly Cox a grant of immunity for her promise of testimony against Fryman. The defendant, meanwhile, elected to drop his insanity plea and stand trial on the evidence. "I was going to fake insanity," Fryman said. "I am well aware of sociology and psychology, and know how to do that. Now, I think I can stand on the facts of the case without having to push things around."

Prosecutors rested their case against Fryman on September 16, 1987, without ever calling Beverly Cox to the witness stand. In effect, they said, Fryman had "confessed five or six different ways. What more to you need?" The jury agreed, and Fryman was convicted of murder, earning a sentence of life imprisonment. The remainder of Monica Leman's body was never found.

FUSCO, THERESA

In 1984 and early 1985, Long Island was the scene of several rapes and murders aimed at teenage girls, with evidence suggesting that the crimes had been committed by a mobile group including three or more young men. Police have solved one case, with indications that the perpetrators—and unknown accomplices—may be responsible for other slayings in the area. New evidence, secured by newsman Maury Terry, further indicates the possible involvement of a devil-worship cult with ties to other lethal groups in New York City and in California.

The first Long Island victim was fifteen-year-old Kelly Morrissey, who vanished on the short walk home from a popular teenage hangout on June 12, 1984. Five months later, a friend of the missing girl—Theresa Fusco—was forced into a van after leaving a skating rink in Lynbrook, one mile from the spot where Morrissey disappeared. Fusco's body, beaten, strangled, and raped by at least three men, was found on December 5, realizing the worst fears of family and friends.

John Kogut, a twenty-one-year-old high school dropout and unemployed landscaper, was jailed on charges of burglary and disorderly conduct when police began asking him questions about the Fusco homicide. Cracking under interrogation, he confessed to the crime, naming two accomplices, and was formally charged with the murder on March 26, 1985. Kelly Morrissey was still missing, but her diary contained entries describing at least one date with Kogut prior to her disappearance.

Eight hours after the announcement of Kogut's arrest, nineteen-year-old Jacqueline Martarella was reported missing from Oceanside, a short four miles from the scene of Theresa Fusco's abduction. Kogut was obviously innocent in that case, but his alleged accomplices were still at large, and police were already collecting evidence of Kogut's alleged participation in a satanic cult that favored the rape of young virgins as a form of "sacrifice." Kogut's friends informed police that he had once burned the mark of an inverted cross on his arm, and acquaintances of Theresa Fusco recalled her discussions of a satanic coven reportedly active in the Long Beach–Oceanside area.

On April 22, Martarella's raped and strangled corpse was found beside a golf course at Lawrence, Long Island. Visiting the scene, journalist Maury Terry discovered a "cult sign" linked with Satanists in Queens and Yonkers, who allegedly participated in the infamous "Son of Sam" murders in 1976 and 1977. Not far from the dump site, searchers discovered an abandoned root cellar, its walls festooned with cult symbols and slogans. Outside, some articles of clothing were found, described by Jacqueline Martarella's parents as "very similar" to items she wore on the night of her disappearance.

John Kogut steadfastly refused to discuss the cult angle, while freely admitting his role in the rape and strangulation of Theresa Fusco. After she was raped, he said, the girl had threatened to tell police, whereupon one of Kogut's associates handed him a rope, with instructions to "Do what you gotta do." On May 9, 1985, authorities went public with their theory that a gang of twelve associates were linked with three

known murders and at least four rapes in which the victims
had survived. By June 21, suspects John Restivo, twenty-six,
and Dennis Halstead, thirty, were in custody on charges of
first-degree rape and second-degree murder in the Fusco case.
Kogut was convicted and sentenced to life in May 1986, with
Restivo and Halstead joining him later that year. Prior to
Kogut's trial, a teenage friend—Bob Fletcher—who had testified to Kogut's Satanism and involvement in pornography
"committed suicide" in Rosedale, Queens. Police have been
unable to explain the disappearance of the gun he used to
shoot himself.

FUSTER ESCALONA, FRANCISCO

A Cuban immigrant who reached the United States at age
twelve, in 1960, Frank Fuster grew up troubled in the Bronx,
barely able to contain his mercurial temper. In January 1969,
following a traffic altercation, he shot and killed another motorist; Fuster called it an "accident," but eyewitnesses described him reloading his .22-caliber rifle for a second shot,
and he was indicted for first-degree murder. Bargaining for a
guilty plea on manslaughter charges, Fuster was sentenced to
ten years in October 1969, winning parole two years later. A
move to Florida was approved in 1974, and Fuster's June
1977 arrest for shoplifting did not prevent his discharge from
parole in 1978.

Some ex-convicts learn from their mistakes, but Fuster
wasn't one of them. In September 1981, Florida prosecutors
charged him with sexual assault on a nine-year-old girl; convicted in November 1982, he got off with a wrist slap of two
years probation. A year later, he was charged with assaulting
a neighbor, threatening the other man with a pistol, but the
frightened victim declined to press charges and the case was
dropped.

Frank Fuster liked his sex partners young, and his third
wife seemed to fit the bill perfectly. Sixteen years old when
they met in 1983, Iliana Fuster was an illegal alien from Hon-
duras who could pass for twelve or thirteen if she dressed
down and dispensed with makeup. She was also the family
breadwinner, at least on paper, managing an unlicensed day-
care facility at their home, in the exclusive Miami neighbor-

hood of Country Walk. Life was sweet for Frank Fuster . . . until it began to unravel in the summer of 1984.

That July, a four-year-old client of the Fuster's baby-sitting service surprised his mother at bath time, asking her to kiss his "body"—the word his parents had agreed on to describe his penis. Under gentle questioning, the boy explained that "Iliana kisses all the babies' bodies." Desperate phone calls and comparison of notes ensued, the circle of reputed victims widening with time to include at least twenty-one children, ranging in age from six months to five years. In conversations with their parents and a team of expert child psychologists, the victims went beyond specific descriptions of sexual acts, their stories quickly lapsing into the macabre.

There were "monsters" at the day-care center, some explained, finally identifying the creatures as Frank and Iliana, dressed up in Dracula and Frankenstein masks. Children were allegedly whipped with a belt, some of them "hypnotized" by Iliana Fuster and told they had demons inside their bodies. Horror movies played constantly on the Fusters' TV, and children were forced to drink a concoction called "demon slime" or "magic punch." They also played bizarre "pee-pee" and "ca-ca" games, involving urination, defecation, and the fondling or consumption of feces. At least two unidentified adults dropped by from time to time, to join in the festivities, passing the children around. When they were not being molested by Frank or Iliana, some of the children were forced to abuse each other, one five-year-old boy tearfully sodomizing his own younger brother and an unrelated girl. Threats guaranteed silence, including the mutilation of birds and a game called "Cut Your Head Off," where Frank ran around the room, pressing a knife to different children's throats. Many of the acts, they said, were photographed or recorded on videotape.

In retrospect, horrified parents recalled various symptoms of abuse—persistent rashes, nightmares, aberrant or sexual behavior in the home. Parents who dropped in ahead of schedule were likely to find nude children running around the Fuster house, and Iliana took an inordinately long time answering the door. Other kids came home groggy, as if sedated, some of them so sleepy they could not be roused for hours. And there was the chanting, quoted verbatim by several young children, recalled from occasions when Frank and Iliana would mutilate living birds in their kitchen.

Devil, I love you. Please take this bird with you and take all the children up to hell with you. You gave me the grateful gifts. God of ghosts, please hate Jesus and kill Jesus because He is the baddest, damnedest person in the whole world. We don't love children because they are a gift of God. We want the children to be hurt. Signed, Iliana and Frank, Amen.

Police were initially skeptical of some allegations, including the "demon slime" and reports from some children that they had been forced to shove "pennies" up Iliana's rectum. Likewise, descriptions of bluebirds slaughtered at the house rang hollow, since they were not native to southern Florida. On the plus side, there was Frank's prior conviction for child molesting and a nasty piece of medical evidence: Fuster's son by a previous marriage, now living with Frank and Iliana, had been diagnosed as suffering from gonorrhea of the throat.

Detectives launched their investigation in August, dropping by the outlaw day-care center where a prophetic sign proclaimed: "We may not be the best but people do talk." Fuster tried to bluff his way through the interviews, insisting he was "never at home" when Iliana had kids in the house, but his answers rang hollow. Still on probation from the 1982 conviction, Frank was arrested on August 10, held without bond pending judicial determination of his status. Police searched his home the same day, hoping to find a pornography stash, but they came away with only "innocent" snapshots, one nail-studded thumb cuff, and a wooden crucifix found underneath the mattress in the master bedroom. Meanwhile, Country Walk parents complained that crates of videotapes and other suspicious material had been removed from the house days earlier, one mother alerting police ... who took no steps to block the exodus of crucial evidence.

At that, police had confirmed Frank's interest in child pornography from an independent source. One of his nieces recalled Fuster trying to recruit her for a "naked movie," but she turned him down. Sadly, the toddlers in his care at Country Walk had no such option.

Accusations continued to pile up with Fuster in jail, and his wife was arrested on August 24, charged with sixteen counts of sexual battery on a child. The two cases were legally severed in May 1985, but Frank wasn't going anywhere prior to trial; an evidentiary hearing before Judge Robert

Newman had already earned him a new prison sentence of fifteen years without parole, on charges of violating his 1982 probation.

On August 23, 1985, Iliana Fuster pleaded guilty on fourteen counts of child molestation, two other counts dropped in return for her promise to testify against Frank. It was Iliana, in fact, who finally drew back the curtain of doubt, helping skeptical police understand what the children had been saying all along. The "magic punch" and "demon slime" they spoke about was Gatorade, spiked with Frank's urine and a hefty dose of tranquilizers. The "pennies" they shoved into Iliana's rectum on command were suppositories, wrapped in copper foil. And the "bluebirds" butchered in her kitchen were actually "blue birds"—a simple description, not at all a species foreign to the Sunshine State.

At his trial, in 1985, Frank Fuster faced sixteen felony counts related to abuse of eleven children. Of twenty-one identified victims, only eight would testify, the others being deemed too young, too frightened, too confused by all that they had suffered at his hands. In addition to specific counts of sexual misconduct, Fuster was confronted with a catchall charge of aggravated assault, alleging that he terrorized his victims "on numerous occasions," with acts "which consisted of, but were not limited to" a display of weapons, masked threats, public urination and defecation, administration of drugs, confinement in closets, and forced consumption of human waste.

In the name of "common sense," prosecutors carefully avoided any mention of occult rituals during Fuster's trial, but part of the mystery was solved when his family turned up in court accompanied by a priest of the santeria cult. Despite the emergency housecleaning, detectives had found several "family" snapshots corroborating some of the victims' testimony. One portrayed Fuster and his wife cuddling on the couch, both wearing monster masks which had miraculously disappeared before the search. Another showed a woman standing at Fuster's kitchen sink with her back to the camera; Fuster's son was lifting up her skirt in back, revealing panties black with fecal stains.

For all the pathos of the children's testimony, it was Iliana Fuster who finally put Frank away. On the witness stand, she described Frank abusing various children and forcing her to do likewise, sometimes beating and raping her while the youngsters looked on. When he was in a *really* bad mood, Fuster smeared her body with feces, rammed a crucifix and other foreign objects into her anus, and threatened to ream out her vagina with an electric drill. Frank, for his part, blandly denied it all, sketching an evil conspiracy hatched by his unfaithful wife, lying brats, and deranged child psychologists. Skeptical jurors convicted him on all counts in November 1985, and Fuster was sentenced to six consecutive life terms. If he discovers the fountain of youth, Fuster will be eligible for parole in A.D. 2150.

Iliana, for her part, received a ten-year prison sentence on November 26, with ten years of probation to follow her release. Police report that Frank has placed a contract on her head from prison, promising to pay the hit man with his prize possession: videotapes. [See Child Abuse; Santeria]

GALIMANIS, PHILIP

When Cynthia McQueen missed work on April 20, 1983, her best friend was concerned. The twenty-three-year-old mother of two normally called to explain any absence, and recent events in her life made the silence more ominous. That spring, Cynthia McQueen was a young woman living in fear.

After work, her friend made a call, and Cynthia's three-year-old daughter picked up the phone. "Mommy's broken," the child said. "She's got a big owie." Police were dispatched to McQueen's apartment in Wheatland, Colorado, and they found her stretched out on a blood-drenched bed, her severed head nearby. Cuts and bruises told the story of a ferocious assault, but autopsy results showed Cynthia was still alive and conscious when her assailant went to work on her neck with an ax and a knife.

Barely coherent, McQueen's young daughter referred to the killer as "Daddy," but Cynthia's friend from work provided a name. For the past several months, McQueen had been dating a neighbor, twenty-year-old Philip Galimanis, but the young man's sadistic temperament made Cynthia fear for her life. Galimanis would sometimes burn her daughter with cigarettes, to amuse himself, or twist McQueen's fingers until she screamed. Cynthia was trying to end the relationship, but Galimanis was persistent in his attentions.

The name of their suspect rang alarm bells at police headquarters. A local thief and "stoner" who dropped out of high school five times in one seven-month period, Galimanis had logged five arrests for burglary, theft, reckless driving, and resisting an officer before his eighteenth birthday. He had also been committed to mental wards four times in the past three years, once for assaulting his mother in December 1981. On that occasion, doctors had described him as a drug-dependent psychotic. In conversations with a staff psychiatrist, Galimanis had referred to himself as a "mean, bad, and devilish person," citing a devotion to witchcraft and Satanism as proof of his claim.

Galimanis was arrested at his sister's home on April 21, and Cynthia McQueen's daughter readily identified him as the "Daddy" who had given Cynthia the "big owie." Filing an insanity plea, Galimanis told court psychiatrists that he "felt like the devil," a sensation he described as "a real powerful feeling, a supernatural high." He was found sane and competent for trial on September 1, 1983, but the actual proceedings were delayed until March 1984. Convicted of first-degree murder on April 9, Galimanis was sentenced to life imprisonment, with eligibility for parole after twenty years.

GAMBLE, LLOYD HAROLD

A seventeen-year-old high school senior in Carleton, Michigan, Lloyd Gamble was sleeping at his family home on February 2, 1986, when two shotgun blasts shattered his skull, killing him instantly. Detectives investigating the murder soon identified Gamble's younger brother as the gunman, and while family slayings constitute the majority of American homicides, this time the motive came as a surprise to all concerned.

In custody, fifteen-year-old Phillip Gamble told police that he had killed his brother as a human sacrifice to Satan, hoping to "release him to a higher plane of consciousness." February 2 had been chosen for the event because it was a recognized satanic holiday, celebrated by cultists as Candlemas. A search of the suspect's room turned up ritual robes, a sword, inverted crosses, numerous heavy metal albums, occult drawings, plus a well-thumbed copy of *The Satanic Bible* and other demonic literature. Chapter 9 of *The Satanic Bible,* "On the Choice of a Human Sacrifice," prophetically listed objects of sibling rivalry as one example of the "ideal sacrifice." As Lt. Mike Davidson reported, "We couldn't come up with any other motive for the killing except devil worship."

Background investigation linked Phillip Gamble with a ten-member "cult" at Airport High School, but officers told the press their prisoner was "the only one who took it seriously." His case was ultimately processed through juvenile court, but it left Monroe County on edge, with nervous adults eyeing teens who displayed pentagrams, "witchy" amulets, or the number "666." Small covens were identified at three area high schools, but their members seemed more preoccupied with heavy metal tunes than any serious study of the occult. To date, no further incidents have been reported from the district.

GARDNER, GERALD B.

The son of an affluent British family, born in 1884 and largely neglected by his parents during childhood, Gardner was delivered to the care of a nanny with a penchant for world travel. In her company, Gardner visited the Canary Islands, Northern Africa, and Ceylon, finally spending most of his early life in the Far East. In adulthood, still living in Ceylon, he served as a British customs agent and earned a substantial income from his tea plantations.

It was also in the East that Gardner first acquired his lifelong taste for occult mysticism, boning up on the available texts in his search for hidden wisdom. Retiring to his native England in 1939, he made contact with a small witches' coven called the Fellowship of Crotona, featuring a mixed membership of Rosicrucians, Theosophists, and Freemasons. Further study drew Gardner into the Ordo Templi Orientis, then led by Aleister Crowley, and he solicited Crowley's help in composing new rituals for his own personalized cult.

The end result of their collaboration was "Wicca," a modern form of witchcraft based in equal parts on the anthropological studies of Margaret Murray and Crowley's peculiar obsession with "sex magick." Some critics have suggested that Gardner's creation of Wicca owed more to his own eccentric sexuality than any religious conviction, with witches required to meet "skyclad"—that is, nude—and participate in rituals that included both sexual intercourse and flagellation. In his published writings, Gardner tried to disguise the sexual thrust of his message, referring to his ritual of the "fivefold kiss" by a capital "S," while an "S" with a diagonal stroke through the letter symbolized flagellation. Rambling discussions of nature, "old gods," and the "wise ones" obscured the main focus of a cult that was, from all appearances, conceived primarily as an excuse to get naked and party.

Gardner's "religion" was limited to a handful of friends and kinky playmates until 1951, when the British witchcraft laws were finally repealed. Three years later, Gardner, published *Witchcraft Today*, a cut-and-paste compendium of standard witch lore and personal philosophy, suggesting that the ancient witch cults of medieval Europe were alive and well in Gardner's loving care. The book brought thousands of inquiries from around the globe, and Wicca blossomed overnight, expanding from a local swingers' circle to a worldwide religion. As with any fringe group, success inspired competition, disciples like Sybil Leek and Alex Sanders spinning off from the parent body with their own revised rituals, but the majority of Wicca devotees still follow Gardner's "original" tenets. At his death in 1964, while cruising the North African coast, Gardner was justly recognized as the father of modern witchcraft and neopaganism. [See: Crowley, Aleister; Sanders, Alexander; Wicca]

GECHT, ROBIN

It was a case with all the grisly drama of a Hollywood production. A serial slayer, predictably dubbed "Jack the Ripper" by newsmen, was stalking young woman in Chicago and environs, discarding their mutilated corpses like so much castoff rubbish. Homicide detectives had no inkling of the killer's motive or identity; they couldn't even manage to agree upon a body count. The speculation published daily in Chicago's press was bad enough; the truth, when finally exposed, was infinitely worse.

On May 23, 1981, twenty-eight-year-old Linda Sutton was abducted by persons unknown from Elmhurst, a Chicago suburb. Ten days later, her mutilated body—the left breast missing—was recovered from a field in Villa Park, adjacent to the Rip Van Winkle Motel. The evidence suggested Sutton had been kidnapped by a sadist, but police had nothing in the way of solid clues.

A year would pass before the next acknowledged victim in the series disappeared. On May 15, 1982, twenty-one-year-old Lorraine Borowski was scheduled to open the Elmhurst relator's office where she worked. Employees turning up for work that morning found the office locked, Borowski's shoes and scattered contents of her handbag strewn outside the door. Police were called at once, but five more months elapsed before her corpse was found, on October 10, in a cemetery south of Villa Park. Advanced decomposition left the cause of death a mystery.

Two weeks later, on May 29, Shui Mak was reported missing from Hanover Park, in Cook County; her mutilated body was recovered at Barrington on September 30. On June 13, prostitute Angel York was picked up by a "john" in a van, handcuffed, her breast slashed open before she was dumped on the roadside, still alive. Descriptions of her attacker had taken police nowhere by August 28, when teenage hooker Sandra Delaware was found stabbed and strangled to death on the bank of the Chicago River, her left breast neatly amputated. Rose Davis, age thirty, was in identical condition when police found her corpse in a Chicago alley, on September 8. Three days later, forty-two-year-old Carole Pappas, wife of the Chicago Cubs pitcher, vanished without a trace from a department store in nearby Wheaton, Illinois.

Detectives got the break they had been waiting for October 6. That morning, prostitute Beverly Washington, age twenty, was found nude and savaged beside a Chicago railroad track. Her left breast had been severed, the right deeply slashed, but she was breathing, and emergency treatment would save her life. Hours later, in a seemingly unrelated incident, drug dealer Rafael Torado was killed, a male companion wounded, when the occupants of a cruising van peppered their phone booth with rifle fire.

Two weeks later, on October 20, police arrested unemployed carpenter Robin Gecht, age twenty-eight, and charged him with the cruel assault on Beverly Washington. Also suspected of slashing eighteen-year-old prostitute Cynthia Smith before she escaped from his van, Gecht was an odd character, ousted from home as a teen for molesting his own younger sister. In later years, he worked for contractor and serial killer John Wayne Gacy, remarking to friends that Gacy's "only mistake" had been planting his victims at home, where the bodies were easily found. Authorities immediately linked Gecht with the "Ripper" slayings, but they had no proof, and he made bail October 26.

Meanwhile, detectives had learned that Gecht was one of four men who rented adjoining rooms at Villa Park's Rip Van Winkle Motel, several months before Linda Sutton was murdered nearby. The manager remembered them as party animals, frequently bringing women to their rooms, and he surprised investigators with one further bit of information. The men had been "some kind of cultists," perhaps devil worshipers.

Two of the Rip Van Winkle tenants, brothers Thomas and Andrew Kokoraleis, had been kind enough to leave a forwarding address for any mail they might receive. Police found twenty-three-year-old Thomas at home when they called, and his inconsistent answers earned him a trip downtown. The suspect promptly failed a polygraph examination, cracking under stiff interrogation to describe the "satanic chapel" in Gecht's upstairs bedroom, where captive women were tortured with knives and ice picks, gang raped, and finally sacrificed to Satan by members of a tiny cult, including Gecht, the Kokoraleis brothers, and twenty-three-year-old Edward Spreitzer. As described by the prisoners, cultic rituals included severing one or both breasts with a thin wire garrote, each celebrant "taking communion" by eating a piece before the relic was consigned to Gecht's trophy box. At one point, Kokoraleis told detectives, he had counted fifteen breasts inside the box. Some other victims had been murdered at the Rip Van Winkle, out in Villa Park. He picked a snapshot of Lorraine Borowski as a woman he had kidnapped, with his brother, for a one-way ride to the motel.

Police had heard enough. Armed with search and arrest warrants, they swept up Robin Gecht, Ed Spreitzer, and twenty-year-old Andrew Kokoraleis on November 5, lodging them in jail under $1 million bond. A search of Gecht's apartment revealed the satanic chapel described by Tom Kokoraleis, and lawmen came away with a rifle matched to the recent Torado shooting. Satanic literature was also retrieved from the apartment occupied by Andrew Kokoraleis. With the suspects in custody, authorities speculated that the gang might have murdered eighteen women in as many months.

Tom Kokoraleis was charged with the slaying of Lorraine Borowski on November 12, formally indicted by a grand jury four days later. Brother Andrew and Edward Spreitzer were charged on November 14 with the rape and murder of Rose Davis. When the mangled body of twenty-two-year-old Susan Baker was found on November 16, at a site where previous victims had been discarded, police were worried that other cult members might still be at large. No charges were filed in that case, and authorities now connect Baker's death with her background of drug and prostitution arrests in several states.

Facing multiple charges of attempted murder, rape, and aggravated battery, Robin Gecht was found mentally competent for trial on March 2, 1983. His trial opened on September 20, and Gecht took the witness stand the next day, confessing the attack on Beverly Washington. Convicted on charges of attempted murder, rape, deviant sexual assault, armed violence, aggravated kidnapping, and aggravated battery, Gecht received a sentence of 120 years in prison.

Tom Kokoraleis had suffered a change of heart since confessing to murder, attorneys seeking to block the reading of his statements in forthcoming trials, but on December 4, 1983, the confessions were admitted in evidence. Meanwhile, on April 2, 1984, Ed Spreitzer pleaded guilty on four counts of murder—including victims Davis, Delaware, Mak, and Torado. Sentenced to life on each count, he received additional time on conviction for charges of rape, deviant sexual assault, and attempted murder.

Tom Kokoraleis was convicted of Lorraine Borowski's murder on March 18, 1984. While awaiting sentencing, he led police to a field where Carole Pappas was allegedly buried, but searchers could find no remains. On September 7, the killer's helpful attitude was rewarded with a sentence of life imprisonment. Eighteen days later, Kokoraleis, his brother, and Ed Spreitzer were indicted for the murder of Linda Sutton. Andrew Kokoraleis and Spreitzer were also named in a second indictment, covering the murder of Lorraine Borowski.

On February 6, 1985, a statement from Andrew Kokoraleis was read to the jury in his trial for the Davis murder. In his confession, the defendant admitted he was "cruising" with fellow cultists Gecht and Spreitzer when they kidnapped Davis, with Andrew stabbing her several times in the process.

Convicted on February 11, he received his life sentence on March 18.

A year later, on March 4, 1986, Edward Spreitzer was convicted of murdering Linda Sutton and formally sentenced to death on March 20. Authorities describe Gecht as the cult's ringleader, with Spreitzer willing to testify against him, but no further charges have been filed in Chicago's grim series of cannibal murders.

GIRI, LAXMAN

A native of India, born in 1911, Laxman Giri was raised in a religious tradition that harked back to the murderous nineteenth century thugs. In later life, as leader of his own rural cult, Giri practiced human sacrifice in ceremonies designed to make his followers immortal. His preferred victims were children below age six, lured with candy to isolated ritual sites, where their throats were cut. No body count was established for Giri's cult, but the number of children slain before his March 1, 1980 arrest must have been considerable. Confined at a Bangalore hospital, the aged swami died of natural causes on March 5, before his trial could begin.

GORDON, CARL and COLLEEN

The crime bore every earmark of a standard family murder: victims slain in middle age, the promise of a rich inheritance, a younger relative indicted as the mastermind. Such homicides are common—eighty-five percent of all domestic murders are committed by a relative or trusted friend—but in November 1984, a sinister new twist was added to the grim equation, and Las Vegans got a glimpse of something dark and terrible at work in their community. Persistent rumors of satanic cult activity were elevated overnight from backyard gossip to the daily headlines, trumpeting the details of a grisly double homicide that stood, some said, as evidence of worse to come.

Carl Gordon and his wife Colleen were native Californians, high school sweethearts who had married, built a life, and raised a family together, finally pulling up their roots in middle age and searching for a new place in the sun. They moved to Las Vegas, Nevada, in 1979, Carl working as an air-traffic controller at McCarran Airport, while Colleen maintained their comfortable, somewhat isolated home on Washburn Road. By 1984, Carl had retired, still vigorous at fifty-eight, prepared to spend his golden years enjoying life and family. The Gordons doted on their grandson, nineteen-year-old Dale Flanagan, and let him park a trailer on their property, a comfortable arrangement that allowed the boy some freedom while maintaining family close at hand.

But Carl and Colleen Gordon never saw their golden years. Near midnight on November 5, intruders smashed a window of their home and took the couple by surprise. Colleen was wrestled to her bed and murdered execution-style, two bullets shattering her skull. A second gunman pumped no less than seven bullets into Carl as he was racing up the stairs to help his wife.

From evidence recovered at the scene, the crime appeared to be burglary gone wrong, but homicide detectives took a closer look and came to quite a different conclusion. On December 10, Dale Flanagan was jailed on open murder charges, and the probe continued. Ten days later, warrants were released for five more suspects: Randy Moore, 18; Roy McDowell, 18; Thomas Akers, 18; Johnny Luckett, 17; and Michael Walsh, 17. According to the charges filed and later proved to a jury in the district court, the six conspired to murder Carl and Colleen Gordon so that Flanagan could net the rich inheritance which he presumed was his. (Ironically, no will was ever found.) The evidence of burglary had been contrived to dupe investigators, but the youths had shown a tendency to boast about their crime, regaling friends with all the gory details, gloating over their accomplishment.

In court, prosecutor Mel Harmon warned jurors not be deceived by the appearance of the young defendants. They looked like "ordinary apple pie boys," who might enjoy "Budweiser, rock music, and chasing chicks," but looks could be deceptive. "Unfortunately," Harmon told the panel, "there was a darker, deviant side to the personalities of these young men." In fact, according to the testimony of assorted witnesses—and Flanagan himself—the homicidal friends were dedicated Satanists.

For Flanagan and Randy Moore, the fascination with satanic ritual began in 1980, while they were attending vocational classes at a local university. They heard some lectures by a visiting occultist who aroused their interest, and in time began to practice on their own. While Flanagan insists that only he and Moore were Satanists, a former girlfriend—summoned as a prosecution witness at his trial—maintains that of the six defendants, only Akers was excluded from satanic ceremonies. "Obviously," she informed the jury, "they were into it to the point where they had no moral values left."

Dale Flanagan—who later "found Jesus" in the county jail—asserts that he achieved the rank of "black magician," nothing to be sneezed at in the overall satanic hierarchy. "Where you stand," he said, "depends on what you've done, what you do, and what you know. A black magician wouldn't be the highest level, but certainly one of the highest. The highest would be a sorcerer or wizard." On his way to wizardry, the teenaged cultist was inclined to "read the [tarot] cards, do research, associate with other people and participate in what others might call covens, but what I would call get-togethers."

During one such get-together, in October 1984, he first suggested to his cronies that substantial wealth might be obtained by murdering his grandparents, thereby hastening his presumed inheritance. No date was set, but methods were discussed, and all concerned were sworn to secrecy, on threat of death from Flanagan. Coincidence prevented cultist Rusty Havens from participating in the murder—he had been arrested on a weapons charge and spent the night in jail—but he would surface as a damning prosecution witness when his cohorts went to trial.

In custody, the "psychic bond" among the killers started showing signs of strain, and finally unraveled altogether. Tommy Akers filed a guilty plea to voluntary manslaughter in August 1985, drawing a suspended sentence and five years probation in return for his promise to testify against the others. In September, Michael Walsh entered a guilty plea for two counts of murder with a deadly weapon; hanging tough in his refusal to become a witness for the state, he was rewarded with a matching set of four life terms. The prosecution scarcely needed him by then, and in a ten-day trial, beginning on September 30, the state buried Flanagan and his remaining codefendants in a withering barrage of evidence. On October 12, jurors took four hours to convict the quartet on all counts; triggermen Flanagan and Moore were sentenced to die, Johnny Luckett drew a term of life without parole, and Roy McDowell pulled straight life, making him eligible for parole around the year A.D. 2035.

Awaiting transport to death row, Flanagan privately admitted inside knowledge of satanic homicides. "I know of human sacrifices that have been done," he told newsmen, "some out at Red Rock, some out at Lone Mountain, and some up at [Lake Mead]. I don't know if it's a myth or reality, but they supposedly cut the human heart out after sacrifices, and then dismember the body." In late 1985, Flanagan corresponded briefly with the author, agreeing to discuss those rituals, but he soon fell silent on advice from counsel. Investigations continue in Las Vegas and environs.

GOYTIA, KIMBERLY

Kim Goytia was eight years old when she sat through a showing of *The Omen* in 1976, emerging from the movie with a fascination for the prince of darkness. Over time, she collected multiple copies of a novel based on the movie's screenplay, as well as a sequel titled *Damien*. Kim's mother, Carol Sommers, reportedly told friends that her daughter also dressed in black, growled like an animal at times, and moaned incantations while burning candles in satanic rituals around their Sacramento, California home.

Five years of prelude somehow left the family unprepared for the events of February 3, 1981. That afternoon, Kimberly—now thirteen—shot and killed her eleven-year-old sister, Stephanie, in front of the apartment complex where they lived. Detained on murder charges, she informed police that Satan had instructed her to fire the fatal shot.

On April 3, Superior Court Judge Mamoru Sakuma dismissed the state's murder charge, declaring that prosecutors had failed to prove the necessary elements of malice or premeditation. Five days later, Kimberly was convicted on the lesser charge of manslaughter, consigned to a juvenile facility for appropriate treatment. Judge Sakuma thereafter sealed the records of her case, citing a California law designed to protect the privacy of minors.

GRAVE ROBBING

From ancient times to the present day, human remains have played a significant role in occult rituals. Early necromancers collected fresh corpses in their attempts to commune with the dead, and no sorcerer's lair was complete without a grinning skull on the altar. Magicians and common thieves alike believed that there were special powers in the "hand of glory"—that is, the severed left hand of a corpse, sometimes converted into a grotesque candle. Preferred donors included condemned criminals, suicides, or other victims of violent death.

The occult fascination with human remains transcends racial and cultural boundaries, with reports of ritual cannibalism on file from every occupied continent. In Africa, human blood and ashes are the primary components for various high-priced salves, soaps, and potions sold by priests of the ju-ju religion. In Haiti, certain vital organs are required to brew the poison that reduces breathing humans to a zombie state. Disciples of palo mayombe stir blood and brains in their magic cauldrons, while some South American witches siphon off fat for special concoctions. In many cases, today as in centuries past, fresh ingredients are obtained through human sacrifice, but more timid practitioners often prefer to rob graves. Even Mexico's Adolfo Constanzo, linked with twenty-three ritual murders, got his start with grave robbery, leaving a handful of pennies and a headless chicken in exchange for the stolen corpse.

Modern grave-robbing incidents seem to fulfill various needs, depending on the cult and culprit involved. For some "black" magicians, an unguarded cemetery is the equivalent of an all-night supermarket, stocked with relics useful in a wide variety of rituals. Another individual or group may view the opening of graves and desecration of remains as an expression of defiance, low-grade terrorism targeting society at large. On yet another plane, reports of cult-related child abuse routinely charge that children have been lowered into open graves or locked in caskets, often with a rotting corpse, as part of a sadistic rite designed to break their spirits.

In the past three decades, there has been no shortage of reports connecting cults with theft or desecration of remains. A sampling includes:

March 1963—Bedfordshire, England: Satanists opened graves in the cemetery of a tenth century church, arranging one woman's bones on the altar for a Black Mass climaxed by the sacrifice of a rooster.

July 1981—Rosemont, West Virginia: The corpse of twenty-one-year-old Timothy Fitzwater was stolen from its grave, found days later in a burning car at nearby Shinnston.

November 1981—Reno, Nevada: Unidentified ghouls stole the body of seven-year-old Katherine Higgins, raped her corpse, and dropped it in a garbage dumpster. Cultists were suspected, but the case remains unsolved.

June 1983—Burnaby, British Colombia: Police blamed Satanists for the nocturnal theft of remains from several graves. No arrests were made.

December 1983—Newport Beach, California: Two urns, containing the ashes of a husband and wife, were stolen from a local mausoleum. A month later, thieves stole the ashes of another married couple in Redlands, sixty miles away. The case broke when a Redlands patrolman stopped a car driven by a teenager from Newport Beach, spotting a *Satanic Bible* on the front seat. Under questioning, the youth confessed his role as high priest of a "black" coven, naming five accomplices to the thefts. Stolen ashes had been used in ceremonies performed on a spit of land off the coast, referred to by Satanists as "Death Island."

July 1984—Hollywood, California: A fire at the RAM Center, an occult retail store, gave police their first glimpse of a back room described as "some kind of satanic worship place." Inside the chamber, officers found a coffin, two human skeletons, and six preserved human fetuses, all apparently for sale. No charges were filed, with the remains officially classified as "medical specimens."

December 1985—Cypress, California: The urns and ashes of a married couple were stolen from a mortuary by six young Satanists. The burglars were caught by security guards, on the roof, before they could flee with their prize.

October 1986—Mt. Airy, Maryland: Ten days before Halloween, five teenage Satanists invaded a rural cemetery, toppling sixty headstones and stealing an infant's corpse for upcoming rituals. All were later arrested and charged with vandalism.

January 1987—Los Angeles, California: Patrolmen found an old, dirt-encrusted coffin lying in the middle of an urban intersection, but no corpse and no suspects were ever discovered.

October 1987—Hendricks County, Indiana: Sheriff's officers confirmed a total of fifteen grave robberies since September, some involving century-old remains. A femur from one grave was found several hundred feet away, near a fire pit suggestive of ritual activity. Local residents phoned in reports of black-robed figures in the nearby woods, and deputies found a tree painted with "Satan" and "666." Close by, a crude altar was discovered, with candles and an empty bag of salt. The only arrest was that of an eighteen-year-old, linked to an unrelated grave robbery dating from 1984.

November 1987—Redwood City, California: Two crypts were opened, with four coffins smashed and teeth removed from the cadavers. An adult and two juveniles were charged with the crime in January 1988.

April 1990—Waterbury, Connecticut: Two sixteen-year-old Satanists were jailed on charges of stealing urns and human ashes from a mausoleum, the remains intended for use in occult ceremonies. A third suspect, age fifteen, was still being sought by police.

September 1990—Providence, Rhode Island: Two adults and four teenagers were arrested for stealing an infant's corpse from a local cemetery. The body was found in an abandoned house used for satanic rituals.

April 1991—Indianapolis, Indiana: A casket and its occupant, the body of a seventy-eight-year-old woman, were removed from a suburban graveyard. No suspects were identified, and the corpse was not recovered.

May 1991—Des Moines, Iowa: Vandals broke into a hundred-year-old mausoleum, removing a woman's skull. The relic was found at an abandoned motel scarred with satanic graffiti, described by neighbors as a regular meeting place for "The Lost Boys," a gang of teenage cultists who borrowed their name from a popular horror film.

July 1991—New York City: Twenty-one-year-old Matias Frias was charged with stealing five skulls from a Brooklyn cemetery and selling them for use in occult rituals.

August 1991—Ft. Wayne, Indiana: Two teenage body snatchers were arrested on burglary charges after they tried to steal a corpse from a local mortuary. Held in lieu of $10,000 bond, eighteen-year-old Adam Barnaba and his seventeen-year-old accomplice reportedly advertised their occult delivery service by word of mouth, running afoul of the law when an undercover detective posed as a Satanist, offering $400 for a fresh body.

September 1991—Brown County, Indiana: Several graves were opened by persons unknown, in an area where cult gatherings and torchlight processions are frequently reported.

Such incidents are often minimized as "childish pranks" in the hope of avoiding bad publicity, even in regions where grave robbing has become routine. As Detective Pat Metoyer told author Larry Kahaner in 1987: "In East Los Angeles, in Calvary Cemetery, every Saturday the fourteenth the grounds keeper has to right tombstones. Some son of a bitch has been trying to dig up bodies. The grounds keeper excuses it by saying it has to be Friday the thirteenth dares. Why does it have to be Friday the thirteenth dares? Why can't it be someone who is there to steal bones, which is in fact what happens."

At the height of a 1987 body-snatching epidemic in Hendricks County, Indiana, religious scholars at nearby Ball State University proclaimed correctly——and irrelevantly— that the incidents were "very probably not associated" with Anton LaVey's Church of Satan. No one had suggested that LaVey's handful of followers traveled two thousand miles from their San Francisco stronghold to rob graves in the Midwest, but the disclaimer was good enough for Sheriff Roy Waddell, who promptly announced that the still-unidentified vandals had no cult connections. Internal controversy finally drove Lt. Michael Nelson to quit the force, telling newsmen: "In a nutshell, without getting in a battle with [Waddell], I believe there is satanic activity and he believes there isn't. He also didn't care for the publicity." [See: Human Sacrifice]

GREEN, HOWARD and MARRON, CAROL

At 7:00 P.M. on Sunday, December 16, 1979, a motorist in West Paterson, New Jersey, sighted the bodies of a man and woman lying on the grassy shoulder of Route 80. Authorities were summoned, and both victims were pronounced dead at the scene. Each had been clubbed on the left side of the head and stabbed in the right eye; a clump of hair was also found clutched in each victim's hand. Autopsy reports show that both bodies were completely drained of blood, the killers employing a veterinarian's syringe.

Police identified the victims as fifty-three-year-old Howard Green and thirty-three-year-old Carol Marron, residents of Brooklyn, in nearby New York City. Green was a cab driver and part-time artist, while Marron held a secretarial position at Brooklyn's Pratt Institute, designing clothes in her spare time. They shared a basement flat on DeKalb Avenue, where a police search turned up various items of occult paraphernalia. The couple was last seen alive in the early evening of December 15, by a friend who met them on a Manhattan subway train.

While motive and suspects remained elusive in the case, NYPD Detective Jim Devereaux told reporters, "It was definitely a satanic murder. And it wasn't a one-man job. In all my years in this business, I've never seen anything like this." Independent confirmation of that judgment comes from newsman Maury Terry, who later received an anonymous letter reading:

Dear Maury Terry. Please look into this double killing. Carol was asking people about the OTO a year prior to the murders. I can't accept that the people responsible for this are still walking around free. I am afraid that the problem will not go away and that minds this unbalanced may perpetrate additional horrors. Forgive me for not signing my name. I haven't gotten over the fear.

Despite this pointer to the Ordo Templi Orientis, a ritual magic society once led by Satanist Aleister Crowley, police have made no further progress on the case. At this writing, the murders of Howard Green and Carol Marron remain unsolved. [See: Ordo Templi Orientis]

GREENE, LINDA and JONES, ARZELL

In 1983, Detroit policewoman Linda Greene and a companion, private investigator Arzell Jones, were arrested and held under $25,000 bond on four counts of kidnapping, first-degree sexual assault, and firearms violations. According to their victim, an adult Caucasian female, Greene and Jones abducted her from a nightclub and drove her to a motel, where she was beaten, sexually abused, and forced to chant "Satan is my master. I denounce the words of Jesus Christ." Before his arrest, Jones allegedly tried to recruit another woman for "some type of ritualistic ceremony" involving black robes. Both defendants were convicted and sentenced to prison in December 1983.

HALL, PATRICIA

In May 1970, New Orleans police arrested eighteen-year-old Patricia Hall and three male drifters for the rape and cat-o'-nine-tails flogging of a teenage girl, carried out in the Hall of Horrors Wax Museum on Bourbon Street. An ardent Satanist who claimed she had been baptized by the "Black Pope" in San Francisco—Anton LaVey denies the claim—Hall was described by detectives as a "hippie-type with tattoos." Before the rape case went to trial, she was extradited to Florida, there convicted and sentenced to prison for the stabbing death of a sixty-six-year-old man.

"HAND OF GLORY"

Documented in crime reports and religious texts as early as the mid–fifteenth century, the "hand of glory" is a classic example of human remains used for magical ends. Generally defined as the severed hand of a corpse—and typically the *left* hand, in accordance with the satanic significance of the "left-hand path"—such a relic, if properly processed and "blessed," was thought to imbue its owner with various powers, including invisibility. That particular property made the talisman attractive to thieves, like the burglars who entered a house at Loughcrew, Ireland, in 1831, armed with a shriveled hand clutching a "magic" candle. Predictably, the charm failed to work, and the burglars fled, leaving their "hand of glory" behind when an alarm was sounded.

A century later, in 1939, a gang of poisoners-for-profit used the "evil eye," witchy hexes, and a "hand of glory" to terrorize witnesses and potential victims in Philadelphia. In that case, superstitious immigrants believed the mummified relic could injure or kill them by magical means, and the homicidal swindlers used it to good effect before meeting a hardheaded witness who scoffed at such legends. More recently, in Roswell, Georgia, during 1988, police raided an abandoned house used for teenage satanic rituals, finding severed human fingers on a makeshift altar, candles affixed to the fingernails.

Various grimoires dictate different techniques for obtaining and processing a "hand of glory," but artificial substitutes are rarely tolerated in the classic texts. It is believed that efforts to obtain such relics may account for many incidents of grave robbing where cultists are involved. Within the past two decades, such cases have been widely documented from all parts of the United States, and from the western provinces of Canada. [See: Grave Robbing]

"HANDS OF DEATH"

The most bizarre and controversial murder case of modern times began in June 1983, with the arrest of a one-eyed drifter on misdemeanor firearms charges. Henry Lee Lucas, age forty-six, was suspected of killing an elderly woman in Montague County, Texas, but the local sheriff had no evidence on which to base a murder charge. Finally jailed for possession of a handgun, illegal for ex-convicts in Texas, Lucas spent four nights in jail before he broke down and confessed *two* recent homicides. In addition to eighty-year-old Kate Rich, Lucas also admitted killing and dismembering his teenage girlfriend, Frieda Powell. He led police to the remains of both victims and later pleaded guilty to the murders in court . . . but there was more.

Before he finished talking, almost two years later, Henry Lucas confessed to a staggering total of 360 murders, allegedly committed over seven years in the United States and Canada. His confessions implicated an accomplice, thirty-six-year-old Ottis Toole—already serving twenty years for an arson conviction in Florida—and Toole chimed in with more confessions of his own, corroborating Henry's statements and adding new crimes to the list. By early 1985, Lucas and Toole had been convicted and sentenced for a total of twelve slayings, with Henry condemned to die for the murder of a Texas hitchhiker. Across the country, more than two hundred other homicides were "cleared" by police on the basis of confessions from Lucas or Toole.

The numbers alone were staggering, but raw statistics were not the worst part of the story. In addition to his marathon confessions, Lucas—later supported by Toole—had begun to describe his participation in a murderous satanic cult he called the "Hands of Death." As sketched by Lucas for a special task force working in his case, the cult had members nationwide, who practiced brutal homicide as both a form of ritual and recreation. On the side, he said, the cultists were involved in organized narcotics traffic, child pornography, and "snuff" films, many of the latter produced in Mexico. One of his duties with the cult, said Lucas, had been snatching children off the street and driving them across the border for delivery to wealthy pedophiles and fellow Satanists.

According to Lucas, his introduction to the "Hands of Death" came sometime in the late 1970s, while he was traveling through Maryland. A relative, Wade Kiser, confirms Henry's meeting with an enigmatic "used car salesman," allegedly from Shreveport, Louisiana, who offered both men well-paid jobs driving stolen cars to Mexico. Kiser declined the offer, while Lucas accepted, learning over time that his deliveries would include more than hot cars. According to Lucas, he was formally initiated into the "Hands of Death" at a camp in the Everglades, where he witnessed acts of human sacrifice and cannibalism remarkably similar to reports of California's satanic "Four P Movement." As a full-fledged member of the cult, Lucas was not only paid for felonious errands, but also encouraged to satisfy his personal taste for serial murder at every opportunity.

There were problems with some of Henry's confessions from the beginning. One alleged victim was found alive and well, while other crimes confessed by Lucas in persuasive detail actually occurred while he was serving jail time. At times, it seemed that Lucas was deliberately toying with police, as when he claimed a homicide in Spain or told authorities that he had carried poison to the Peoples Temple cultists for their 1978 mass suicide in Guyana, but other statements had the solid ring of truth, complete with hand-drawn maps and floor plans, detailed descriptions of mutilations, and recollection of stolen items omitted from original police reports. Ottis Toole, a self-admitted cannibal and pyromaniac, was equally convincing in his description of crimes committed without Henry's knowledge.

In April 1985, the roof fell in, with Lucas suddenly recanting all of his confessions, pleading total innocence. Overnight, he denied killing anyone but his mother, a crime that had sent him to prison for a decade back in 1960. The "new" Henry could not understand how Kate Rich's bones wound up in his wood-burning stove. Police were lying when they said he led them to the pitiful remains of Frieda Powell in Denton county. And, of course, there was no cult at all.

Henry's turnabout stunned detectives from coast to coast, and ninety of the murders he had "cleared" would be reopened for investigation in the next few months. Critics began to speak of the "Lucas hoax" as an established fact, but Henry wasn't finished talking yet. The ink was barely dry on headlines trumpeting his claims of innocence when Lucas sent a letter out of jail, insisting that his latest story was the hoax, his previous confessions true. Bob Larson, a fundamentalist minister, broadcast a tape of an interview with Lucas, Henry claiming that his jailers had drugged and coerced him into changing his story.

What, finally, is the truth of the matter? At this writing, none of Lucas's convictions have been overturned, and he remains the prime suspect in more than one hundred homicides across the nation. In September 1991, Ottis Toole pleaded guilty to four more murders in Florida and received yet another life sentence; Henry's scheduled trial in the same four cases was canceled on economic grounds, as a waste of tax money. As for the allegations of a cult . . .

In early 1984, some detectives aired their opinion that the "Hands of Death" was simply a nickname applied by Lucas and Toole to each other, part of a sick game wherein the first man to touch a woman had the "right" to take her life. Author Sondra London confirmed that suspicion in interviews with Toole during 1991, but her research also revealed an apparent cult connection in the case. Toole not only described his late grandmother as a "devil-worshiper," but he also spoke of personal visits to the New Orleans headquarters of the satanic Process Church of Final Judgment, elsewhere linked to such diverse killers as the Charles Manson "family" and New York's "Son of Sam." More to the point, London discovered independent evidence of a satanic, drug-dealing cult active in Toole's hometown of Jacksonville, Florida. In fact, as revealed by London's tireless digging, the mysterious "used car dealer from Shreveport" appears to be a real-life car salesman, now deceased, who was well-known for his cult and criminal ties around Jacksonville prior to his unsolved murder in the 1980s.

After so much controversy, *any* statement from Lucas or Toole is naturally suspect, but portions of Henry's original confessions are supported by independent evidence. As early as 1978, five years before the arrest of Lucas and Toole, authorities in Texas and Washington, D.C., published reports on the traffic in kidnapped children between Mexico and the United States, with specific references to child pornography and "snuff" films. Lucas himself drew a map of cult hideouts and headquarters along the Mexican border, but it got lost in the shuffle when he began recanting his statements in 1985. Four years later, with the exposure of drug-related human sacrifices around Matamoros, Texas Rangers dusted off the map and found that one site marked by Lucas corresponded precisely with Adolfo Constanzo's ritual killing ground at Rancho Santa Elena.

Most discussions of the Lucas case and Satanism meet a brick wall with the claim that FBI agents investigated Henry's cult allegations and "found no supporting evidence." Author Max Call describes futile airborne searches of the Everglades, with an implication that the cultists must have pulled up stakes and moved their hidden compound in the nick of time. Each reference to a sweeping FBI investigation further reduces Henry's credibility ... or it would, if any such investigation had ever occurred.

Unfortunately, such is not the case.

In 1987, I approached the FBI with a Freedom of Information Act request for access to official records on the "Hands of Death." The FBI's response, dated May 12, acknowledges the existence of *one* file by that title, involving a 1937 extortion case from Kentucky! No other mention of the cult was found anywhere in the FBI files or computers, a circumstance confirmed by author Mike Cox in 1991, with his report that the FBI took no part in the ongoing Lucas investigation between 1983 and 1985. FBI "cult expert" Ken Lanning affirmed the Bureau's lack of interest in a 1991 interview with Sondra London. Lanning's backward premise: "There's nothing to it, so we're not wasting time on an investigation."

After nearly a decade of controversy and name-calling, the

final truth in this puzzling case remains elusive. With Lucas changing stories on a daily basis, newsmen competing for banner headlines, and detectives scrambling to save their reputations, only two things can be said about the case with any certainty. First, a number of events and rituals described by Lucas dovetail perfectly with independent information gained from other crimes. And second, the alleged "proof" of his "hoax" proves nothing at all. [See: "Four P Movement"; Pornography; Process Church of Final Judgment; Serial Murder; Slavery; "Snuff" Films]

HAYSOM, ELIZABETH ROXANNE and SOERING, JENS

On March 30, 1985, steel executive Derek Haysom, age seventy-two, and his wife Nancy, fifty-three, were found slain in the kitchen of their country home near Lynchburg, Virginia. Both victims had been stabbed repeatedly, with their throats slashed and bodies mutilated after death. Police who searched the lavish home could find no evidence of robbery, but they did note a triangle painted in blood at the scene, along with the satanic numerals "666" carved into the wooden floor.

Daughter Elizabeth, then twenty-two, was routinely questioned by police in the wake of the crime, but no charges were filed. Family members described her as "headstrong" and "a strange little girl," who once ran away from an English boarding school and surfaced six months later, living in Germany. Her latest boyfriend, in fact, was the son of a German diplomat. Born in Bangkok, eighteen-year-old Jens Soering had graduated with honors from an exclusive prep school in Atlanta, where he was known as "eccentric and extremely bright." Elizabeth and Jens were freshmen at the University of Virginia when they met, in early 1985, and soon became inseparable.

It was a strange relationship, at that. Acquaintances noted that Elizabeth seemed to dominate Jens, directing his every thought and deed. "She was his Svengali," one friend told the press, "and he just sort of fluttered around her." Their peculiar interests included a fascination with the occult.

Still, locals felt more sympathy than suspicion for Elizabeth Haysom, until she and her lover vanished without a trace in October 1985. As the story was later pieced together by authorities, the couple fled to Thailand, and from there to London, renting a Baker Street flat as "Mr. and Mrs. Christopher Noe." On April 30, 1986, they were arrested in a London department store, suspicious behavior and a lack of valid ID giving way to proved connections with a series of fraudulent checks. Both suspects were held without bond, pending interrogation by American authorities in the death of Elizabeth's parents. Letters found in their apartment, written by Jens to Elizabeth before the double murder, reportedly contained "inferences" of the crime to come, and a Virginia grand jury indicted both suspects on charges of first-degree murder.

Extradition of Elizabeth Haysom, as a U.S. citizen, was routine. Convicted of double murder in Virginia, she was sentenced to a prison term of ninety years. The British government also agreed to extradite Soering, in 1985, but Jens appealed his case to the European Court of Human Rights. On July 7, 1989, that body ruled that he could not be extradited to a jurisdiction where he might be executed for his crimes.

HEAVY METAL MUSIC

Rock and roll has enjoyed a strange, symbiotic relationship with the occult since the 1960s, when the Beatles included a photo of Aleister Crowley on their *Sgt. Pepper* album, and the Rolling Stones credited Anton LaVey or Haitian voodoo priests with the inspiration for such albums as "Goat's Head Soup," "Sympathy for the Devil," and "Satanic Majesties Request." It was, perhaps, inevitable that the hippie era of the latter Sixties, with its emphasis on "acid rock" and Eastern mysticism would initiate a change in classic rock and roll, evolving over time into the current "heavy metal" scene.

Heavy metal music—so called for its reliance on electric guitars cranked to ear-splitting decibels—has become inextricably linked with Satanism in the public eye, thanks in equal parts to lyrics, deliberate marketing strategy, and the sometimes exaggerated claims of Christian fundamentalist groups. Beyond the footlights and the amplifiers, in the daily world of "metal heads" and "stoners" who become obsessed with heavy metal to the point that it controls their lives, police contend that crimes ranging from petty vandalism to multiple murder are directly inspired by the message of cult-oriented bands.

The direct ancestor of modern heavy metal groups is Led Zeppelin, a band known as much for its occult connections as for its trend-setting sound. Associates and survivors of the original group still debate an alleged pact with Satan, reportedly signed in blood by band members during the mid-1960s. Whatever the truth of that story, guitarist Jimmy Page once owned an occult bookstore in London and professed himself a disciple of Aleister Crowley. After purchasing Crowley's old mansion at Boleskin, in Scotland, Page retained Satanist Charles Pace to decorate the house in a motif depicting various aspects of ritual magic. (Page's nickname—"Zoso"—was shared with a three-headed dog, supposed to guard the gates of Hell.) Lead singer Robert Plant also professed a fascination with witchcraft, and it comes as no surprise that Led Zeppelin was one of the first bands charged with inserting subliminal prayers to Satan in their recorded tunes.

As the 1970s progressed, performers like Alice Cooper and the band Black Sabbath made more deliberate appeals to the occult/satanic image in their stage performances and advertising. Cooper, born Vincent Furnier, allegedly borrowed his stage name from a seventeenth century witch, after consulting a Ouija board. Black Sabbath, first introduced to the press with a mock sacrifice of a seminude woman, took the game a step further, becoming the prototype of modern "satanic" bands, sporting devilish figures, pentagrams, and the number "666" on albums devoted largely to themes of death, sacrifice, and demonic possession. Lead singer Ozzy Osbourne broke with the group in 1979 to become a solo artist, but he continued the hell-bent tradition with songs like "Mr. Crowley" and "Bark at the Moon." In 1982, Osbourne underwent precautionary treatment for rabies after biting off a bat's head at a concert; later the same year, he was briefly committed to a London sanitarium after removing his clothes in the midst of a business meeting. As he told one interviewer: "I don't know if I'm a medium for some outside source. Whatever it is, frankly I hope it's not what I think it is—Satan."

By that point, showmanship was clearly the key for heavy metal bands, epitomized by the fire-spitting, tongue-wagging performances of KISS. Guitarist Gene Simmons described the

band's style thusly for one interviewer: "We wanted to look
like we crawled out from under a rock somewhere in hell. We
wanted parents to look at us and instantly want to throw up."
To that end, singer Peter Criss told *Rolling Stone,* in 1977, "I
find myself evil. I believe in the devil as much as God. You
can use either one of them to get things done."

Within a few short years, satanic emblems, lyrics, and tattoos became the standard trappings of successful heavy metal
bands. Taking their cue from Black Sabbath, would-be overnight successes began to advertise themselves as Iron
Maiden, Venom, Slayer, Sodom, Voi Vod, Anti Christ, Hell-
hammer, Nocticula, Megadeth, Possessed, and Bathory
(named for a seventeenth century Romanian countess who
bathed in the blood of murdered virgins). A small-time band
from Denver, Satan's Host, boasted performers with stage
names like Satan Patrick Evil, Belial, D. Lucifer Steele,
and Leviathan Thisiren. Heavy metal publicists worked overtime exploiting the "witchy" angle, creating a semantic
snarl with published references to "thrash metal," "black
metal," "speed metal," and "death metal"—each presumably more awesome (and more profitable) than its predecessor.

Critics of the new wave noted its preoccupation with
demonic themes and kinky sex, brute force and bloodshed.
On the Christian talk show circuit, word began to circulate
that certain heavy metal bands were hiding secret messages
within their very names, as well as in their lyrics. Thus, it
was suggested that KISS *really* stood for "Kids (or Knights)
In Satan's Service." AC/DC's logo was described as short-
hand for "Anti-Christ, Devil's Child," or perhaps "After
Christ, the Devil Comes." By the same logic, WASP becomes
an acronym for "We Are Satan's People." Heavy metal performers uniformly deny such claims, to which their critics
reply that the "real" meanings are widely "understood" by
teenage fans.

It is difficult, if not impossible, to gauge the true measure
of occult/satanic belief among heavy metal performers. For
some bands, like the effeminate Motley Crue, pentagrams and
inverted crosses are simply part of the act, along with lipstick, eye shadow, and women's underwear. At the other end
of the spectrum, lead singer King Diamond, with the band
Mercyval Fate, openly proclaims his devotion to Satan. Likewise, the members of Venom—performing under the "infer-

nal names" of Abaddon, Cronus, and Mantas—admit that black magic rituals provide the underpinning for songs like "Welcome to Hell."

In the final analysis, it probably matters less how heavy metal singers view Satan, than it does how young prospective Satanists view heavy metal rock. Michael Aquino, founder of the Temple of Set, has compared heavy metal to the torch-light processions of Nazi Germany, "an explosion of fury" designed to release inhibitions and compensate for frustration. Some metal heads, like "Night Stalker" Richard Ramirez, allow a particular song or band to dominate their lives, becoming a personal anthem that speaks to their darkest desires. It is, perhaps, no coincidence that names of heavy metal bands and artists dominate graffiti at many ritual sites and scenes of cult-related vandalism. Within the past decade, heavy metal's message of "sex, drugs, and rock 'n' roll" has taken its place as the modern equivalent of Aleister Crowley's "Do What Thou Wilt."

From coast to coast, police blame roving gangs of "stoners" or "satanic heavy metal rockers" for crimes including church and cemetery desecration, grave robbing, burglary, arson, assault, drug dealing, and murder. Across America, in cult-related killings where the murderers are under twenty years of age, it is a standard rule of thumb that heavy metal tapes and records, posters, T-shirts and the like will be retrieved among the killers' personal effects. And in the heart of London, several victims of marauding rapists have reported their attackers bearing hand tattoos depicting spider webs and the initials MAR—both symbols of a heavy metal band, Marillion, whose albums feature songs of violent rape and mayhem.

It would be unfair to say that all—or even most—devoted fans of heavy metal rock are criminals, much less devoted Satanists. Charles Manson's twisted adoration of the Beatles and his personal, bizarre interpretation of their songs does not indict the millions who enjoyed performances by John, Paul, George, and Ringo through the years. In any fad, from "Dungeons & Dragons" to ghetto rap music, there are unstable individuals who lose track of the dividing line between entertainment and reality. Unfortunately, in the case of heavy metal and its message of apocalypse, the price of fantasy is sometimes paid in blood. [See: Backward Masking; "Hell Crew"; Ramirez, Richard; "Stoners"]

"HELL CREW"

In the first five months of 1986, unknown vandals caused more than $300,000 damage in Middlesex County, New Jersey, striking solely at religious targets. The Holy Spirit Church in Perth Amboy was first to feel the night prowlers' wrath, with damage including smashed statues and extensive spray-painted graffiti, mingling satanic symbols with the names of heavy metal bands like Venom and Slayer. In April, authorities were called to Our Lady of the Most Holy Rosary Cemetery, where an estimated $100,000 damage was done, primarily in the toppling and defacing of several dozen headstones. A month later, the vandals struck at Beth Israel Memorial Park, in Woodbridge, uprooting seventy markers and adding backward swastikas to their repertoire of graffiti, for an estimated $60,000 damage.

County prosecutor Alan Rockoff responded to the wave of attacks by organizing a Joint Unit to Stop Terrorism (JUST). Calling on participants from twenty-five police agencies countywide, JUST began its search for suspects with the symbols pointing to satanic ideology and heavy metal rock, a trail that ultimately led investigators to an eighteen-member gang that called itself the "Hell Crew." Members and associates dressed in black leather, sported satanic jewelry or tattoos, and doted on the "thrash" music of "black metal" bands, typified by Venom—a group whose members openly admit participation in demonic rituals.

Under police questioning, members of the Hell Crew described their favorite pastime as gathering by night in wooded areas or cemeteries, where they threw "hell parties." As described by one participant, "You're around your friends, listening to music, you light a fire, and it reminds you of hell. We don't like to bother people. We don't like to vandalize nothing. We just like to hang out and have a good time."

Prosecutor Rockoff took a different view of the festivities. "They are rebelling against society, and this is the way they are showing it," he told newsmen. "They have a creed to deface and defame wherever and whatever they can for the purpose of shocking society. They meet in cemeteries, in a sewer pipe in Woodbridge, behind a closed refinery in Port Reading, and in the trash area of a supermarket in Hopelawn. They do their drinking, their consumption of drugs, and listen to heavy metal on cassettes. I guess they beat themselves into a frenzy.

They're baying at the moon like a pack of jackals. These kids hang out in cemeteries, and they hang out near churches because they feel with the devil or Satan because of this music. They feel they're doing their part for the satanic cult by destroying God's temples and monuments. They're groupies. They wear the shirts, they wear the hair, they wear the make-believe studs on their wrists. Some of the drawings we've picked up from the homes reveals a strong influence of a group at play at being cultists, Satanists, a kind of anti-Christ movement."

In June, Middlesex officers arrested two Hell Crew members, aged sixteen and seventeen, on charges of vandalizing the Beth Israel cemetery. Both were convicted in juvenile court, with the seventeen-year-old also pleading guilty to the raid on Holy Spirit Church. Rockoff described the convicted vandals as "devotees, totally immersed in, and totally influenced by, heavy metal rock music and alcohol." [See: Heavy Metal Music; "Stoners"]

HELL-FIRE CLUBS

Similar in some respects to the aristocratic devil-worship cults that once scandalized France, the so-called "hell-fire clubs" were apparently restricted to Great Britain in the eighteenth century. Unlike their continental predecessors, though, the British Satanists refrained from animal and human sacrifice, preferring to amuse themselves with liquor, drugs, and sexual debauchery.

The precise origins of British hell-fire clubs is unclear, but they were already infamous enough in 1721 for King George I to issue an edict denouncing the sort of "scandalous society" where young men gathered to "insult in the most impious and most blasphemous fashion those principles which are most sacred in our Holy Religion, where they brave even the person of the All-Powerful Lord and mutually corrupt one another." Despite royal disapproval, groups like the Bold Backs, the Demoniacs, the Dublin Blasters, and the Edinburgh Sweating Club were active well into the next decade, with stylized Black Masses predictably degenerating into drunken orgies.

The most significant and infamous of all the hell-fire clubs was organized around 1745 by Sir Francis Dashwood, a wealthy young libertine. Well known for his interest in Satanism and the occult, Dashwood had posed for a portrait three years earlier, depicting himself in a friar's robe, kneeling before a statue of Venus, while a halo overhead mirrors the face of Satan. Second-in-command of the new hell-fire club, serving as assistant to Dashwood's "Father Superior," was a wealthy eccentric named George Bubb, whose home in Hammersmith, London, provided the group with its first meeting place. Other recruits from the British upper crust included: the Earl of Sandwich, First Lord of the Admiralty; the Earl of Bute; Thomas Potter, son of the Archbishop of Canterbury; poet Charles Churchill; satirist George Selwyn, expelled from Oxford, who often disguised himself as an old woman to attend public executions; John Wilkes and Paul Whitehead, both members of Parliament; famed novelist Lawrence Sterne; and Robert Lloyd, a wastrel whose claim to fame was the largest one-man debt in London. With two members of the local gentry, these comprised Dashwood's "Unholy Twelve," but other members were welcomed. One such, a personal friend of "Saint Francis," was Benjamin Franklin, said by modern biographers to have enjoyed sex with underage girls.

In 1750, Dashwood leased the Cistercian abbey at Medmenham, in Buckinghamshire, and financed extensive renovations. When complete, his new "abbey" featured pornographic art work, satanic ornaments, and a vast library of erotic literature. Black Masses were performed by the "Monks of Medmenham," complete with mockery of standard Christian rituals, but the main thrust of club gatherings was patently sexual. Members of the club were serviced by prostitutes dressed in nuns' habits, and they also practiced sexual abuse of children purchased from the slums of London. Incest was a common "sacrament" at Dashwood's abbey, but freewheeling indulgence had its price, with several members falling prey to fatal cases of venereal disease through the years.

By 1762, the membership roster of the hell-fire club read like a *Who's Who* of British government. Lord Bute had become prime minister, Bubb was a cabinet minister, and Dashwood himself was serving as Chancellor of the Exchequer. With Wilkes and Churchill in Parliament, the secret society seemed untouchable . . . but partisan politics finally ruined the game. In his bid to become prime minister, Wilkes leaked details of the hell-fire club's demonic rituals, persuading Churchill to do likewise. The resultant scandal toppled Lord Bute's government, but Wilkes would not succeed him, as the taint of rampant Satanism ruined all concerned. Dashwood tried to revive the order in new quarters, leading poorly attended rituals in the caves under Wycombe Hill, but the moment had passed. Age and disease claimed Dashwood and most of his "monks" in the next two decades, writing *finis* to the hell-fire club. Ironically, Wilkes would outlive them all, dying in 1797, a victim of self-imposed exile to France. [See: Black Mass]

HERNANDEZ, CAYETANO and SANTOS

Unscrupulous scam artists from Yerba Buena, in the Mexican state of Tamaulipas, the Hernandez brothers organized a local cult in early 1963, persuading gullible farmers that the "mountain gods" would shower them with riches if they demonstrated proper piety and made unselfish sacrifices. Sex was the prescribed form of devotion, with women submitting themselves to Santos, while Cayetano serviced the men. Dissension spread over time, when the promised riches failed to materialize, and the brothers went shopping for a solution in Monterrey. There, they met Magdalena Solis, a blond lesbian prostitute, persuading her and her brother Eleazor to impersonate the mountain gods for a share of the take.

Villagers in Yerba Buena were briefly appeased by the ruse, but even steamy sex with deities paled in comparison to hard cash. When their disciples grew restless again, the Hernandez brothers called for a human sacrifice, with two of their most vocal critics beaten to death, their blood consumed by the faithful from ceremonial bowls. Over the next few weeks, six more doubters were dispatched in similar style.

Old-fashioned jealousy finally doomed the cult, Magdalena Solis flying into a rage when one of her female devotees began sharing sexual favors with Santos Hernandez. The "goddess" demanded an immediate sacrifice, with the teenage girl bound to a cross and beaten to death. While her body was being burned, Magdalena fingered another member of the cult as a heretic, watching her disciples hack the man to pieces with machetes on the spot.

Unknown to participants in the ghoulish rite, they were

also observed by a teenage witness not affiliated with the sect. Police were skeptical, but they dispatched a patrolman to check out the cult's mountain lair, just in case. When the officer disappeared, along with his guide, a flying squad was sent to Yerba Buena from the capital at Ciudad Victoria. They found two mutilated corpses, the policeman's heart ripped from his chest, and rifle fire erupted when the squad approached a cave the cult had fortified. Three officers were wounded in the shootout, but the odds were on their side. When the smoke cleared, police found Santos Hernandez dead from bullet wounds. His brother was missing, later identified as a victim of assassination by a rival candidate for priesthood in the cult. The resident "gods" and twelve disciples were convicted of murder, earning long terms in prison.

HUBBARD, LAFAYETTE RONALD

The son of a navy commander, born in Nebraska on March 13, 1911, L. Ron Hubbard finished one year of study at George Washington University before dropping out of college in 1932 to become a moderately successful writer of pulp science fiction and westerns. With the outbreak of World War II, he followed family tradition by joining the U.S. Navy and served in the Pacific Theater. Wounded in action and discharged from the service, he would later complain to Veterans Administration physicians about his "seriously affected" mind and "suicidal inclinations."

Hubbard's tour of duty had included visits to China and India, where he reportedly witnessed "miracles done by holy men." In pursuit of their secret, during 1945 and 1946, he turned to Aleister Crowley's Ordo Templi Orientis. Bearing the rank of "frater" in the OTO's southern California Agape Lodge, led by John Parsons, Hubbard was impressive enough to rise through the ranks in short order, soon becoming Parsons's trusted assistant. In one ceremony, designed to created a magical "moonchild," Parsons engaged in ritual intercourse with a female disciple, while Hubbard acted as a "seer" to describe concurrent events on the "astral plane." By all accounts, the effort was a bust.

Parsons and Hubbard had a falling-out in 1946, the circumstances still contested by opposing sides. OTO spokesmen claim that Hubbard persuaded Parsons to sell off property belonging to the lodge, whereupon Hubbard promptly de-camped with the money and Parsons's sister-in-law Betty. Hubbard's wife sued for divorce, but "Elron" was on a roll, turning up on the Florida coast with a brand-new yacht in early July, preparing for an extended pleasure cruise. The ship set sail at 5:00 P.M. on July 5, and Parsons reportedly performed an invocation of the demon "Bartzabel" three hours later, whipping up a squall that drove the yacht back to port with serious damage. A small portion of the missing cash was later returned, and Hubbard was ultimately "forgiven," returning to work with Parsons by year's end.

Hubbard, in all fairness, had a different version of events, his story sounding more like James Bond than Merlin the ma-gician. In the alternate account, shadowy persons unknown recruited Hubbard to investigate the OTO's relationship with certain nuclear physicists at Cal Teach University. Heroic Hubbard, doubtless chosen for the secret mission on the basis of his vast experience, managed to crack the cult and save America's atomic secrets from the Prince of Darkness. Grant-ing that the OTO is widely known for flights of fancy—some would say hallucinations—Hubbard's subsequent behavior and the accusations filed against him tend to ratify the story told by Parsons of a rip-off gone to pot.

In any case, the OTO had taught Hubbard a crucial lesson in cult management: Suckers are born to be taken. In short or-der, Hubbard began to reconstruct his image, picking up a mail order doctorate from "Sequoia University" and billing himself as an "extensively decorated" war hero. (Years later, in a 1984 lawsuit, a California judge would describe Hubbard as "a pathological liar.") His book *Dianetics,* written in 1948 and commercially published two years later, advanced a new psychotherapeutic technique called "auditing," wherein a simplified polygraph machine called an "E-meter" is used to pinpoint "engrams"—mental problems accruing from past lives—and points the way toward progressive stages of coun-seling which leave the cured patient "clear."

Dianetics sold 1.5 million copies within a brief period, though critics insist that the best-seller status of this and other Hubbard tomes has been artificially inflated by teams of his disciples who buy up each new book in mass quantities. In any case, initial sales were hopeful enough to launch the New Jersey–based Hubbard Dianetics Research Foundation in 1950, with chapters spreading nationwide by the end of the year. Financial success was one thing, but Hubbard also craved respectability, and the medical community's stern rejection of Dianetics paved the way for a war of propaganda and litigation, continuing to the present day.

In 1952, Elron moved his headquarters to Phoenix and set up shop as the Hubbard Association of Scientologists. The Church of Scientology was incorporated a year later, with the first two congregations organized in Los Angeles and Auckland, New Zealand, during 1954. In practice, Hubbard had trouble deciding whether his message represented a science, a philosophy, or a religion—but the bottom line was always money. Free "personality tests" inevitably diagnosed potential recruits as "preclear"—that is, in need of "auditing"—but none of the treatments were free from that point on. By 1991, the church's "Bridge to Enlightenment" included eight progressive stages of counseling, each more costly than the last, with committed disciples shelling out an average $300,000 each to become "clear." Hubbard referred to the new recruits as "raw meat," and his profiteering was blatant enough that the IRS stripped his church of its tax-exempt status in 1958. Elron responded by creating numerous front groups, including Narconon, the Citizens Commission on Human Rights, the Committee on Public Health and Safety, American Citizens for Honesty in Government, the Committee for a Safe Environment, and the National Commission on Law Enforcement and Social Justice.

Church philosophy took another bizarre turn in the 1960s, with Hubbard's "discovery" that all human beings are occupied by alien spirits called "Thetans," banished to earth some seventy-five million years ago by the intergalactic tyrant Xenu. As described in a report on Scientology in the AMA publication *Today's Health*, from December 1968:

One preclear said that this Thetan had inhabited the body of a doll on the planet Mars, 469,476,600 years ago. Martians seized the doll and took it to a temple, where it was zapped by a bishop's gun while the congregation chanted "God is Love." The Thetan was then put into an ice cube, placed aboard a flying saucer, and dropped off at Planet ZX 432, where it was given a robot body, then put to work unloading flying saucers. Being a bit unruly, it zapped another robot to death, and was shipped off in a flying saucer to be punished. But the saucer exploded, and the Thetan fell into space.

Ridiculous as it may seem, the new sci-fi twist was immensely popular with recruits, and church membership nearly quadrupled in the last three years of the 1960s. At the same time, publicized success inspired competition, including some defectors from the ranks. Robert Moore and Mary Anne MacLean were students at the London Hubbard Institute of Scientology when they met and married, branching off to form their own cult—the satanic Process Church of Final Judgment—in 1963. The Process, in turn, would give birth to California's homicidal, Satan-worshiping "Four P Movement," prompting some critics to say that Hubbard's early fascination with black magic had finally come full circle.

Another student of both Scientology and the Process was killer cultist Charles Manson. Serving federal time for auto theft, Manson reportedly sat for 150 "auditing" sessions in prison, pronouncing himself a "Theta clear" by the time he left McNeil Island Penitentiary in 1967. Los Angeles prosecutor Vincent Bugliosi later claimed that he could find "no evidence" linking Manson with Scientology after his parole, but surviving members of the drugged-out guru's homicidal "family" report that Charlie often lapsed into "Scientology raps" around the campfire. In 1968, disciple Bruce Davis— later convicted of murder—was sent to visit Process headquarters in London, where he also spent time in a Scientology training school. In fact, the Mansonoids heard so much about Scientology from Charlie that several of his followers defected to the cult in June 1969, irritating Manson no end. Five months later, "family" members were suspected when two Scientologists were murdered in L.A., their bodies torn by more than fifty stab wounds each. One victim, twenty-one-year-old Doreen Gaul, had dated Bruce Davis before his trip to London.

It should not be presumed that Hubbard or his church supported Manson's "family" in any way, but such publicity— combined with nonstop "persecution" by the federal government, inspired Hubbard to create a new Guardian's Office, specifically designed to investigate and harass perceived enemies of Scientology. Multimillion-dollar lawsuits were a favorite means of silencing critics, but Hubbard cultists were not above criminal harassment, death threats, burglary, and other forms of "free expression" when it came to polishing the church's image. In the 1980s, eleven ranking members of the cult—including Hubbard's wife—were sent to prison for infiltrating, burglarizing, and wiretapping more than one hundred private and government agencies, all with the aim of scuttling investigations into church affairs. It was the kind of operation which has moved American judges to describe Scientology as "schizophrenic and paranoid," and "corrupt, sinister, and dangerous."

A special challenge for the Guardian's Office arose in 1982, with new investigations of New York's "Son of Sam" serial killings. An unindicted suspect in the case, Satanist Michael Carr, was also a counselor for the Church of Scientology in New York, and convicted triggerman David Berkowitz described Carr's murderous cult as an "offshoot of Scientology." Following that January interview with lawyer Harry Lipsig and journalist Maury Terry, the Guardian's Office launched a covert campaign to smear both men. As revealed in church memos secured by Terry and published in 1987, Scientologists were anxious to link the attack with their ongoing federal feud.

Exposé on Terry: At some point we are going to have to do an exposé on Terry and his false reports and do a full invalidation of his investigation into this whole Berkowitz affair. He is the mouthpiece for Berkowitz and he has to be discredited. This would preferably be done off their lines. The reason for this is obvious. If we do it, then we have such a vested interest that it will simply be our word against Maury Terry's, so some credible source will have to be found. This is something that should be researched immediately.

Exposé on Lipsig: This activity will also be conditional on his relationship with Terry. If they are really tight, then we will have to expose them both together. The value of this exposé on Lipsig will be enhanced by any connection we can prove to any government agency and of course any psych agency.

As for Hubbard, his main worry was the IRS, with audits from the 1970s documenting a massive skim of church funds, laundered through dummy corporations in Panama, salted away in banks scattered from Switzerland and Liechenstein to Cyprus. Indictments for criminal tax evasion were pending at the time of Elron's reported death in 1986. (A continuing stream of new Hubbard novels has led some observers to question his demise, but no evidence of the cult leader's survival has been produced to date.)

Most cults of personality die with their leader, but Scientology has proved itself an exception, hanging tough with a reported income of $503 million in 1987 alone. By 1991, still a lightning rod for controversial accusations of fraud and worse, the cult maintained seven hundred centers in some sixty-five countries around the world. [see: Berkowitz, David; Carr, Michael; "Four P Movement"; Manson "Family"; Ordo Templi Orientis; Process Church of Final Judgment]

HUMAN SACRIFICE

Chanting cultists. Writhing victims. Flashing knives. An altar stained with blood. A heart, still throbbing, lifted to the high priest's lips. It is the stuff of nightmares, relegated to the kind of horror films that usually turn up on the Late, Late Show. Such grisly images have no connection with reality.

Or, do they?

Human sacrifice, as a religious ritual, is firmly rooted in our history. Without regard to race, creed, or geography, it is a simple fact that residents of every continent, at one time or another, have indulged in ceremonial assassination of their fellow men. Ancient Greeks dismembered and cannibalized a child each year, atop Mt. Lykaion, and their Roman successors elevated ritual bloodshed to an art form. The Old Testament places recurring emphasis on sacrifice of the firstborn, both human and animal, a command from Jehovah which Jews honored in festivals at their Great Temple on Mt. Moriah. Druids sacrificed human victims and planted their charred bones at Stonehenge, while Celtic witch covens executed their own leaders in nine-year cycles. Sanskrit and Vedic texts required human sacrifice to insure prosperity and sanctify new buildings. Mayan priests were decapitating victims, carving out their hearts and rolling the corpses down pyramid steps a thousand years before Aztecs and Incas saw fit to follow their example.

Nor should we assume that sacrifice of human beings was eliminated with the spread of Christianity or exploration of the New World by "civilized" Europeans. Indian disciples of the goddess Kali slaughtered millions of victims between the mid–thirteenth century and their eventual suppression in the 1840s. Medieval witch cults sacrificed and cannibalized infants, some witches believing they would be speechless as babies if called upon to confess. Before her exposure in the late seventeenth century, a mistress of King Louis XIV hired renegade priests to sacrifice children in stylized Black Masses. As recently as 1841, Italian treasure hunters sacrificed a young boy to a demon they believed would help them find a buried cache of gold. In 1910, Oklahoma sheriff's deputies interrupted the crucifixion of a young woman, planned as a sacrifice to Halley's Comet.

That said, it would be comforting to think that we, as modern men and women, are beyond such lapses into lethal superstition. Living in the space age, with computers in our homes and footprints on the moon, it seems impossible that *anyone* could still have faith in human sacrifice.

Unfortunately, such presumptions of enlightenment are premature. In Thailand, Sila Wongsin's cult of devil worshipers was broken up in 1959, its leader executed for conducting human sacrifices. Similar charges were filed against elderly Laxman Giri, in India, during 1980. In Spain, a self-styled witch was put to death in 1912 for murdering children and using their remains in "magic" potions. A half century later, at Figueras, Spanish officials blamed the disappearance of young Maria Diaz on a local satanic cult.

In Africa, practitioners of ju-ju typically sacrifice goats and other animals, but they also have ritual uses for man—"the animal that eats salt." Rampant promiscuity encouraged during periodic harvest festivals results in the birth of "throw-away babies" who are donated to the cult by their unmarried mothers, subsequently murdered by ju-ju priests, and processed into various potions, powders, soaps, and lotions. Adult victims are preferred for the ritual of *iko-awo,* in which a man or woman is flayed alive, then gutted, the liver preserved in a plastic box, while the corpse is washed and hung in a portable wardrobe, taken home as a "spirit slave" by the client who sponsored the sacrifice. Retired ju-ju priest Isaiah Oke describes one such ritual in which he assisted, performed on behalf of a colonel in the Nigerian army. In July 1987, the *Nigerian Tribune* reported the case of a man who hired a ju-ju priest to sacrifice his own thirteen-year-old nephew. The boy was decapitated, his body dumped in a canal, while his head reposed in a box at his uncle's home. The relic was later introduced as evidence in court, with the uncle and his parents—the victim's grandparents—convicted of murder. Six months later, in Onitsha, Nigeria, a thirty-four-year-old man was found at home with his throat cut, his ears and genitals removed, and the room "sprayed with blood." A ritually decorated machete lay beneath a cushion, near the corpse. In May 1988, the *African Guardian,* published in Lagos, Nigeria, declared that native shamans were using human blood, plus the breasts and pubic hair of murdered women, to produce magic charms. A short time later, Nigerian essayist Wilson Asekombe wrote that "human sacrifice will soon become the number two cause of accidental death in West Africa, second only to automobile accidents."

In the western hemisphere, ju-ju traditions survive in such variant forms as voodoo, santeria, abaqua, macumba, and others, while the Bantu religion of palo mayombe has also taken root with rituals involving human sacrifice. Reports of ritual murder emanate periodically from Haiti, where voodoo is the dominant religion, and a young Cuban girl was sacrificed as far back as 1903, by practitioners of palo mayombe. More recently, around Havana in 1978, devotees of abaqua murdered the entire twenty-member cast of a play that publicized their cult's secret rituals.

Mexico, home of the Aztecs, has also experienced its share of human sacrifice in modern times, from the ritual bloodletting of the Hernandez brothers in the 1960s, to the grisly deeds of Adolfo Constanzo, linked with at least twenty-three sacrificial murders between 1987 and 1989. Police in Mexico City investigated ritual slayings of sixty adults and fourteen infants during the same period, with more deaths reported around Veracruz. With the exposure of Constanzo's cult in 1989, it was tempting to blame him for all such crimes, but in fact, the ceremonies have continued since his death in a shootout with police. As prosecutor Guillermo Ibarra explained, "We would like to say, yes, Constanzo did them all, and poof, all those cases are solved. And the fact is, we believe he was responsible for some of them, though we'll never prove it now. But he didn't commit all of those murders, which means someone else did. Someone who is still out there."

Farther south, in Peru, human sacrifice remains a daily fact of life, dating back to the time of the Incas. For some practitioners, the ritual offering of human lives is believed to insure bountiful crops, control the weather, and prevent such natural catastrophes as floods and earthquakes. Such rituals, called "paying the earth," are also employed by wealthy businessmen, ranging from mine owners to beer distributors, to insure continued prosperity. Various local festivals and holidays demand a human sacrifice, and regional narcotics smugglers—as in Mexico and elsewhere—rarely make a move without spilling blood to appease the gods in advance. In parts of Peru, a sect of cultists called *liquichiri* devote themselves solely to the extraction of fat from human victims. The end product, called *cebo,* is believed to be especially useful in rituals aimed at acquiring new vehicles, ranging from automobiles to airplanes and even spacecraft.

While isolated human sacrifices have been documented throughout Peru from the 1940s to the present day, some *yatiri*—shamans for hire—have traditional killing grounds of their own. One such, near Puno, is Mt. Santa Barbara, the site of several sacrifices in the early 1980s. A female victim, killed there in 1982, was found with her breasts cut off, her vagina slashed, and her face painted black. Around Yunguyo, ritual murders are so common that Mayor Horacio Benavides circulated a petition in May 1988, calling on the provincial prosecutor's office to investigate. Signed by local nuns, together with civil and military authorities, the petition charged that "around these places there are abnormal elements or people who are practicing paganism or perhaps the narcotrafficker *pistacos* [vampires]." To date, despite several well-publicized cases resulting in prosecutions and convictions, the ceremonial murders continue.

In neighboring Chile, human sacrifice is such an established tradition that the courts recognize "compulsion by irresistible psychic forces" as grounds for acquittal in cases of ritual murder. Where police have tried to discourage the practice, Mapuche Indians complain of more frequent droughts and earthquakes, now that fewer children are offered to the gods. In 1960, following a period of earthquakes near Puerto Dominguez, Clara Huenchillan decapitated two of her own children as a sacrifice; prosecutors declined to press charges when Clara blamed the murders on a dream, inspired by "many witches" in the neighborhood. A quarter century later, at Lago Budi, Juana Namuncura was suspected—but never charged—with sacrificing her own great-grandchild to appease the elements. A year later, in August 1986, cultists in Vista Hermosa blamed Osvaldo Salamanca's chronic illness on a "vampire demon," which they exorcised by driving a wooden stake through the heart of his nine-year-old nephew.

With the spread of Afro-Caribbean cults in the United States, most notably since the Mariel boatlift of 1980, police have been confronted with a dramatic rise in ritual homicides. Spokesmen for the santeria and palo mayombe religions staunchly deny involvement in human sacrifice, but the grim facts speak for themselves. In February 1981, victim Leroy Carter was found decapitated in San Francisco's Golden Gate Park, with typical santeria offerings of fried corn and mutilated chickens nearby. Five years later, in Miami, a murdered infant was discovered with its tongue and eyelids severed, offered to appease the Afro-Caribbean *orishas*. A similar case was reported from Fairfield, Connecticut, in March 1986, with a day-old infant found in a city park, smothered and mutilated, its body surrounded by pennies, fruit, and other trinkets typical of santeria. In 1987, three bodies were dredged from the Miami River, bound and shot, along with the carcass of a sacrificial goat. Around the same time, in Fort Myers, Florida, a search of a drug dealer's home turned up a *nganga*—the traditional palo mayombe cauldron of blood—with the severed heads of two black men and internal organs from a human body. Lack of embalming ruled out a grave robbery, but no charges were filed, since the cause of death was unclear. Houston narcotics detectives blame cult-related killers for at least a dozen murders in their city, and officers of the New Jersey Port Authority, investigating a child pornography ring in 1988, discovered a santeria altar with jars of human blood at one suspect's home. Detectives believe the blood belonged to one of the pornographer's young "movie stars," still missing, but again prosecution was scuttled for lack of hard evidence. Four months after the discovery of Adolfo Constanzo's heart-eating cult in Matamoros, Mexico, a similar case was reported from the Florida Keys. In July 1989, thirty-nine-year-old Sherry Perisho was found floating in the ocean with her heart cut out. A short time earlier and ten miles away, twenty-year-old Lisa Sanders had been found in a rock grotto on No Name Key, strangled and stripped of her heart. As detectives told the press, "All we can determine is that someone killed her for her heart."

Modern Satanists adopt contradictory attitudes on the subject of ritual murder. Anton LaVey devotes four pages of his *Satanic Bible* to the "choice of a human sacrifice," with readers halfway through the chapter before they discover LaVey's sacrifice is merely "symbolic," amounting to a mumbo jumbo death curse. Even so, the Black Pope's language is ambiguous enough that killers like Ricky Kasso, Scott Waterhouse, Phillip Gamble, and Bunny Dixon have seen fit to take LaVey literally. The writings of Aleister Crowley are more to the point: "For the highest spiritual working one must accordingly choose that victim which contains the greatest and purest force. A male child of perfect innocence and high intelligence is the most satisfactory and suitable victim." Crowley's false bravado aside, it is perhaps no coincidence that alleged victims of ritual child abuse routinely describe acts of infant sacrifice, while middle-aged occult survivors speak of "breeders," deliberately impregnated in satanic rituals, who donate their offspring to the cult. In 1987, a spokesman for the Royal Canadian Mounted Police publicly blamed Satanists for the abduction of several children in Alberta, where the crimes remain unsolved.

In some cases, like those of Ricky Kasso in New York and Carl Drew in Massachusetts, authorities deliberately suppress evidence of ritual murder, preferring to prosecute "sex crimes" or "drug-related" killings which an average jury can more easily absorb. In other cases, though, the ritual motives are less easily ignored.

July 1970—Big Sur, California: Satanist Stanley Baker was jailed for killing a Montana park ranger and eating the victim's heart. In custody, Baker confessed other ritual crimes committed as a member of the "Four P Movement."

July 1970—Los Angeles: Steven Hurd and four other Satanists were held in connection with two local murders involving ritual dismemberment and cannibalism.

October 1981—Chicago: Robin Gecht and three fellow Satanists were jailed for a series of murders involving young women who were abducted, raped, and murdered in a satanic chapel, then mutilated with their breasts severed and cannibalized.

January 1984—Granbury, Texas: Narcotics raiders seized eight jars containing human fetuses, along with two partial infant skeletons. Suspect Timothy Newsome, nineteen, explained that he stole the remains from a "cult house" in

Lake County, Indiana, where he earlier attended rituals with an estimated fifty to sixty outlaw bikers. Lake County authorities confirmed satanic activity in the area, but no arrests resulted.

January 1986—Houston, Texas: Satanist Harold Smith and four of his disciples were apprehended for a series of homicides, including the recent torture-slaying of a young man in a local cemetery.

February 1986—El Paso, Texas: Jesse Villalobos told police that he had witnessed three human sacrifices by Satanists in west Texas, along with the decapitation of a ten-year-old girl in southern California. When police failed to track down the alleged perpetrators, Villalobos said, "They'll kill again, if the rituals keep on. They'll just keep killing."

December 1986—Texas: Four days before the occult Yule holiday, a thirty-nine-year-old prostitute was abducted, beaten, and stabbed to death, her body drained of blood, with her nipples, vagina, and rectum removed. Less than a mile away, construction workers found the decomposed body of a second female victim, whose death would have roughly coincided with Halloween. The crimes remain unsolved.

1987—Toronto, Canada: Two men tortured, mutilated, and murdered a male victim for no apparent motive. Police wiretaps recorded both suspects discussing the pleasure they derived from "committing satanic acts."

May 1988—San Francisco: Satanist Clifford St. Joseph was convicted in the 1985 ritual slaying of an unidentified transient, found tortured to death, with an inverted pentagram carved on his chest.

March 1989—Brantford, Ontario: A man who frequently conducted satanic rituals in his home told police the devil had ordered him to rape his own sister, after which he stabbed her to death. The defendant was convicted of murder.

These cases and others clearly refute the claims of skeptics like FBI "cult expert" Ken Lanning, who insists "There are no bodies and there is not one conviction." In the cases that remain unsolved, alleged witnesses to human sacrifice report that bodies are often cremated, either in portable ovens mounted on trucks—a possibility confirmed in 1985 by California manufacturers of crematoria—or in the facilities of licensed mortuaries owned by Satanists. A similar disposal service, without the cult connection, was exposed at Hesperia, California, in February 1987, when neighbors complained of noxious odors emanating from the Oscar Ceramics plant. Police investigated and discovered that the plant had been receiving corpses from local morticians, cremating them at bargain rates in violation of state law. The plant was closed, and two proprietors of a Pasadena funeral home were jailed for stealing gold teeth from their lifeless customers. [See: Animal Sacrifice; Blood Rituals; Carter, Leroy; "Chambre Ardente Affair"; Chipana, Nieves; Constanzo, Adolfo; Copa, Rolando; Diaz, Maria; Enriqueta, Marti; "Four P Movement"; Gamble, Lloyd; Gecht, Robin; Giri, Laxman; Hernandez, Cayetano; Hurd, Steven; Jones, Dana; Limachi, Clemente; Loza, Camilo; "Maxwell's Silver Hammer"; Montoya, Simon; Painecur, Jose; Perry, Arliss; Rais, Gilles de; Smith, Harold; Uriarti, Juan]

HURD, STEVEN CRAIG

A barbiturate addict and native of southern California, born in 1950, by age twenty Steven Hurd was a rootless drifter who never stayed long in one place. Part of the problem was money, squandered on drugs as soon as he got it, and Hurd was often reduced to the scavenging life of a "troll," sleeping in open fields and highway culverts, scrounging in trash cans for edible scraps. Somewhere along the way from childhood to the pits he had discovered Satanism, and he preached its doctrines with enough persuasive zeal to win himself a small group of disciples from the streets. When they grew tired of chanting and dismembering small animals, they looked around for larger game, a greater "kick," and found it in the form of human sacrifice. As Hurd would later tell police, his cult believed it was permissible to "snuff people out," as long as certain body parts were saved for Lucifer.

The group's first homicide began as simple robbery. Hurd wished to visit San Francisco for a private consultation with "Head Devil" Anton LaVey, but he was predictably short of cash. While he was at it, Hurd would have to fill his gas tank, and the cultists chose a Santa Ana service station as their target on the night of June 2, 1970. By the time they left, atten-

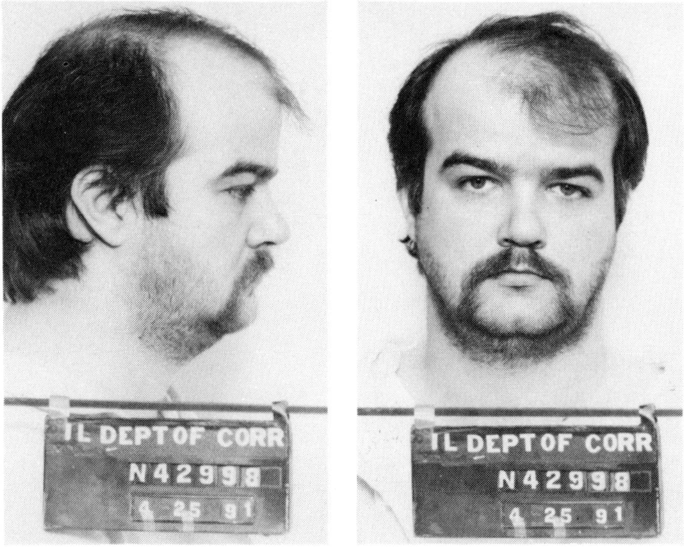

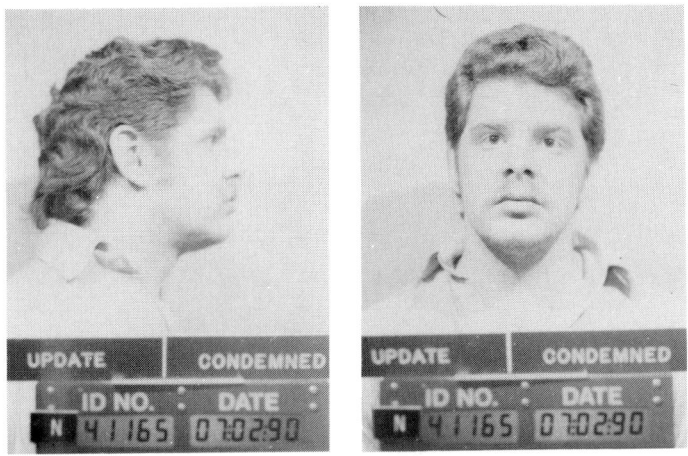

Thomas Kokoraleis (Robin Gecht case)
(Courtesy of the Illinois Department of Corrections)

Edward Spreitzer (Robin Gecht case)
(Courtesy of the Illinois Department of Corrections)

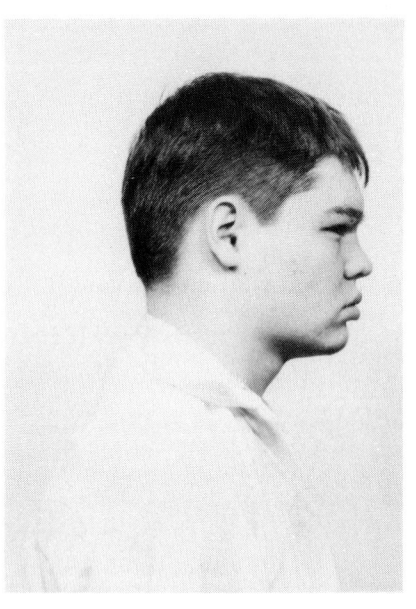

John-Michael Trimmer
(Harold Smith case)
(Courtesy of the Texas
Department of Corrections)

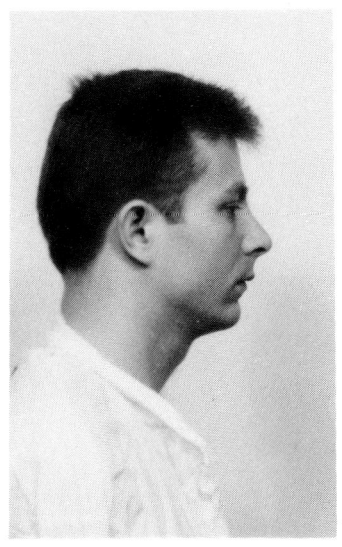
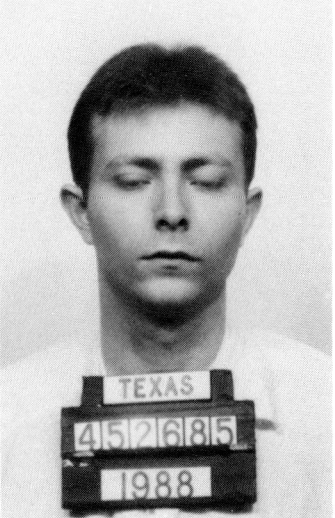

Michael Cravey (Harold Smith case)
(Courtesy of the Texas Department of Corrections)

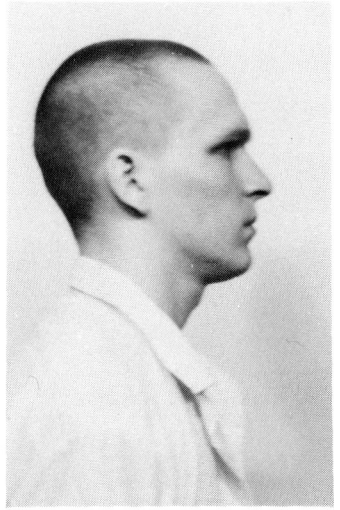

Martin Tosh (Harold Smith case)
(Courtesy of the Texas Department of Corrections)

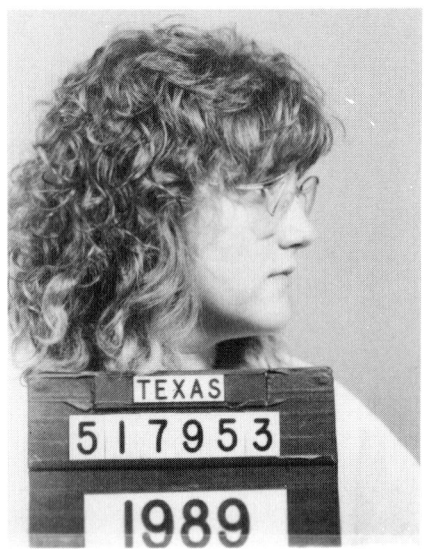

Shannon Rivera
(Harold Smith case)

(Courtesy of the Texas
Department of Corrections)

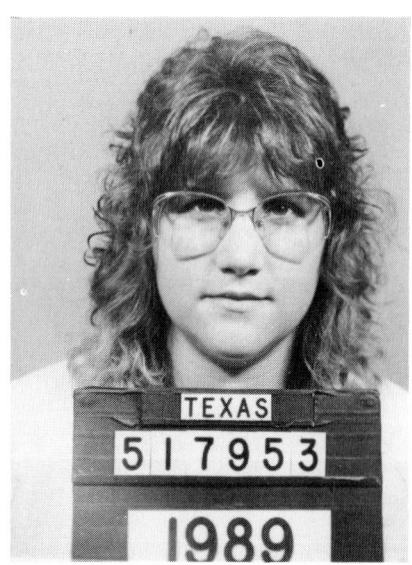

Satanic goat and pentagram combined, called "Baphomet" by some groups

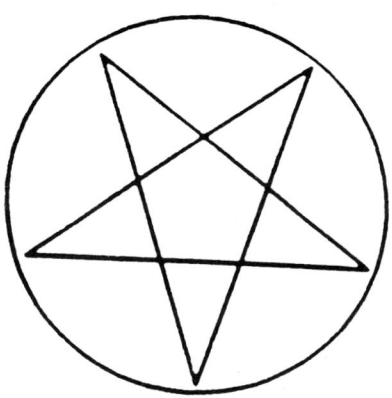

Satanic inverted pentagram

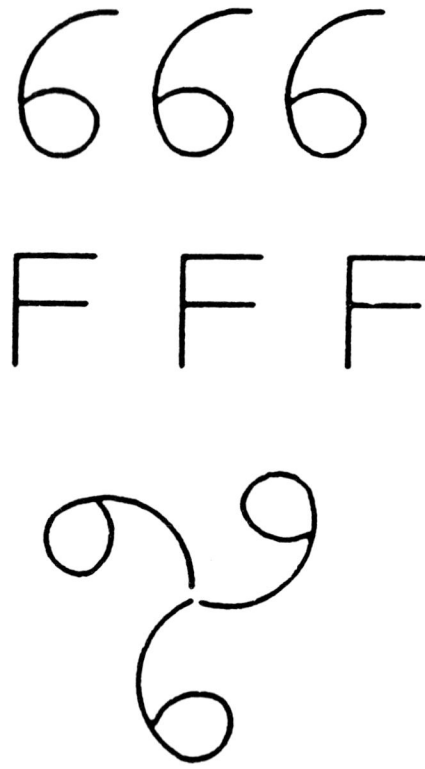

Variations of the "666" number said to identify Satan or the "Great Beast" (Anti-Christ) from the Biblical *Book of Revelations*

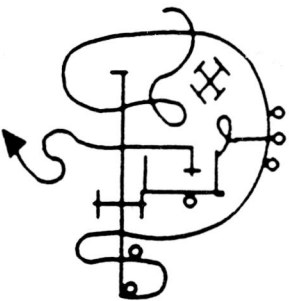

Symbol for the demon Asmodeus

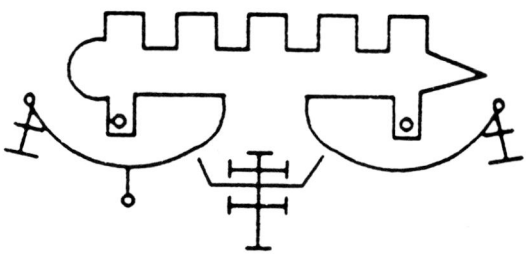

Symbol for the demon Beli

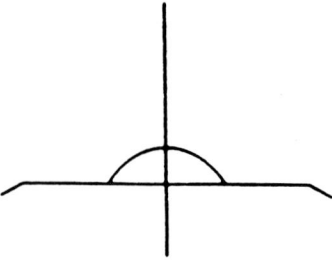

Mark denoting a "satanic traitor," used in threats and cursing rituals, occasionally found on corpses

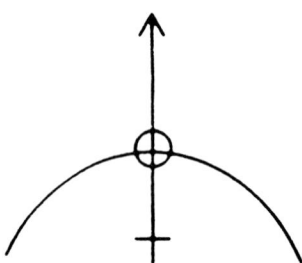

Symbol denoting an area used for sex-magic rituals

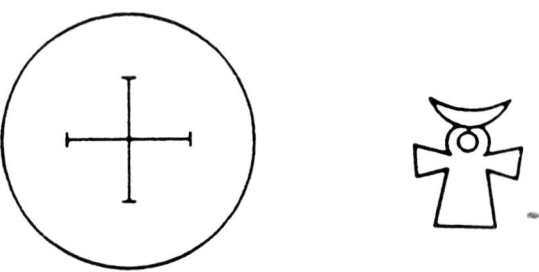

Symbols denoting an area used for Black Masses

infiltrating, burglarizing, and wiretapping more than one hundred private and government agencies, all with the aim of scuttling investigations into church affairs. It was the kind of operation which has moved American judges to describe Scientology as "schizophrenic and paranoid," and "corrupt, sinister, and dangerous."

A special challenge for the Guardian's Office arose in 1982, with new investigations of New York's "Son of Sam" serial killings. An unindicted suspect in the case, Satanist Michael Carr, was also a counselor for the Church of Scientology in New York, and convicted triggerman David Berkowitz described Carr's murderous cult as an "offshoot of Scientology." Following that January interview with lawyer Harry Lipsig and journalist Maury Terry, the Guardian's Office launched a covert campaign to smear both men. As revealed in church memos secured by Terry and published in 1987, Scientologists were anxious to link the attack with their ongoing federal feud.

Exposé on Terry: At some point we are going to have to do an exposé on Terry and his false reports and do a full invalidation of his investigation into this whole Berkowitz affair. He is the mouthpiece for Berkowitz and he has to be discredited. This would preferably be done off their lines. The reason for this is obvious. If we do it, then we have such a vested interest that it will simply be our word against Maury Terry's, so some credible source will have to be found. This is something that should be researched immediately.

Exposé on Lipsig: This activity will also be conditional on his relationship with Terry. If they are really tight, then we will have to expose them both together. The value of this exposé on Lipsig will be enhanced by any connection we can prove to any government agency and of course any psych agency.

As for Hubbard, his main worry was the IRS, with audits from the 1970s documenting a massive skim of church funds, laundered through dummy corporations in Panama, salted away in banks scattered from Switzerland and Liechenstein to Cyprus. Indictments for criminal tax evasion were pending at the time of Elron's reported death in 1986. (A continuing

Ridiculous as it may seem, the new sci-fi twist was immensely popular with recruits, and church membership nearly quadrupled in the last three years of the 1960s. At the same time, publicized success inspired competition, including some defectors from the ranks. Robert Moore and Mary Anne MacLean were students at the London Hubbard Institute of Scientology when they met and married, branching off to form their own cult—the satanic Process Church of Final Judgment—in 1963. The Process, in turn, would give birth to California's homicidal, Satan-worshiping "Four P Movement," prompting some critics to say that Hubbard's early fascination with black magic had finally come full circle.

Another student of both Scientology and the Process was killer cultist Charles Manson. Serving federal time for auto theft, Manson reportedly sat for 150 "auditing" sessions in prison, pronouncing himself a "Theta clear" by the time he left McNeil Island Penitentiary in 1967. Los Angeles prosecutor Vincent Bugliosi later claimed that he could find "no evidence" linking Manson with Scientology after his parole, but surviving members of the drugged-out guru's homicidal "family" report that Charlie often lapsed into "Scientology raps" around the campfire. In 1968, disciple Bruce Davis—later convicted of murder—was sent to visit Process headquarters in London, where he also spent time in a Scientology training school. In fact, the Mansonoids heard so much about Scientology from Charlie that several of his followers defected to the cult in June 1969, irritating Manson no end. Five months later, "family" members were suspected when two Scientologists were murdered in L.A., their bodies torn by more than fifty stab wounds each. One victim, twenty-one-year-old Doreen Gaul, had dated Bruce Davis before his trip to London.

It should not be presumed that Hubbard or his church supported Manson's "family" in any way, but such publicity—combined with nonstop "persecution" by the federal government, inspired Hubbard to create a new Guardian's Office, specifically designed to investigate and harass perceived enemies of Scientology. Multimillion-dollar lawsuits were a favorite means of silencing critics, but Hubbard cultists were not above criminal harassment, death threats, burglary, and other forms of "free expression" when it came to polishing the church's image. In the 1980s, eleven ranking members of the cult—including Hubbard's wife—were sent to prison for stream of new Hubbard novels has led some observers to question his demise, but no evidence of the cult leader's survival has been produced to date.)

Most cults of personality die with their leader, but Scientology has proved itself an exception, hanging tough with a reported income of $503 million in 1987 alone. By 1991, still a lightning rod for controversial accusations of fraud and worse, the cult maintained seven hundred centers in some sixty-five countries around the world. [see: Berkowitz, David; Carr, Michael; "Four P Movement"; Manson "Family"; Ordo Templi Orientis; Process Church of Final Judgment]

HUMAN SACRIFICE

Chanting cultists. Writhing victims. Flashing knives. An altar stained with blood. A heart, still throbbing, lifted to the high priest's lips. It is the stuff of nightmares, relegated to the kind of horror films that usually turn up on the Late, Late Show. Such grisly images have no connection with reality.

Or, do they?

Human sacrifice, as a religious ritual, is firmly rooted in our history. Without regard to race, creed, or geography, it is a simple fact that residents of every continent, at one time or another, have indulged in ceremonial assassination of their fellow men. Ancient Greeks dismembered and cannibalized a child each year, atop Mt. Lykaion, and their Roman successors elevated ritual bloodshed to an art form. The Old Testament places recurring emphasis on sacrifice of the firstborn, both human and animal, a command from Jehovah which Jews honored in festivals at their Great Temple on Mt. Moriah. Druids sacrificed human victims and planted their charred bones at Stonehenge, while Celtic witch covens executed their own leaders in nine-year cycles. Sanskrit and Vedic texts required human sacrifice to insure prosperity and sanctify new buildings. Mayan priests were decapitating victims, carving out their hearts and rolling the corpses down pyramid steps a thousand years before Aztecs and Incas saw fit to follow their example.

Nor should we assume that sacrifice of human beings was eliminated with the spread of Christianity or exploration of the New World by "civilized" Europeans. Indian disciples of the goddess Kali slaughtered millions of victims between the mid–thirteenth century and their eventual suppression in the 1840s. Medieval witch cults sacrificed and cannibalized infants, some witches believing they would be speechless as babies if called upon to confess. Before her exposure in the late seventeenth century, a mistress of King Louis XIV hired renegade priests to sacrifice children in stylized Black Masses. As recently as 1841, Italian treasure hunters sacrificed a young boy to a demon they believed would help them find a buried cache of gold. In 1910, Oklahoma sheriff's deputies interrupted the crucifixion of a young woman, planned as a sacrifice to Halley's Comet.

That said, it would be comforting to think that we, as modern men and women, are beyond such lapses into lethal superstition. Living in the space age, with computers in our homes and footprints on the moon, it seems impossible that *anyone* could still have faith in human sacrifice.

Unfortunately, such presumptions of enlightenment are premature. In Thailand, Sila Wongsin's cult of devil worshipers was broken up in 1959, its leader executed for conducting human sacrifices. Similar charges were filed against elderly Laxman Giri, in India, during 1980. In Spain, a self-styled witch was put to death in 1912 for murdering children and using their remains in "magic" potions. A half century later, at Figueras, Spanish officials blamed the disappearance of young Maria Diaz on a local satanic cult.

In Africa, practitioners of ju-ju typically sacrifice goats and other animals, but they also have ritual uses for man—"the animal that eats salt." Rampant promiscuity encouraged during periodic harvest festivals results in the birth of "throwaway babies" who are donated to the cult by their unmarried mothers, subsequently murdered by ju-ju priests, and processed into various potions, powders, soaps, and lotions. Adult victims are preferred for the ritual of *iko-awo,* in which a man or woman is flayed alive, then gutted, the liver preserved in a plastic box, while the corpse is washed and hung in a portable wardrobe, taken home as a "spirit slave" by the client who sponsored the sacrifice. Retired ju-ju priest Isaiah Oke describes one such ritual in which he assisted, performed on behalf of a colonel in the Nigerian army. In July 1987, the *Nigerian Tribune* reported the case of a man who hired a ju-ju priest to sacrifice his own thirteen-year-old nephew. The boy was decapitated, his body dumped in a canal, while his head reposed in a box at his uncle's home. The relic was later introduced as evidence in court, with the uncle and his parents—the victim's grandparents—convicted of murder. Six months later, in Onitsha, Nigeria, a thirty-four-year-old man was found at home with his throat cut, his ears and genitals removed, and the room "sprayed with blood." A ritually decorated machete lay beneath a cushion, near the corpse. In May 1988, the *African Guardian,* published in Lagos, Nigeria, declared that native shamans were using human blood, plus the breasts and pubic hair of murdered women, to produce magic charms. A short time later, Nigerian essayist Wilson Asekombe wrote that "human sacrifice will soon become the number two cause of accidental death in West Africa, second only to automobile accidents."

In the western hemisphere, ju-ju traditions survive in such variant forms as voodoo, santeria, abaqua, macumba, and others, while the Bantu religion of palo mayombe has also taken root with rituals involving human sacrifice. Reports of ritual murder emanate periodically from Haiti, where voodoo is the dominant religion, and a young Cuban girl was sacrificed as far back as 1903, by practitioners of palo mayombe. More recently, around Havana in 1978, devotees of abaqua murdered the entire twenty-member cast of a play that publicized their cult's secret rituals.

Mexico, home of the Aztecs, has also experienced its share of human sacrifice in modern times, from the ritual bloodletting of the Hernandez brothers in the 1960s, to the grisly deeds of Adolfo Constanzo, linked with at least twenty-three sacrificial murders between 1987 and 1989. Police in Mexico City investigated ritual slayings of sixty adults and fourteen infants during the same period, with more deaths reported around Veracruz. With the exposure of Constanzo's cult in 1989, it was tempting to blame him for all such crimes, but in fact, the ceremonies have continued since his death in a shootout with police. As prosecutor Guillermo Ibarra explained, "We would like to say, yes, Constanzo did them all, and poof, all those cases are solved. And the fact is, we believe he was responsible for some of them, though we'll never prove it now. But he didn't commit all of those murders, which means someone else did. Someone who is still out there."

Farther south, in Peru, human sacrifice remains a daily fact of life, dating back to the time of the Incas. For some practitioners, the ritual offering of human lives is believed to insure bountiful crops, control the weather, and prevent such natural catastrophes as floods and earthquakes. Such rituals, called "paying the earth," are also employed by wealthy businessmen, ranging from mine owners to beer distributors, to insure continued prosperity. Various local festivals and holidays demand a human sacrifice, and regional narcotics smugglers—as in Mexico and elsewhere—rarely make a move without spilling blood to appease the gods in advance. In parts of Peru, a sect of cultists called *liquichiri* devote themselves solely to the extraction of fat from human victims. The end product, called *cebo,* is believed to be especially useful in rituals aimed at acquiring new vehicles, ranging from automobiles to airplanes and even spacecraft.

While isolated human sacrifices have been documented throughout Peru from the 1940s to the present day, some *yatiri*—shamans for hire—have traditional killing grounds of their own. One such, near Puno, is Mt. Santa Barbara, the site of several sacrifices in the early 1980s. A female victim, killed there in 1982, was found with her breasts cut off, her vagina slashed, and her face painted black. Around Yunguyo, ritual murders are so common that Mayor Horacio Benavides circulated a petition in May 1988, calling on the provincial prosecutor's office to investigate. Signed by local nuns, together with civil and military authorities, the petition charged that "around these places there are abnormal elements or people who are practicing paganism or perhaps the narcotrafficker *pistacos* [vampires]." To date, despite several well-publicized cases resulting in prosecutions and convictions, the ceremonial murders continue.

In neighboring Chile, human sacrifice is such an established tradition that the courts recognize "compulsion by irresistible psychic forces" as grounds for acquittal in cases of ritual murder. Where police have tried to discourage the practice, Mapuche Indians complain of more frequent droughts and earthquakes, now that fewer children are offered to the gods. In 1960, following a period of earthquakes near Puerto Dominguez, Clara Huenchillan decapitated two of her own children as a sacrifice; prosecutors declined to press charges when Clara blamed the murders on a dream, inspired by "many witches" in the neighborhood. A quarter century later, at Lago Budi, Juana Namuncura was suspected—but never charged—with sacrificing her own great-grandchild to ap-

pease the elements. A year later, in August 1986, cultists in Vista Hermosa blamed Osvaldo Salamanca's chronic illness on a "vampire demon," which they exorcised by driving a wooden stake through the heart of his nine-year-old nephew.

With the spread of Afro-Caribbean cults in the United States, most notably since the Mariel boatlift of 1980, police have been confronted with a dramatic rise in ritual homicides. Spokesmen for the santeria and palo mayombe religions staunchly deny involvement in human sacrifice, but the grim facts speak for themselves. In February 1981, victim Leroy Carter was found decapitated in San Francisco's Golden Gate Park, with typical santeria offerings of fried corn and mutilated chickens nearby. Five years later, in Miami, a murdered infant was discovered with its tongue and eyelids severed, offered to appease the Afro-Caribbean *orishas*. A similar case was reported from Fairfield, Connecticut, in March 1986, with a day-old infant found in a city park, smothered and mutilated, its body surrounded by pennies, fruit, and other trinkets typical of santeria. In 1987, three bodies were dredged from the Miami River, bound and shot, along with the carcass of a sacrificial goat. Around the same time, in Fort Myers, Florida, a search of a drug dealer's home turned up a *nganga*—the traditional palo mayombe cauldron of blood—with the severed heads of two black men and internal organs from a human body. Lack of embalming ruled out a grave robbery, but no charges were filed, since the cause of death was unclear. Houston narcotics detectives blame cult-related killers for at least a dozen murders in their city, and officers of the New Jersey Port Authority, investigating a child pornography ring in 1988, discovered a santeria altar with jars of human blood at one suspect's home. Detectives believe the blood belonged to one of the pornographer's young "movie stars," still missing, but again prosecution was scuttled for lack of hard evidence. Four months after the discovery of Adolfo Constanzo's heart-eating cult in Matamoros, Mexico, a similar case was reported from the Florida Keys. In July 1989, thirty-nine-year-old Sherry Perisho was found floating in the ocean with her heart cut out. A short time earlier and ten miles away, twenty-year-old Lisa Sanders had been found in a rock grotto on No Name Key, strangled and stripped of her heart. As detectives told the press, "All we can determine is that someone killed her for her heart."

Modern Satanists adopt contradictory attitudes on the sub-

ject of ritual murder. Anton LaVey devotes four pages of his *Satanic Bible* to the "choice of a human sacrifice," with readers halfway through the chapter before they discover LaVey's sacrifice is merely "symbolic," amounting to a mumbo jumbo death curse. Even so, the Black Pope's language is ambiguous enough that killers like Ricky Kasso, Scott Waterhouse, Phillip Gamble, and Bunny Dixon have seen fit to take LaVey literally. The writings of Aleister Crowley are more to the point: "For the highest spiritual working one must accordingly choose that victim which contains the greatest and purest force. A male child of perfect innocence and high intelligence is the most satisfactory and suitable victim." Crowley's false bravado aside, it is perhaps no coincidence that alleged victims of ritual child abuse routinely describe acts of infant sacrifice, while middle-aged occult survivors speak of "breeders," deliberately impregnated in satanic rituals, who donate their offspring to the cult. In 1987, a spokesman for the Royal Canadian Mounted Police publicly blamed Satanists for the abduction of several children in Alberta, where the crimes remain unsolved.

In some cases, like those of Ricky Kasso in New York and Carl Drew in Massachusetts, authorities deliberately suppress evidence of ritual murder, preferring to prosecute "sex crimes" or "drug-related" killings which an average jury can more easily absorb. In other cases, though, the ritual motives are less easily ignored.

July 1970—Big Sur, California: Satanist Stanley Baker was jailed for killing a Montana park ranger and eating the victim's heart. In custody, Baker confessed other ritual crimes committed as a member of the "Four P Movement."

July 1970—Los Angeles: Steven Hurd and four other Satanists were held in connection with two local murders involving ritual dismemberment and cannibalism.

October 1981—Chicago: Robin Gecht and three fellow Satanists were jailed for a series of murders involving young women who were abducted, raped, and murdered in a satanic chapel, then mutilated with their breasts severed and cannibalized.

January 1984—Granbury, Texas: Narcotics raiders seized eight jars containing human fetuses, along with two partial infant skeletons. Suspect Timothy Newsome, nineteen, explained that he stole the remains from a "cult house" in

Lake County, Indiana, where he earlier attended rituals with an estimated fifty to sixty outlaw bikers. Lake County authorities confirmed satanic activity in the area, but no arrests resulted.

January 1986—Houston, Texas: Satanist Harold Smith and four of his disciples were apprehended for a series of homicides, including the recent torture-slaying of a young man in a local cemetery.

February 1986—El Paso, Texas: Jesse Villalobos told police that he had witnessed three human sacrifices by Satanists in west Texas, along with the decapitation of a ten-year-old girl in southern California. When police failed to track down the alleged perpetrators, Villalobos said, "They'll kill again, if the rituals keep on. They'll just keep killing."

December 1986—Texas: Four days before the occult Yule holiday, a thirty-nine-year-old prostitute was abducted, beaten, and stabbed to death, her body drained of blood, with her nipples, vagina, and rectum removed. Less than a mile away, construction workers found the decomposed body of a second female victim, whose death would have roughly coincided with Halloween. The crimes remain unsolved.

1987—Toronto, Canada: Two men tortured, mutilated, and murdered a male victim for no apparent motive. Police wiretaps recorded both suspects discussing the pleasure they derived from "committing satanic acts."

May 1988—San Francisco: Satanist Clifford St. Joseph was convicted in the 1985 ritual slaying of an unidentified transient, found tortured to death, with an inverted pentagram carved on his chest.

March 1989—Brantford, Ontario: A man who frequently conducted satanic rituals in his home told police the devil had ordered him to rape his own sister, after which he stabbed her to death. The defendant was convicted of murder.

These cases and others clearly refute the claims of skeptics like FBI "cult expert" Ken Lanning, who insists "There are no bodies and there is not one conviction." In the cases that remain unsolved, alleged witnesses to human sacrifice report that bodies are often cremated, either in portable ovens mounted on trucks—a possibility confirmed in 1985 by California manufacturers of crematoria—or in the facilities of licensed mortuaries owned by Satanists. A similar disposal service, without the cult connection, was exposed at Hesperia, California, in February 1987, when neighbors complained of noxious odors emanating from the Oscar Ceramics plant. Police investigated and discovered that the plant had been receiving corpses from local morticians, cremating them at bargain rates in violation of state law. The plant was closed, and two proprietors of a Pasadena funeral home were jailed for stealing gold teeth from their lifeless customers. [See: Animal Sacrifice; Blood Rituals; Carter, Leroy; "Chambre Ardente Affair"; Chipana, Nieves; Constanzo, Adolfo; Copa, Rolando; Diaz, Maria; Enriqueta, Marti; "Four P Movement"; Gamble, Lloyd; Gecht, Robin; Giri, Laxman; Hernandez, Cayetano; Hurd, Steven; Jones, Dana; Limachi, Clemente; Loza, Camilo; "Maxwell's Silver Hammer"; Montoya, Simon; Painecur, Jose; Perry, Arliss; Rais, Gilles de; Smith, Harold; Uriarti, Juan]

HURD, STEVEN CRAIG

A barbiturate addict and native of southern California, born in 1950, by age twenty Steven Hurd was a rootless drifter who never stayed long in one place. Part of the problem was money, squandered on drugs as soon as he got it, and Hurd was often reduced to the scavenging life of a "troll," sleeping in open fields and highway culverts, scrounging in trash cans for edible scraps. Somewhere along the way from childhood to the pits he had discovered Satanism, and he preached its doctrines with enough persuasive zeal to win himself a small group of disciples from the streets. When they grew tired of chanting and dismembering small animals, they looked around for larger game, a greater "kick," and found it in the form of human sacrifice. As Hurd would later tell police, his cult believed it was permissible to "snuff people out," as long as certain body parts were saved for Lucifer.

The group's first homicide began as simple robbery. Hurd wished to visit San Francisco for a private consultation with "Head Devil" Anton LaVey, but he was predictably short of cash. While he was at it, Hurd would have to fill his gas tank, and the cultists chose a Santa Ana service station as their target on the night of June 2, 1970. By the time they left, atten-

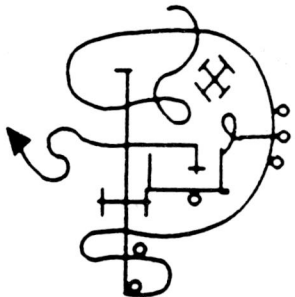

Symbol for the demon Asmodeus

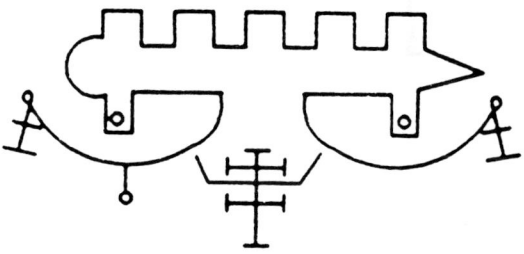

Symbol for the demon Beli

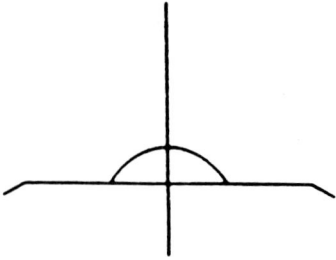

Mark denoting a "satanic traitor," used in threats and cursing rituals, occasionally found on corpses

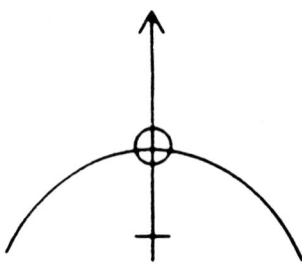

Symbol denoting an area used for sex-magic rituals

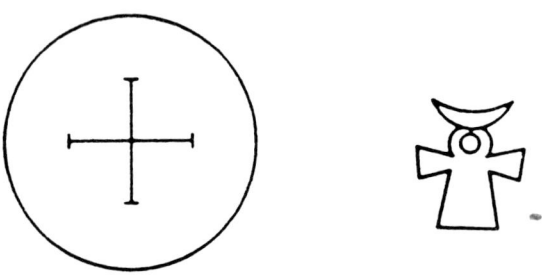

Symbols denoting an area used for Black Masses

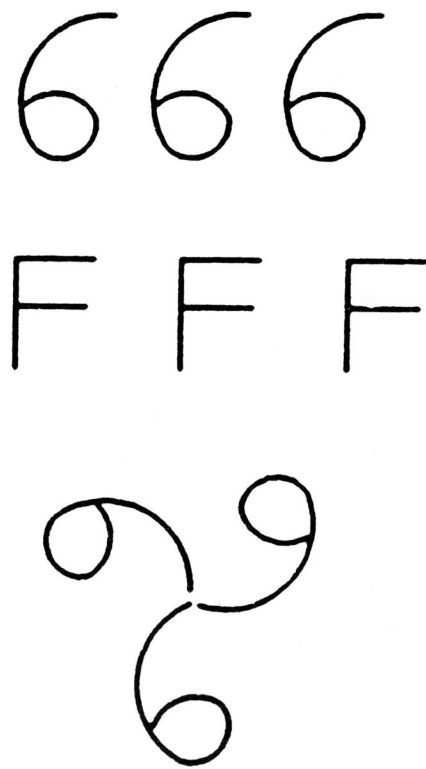

Variations of the "666" number said to identify Satan or the "Great Beast" (Anti-Christ) from the Biblical *Book of Revelations*

Satanic goat and pentagram combined, called "Baphomet" by some groups

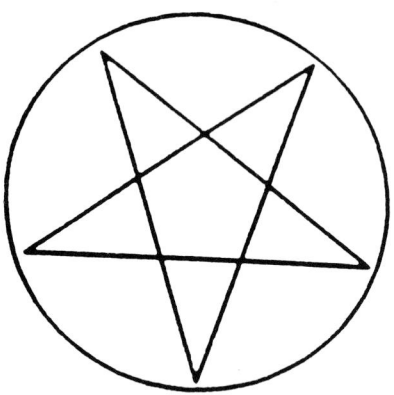

Satanic inverted pentagram

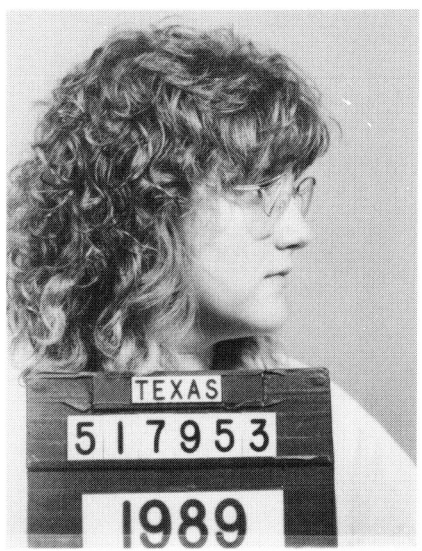

Shannon Rivera
(Harold Smith case)

(Courtesy of the Texas
Department of Corrections)

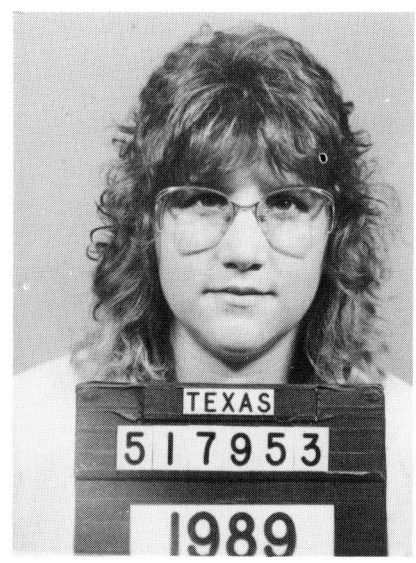

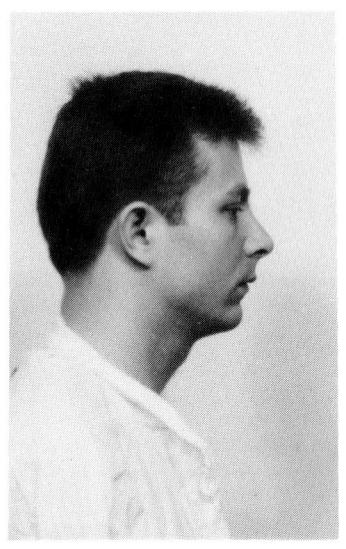
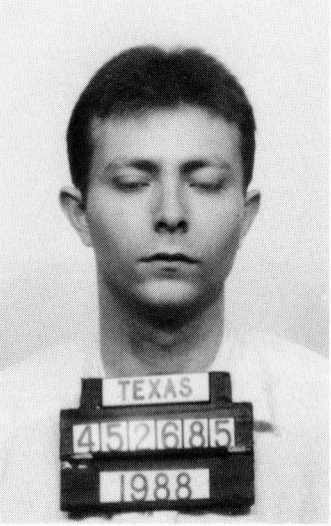

Michael Cravey (Harold Smith case)
(Courtesy of the Texas Department of Corrections)

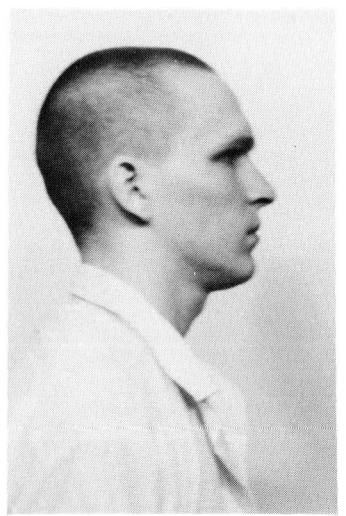

Martin Tosh (Harold Smith case)
(Courtesy of the Texas Department of Corrections)

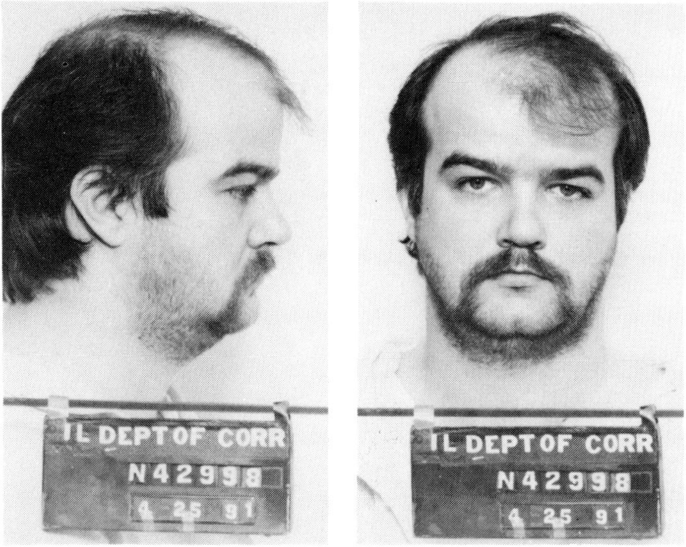

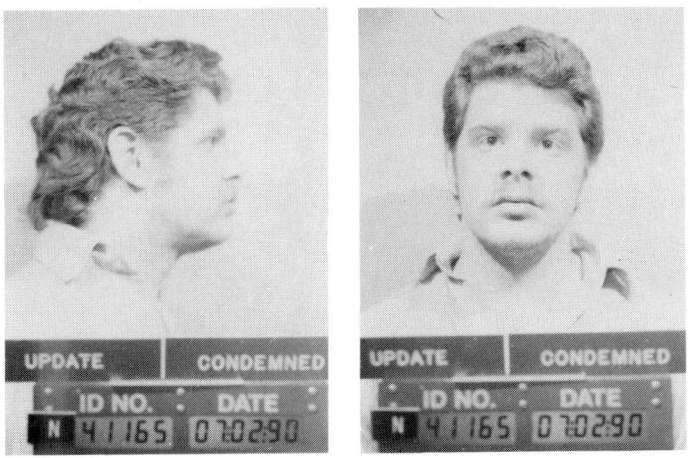

Thomas Kokoraleis (Robin Gecht case)
(Courtesy of the Illinois Department of Corrections)

Edward Spreitzer (Robin Gecht case)
(Courtesy of the Illinois Department of Corrections)

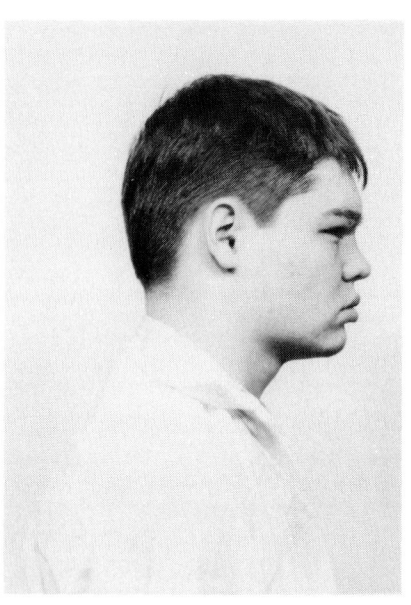

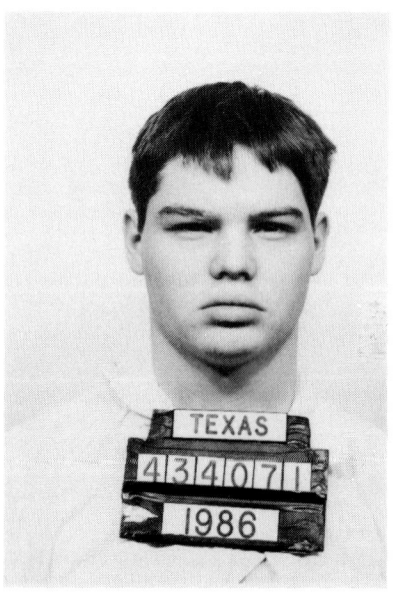

John-Michael Trimmer
(Harold Smith case)
(Courtesy of the Texas
Department of Corrections)

mum term of three years. The unrepentant killer was released in February 1988, despite a massive public outcry. As police staff sergeant Joe Cziraky told the press, "He's fulfilled his obligations as far as the law goes, but nobody can say there's nothing to fear."

JONES, DANA SUE

On February 4, 1986, Denver police received a telephone call from an hysterical woman, who proclaimed, "I have a man tied up on my bed, and if you don't come and get him, I'm going to kill him." The woman hung up without giving her name or address, but she called back moments later, repeating: "I'm going to kill this son of a bitch if you don't get over here." Again the line went dead, and operators were inclined to dismiss the caller as a harmless crank . . . until a practicing attorney called in and directed patrolmen to the home of Dana Jones, on South Pennsylvania Street.

Officers arrived to find Jones, age twenty-three, drenched in blood and brandishing a large kitchen knife. Tense negotiations finally persuaded her to lay the weapon down, whereupon she was handcuffed and driven to Denver General Hospital, spitting and kicking all the way. Staff physicians sedated the subject, determined that she was uninjured, and held her for psychiatric observation.

Back on Pennsylvania Street, detectives found themselves examining a slaughterhouse. The walls were streaked with blood, and crimson footprints led investigators to a bedroom, where a naked man was lying on the bed, a carving knife still buried in his back. Bound hand and foot when he died, the man had been stabbed a total of 117 times. A large "D" with an arrow through it had been carved on his chest, with four small numeral 7s inside the "D."

Aside from the obvious ritual mutilations, detectives found a plate marked with a pentagram at the foot of the bed. Downstairs, a basement altar was surrounded by candles, crucifixes, and occult-type drawings. (A lesbian roommate of Jones's claimed most of the paraphernalia as her own, admitting membership in the Astrum Argentium, a sex-magic cult founded by Aleister Crowley in 1907.) Police noted that the murder occurred two days after the occult holiday of Candlemas, and acquaintances of the victim—twenty-nine-year-old

Raymond Terry—described his passionate interest in Satanism and black magic. Autopsy reports indicated blood found in Terry's stomach had been deliberately swallowed, and was not produced by any of his wounds, suggesting his participation in a ritual gone wrong.

As homicide investigators put the sequence of events together, Jones had twice called police before phoning a girlfriend, reporting the murder as an accomplished fact. Her friend, in turn, had called the lawyer, who dispatched police to Pennsylvania Street. The motive remained unclear, but Jones had a long history of mental problems dating from childhood, with a suicide attempt at age eight and subsequent evidence of drug abuse. Detectives also learned that Jones had been molested by her father at an early age. The father, incidentally, was tattooed with an inverted pentagram, as was one of Jones's uncles, suggesting a history of ritual abuse in the family.

Two days after her arrest, Jones tried without success to hang herself. At her trial on murder charges, Jones was acquitted on grounds of insanity and confined for treatment at the Colorado State Hospital in Pueblo. She remained preoccupied with suicide, making two more failed attempts in subsequent months. On April 23, 1988, Jones wrote to a friend: "I've found that answer that will take away the heartache. I know that my death is the only guarantee that I won't kill again."

Less than three weeks later, on June 10, Dana Jones escaped from the hospital with help from Doris Frost, a fifty-six-year-old nurse on the staff. The two women drove to Albuquerque, New Mexico, where they rented a studio apartment. On June 20, police responded to reports of a gunshot fired in the apartment, finding Jones half-naked on the bed, a .38 revolver in her hand, a fresh wound in her skull. Doris Frost, also present at the scene, admitted helping Jones position the revolver; she was jailed on charges of contributing to suicide and held for extradition to Colorado, pending indictment on felony counts related to Jones's escape.

JORDAN, MN—CHILD ABUSE

On the afternoon of September 26, 1983, Judith Kath and Christine Brown marched their ten-year-old daughters into the Jordan, Minnesota, police station, complaining that Kath's ex-fiancé, twenty-seven-year-old James Rud, had sexually abused both girls. Jordan, a suburb of Minneapolis, had no child abuse experts on its five-man police force, but officers were familiar with Rud's unsavory reputation. A trash collector and resident of Jordan's Valley Green Trailer Park, Rud had a record of prior convictions for child molesting in Virginia and Minnesota. Arrested that evening, Rud was lodged in jail while police quizzed other children in the neighborhood. By October 1, Rud was charged with thirteen counts of sexual abuse involving four separate victims . . . and the case had barely gotten underway.

On October 5, Patrolman Larry Norring visited Rud's trailer, seeking evidence to support accusations of child pornography. As later described in his report, Norring found "numerous items of children's clothing," along with "a stack of approximately 12 VCR cassette tapes, a large box containing pornographic magazines in the living area and two green garbage bags of pornographic material in the bedroom area." Before he could examine the stash in more detail, Rud's parents arrived, their behavior so "abusive and threatening" that Norring left the scene "to avoid an altercation." Before he drove away, the officer observed Rud's parents carrying "unknown items of personal property in boxes and bags," from the trailer. When he returned at nine o'clock the next morning, all videotapes and pornography had vanished, along with most of the children's clothes. It was the first critical mistake in an epic investigation, but it would not be the last.

As police canvassed Rud's circle of friends, they kept coming up with more victims, enough to add eighty-five new charges on November 18. In the meantime, alleged victims were also naming multiple abusers, sometimes including their own parents. On November 14, Judith Kath and another trailer park resident, Marlene Germundsen, were arrested, Kath on five counts of promoting a minor to engage in "obscene works," Germundsen on seventeen counts of sexual abuse (including subjecting her own children to abuse by Rud). Two days later, Christine Brown was jailed on ten counts of child molestation, and Rud's parents were picked up on November 17, charged with eight counts each. By June 1984, the expanding list of accused molesters included: Robert Rawson, four counts of sex with a ten-year-old girl; Coraline Rawson (Robert's wife), ten counts; Irene Meisinger, eleven counts involving four children; Tom and Helen Brown (Christine's sister), charged with abusing seven children; Robert and Lois Bentz, twelve counts, including molestation of their own son; Greg and Jane Myers, eight counts each; Duane and Dee Rank, six counts each; Charles and Carol Lallak, six counts each; Donald and Cindy Buchan; and Terry Morgenson. Occupationally, the suspects ranged from a waitress, truck driver, and auto-body painter to a deputy sheriff, an eight-year veteran of the Jordan police force, and an employee of the Scott County assessor's office.

Children involved in the case had described every imaginable sex act and combination, including incest and bestiality. Some reported they were given drugs or liquor prior to sexual assaults, while others recalled threats of jail, injury, or death if they refused to submit. Sex parties were described, at which adults played innocuous games like baseball or hide-and-seek with a twist, the winners were permitted first choice of the children they would molest. By the early summer of 1984, with the alleged victims lodged in foster homes and undergoing therapy for trauma, darker allegations had begun to surface, including satanic rituals, mutilation of animals, and the murder of several black or "dark" children, their bodies dumped in the Minnesota River by night.

For such a major case, the police response was incredibly haphazard. FBI agents would later describe the sweeping arrests as hasty, conducted without prior surveillance or much investigation beyond victim interviews. Despite widespread allegations of pornography and ritual murder, most of the suspects' homes were never searched for evidence at all. One woman who admitted sexually abusing her son was released without charges when authorities failed to link her with their established suspects. On the flip side, each new allegation prompted fresh, repetitive interviews with the troubled children; one girl was interrogated fifty times, and contradictions inevitably surfaced as the witnesses were repeatedly questioned.

Police negligence left prosecutor Kathleen Morris dangerously short of evidence as the first trial approached, and she tried to bolster her case by cutting a controversial deal with James Rud. Promised leniency in return for truthful testimony, on August 15, 1984, Rud pleaded guilty to ten counts of sexual abuse and agreed to testify against alleged accomplices. By August 20, he had named eighteen of the twenty-three accused suspects as participants in child-sex orgies, corroborating the children's stories in many details.

Defense attorneys, meanwhile, called the investigation a witch-hunt, blaming therapists from Minneapolis for "brainwashing" the children and planting false tales of satanic abuse in their minds. The therapists were unconcerned with discrepancies in the children's reports. "Five-year-olds change their stories," one explained. "When you discover the cookie on the floor and he's the only one in the room, you'll give five different stories on something as innocent as that. Now imagine your son being severely sexually abused over a long period of time, and you can imagine why they are telling different stories at different times." Another therapist said of the children in Jordan, "They tell you what sex is like. They say, 'He put lotion on his penis before he put it in my butt.' When a three-year-old tells you that, there's nothing for me to conclude other than the kid is relating something that really happened to them."

Indeed, there was *some* evidence supporting charges of abuse in Jordan. Two victims described anal penetration with candles and miniature bowling pins at one defendant's house, and police broke their usual pattern by actually searching the home. Candles and a miniature bowling pin were found, all described in lab reports as being coated with an "organic material" that could have been feces, but the reports could not say how or by whom the implements were used. A panel of doctors found fourteen children with physical symptoms of abuse—including one girl so injured she could not control her bowels or bladder—but again, physical damage would not identify specific rapists.

The first trial, that of Bob and Lois Bentz, began on August 27, with James Rud on the witness stand. Asked to identify Bob Bentz for the record, Rud was unable to do so, and his rambling testimony left the confessed child abuser largely discredited. Things went from bad to worse as successive children were called to testify, one admitting lies in a previous statement to police, another describing how several children had discussed their stories over dinner, the night before the trial. Through it all, Kathleen Morris was unaccountably distracted, failing to object when defense lawyers badgered the children, neglecting to question the dubious credentials of "expert witness" Ralph Underwager, called for the defense to attack prosecution "brainwashing" techniques. Judge Martin

Mansur dismissed half of the charges on September 5, and two weeks later, jurors acquitted the Bentzes on all remaining counts.

On October 15, in the midst of opening arguments for the trial of Don and Cindy Buchan, prosecutor Gehl Tucker suddenly dropped the pending charges. A short time later, Kathleen Morris dismissed sex abuse charges against the other nineteen defendants, saying the surprise move was designed to protect "an investigation of great magnitude," involving ritual murder. As the erstwhile suspects lined up to file lawsuits, Morris turned the case over to Minnesota's state attorney general, a move that brought FBI agents and officers of the state's Bureau of Criminal Apprehension (BCA) into Jordan overnight.

The new probe got off to a rocky start, with James Rud recanting his 113-page confession on October 30. The turnaround scuttled Rud's deal for a six-year sentence, leaving him open to forty years' hard time, and authorities could only guess at his motive following an inconclusive polygraph test. "He's got so many stories," one agent complained, "who knows what he's saying any more?"

State and federal investigators were primarily interested in murder allegations, but they approached the case in a curious manner. Retired sheriff's deputy Gordon Gelhaye was called out to organize a river-dragging expedition on October 31, but the plans were scuttled at the last minute. "We had six boats, all the equipment we needed," Gelhaye said, "but suddenly the BCA agent made a call, and said it was all off. We could go home. Who was I to disagree? It was their baby."

Over the next two weeks, contradictory statements from various children convinced FBI and BCA agents that there was "no credible evidence" of ritual murders in Jordan, hence no need to waste time searching for bodies. Even so, investigators were not ready to brand the case an all-out witch-hunt. "Some of the kids are liars," one agent reported. "Some are telling the truth. We just don't know which is which." A senior investigator on the case agreed that "It isn't just James Rud who's involved in this." A third agent described three or four of the recent defendants as genuine psychopaths, with some of the others—including most of the women—designated as "followers." "Maybe they didn't do anything," he said, "but they knew what was happening. They went along with what their husbands wanted. They were very passive, dependent people who had had hard lives. They were victims like their children."

On December 20, 1984, BCA spokesmen announced that information obtained from a sixteen-year-old victim might result in new charges against several adults, but none were ever filed. A report from the state attorney general's office, issued in February 1985, found "a lack of credible evidence which would provide a basis for pursuing any criminal charges in these cases."

The description of black or dark-skinned murder victims was always a puzzling feature in Jordan, which had no black families and no reports of missing children in 1983 or 1984. Journalist William Inman noted that one sacrificial victim allegedly wore an Iowa baseball cap, identical to one worn by a missing newspaper boy from Des Moines, Iowa, while others closely matched descriptions of children who vanished from Chicago during 1983. In the absence of bodies, however, no firm connection with known missing children was ever established. Doubts still linger in Jordan, where BCA chief Jack Erskine told the press in 1984, "These kids have seen something. What it is, we're not sure of. It's not just a bunch of kids getting together and fabricating a story." [See: Child Abuse]

JU-JU

The spiritual ancestor of voodoo, santeria, macumba, and other Afro-Caribbean cults, ju-ju is the historic religion of the Yoruba tribe, in central Africa. Multiple deities, called *orishas,* are worshiped by ju-ju devotees, with the supreme being designated as Olodumare. A python is the symbol or "mascot" of the cult, as in the derivative Haitian voodoo. Sacrifices of various kinds are deemed necessary for most of the cult's rituals.

As described by ex-*babalawo* (junior priest) Isaiah Oke, ju-ju is a religion that presents two faces to the world. One, the public face, is law-abiding and serene, with temples open to tourists, sacrifices limited to money, fruit and grain, or an occasional small animal. On another level, unknown even to many ju-ju adherents, the cult deals in magic for money, offering "lucky" soaps, powders, and lotions produced with ingredients including animal and human remains. Human sacrifice, a sadistic ritual called *iko-awo*, has been documented from Nigeria and elsewhere as recently as 1989, with clients hiring ju-ju priests to kidnap and execute selected "spirit slaves."

Sex is also an important part of many ju-ju rituals, with one branch of the cult devoted to worship of the god Esu, elevating sexual perversion to "an almost sacramental status." In Uganda, worshipers of Esu regard bestiality as an "essential element" of their private rituals, afterward slaughtering the hapless animals and eating them raw. Drunken four-day harvest festivals often degenerate into full-scale orgies, with resultant pregnancies blamed on seduction or rape by "evil spirits." Children produced from such unions are prime candidates to become "throwaway" babies, donated to the cult for sacrifice.

In Nigeria, followers of the *egungun* ju-ju faction celebrate reincarnation of their ancestors in a ceremony called *ikunle*—"the night of kneeling." Ritual prayers are followed by a seven-day festival, during which cultists believe themselves "possessed," generally with the aid of liquor, marijuana, and cocaine. Anthropologists have compared the ritual to Mardi Gras in New Orleans, but it also has a dark side, including hundreds of assaults, rapes, robberies, and murders by "possessed" cultists. Prosecution is rare, since even the police blame ghosts or demons for their crimes, and municipal authorities are more concerned with protecting nonmembers of the cult from attack on the streets. In most Nigerian cities, police guarantee safe conduct for nonparticipants during the first six days of the festival, but a twenty-four-hour curfew is imposed on the seventh day, with no uniforms in sight. In Kwara, during February 1988, the festival produced so many homicides that the governor called for an indefinite statewide curfew, imposing martial law to restore some semblance of order. [See: Human Sacrifice; Santeria; Voodoo]

KASSO, RICHARD, Jr.

The son of affluent parents, born in March 1967, Ricky Kasso grew up rebellious and bored with his life in the upscale community of Northport, Long Island. By age twelve or thirteen he had begun to experiment with drugs, later dubbing himself "The Acid King," cultivating a reputation as a "stoner" who always pushed the limits of his physical endurance, gobbling more pills than anyone else in his circle of friends. Counselors at Northport Junior High considered him "antisocial" and "emotionally handicapped," but Ricky still managed to have a good time, as long as there were chemicals involved.

In 1981, Kasso purchased his one and only book, a copy of Anton LaVey's *Satanic Bible*, poring over its pages in a search for the meaning of life. He attached himself to the fringes of a local high school cult, the Knights of the Black Circle, and while Kasso was never a formal member, the group's clandestine activities—from vandalism and malicious mischief to drugged-out "hell parties" in Aztakea Woods—doubtless helped set the course of his life. By age sixteen, the "Acid King" was a legend of sorts among Northport's disaffected youth. When he was not immersed in drug deals, Ricky lectured his associates on Satanism, holding forth for hours on end at the gazebo in Cow Harbor Park, lavishing praise on Lucifer, his "number-one man." On one occasion, flying high on who knows what, he raised his arms and shouted at the darkness, "I am Satan! God will burn!"

Kasso's closest friend was James Troiano, affectionately known as "Dracula" (for his elongated canines) or "Scarface" (from the damage suffered in a childhood swing set accident). Another heavy drug abuser with a string of burglary convictions, Troiano was a perfect match for Kasso, the two of them teaming up to import large quantities of LSD, mescaline, and PCP from the Bronx. If Jimmy ever questioned Ricky's Satan rap, he kept his skepticism to himself.

Another tenuous member of the Kasso-Troiano circle, in early 1984, was seventeen-year-old Gary Lauwers. Gary idolized the "Acid King," following his lead as a high school dropout and fledgling Satanist, perhaps more interested in drugs and alcohol than any trappings of religion. A theft of mescaline put Lauwers on the outs with Kasso, but he tried to patch things up by paying back the debt with cash and drugs. It seemed to do the trick . . . but you could never really tell, with crazy Ricky.

By the spring of 1984, Kasso's behavior had grown increasingly bizarre. On Walpurgisnacht (April 30), he led Troiano and another friend to nearby Amityville, for a visit to the "haunted" house where Ronald De Feo had massacred his family ten years earlier. There, before a makeshift altar,

Kasso knelt and prayed to Satan for the strength to offer Gary Lauwers as a human sacrifice.

On the night of June 17, Kasso and Troiano left the gazebo with Lauwers and seventeen-year-old Albert Quinones in tow, bound for Aztakea Woods. Ricky and Scarface were already high on PCP and mescaline, much in the mood for a "hell party," the others tagging along for something to do. As the night wore on and Kasso took more drugs, he became increasingly abusive toward Lauwers, recalling their old grievance, finally attacking him with a hunting knife. Lauwers tried to run, but Troiano tackled him and held him down, watching Kasso stab his victim more than three dozen times, forcing Lauwers to profess his love for Satan as he bled to death. Quinones fled before the killers got around to covering their victim's corpse with leaves, and while Kasso boasted of the murder to numerous friends, it would be July 4 before one of them spoke to police. Although prosecutors would later sidestep the satanic question, Detective Lt. Robert Dunn, chief of the Suffolk homicide division, told newsmen: "This was a sacrificial killing. It's pure Satanism."

Arrested on July 5, Kasso and Troiano were lodged at the Riverhead jail, where Ricky hung himself with a bed sheet two days later. On July 11, Troiano was indicted for second-degree murder by "depraved indifference," Albert Quinones turning state's evidence in return for a grant of immunity from prosecution. At Troiano's trial, in April 1985, the defense cast doubt on Albert's testimony, the witness admitting his own use of drugs on the night of the crime. Troiano's signed confessions were described as "doctored" by police, obtained before the young man sought advice from an attorney. Acquitted of murder on April 25, Troiano remained in jail on an unrelated burglary charge, and has since described himself as a "born-again" Christian. [See: Knights of the Black Circle]

KELLUM, GEORGE DAVID

A native of Tupelo, Mississippi, born July 13, 1943, George Kellum remains one of the more elusive figures in America's occult underground. If half the stories spun around his name are true—including tales spread by Kellum himself—he may hold answers to a number of the nagging mysteries surrounding the Charles Manson "family," the Process Church of Final Judgment, and allegations of satanic child abuse. Unfortunately, Kellum—like so many witnesses and bits of evidence involved in cases linked to the occult— has disappeared.

An indifferent student at Mississippi's Delta State College, Kellum spent his freshman year on academic probation, flunked out in early 1963, and finally completed his four-year stint on continuous probation for marginal grades. From college, he enlisted in the army and was stationed in California, where matters apparently went from bad to worse. In later years, he would boast of a drunk-driving incident that allegedly claimed the life of a two-year-old boy; no record of the incident exists today, but there is written evidence on Kellum's service buddies dubbing him "Killer" in 1968 and early 1969.

It was during this same period, apparently, that Kellum first made contact with Charles Manson, through a satanic cult that operated out of San Francisco's infamous "Devil House." Alternately known as the Companions of Life or the Final Church of Judgment, the cult was led by a globe-hopping guru who billed himself as "Father P the 66th." As described by author Ed Sanders and others, the cult was homosexual, with sadomasochistic overtones. In his book *The Family*, Sanders describes the ritual trial of one member, named Sadyi, who stood accused of "cursing Haight-Ashbury," violating nature's law by "consorting with a woman," and causing a demon to invade the body of Father P's lover, a young cultist known as Pussycat. According to eyewitnesses, participants in the trial-cum-exorcism included Manson and a cultist identified by the initials "D.K." Together, these two were dispatched by Father P to steal holy water from a nearby church, and they later joined in the ritual beating of Pussycat, designed to drive out any lurking demons. "D.K." was prepared to go further, sharpening a wooden stake and muttering "He must die," but other members of the group restrained him, thus sparing Pussycat's life.

Years later, at home in his native Mississippi, Kellum would show his wife Sandra the relevant passage in *The Family*, boasting that he was the selfsame "D.K." (The same initials—for "David Kellum," his preferred form of address— are also inked inside copies of his favorite books, retained by Sandra at the time of their divorce.) Elaborating on the story,

Kellum allegedly spoke of his undying admiration for Manson, whom he always referred to as "The Master."

In spite of his undistinguished college career, Kellum wound up as a high school teacher in Grenada, Mississippi, promoted over time to the position of assistant principal. (Kellum's students were reportedly encouraged to call him "The Wizard"—also a favorite nickname of Manson's in the Helter Skelter period.) His marriage to Sandra produced a son, but the couple separated in early 1983, with Sandra accusing her husband of physical and mental abuse. In July of that year, the relationship took a bizarre turn which leaves Grenadans divided by bitter controversy to the present day.

An alleged victim of spousal abuse in her own right, Sandra Kellum had been slow to report her husband's violence, and her reaction to signs of abuse in their three-year-old son was slower yet. She first began putting two and two together in July 1983, when the boy spoke of frightening sessions with his father, enduring severe pain as a tubular object was forced into his rectum. (A year later, scanning sex catalogues in a search for similar items, the boy identified an object known in homosexual circles as a "butt plug.") Local physicians displayed a peculiar reluctance to examine the boy, one accusing Sandra of mounting a "witch-hunt" against her estranged husband, but the bizarre stories continued. In August, following another visit with his father, the boy described a trip to Greenwood, Mississippi, where he was reportedly molested and given enemas by "mean doctors." By October, around the time Sandra's divorce from David was finalized, their son was describing masked rituals with human skulls, his face mashed into feces at the high point of the ceremony. In November, he reported a trip to a "bad-smelling" funeral home, where "mean adults" dunked him in a vat of cold water. A month later, following yet another paternal visit, the boy described a ritual chamber complete with a silver likeness of Satan nailed to a cross. Kellum angrily denied driving his son to a shabby mobile home for still more sessions of abuse, but the child was able to point out a specific trailer, occupied by a woman later identified as Kellum's new girlfriend.

Meanwhile, preschool teachers noted changes in the little boy's behavior, and his sleep was torn apart by nightmares. Child psychologists identified the classic symptoms of abuse, but they could offer little help. Sandra Kellum vowed to keep her son from David at any cost, earning a beating for her trouble in March 1984. The assault landed Kellum in court, where he was convicted and fined on reduced charges of trespassing and disturbing the peace.

That April, following what proved to be his last paternal visit, Sandra noted fresh blood in her son's stool. Under questioning, the boy produced more tales of ritual abuse, including threats of death directed at himself and Sandra if he ever told his father's secret. By June, Sandra was receiving phone calls from a local prostitute who admitted starring in a porno film with Sandra's son. A year later, the hooker would repeat her story under oath, in chancery court, but by that time the "movie studio"—an abandoned motel—had been demolished, and no physical evidence remained.

Sandra Kellum seemed to get a break in January 1985, when the oldest son of David's girlfriend came forward voluntarily, corroborating and expanding on the stories of satanic ritual abuse. Investigators from the district attorney's office tagged along one afternoon when the children pointed out a vacant house alleged to be the scene of child-sex parties, but no search warrant was ever obtained. Indeed, local apathy was so monumental that Sandra Kellum began to suspect a conspiracy. State narcotics officers hinted at a connection between wealthy pedophiles and the narcotics trade, dropping names as Sandra worked her way into their confidence. In time, besides her husband, Sandra would point the accusing finger at two attorneys, two bank officers, a former state legislator, three policemen, a chiropractor, two ministers, and the proprietors of four nearby mortuaries. District Attorney Ed Snyder, for his part, was unimpressed, ordering his subordinates to put Kellum's case "on the back burner."

Nor was the FBI much help, when Sandra called the Jackson field office in January 1985. An agent listened to her story, promised to stay in touch . . . and the rest is silence. When Sandra called back to check on his progress, she says the agent "became quite rude. He said he had all the information he wanted and didn't care about getting any more." By August, when Sandra reported someone's opening her mail, Grenada authorities were inclined to dismiss the claim as a paranoid delusion. When the D.A. refused to present her case to the grand jury, Sandra took up the fight on her own, working her way through the lower courts to win a true bill of indictment without the prosecutor's help. David Kellum was arrested on charges of child molesting and briefly held in lieu of $200,000 bond, later reduced by a judge over Sandra's objections ... at which time Kellum promptly disappeared. At this writing, the case remains open, no end in sight. Charles Manson has no comment on his alleged relationship with Kellum, and "D.K." is permanently unavailable for interviews. Letters sent to his last known address, in care of a relative linked to the Church of Scientology, are neither answered nor returned. [See: Child Abuse; Manson "Family"; Process Church of Final Judgment]

KERK DU SATAN

A Dutch affiliate of Anton LaVey's Church of Satan, also known as the Magistralis Grotto, the Kerk du Satan was founded by Martin Lamers in 1972. A retired actor from the Netherlands, Lamers picked up a copy of *The Satanic Bible* in 1971, on a visit to New York, and was impressed enough to seek a private meeting with the author. Winging off to San Francisco on a whim, he huddled with LaVey, emerging with a charter for his own satanic "grotto" overseas.

The kerk's first base of operations was in Etersheim, where Lamers and his cultists occupied one of the oldest Protestant churches in Holland. Shifting to Amsterdam in 1976, Lamers purchased two adjacent buildings in the red-light district, facing the city's oldest church across a polluted canal. One building serves the kerk for rituals, while its companion opened as Walburga Abbey, a sex club where patrons pay by the minute and the cult's "monastic sisters" masturbate on stage.

Dutch liberalism aside, Lamers and company ran afoul of police when the kerk and adjacent "abbey" filed for tax exemption, calling the strip club's stage an "altar" where the "sisters" performed "acts of symbolic communion with Shaitan" in return for voluntary "religious donations." Lamers won the first round of his battle in court, but the resultant publicity caused a rift with LaVey, a staunch opponent of tax exemption for any church. Terse negotiations saved the kerk's charter, but relations with San Francisco remain strained.

Meanwhile, flamboyant publicity has brought the kerk no rush of new recruits, a dependable forty or fifty hard-core members turning out for "sabbaths" at nine-day intervals. Special holidays like Walpurgisnacht draw larger turnouts, but many sympathizers steer clear of formal membership. "There are groups that should be part of the church," Lamers says, "but they don't dare affiliate because they are afraid. We're treated as a student's joke." [See: Church of Satan]

KIMBALL, MICHELLE

A bright and popular high school student in Bristol, Vermont, Michelle Kimball stunned friends and family when she shot herself to death on January 6, 1988. Her boyfriend, sixteen-year-old dropout George Steady, suffered a bruised head in the same incident and was committed to a psychiatric ward for observation. Police were at a loss to find a motive in the case, until they glanced at Kimball's diary, filled with lavish praise for Satan and his works. Lately obsessed with heavy metal music of the mock-satanic bands like Judas Priest and Black Sabbath, Kimball had been fond of telling friends "The devil is the person to worship." A suicide note, paraphrased by Lt. George Dean of the Vermont State Police, explained that Michelle "believed in the devil and worshiped the devil, and that was something her parents wouldn't understand, but she wanted them to understand."

KIRKE ORDER OF DOG BLOOD

One of several California cults practicing canine sacrifice in the 1960s, this group reportedly worshiped a red-haired Englishwoman who billed herself as the reincarnation of Circe, the goddess who transformed Odysseus's crewmen in *The Odyssey*. Named for its favorite ritual beverage, the Order of Dog Blood made a special point of recruiting members from the Satan Slaves motorcycle gang. The Satan Slaves were also closely affiliated with Charles Manson's homicidal "family," and author Ed Sanders cites the Circe cult as one of several "sleazo inputs" that contributed to Manson's mix-and-match occult philosophy. Although the leader of this cult was never publicly identified, authorities assume the group dissolved some time in 1969 or 1970. [See: Manson "Family"; Motorcycle Gangs]

KIRKMAN, JASON

In April 1986, New Mexico police arrested fifteen-year-old Jason Kirkman for the murder of his father at the family home, in Albuquerque. A hard-core occultist, Kirkman quarreled with his father repeatedly prior to the killing, throwing a tantrum when his father shredded a copy of *The Satanic Bible*. Enraged, Jason vowed revenge and started practicing with his archery set. As police reports described the forty-year-old victim, he "appeared to have been shot with a bow and arrow, possibly stabbed, and possibly mutilated to some degree."

Searching Jason's bedroom, police found ample evidence of his fascination with Satan. His home decorations included "a satanic symbol, a star with the number 666 inside, drawn on the carpet in red. An identical symbol was drawn on the closet door and below it was written 'Satan Rules.' " Kirkman's case was processed through the juvenile system.

KNIGHTS OF THE BLACK CIRCLE

A teenage satanic gang or cult, the Knights of the Black Circle was organized around 1979 in Northport, Long Island. At its peak, the group claimed an estimated sixty members from the local high school student body, ardent disciples defacing public buildings with occult symbols and the sage advice that "Satan Rules." Some of the gang members sported black jackets with the group's name and demonic insignia on the back, cultivating a reputation for unpredictable violence. As one high school senior explained, "It was like, if you saw the Knights in the halls, you wouldn't look them in the eye."

Aside from random vandalism and pervasive drug abuse, the youthful cultists liked to gather for "hell parties" in nearby Aztakea woods, lounging around bonfires, blasting heavy metal music from a boom box, often tripping out on drugs while someone read selected passages from *The Satanic Bible* or similar texts. The group's influence declined as members began to graduate or drop out of high school in 1982 and 1983, but the specter of local satanic activity was revived in July 1984, with the arrest of fringe associate Richard Kasso, Jr., on charges of ritual murder. Even after Kasso's suicide in jail, some classmates were reluctant to discuss the

Knights with journalists or homicide detectives, claiming that "they're still around." [See: Kasso, Richard; "Stoners"]

KOGUT, JOHN: See FUSCO, THERESA

KOKORALEIS, ANDREW and THOMAS: See GECHT, ROBIN

KU KLUX KLAN

Organized at Pulaski, Tennessee, in early 1866, the original Ku Klux Klan was a harmless social club for upper-crust veterans of the late Confederate army. Beginning with six founders and growing from there, the early Klan catered to "Southern gentlemen" who enjoyed donning costumes and tipping a jug on occasion—much like the latter-day Shriners or American Legion. Given the time and place, however, it was probably inevitable that the KKK's effect on superstitious former slaves took precedence over the founders' interest in fun and frolic.

By early 1867, the Deep South was immersed in Reconstruction, a revolution in society and politics that terrified many whites with paranoid visions of a "black uprising" in government and compulsory race mixing in the bedroom. That April, delegates from several Southern states convened in Nashville to reorganize the KKK as a resistance movement, armed for war against "carpetbaggers," "scalawags," and "radicals." One author of the new Klan's constitution was Albert Pike, an ex–Confederate general and chief of army intelligence for Robert E. Lee, who had gone on from military service to command the Southern Jurisdiction of Scottish Rite Masons. Pike was also an intellectual disciple of the French occultist Eliphas Levi, whose influence lingers in the choice of KKK regalia and selection of titles like "grand wizard," "goblin," and "ghoul."

It took federal authorities five years to suppress the original Klan, at a cost of several thousand lives and many times that number maimed or injured. Relative peace was restored in the occupied states after 1872, but Klansmen were eulogized throughout Dixie as saviors of society and "white womanhood." Author Thomas Dixon lighted a candle to that distorted, chivalrous memory in 1905, with his novel *The Clansman,* filmed ten years later by D.W. Griffith as America's first epic movie, *The Birth of a Nation.* Modern entrepreneurs resuscitated the Klan in 1915, to cash in on Griffith's success, and by 1925 the so-called Invisible Empire had recruited some four million members across the nation. Dwindling through the 1930s in the face of bad publicity, persistent monetary scandals, and endemic violence, the KKK survives today as America's oldest, most persistent terrorist organization ... and its occult origins have not been forgotten. If anything, visible links between "white power" and the black arts have increased in the past quarter century.

According to journalist Arthur Lyons, himself a close friend of Anton LaVey, Imperial Wizard Robert Shelton tried to link his Alabama-based United Klans of America with LaVey's Church of Satan in the late 1960s, fuming when LaVey dismissed the offer out of hand. In California, during 1968 and 1969, the KKK was found to be affiliated with a gang of outlaw bikers called the Satan Slaves—who also fraternized with Charles Manson's "family" and the bizarre Kirke Order of Dog Blood. Eight years later, when Shelton's UKA sought to colonize Illinois, most of the recruits were drawn from another motorcycle gang, the Devil's Advocates.

In the 1970s and 1980s, Klansmen were linked with a series of child murders in Atlanta, Georgia—a case that also had apparent ties to drugs and Satanism. Klan rallies in Florida have featured an orator who identifies himself from the dais as "Aleister Crowley." In Indiana, death row inmate Terry Lowery, condemned for the murder of a thirteen-year-old girl in 1985, describes Klan members sacrificing infants in the dead of night. Teenage Satanists in Joplin, Missouri, practiced Klan-style cross burnings before they moved on to animal sacrifice and the murder of classmate Steven Newberry in 1987. A similar underage coven in American Fork, Utah, listed fifty stipulations for prospective members, including cross burnings and adoration of the KKK among more traditional forms of "worship" like drug abuse and oral sex. In San Francisco, Robert Heick—the brains behind "Radio Werewolf" and a self-proclaimed member of Anton LaVey's "new order"—displays Klan posters in his home and broadcasts racist music to promote his goal of a militant "skinhead nation."

Ironically—or, perhaps, appropriately—black magic has also been used against the Klan on occasion. In the 1960s, following a public rally of the KKK in Montgomery, Alabama, selected members found black candles on their doorsteps, ringed with greenish powder. Painted on each candle, in blood, was a skull-and-crossbones design, along with the imprecation "Death Unto My Enemy." [See: Aryan Brotherhood; Nazism]

LaVEY, ANTON SZANDOR

The son of a Chicago bootlegger, America's future high priest of Satanism was born Howard Anton LaVey on April 11, 1930. Following Repeal, his family moved to San Francisco, and LaVey left home at age sixteen to join Clyde Beatty's circus, working his way up from cage boy to assistant lion tamer, sometimes playing the calliope for acts like the Flying Wallendas and Hugo Zachini, the "human cannonball." By 1947, he was working at the Pike Amusement Park in Long Beach, California, picking up stage magic from experts, mixing a new interest in the occult with a burgeoning contempt for Christianity.

As LaVey later described his sideshow experience to biographer Burton Wolfe, "On Saturday night I would see men lusting after half-naked girls at the carnival, and on Sunday morning, when I was playing organ for tent show evangelists at the other end of the carnival lot, I would see these same men sitting in the pews with their wives and children, asking God to forgive them and purge them of carnal desires. And the next Saturday night they'd be back at the carnival or some other place of indulgence. I knew then that the Christian church thrives on hypocrisy and that man's carnal nature will out no matter how much is purged or scourged by any white-light religion."

Married to a banker's daughter in 1950, LaVey quit the carnival a year later and enrolled at San Francisco City College, with an automatic draft deferment and a major in criminology. His studies led to a job with the San Francisco Police Department in 1952, LaVey serving as a crime scene photographer, until the gruesome, depressing experience forced him to quit three years later. Falling back on his show business training, LaVey found work playing the organ in various nightclubs, dabbling in black magic on the side. When he had saved sufficient cash, LaVey purchased an eighty-year-old former brothel, moved in and painted it black, as a symbol of his growing devotion to the "left-hand path."

Divorced and remarried in 1960, LaVey began holding regular Friday night lectures on witchcraft, demonology, and other esoteric subjects, attracting a steady audience which he began to call his Magic Circle. On Walpurgisnacht—April 30—1966, LaVey shaved his head, donned a clerical collar, and proclaimed a new "Age of Satan," members of the Magic Circle joining him to found the First Satanic Church. LaVey pulled out all the stops to court publicity for his new cult, including employment of topless "witches" who cavorted in the nude to lure male recruits. (One of LaVey's dancers, Susan Atkins, would be sentenced to death four years later for her role in the Manson "family" murders around Los Angeles.) By late 1967, a series of well-publicized satanic weddings, baptisms, and funerals had earned international notoriety for LaVey and his cult. Celebrities like Kenneth Anger and Sammy Davis, Jr., were drawn to the Church of Satan, while LaVey took Hollywood by storm, serving as a paid "technical advisor" on horror films like *Rosemary's Baby* and *The Devil's Rain*. Along the way, he claimed affairs with sex symbols Marilyn Monroe and Jayne Mansfield—the latter a practicing Satanist for several months prior to her death in a June 1967 car crash. (LaVey once blamed himself for the accident, citing a "death curse" aimed at Mansfield's lover, but he now dismisses the incident as a "weird coincidence.")

More huckster than evangelist, by the mid-1970s LaVey was openly selling satanic charters and priesthoods to the highest bidder, a crass approach to religion that prompted defectors to organize "more sincere" cults like Michael Aquino's Temple of Set. San Francisco's "Black Pope," meanwhile, developed a new passion for privacy, forsaking interviews and retreating into quiet introspection, while his church continued its recruiting efforts by mail. Further embarrassment derived from LaVey's personal acquaintance with the likes of Susan Atkins and serial killer Richard Ramirez, whom LaVey remembers as "very polite." In southern California, deranged cannibal-killer Steven Hurd claims several one-on-one meetings with the "Head Devil," an association which LaVey and his attorneys firmly deny.

How seriously should we treat the Satanism of a one-time stage magician? Following an interview with LaVey in 1975, journalist Dick Russell wrote: "Anton Szandor LaVey has a master plan, and he doesn't think he will need force to achieve it. He expects it might come to him as naturally as the 25,000 followers who already carry his red card declaring themselves CITIZENS OF THE INFERNAL EMPIRE. Before he dies, Anton LaVey believes that he and an elite force of Satanists will rule the world."

A decade later, writing for the *Washington Post,* Walt Harrington took a somewhat different view. "LaVey," he wrote, "is a junkyard intellectual, a philosopher of the sordid, a savant, an ingratiating and funny man. He's a man who could find no faith, until he discovered magic. But Anton LaVey worships only Anton LaVey. His religion is egotism, and that, as LaVey would say, is truly Satanic." [See: Church of Satan]

LeGEROS, BERNARD

On March 17, 1985, a group of teenage hikers found more than they bargained for while trespassing on a rural estate near Tompkins Cove, New York. Intrigued by an old stone smokehouse built into a wooded hillside, one of the youths poked his head through the open doorway . . . and quickly recoiled from the sight of a charred human corpse. Police retrieved the blackened body, noting that it wore a tight-fitting leather hood of the sort favored by sadomasochists and bondage freaks. Whatever its design and purpose, the mask was not bulletproof, and postmortem test results identified the cause of death as two gunshots to the back of the head.

Medical examiners concluded that the body had been set on fire in an attempt to destroy evidence, but the tight leather mask had ironically preserved the victim's face. Photographs were circulated, and detectives scored an immediate hit from New York City, where Norwegian model Eigil Dag Vesti, age twenty-six, had last been seen on February 22, reported missing two days later with a suspicion of foul play involved. Research into Vesti's background soon identified him as a homosexual and frequent visitor to sleazy bars with an S&M clientele.

In early March, Rockland County detectives began receiving calls from Bernard LeGeros, a twenty-two-year-old resident of Manhattan. LeGeros's father owned the land where Vesti's corpse was found, but mere coincidence did not explain Bernard's apparent knowledge of the case. In conversations on the telephone, LeGeros told police their killer was a "chicken hawk" who preyed on younger men for sex. Not only that, but he had killed before, and homicide investigators could expect to find more corpses planted within a fifty-mile radius of the latest crime scene. Invited to visit the Stony Point police station on March 22, LeGeros began his recitation as a helpful citizen but wound up in a cell hours later, after signing the first of several confessions to Vesti's murder.

The son of a United Nations employee in New York, Bernard LeGeros was a troubled youth who attempted suicide in 1980, at age seventeen, and again three years later. Relatives shied away from seeking professional help, and the problem seemed to resolve itself in 1983, when Bernard went to work for millionaire Manhattan art dealer Andrew Crispo. Far from stabilizing the young man's life, however, Crispo actually introduced him to cocaine in massive quantities, using chemical dependency to mold himself a private slave.

According to testimony from LeGeros and mutual acquaintances, Crispo supplied Bernard with an average 3.5 to 7 grams of cocaine each day between August 1984 and March 1985. LeGeros did not share his employer's taste for violent homosexual action, but the drugs apparently reduced him to a point where he would act upon commands from Crispo, never thinking of the consequences. A self-described enforcer for the forty-year-old businessman, LeGeros "muscled" younger men whom Crispo lured to his gallery for rough, coercive sex. More to the point, Bernard's confessions described Crispo as "part of a satanic cult which drank the blood of its victims"—including Eigil Dag Vesti.

As LeGeros reconstructed the crime for authorities, he and Crispo were cruising Manhattan S&M bars on the night of February 22, when they met Vesti in a club appropriately called Hellfire. After snorting a few lines of coke, the trio drove out to Rockland County and the estate owned by John LeGeros. While Crispo and Vesti amused themselves in the smokehouse, Bernard remained outside, assembling a .22-caliber "survival rifle." When Crispo called him into the hut, he found Vesti kneeling, nude except for the black leather mask.

"If he had never worn that mask," LeGeros wrote from jail, "it never would have happened. It awoke my childhood fears. Anyone who wore that mask became a monster. Crispo used my childhood fears of the mask."

According to LeGeros, Crispo pointed to the kneeling man and said, "He wants to die." Like any good slave, LeGeros took it from there, shooting Vesti twice in the head, allegedly drinking some of the victim's blood and watching while Crispo cut out his heart. Afterward, the body was set on fire and left for scavengers, LeGeros returning on March 2 for another failed attempt at total cremation.

LeGeros was indicted for second-degree murder on March 26, after detectives found the murder rifle hidden in an air-conditioning duct at Crispo's art gallery. Crispo's lawyer professed shock, blaming LeGeros for planting the weapon, but he needn't have bothered. Under New York law, suspects may not be charged on the unsupported accusation of accomplices, and Crispo was never tried for Vesti's murder. He *was* indicted for the September 1984 kidnapping and sexual assault of a male college student, surrendering and posting $100,000 bond on May 17, 1985.

As the investigation proceeded, Crispo's acquaintances were more inclined to talk, describing the art dealer as a neo-Nazi who enjoyed donning SS togs or an ersatz police uniform before beating his homosexual playmates. Others recalled conversations dealing with "snuff" films, produced by connections in Houston, and journalist Maury Terry unearthed Crispo's link to drug-dealing entrepreneur Roy Radin, whose 1981 murder in California had strong satanic overtones. Crispo, meanwhile, never denied being present when Vesti was killed, though he staunchly rejected any suggestion that he might have ordered the murder. Called as a witness at LeGeros's murder trial in September 1985, Crispo stood firm behind the Fifth Amendment's ban on self-incrimination and was finally excused.

Bernard LeGeros, for his part, was convicted on September 26, 1985, and received the maximum penalty of twenty-five years to life. He later appeared as a prosecution witness at Crispo's kidnapping trial, in 1987, but the combined testimony of witness and victim was insufficient to sway twelve jurors toward conviction. By that time, the IRS had intervened, and Crispo was facing seven years in prison on a February 1986 conviction for evading some $4 million in federal income tax. From prison, LeGeros wrote of his one-time master: "He belongs in hell. The only thing is that he would enjoy it."

LEVI, ELIPHAS

A Catholic seminarian in the early 1800s, Alphonse-Louis Constant was always fascinated by the dark side of religion, dabbling in occult lore whenever time allowed. His life's course was set when he rediscovered the ancient Hebrew Kabbalah, adding a twist of his own as he merged Jewish ritual magic with traditional European sorcery and the secrets of the tarot. Finally abandoning the Roman church entirely, he joined an occult group called the Saviors of Louis XVII, whose leader believed himself the reincarnation of said monarch, but something was obviously lacking, and Constant soon dropped out to go his own way.

In the 1850s, using the kabbalistic pen name of "Eliphas Levi," the renegade priest published such occult classics as *Dogma and Ritual of High Magic,* a *History of Magic,* and the *Key of the Great Mysteries.* The hand-drawn illustrations were even more dramatic than his prose, and Levi's rendition of Baphomet still graces the pages of countless modern grimoires. Touting ritual magic as the only universally valid religion, Levi influenced a whole generation of occultists, including Rosicrucians, witches, and the founders of such groups as the Ordo Templi Orientis and the Order of the Golden Dawn. One of his long-distance disciples, American Albert Pike, incorporated Levi's mumbo jumbo when he helped compose the 1867 constitution of the Ku Klux Klan.

More recently, Levi's work has provided inspiration for such occult superstars as Aleister Crowley, Gerald Gardner, and Anton LaVey. In New York, "Son of Sam" triggerman David Berkowitz admits to staring at Levi's Baphomet "for hours on end," and journalist Maury Terry finds significance in the fact that one of "Sam's" murders—committed three days after the occult holiday of Midsummer's Eve, in 1977—took place outside the *Elephas* Disco in Queens. Indeed, the cryptic symbol used by Berkowitz to sign his taunting "Sam" letters was apparently lifted from Levi's dusty texts. Questioned about his choice of insignia, Berkowitz admitted the symbol's "significance," adding: "I believe somebody put it in my mind to write that." [See: Baphomet; Berkowitz, David]

LIMACHI SIHUAYRO, CLEMENTE

A thirty-seven-year-old resident of Yunguyo, Peru, Clemente Limachi vanished on February 16, 1986, after leaving home to sell a donkey at the village marketplace. His disappearance coincided with the last day of the pre-Lenten festival, a mystic connection confirmed when his mutilated corpse was found the next morning, at a ritual site on nearby Mt. Incahuasi. Limachi's killers had removed his ears and tongue, slicing the skin from his face and draping it over his head like a mask, the body reclining in a hollowed-out stone. His blood was also drained and removed from the scene, as if for use in future rituals.

In 1982, a young woman had been sacrificed at the same location, and while police had no doubt of the killing's religious significance, they disagreed on motives. Yunguyo had been punished by torrential rains before Limachi's death, and human sacrifice was still a favorite peasant method of appeasing the unruly elements, but Limachi's widow placed the blame on local narcotraffickers. Two cousins of the victim, Fausto Quispi and Alejandro Lopez, were jailed on suspicion of murder, but their first visitor—a wealthy merchant named Simon Montoya—pulled strings with the court to secure their release. Leucaria Limachi publicly denounced Montoya as the man behind her husband's murder, but the victim's own father—ranking shaman and suspected drug runner Angelino Limachi—was also suspected by authorities. Off the record, police fingered another *yatiri*, Limachi's uncle Clemente Fargin, as coordinator of the sacrifice, but the case remains officially unsolved today. [See also: Montoya, Simon]

LIVESTOCK MUTILATIONS

Since the early 1970s, millions of Americans have been intrigued, titillated, and sometimes terrorized by widespread reports of dead and curiously mutilated barnyard animals. The explanations offered by investigators range from scavenging coyotes to sadistic teenagers, secret germ warfare experiments, UFOs ... and cults.

In fact, the livestock mutilation problem is not, strictly speaking, an American phenomenon. In Guilford, England, during 1964, police found sheep's hearts pierced with wooden stakes atop a crude satanic altar. Nine years later, in Sweden, several calves were found with their hearts cut out; others had their throats slashed, while pigs and bullocks vanished from surrounding farms under mysterious circumstances. Unlike many of the later North American cases, there was clear-cut evidence of human agency, including spattered blood, footprints, and tire tracks found around the death scenes. Even so, the crimes remain unsolved and no arrests were made.

Isolated individual reports aside, livestock mutilations crossed the Atlantic with a vengeance in early 1973. That March, two sheep were found drained of blood near Jonestown, Pennsylvania, and the body count would escalate over the coming year. In May, authorities from Lincoln County, Minnesota, reported a bloodless cow, two of its teats cleanly severed as if with a sharp knife. Six months later, in neighboring Yellow Medicine County, another cow was found, missing its udder, ears, tongue, and tail; hair from the tip of the vanished tail had been clipped and neatly piled beside the carcass. Beginning in late November, more than forty cattle were reported slain and mutilated in a dozen counties of north-central Kansas. Only nine specimens were officially examined by pathologists, all reported dead from natural causes—specifically, blackleg disease. Experienced ranchers, meanwhile, refused to accept the blanket verdict that missing blood and neatly severed organs were the work of prairie predators.

The mutilations spread to Nebraska in April 1974, beginning with a cow in Custer County, nearly drained of blood, two teats severed, a small cut on its belly. By September, some 50 head of stock were involved, and Knox County Sheriff Herb Thompson declared: "The mutilation of these animals was neater than if a butcher had done it. It was more like the work of a surgeon." By 1979, the Nebraska Highway Patrol would investigate an estimated 150 mutilation reports, but only 20 specimens were selected for necropsy, and only one of those reportedly displayed clear-cut knife wounds. As for the 130 that were never examined ...

Texas logged its first mutilation in June, and Iowa followed a month later, adding a new twist to the puzzle. On July 15, near Honey Creek, farmer Robert Smith was plowing his field when an unmarked helicopter skimmed past, a passenger firing several gunshots at Smith through the open side door. Reports of cattle mutilations and phantom choppers went hand-in-hand from that point on, spreading from Iowa to encompass other states. By autumn 1974, mutilation reports were emanating from South Dakota, and the death toll in Minnesota was rapidly climbing. One Minnesota specimen, a full-grown bull, was found that October with its ears severed and a long strip of hide peeled from its hindquarters. A veterinarian's report confirmed the mutilation as human handiwork, but blamed the animal's death on natural causes.

The year 1975 saw a dramatic increase in livestock mutilations, with eighteen hundred cases reported by year's end. Oklahoma and Texas both suffered fresh outbreaks in February, with Oklahoma Governor David Boren creating a special investigative task force on February 22. Nine days later, after allegedly studying twenty-six cases, the task force issued its final report with such unseemly haste that some critics still suspect a deliberate whitewash. According to the report, all twenty-six cattle died of natural causes, and while the mutilations were clearly deliberate, the investigators ruled that "human involvement can be attributed to individuals attempting to get in on a fad or young people dissecting dead carcasses for biological or experimental purposes." Few biology classes conduct lab sessions in open pastures at midnight, but the report was clearly aimed at calming local farmers, closing with a prediction that the ghoulish "fad" was "generated by publicity and is only temporary."

There was no such complacency in Kaufman, Texas, where a dead cow was found sitting upright, drained of blood, its lips, tongue, and sex organs removed. As described by Police Chief Caggie Evans, "It was like they used a suction device to get the blood out." In March, at Whiteface, the mutilations performed on another cow included excision of the navel in a perfect circle . . . along with the typical draining of blood. Necropsies performed on several Texas specimens revealed traces of nicotine, typically used as a sedative in tranquilizer guns.

Colorado recorded its first mutilations in May 1975, coupled with more reports of unmarked aircraft, and police had

132 reports on file by August. Several of the dead animals had precise foot-wide circles cut around their rectums or udders, with clean strips of hide peeled from the hindquarters. One animal, an adult bull found in the middle of an open field, was apparently dropped from a great enough height to break all four legs. Authorities in Teller County pursued and photographed one "phantom" helicopter—a powerful Hughes 500 model—but despite multiple sightings, the aircraft and its pilots eluded capture. In July, a Lincoln County rancher found a blue plastic zipper bag, marked with a U.S. government property stamp; a peek inside revealed a severed cow's ear and tongue, a government-issue scalpel, and several pairs of bloody rubber gloves. At Colorado Springs, a female bison, killed and mutilated in the Cheyenne Mountain Zoo, was missing one ear, its udder, and a circular patch of hide. Meanwhile, pathologists at Colorado State University insisted that all damage to the cattle they examined was caused by natural predators. One skeptic, Sheriff George Yarnell of Elbert County, deliberately mutilated a carcass and sent it to CSU for analysis. The verdict: "Predator damage." The Colorado Bureau of Investigation reached a somewhat different conclusion. In 206 reported cases spanning eight months, 35 animals were posthumously tested; of those, 9 had obvious knife wounds, 2 displayed man-made cuts *and* bites from predators, while decomposition ruled out findings on the other 24.

In April 1975, with mutilations continuing in Minnesota, the *Minneapolis Tribune* reported that a federal agent had been specially assigned to check for any links with a satanic cult. Though working undercover, the agent had already been threatened with death by anonymous callers, his house smeared with blood overnight. When reporters asked the U.S. Attorney in Minneapolis for clarification, they were told: "No comment, and I can't even tell you *why* I can't comment." A month later, the mutilations began in Montana, with nearly one hundred cases reported by year's end. Horses were the target around Seattle, with unidentified night prowlers castrating twenty stallions over the next five years.

By early 1976, frequent mutilation reports were emanating from at least fourteen states, with half a dozen others logging scattered incidents. Aside from cattle, the four-footed victims included ponies, pigs, dogs, sheep, goats, deer, and a llama. The unmarked choppers were flying in New Mexico and elsewhere, seemingly unhampered by a sweeping FAA investigation. One of the New Mexico specimens had a broken leg, the flesh marked as if by a metal clamp, its tongue, anus, and genitals sliced away. In 1977, Iowa experienced a new rash of attacks, and reports began to flow from Missouri, initially centered around the aptly named town of Peculiar. At least twelve mutilations from Iowa were described by experts as "human-induced," as were two cases from Nevada.

January 1978 opened with a new rash of incidents around Dulce, New Mexico. In October, four mutilated steers were found on the Jicarilla Apache reservation in a single day, all within a one-mile radius, at least one marked with eighteen-inch burned patches on its hide. That spring, mutilations also began in Benton County, Arkansas, where state police reported evidence of deliberate knife wounds, along with traces of drugs—including mescaline and succinylcholine, an artificial form of curare—found in several animals. At another Benton County site, police found a twelve-foot circle of calcium sulfate (an ingredient of gypsum and plaster) laid out near a mutilated cow, with more sprinkled on the carcass itself. A September necropsy from La Plata County, Colorado, attributed the death of a Hereford steer to "fatal anoxia from near total exsanguination"; the animal's left eye, rectum, and penis had been "cleanly severed with a sharp instrument in practiced fashion" . . . while the beast was still alive.

The action shifted to Alberta, Canada, in 1979, with a spate of cattle mutilations reported around Calgary in August, claiming 150 animals by the end of the year. Veterinarians tested 50 of those, deciding that 3 had been killed with massive doses of the anesthetic ketamine hydrocholride, then mutilated with knives; another 13 were deliberately mutilated after dying from natural causes, and knife wounds were apparent on 10 other carcasses, where cause of death remained unknown. Between January and August 1980, another 100 cases were reported from Alberta, but only 20 animals were scientifically examined; of those, at least 3 had died from overdoses of succinylcholine, apparently administered with dart guns.

And the beat goes on. In Iowa, during the last four months of 1979, nine more cattle were mutilated with knives, missing various combinations of eyes, ears, tongues, and genitals; all nine had needle marks over their jugular veins, corresponding to traces of ketamine found in the blood. A bull and a fifty-pound pig were robbed of their hearts in San Antonio, Texas, during 1980, with more horses castrated around Seattle in 1982 and 1984. A 1980 report from the New Mexico State Police contends that "hovering aircraft" were used in at least some of the state's cattle mutilations, with blood drained from the jugular and "the cow's own heart used as a pump." Similar carnage was reported from north-central Alabama in 1984 and 1986. Granting that many reports of livestock mutilation are exaggerated or misinterpreted, others are clearly the deliberate work of human hands . . . but is there any link between the killings and occult satanic ritual?

1973—Kansas: Following press reports on the mutilation of a steer owned by state senator Ross Doyen, Doyen received a letter from A. Kenneth Bankston, a federal prisoner at Leavenworth. Bankston claimed intimate knowledge of a satanic cult which mutilated stock and used the stolen organs in "fertility rites." A list of names provided by Bankston included a woman arrested for grave robbery in 1969, but authorities dismissed the story as a hoax in early 1975.

1975—Montana: Cult ritual sites, including makeshift altars marked with the name of the goddess Isis, were found by police in rural areas where cattle had been lately killed and mutilated. No arrests were made.

1975—Idaho: A forest service employee reported several persons dressed in black, hooded robes, walking along Cove Creek in September; the next day, mutilated cattle were found nearby. State investigator Steve Watts blamed these and other mutilations on Satanists, describing the case as "solved," despite the absence of arrests. According to Watts, the suspect cult was infiltrated in 1975 and disbanded a year later, its members scattering to avoid police scrutiny.

1976—Minnesota: Police in Lark Park filed the report of a motorist who swerved off a country road to avoid a group of ten white-robed figures. By the end of the month, several cattle had been mutilated in the same area.

1978—Arkansas: Authorities investigating mutilations in Benton County discovered a crude stone altar near the site where several cattle were stolen. Adorned with candles and animal skulls, the altar was also marked with symbols from the "Theban" alphabet, used by many practitioners of Wicca.

1979—Oklahoma: A twenty-three-year-old woman told

police of her five-year involvement with a satanic cult in Tulsa, describing cattle-killing forays that sometimes included use of a helicopter. Blood from the carcasses was reportedly used to baptize new members, while eyes and sex organs were eaten or otherwise used in occult rituals.

1979—Idaho: State police infiltrated another satanic cult with civilian informants, collecting data on five new mutilations. Evidence included correspondence between cultists, boasting of participation in cattle mutilations, but no arrests resulted.

1979—Colorado: *Jay's Journal,* the published diary of a teenage cultist who committed suicide in Nevada during January 1977, describes a December 1976 trip to Colorado, where several bulls were stunned with electric shocks, drained of blood, stripped of their eyes, tongues, and testicles.

1979—Alberta, Canada: Authorities found a fringed rubber skullcap, resembling ceremonial voodoo headgear, near the carcass of a mutilated steer.

1980—Oregon: An eighteen-year-old informant told police of a group called The Gray Witches, which tried to recruit him for cattle-killing forays into Colorado. The group was also interested in human sacrifice, if they could ever find the nerve.

1980—Iowa: The Iowa Division of Criminal Investigation blamed Satanists for a series of cattle mutilations dating back to 1974, citing medical evidence of drug overdoses and clear-cut knife wounds. No arrests were made.

1984—Alabama: Authorities at Walnut Grove interrupted a satanic ritual, scattering cultists from a crude altar and bonfire including animal skulls and bones. Livestock mutilations were reported in the same area.

1985—Utah: A teenage Satanist in Provo confessed membership in a cult that steals and sacrifices pigs and goats, the leader carrying severed ears and cloven hooves in a special "magic bag."

1986—Alabama: Guntersville police blamed Satanists for a new rash of cattle mutilations in rural areas of Marshall County.

Some occultists, like practitioners of santeria and palo mayombe, openly admit their participation in animal sacrifice, while others—including "white" witches and Satanists—

publicly deny any link with such crimes. At present, it remains for law enforcement to persevere and build cases that meet the standards required in a court of law [See: Animal Sacrifice]

LOZA UCEDA, CAMILO

A twenty-year-old resident of Peru's Yunguyo district, Camilo Loza disappeared from his rural home on Good Friday, March 15, 1988. Shepherds found his mutilated body on the slopes of nearby Mt. Kapia on April 1, but they recognized the evidence of human sacrifice and made no report to authorities. Little more than skeletal remains were left by May 14, when two boys stumbled on the corpse and brought one of Loza's shoes back as evidence. His family identified the relic, but the Investigating Police of Peru showed little interest in the case. On May 17, disgusted relatives set off without police to retrieve the skeleton, noting that several men followed them from a distance. Returning to the village with Loza's remains, the party was stopped by angry farmers from Choquechaca, demanding that the sacrifice be left in place to help their crops. When they were shown bleached bones, the farmers relaxed, one remarking, "Oh, this is an old sacrifice." Two freshly killed females, one twenty-year-old and another aged sixteen, were reportedly staked out closer to the mountain's peak.

Despite advanced decomposition, it was clear that Loza had been sacrificed according to some mystic ritual. The shepherds who had seen his body back on April 1 reported he was disemboweled, and family members found a plastic hood pulled tight over his head, secured with a knotted cord. Beneath the hood, his face had been completely flayed, as in the earlier case of sacrificial victim Clemente Limachi.

Police discovered that Camilo Loza had been lured from his home by a reputed friend, one Rufo Lerma, who attempted suicide on Mt. Kapia shortly after the corpse was discovered. No charges were filed, as Yunguyo's mayor could not decide on whom to blame for Loza's murder. The official suspects were described as either cocaine smugglers or elusive *liquichiri*—ritual practitioners who draw the fat from human bodies with syringes for their ceremonies. Loza's own family, in fact, had a long reputation as *liquichiri*, and were not above suspicion in the case. A group of Yunguyo nuns, investigating half a dozen sacrificial murders during recent years, blamed most of the deaths on four competing narco-smuggling gangs.

LUCAS, HENRY LEE:
See "HANDS OF DEATH"

LYLES, ANJETTE DONOVAN

A self-styled practitioner of black magic and voodoo, Anjette Lyles was born in Georgia during 1917. In 1958, authorities in Macon received an anonymous letter, charging that Lyles's daughter Marcia was being poisoned at home, and they felt obliged to investigate. The girl died before police intervened, but an autopsy revealed lethal traces of arsenic. The grieving mother spun a tale of accidental death with Marcia eating poison during a game of "doctor and nurse," but homicide investigators weren't convinced. Their background search had turned up other family skeletons, including Anjette's last two husbands and one of her mothers-in-law. On exhumation, all three victims tested positive for arsenic, and Lyles was shown to have received insurance benefits upon the death of each. Convicted and sentenced to death at her trial, the defendant was later ruled insane by court psychiatrists and packed off to the state hospital at Milledgeville for life.

"MAGICK"

Spelled with a "k" by Aleister Crowley and his latter-day disciples, to distinguish serious occult activity from the stage magician's sleight of hand, "magick" was defined by Crowley as "the science and art of causing change to occur in conformity of the will." Believers view man as a pawn of nature, manipulated by forces beyond his control, until such time as he acquires the arcane skill to practice some manipulation of his own, producing desired effects through incantations, spells, and curses.

Collective and solo practitioners of "magick" are highly individualistic, but all share three common traits, as outlined by religious scholar J. Gordon Melton. Those traits include: (1) the performance of established rituals; (2) a belief in secret, ancient wisdom; and (3) traditions allegedly rooted in pre-Christian history. Ritual is the key ingredient of "magick," incorporating special garb or implements—like the "nine tools of witchcraft"—to invoke deities or demons for specific purposes. When properly performed, occult ritual produces an altered state of consciousness, often achieved with the help of psychedelic drugs.

Modern followers of "magick" generally derive their inspiration from the twelfth century Knights Templar and/or the Hebrew Kabbalah of the Middle Ages, with specific texts interpreted and modified by such latter-day practitioners as Eliphas Levi, Francis Barret, S.L. McGregor Mathers, Aleister Crowley, and Gerald Gardner. Crowley and Gardner were especially prone to emphasize "sex magick," with Crowley creating a homosexual "eleventh degree" of the Ordo Templi Orientis, while Gardener's "Wicca" religion incorporates phallic initiation ceremonies and other sex-oriented rites.

The chief controversy surrounding modern "magick" is not so much its existence, as the distinction between disciples of "black" and "white" lore. In simple terms, "white magick" is defined as benign, even altruistic, while "black magick" is generally regarded as selfish or deliberately malicious. Self-serving propaganda aside, it appears, on closer inspection, that most practitioners fall somewhere in between, occupying a "gray" zone where ethics are extremely flexible. Indeed, as author Owen Rachleff points out in *The Occult Conceit,* the roots of *all* "magick" rituals include:

1. The need for power, the hope that one may harness unearthly forces to produce wealth or to dominate man and the universe.
2. The need to act out an anti-establishment fantasy; the chance to cut loose sexually, morally, and otherwise, while excusing one's anti-social behavior by saying that it's all part of a sacred ritual.
3. The desire to thumb one's nose at science and reason by steeping one's "faith" in astrology, sorcery, and the prattlings of cultism.

4. The craving for danger and psychedelic experience.
5. The need to belong, even to an outcast but nonetheless disciplinary clan.

Thus, we find practitioners of "Christian" santeria who devote themselves to casting spells for the protection of narcotics dealers, child pornographers, and contract killers. "White" witches deny any selfish motives, while undertaking rituals designed to win new lovers or promotions on the job. Disciples of voodoo, palo mayombe, and other Afro-Caribbean cults must slaughter helpless animals—and sometimes human beings—to maintain communication with the spirit world. In *The Modern Witch's Spellbook,* "white" witch Sarah Lyddon Morrison devotes 59 of her text's 240 pages to "hate magic," including recipes for spells designed "to torment but not permanently injure," "to cause a lot of agony," and "to maim and kill." The chapter closes with instructions for the preparation of "a full-dress black ceremony." [See: Brujeria; Ju-Ju; Palo Mayombe; Santeria; Satanism; Voodoo; Wicca]

MANSON "FAMILY"

Born "no name Maddox" in Cincinnati, Ohio, on November 12, 1934, Charles Manson was the illegitimate son of Kathleen Maddox, a sixteen-year-old prostitute. His surname was derived from one of Kathleen's many lovers, whom she briefly married, but it signified no blood connection. During 1936, Kathleen filed a paternity suit against one "Colonel Scott" of Ashland, Kentucky, winning the grand monthly sum of five dollars for the support of "Charles Milles Manson." Scott instantly defaulted on the judgment, and he died in 1954, without acknowledging his son.

In 1939, Kathleen and her brother were sentenced to five years in prison for robbing a West Virginia gas station. Charles was packed off to live with a strictly religious aunt and her sadistic husband, who constantly berated the boy as a "sissy," dressing him in girl's clothing for his first day of school in an effort to help Manson "act like a man." Paroled in 1942, Maddox reclaimed her son, but she was clearly unsuited to motherhood. An alcoholic tramp who brought home lovers of both sexes, Kathleen frequently left Charles with neighbors "for an hour," then disappeared for days or weeks on end, leaving relatives to track the boy down. On one occasion, she reportedly gave Charles to a barmaid in payment for a pitcher of beer.

By 1947, Kathleen was seeking a foster home for her son, but none was available. Charles wound up in the Gibault School for Boys, in Terre Haute, Indiana, but fled after ten months, rejoining his mother. She still didn't want him, so Manson took to living on the streets, making his way by theft. Arrested in Indiana, he escaped from the local juvenile center after one day's confinement. Recaptured and sent to Father Flanagan's Boys Town, he lasted four days before his next escape, fleeing in a stolen car to visit relatives in Illinois. He pulled more robberies en route and on arrival, leading to another arrest at age thirteen. Confined for three years in a reform school at Plainfield, Indiana, Manson recalls sadistic abuse by older boys and guards alike. If we may trust his memory, at least one guard incited other boys to rape and torture Manson, while the officer stood by and masturbated on the sidelines.

In February 1951, Manson and two other inmates escaped from the Plainfield "school," fleeing westward in a series of stolen cars. Arrested in Beaver, Utah, Manson was sentenced to federal time for driving hot cars across state lines. Starting off in a minimum security establishment, Manson assaulted another inmate in January 1952, holding a razor blade to the boy's throat and sodomizing him. Reclassified as "dangerous," Manson was transferred to a tougher lockup, logging eight major disciplinary infractions—including three homosexual assaults—by August 1952. He was moved to the Chilicothe, Ohio, reformatory a month later, and suddenly turned over a new leaf, becoming a "model" prisoner almost overnight. The cunning act was rewarded with parole in May 1954.

Arrested a second time for driving hot cars interstate, in September 1955, Manson got off easy with five years probation. He celebrated by skipping a court date in Florida on pending charges of auto theft, and his probation was promptly revoked. Picked up in Indianapolis on March 14, 1956, he was sent to the federal prison at Terminal Island, California, winning parole again on September 30, 1958. Seven months later, on May 1, 1959, he was jailed in Los Angeles, on charges of forging and cashing stolen U.S. Treasury checks. Once more, he escaped with probation, swiftly revoked with his

April 1960 arrest for pimping and transporting whores inter-state. Entering the lockup at McNeill Island, Manson listed his religion as "Scientologist"; his IQ was tested at 121. Paroled for the last time on March 21, 1967, over his own objections, Manson was drawn to San Francisco and the teeming Haight-Ashbury district.

It was the "Summer of Love," when thousands of young people flocked to the banner of drugs and "flower power," heeding Timothy Leary's advice to "tune in, turn on, drop out." The streets and crash pads overflowed with teenage runaways and drifters, seeking insight on the world and on themselves. Behind the scenes, a small army of manipulators—gurus, outlaw bikers, pushers, pimps, and Satanists—stood ready to squeeze a grim profit from the Age of Aquarius.

In San Francisco, Manson displayed a surprising charisma, attracting young dropouts of both sexes, drawn from all strata of white society. Some, like Mary Brunner, were college graduates. Others, like Susan Atkins and Robert Beausoleil, were already involved with satanic cults. Most were hopelessly confused about their lives, adopting Manson as a combination mentor, father figure, lover, Christ incarnate, and the self-styled "God of Fuck." They drifted up and down the state in fluctuating numbers, with the "family" topping fifty members at its peak, following their chosen leader as the Summer of Love became a waking nightmare.

From Scientology to Satanism, Manson was a collector of notions and doctrines, blending the best—or worst—of what he learned in a bizarre, hodgepodge philosophy of his own. In 1967, hanging out around a San Francisco landmark called the "Devil House," he started rubbing shoulders with a morbid cult from England called the Process Church of Final Judgment. As one "family" member described the scene for author Ed Sanders: "The Devil House people said it was a religious order, and it went under many ancient names, one of them being the Companions of Life, another one being the Final Church of Judgment. The Final Church is the name Manson chose for the church he would eventually found." Aside from its name, Manson also borrowed his concept of "The Fear" from Process spokesmen, along with the cult's program for recruiting outlaw biker gangs to "terrorize society" on the eve of Armageddon.

Near the end of 1967, Manson moved his "family" south

to Los Angeles, meeting an even more sinister cult at a house called the Spiral Staircase, in Topanga Canyon. Manson described the scene in his autobiography, published twenty years after the fact.

> Each time I returned, I would observe and listen to all of the practices and rituals of the different groups that visited the place. I'm not into sacrificing some animal or drinking its blood to get a better charge out of sex. Nor am I into chaining someone and whipping them to get my kicks like some of those people were.
>
> The day we first drove up, we were innocent children compared to some of those we saw during our visits there. In looking back, I think I can honestly say our philosophy—fun and games, love and sex, peaceful friendship for everyone—began changing into the madness that eventually engulfed us in that house.

It was around this time that Manson's "family" began associating with black magic groups like the Kirke Order of Dog Blood and the homicidal "Four P Movement," itself a spin-off from the Process Church of Final Judgment. By mid-1968, Manson was calling himself Christ and Satan, with the titles used interchangeably. At the Spahn movie ranch, he told visitors, "All my women are witches and I'm the Devil." In May, Susan Atkins led several "family" members northward on a recruiting mission, billing themselves as the "Witches of Mendocino." A month later, one of Manson's followers flew to Australia, hoping to organize the "Final Church" down under.

Back at the ranch, Manson was busy recruiting outlaw bikers, concentrating on gangs like the Straight Satans and Satan Slaves. One Straight Satan, Danny DeCarlo, moved in with the "family" and became Manson's personal gunsmith. On the side, Manson orchestrated weird rituals for the faithful, later recalled secondhand by a cell mate of Susan Atkins in Los Angeles.

> She described to me that on various occasions Charlie would put himself on a cross, and a girl would kneel at the foot of the cross, and that he would moan, cry out as though he was being crucified. They

also would sacrifice animals and drink their blood as a fertility rite.

From animals, it was a short step to human beings. On October 13, 1968, two women were found beaten and strangled to death near Ukiah, California. One, Nancy Warren, was the pregnant wife of a highway patrol officer. The other victim, Clida Delaney, was Warren's sixty-four-year-old grandmother. The murders were ritualistic in nature, with thirty-six leather thongs wrapped around each victim's throat, and several members of the Manson "family"—including two later convicted of unrelated murders—were visiting Ukiah at the time.

Two months later, on December 30, seventeen-year-old Marina Habe was abducted outside her West Hollywood home; her body was recovered on New Year's Day with multiple stab wounds in the neck and chest. Investigators learned that Habe was friendly with various "family" members, and police believe her ties with the Manson group led directly to her death.

On May 27, 1969, sixty-four-year-old Darwin Scott—the brother of Manson's alleged father—was hacked to death in his Ashland, Kentucky, apartment, pinned to the floor by a long butcher knife. Manson was out of touch with his parole officer between May 22 and June 18, 1969, and an unidentified "LSD preacher from California" set up shop with several young women in nearby Huntington, Kentucky, around the same time.

On July 17, 1969, sixteen-year-old Mark Walts disappeared while hitchhiking from Chatsworth, California, to the pier at Santa Monica, to do some fishing. His battered body, shot three times and possibly run over by a car, was found next morning in Topanga Canyon. Walts was a frequent visitor to Manson's commune at the Spahn ranch, and the dead boy's brother publicly accused Manson of the murder, though no charges were filed.

Around the time of Walts's death, a "Jane Doe" corpse was discovered near Castaic, northeast of the Spahn ranch, tentatively identified from articles of clothing as Susan Scott, a "family" member once arrested with Manson's "witches" in Mendocino. Scott was living at the Spahn ranch when she dropped out of sight, and while the Castaic corpse remains technically unidentified, Susan has not been seen again.

In the course of these events, Manson had become obsessed with death and "Helter Skelter," his interpretation of a Beatles song predicting race war in America. In Manson's view, once "blackie" had been driven to the point of violence, helpless whites would be annihilated, leaving Manson and his "family" to rule the roost. Unfortunately, blacks were not as militant in 1969 as Manson thought they should be, and he hatched a scheme to hurry things along.

In the month between July 27 and August 26, 1969, Manson's tribe slaughtered at least nine persons in southern California. Musician Gary Hinman was the first to die, hacked to death in retaliation for a drug deal gone sour, "political" graffiti scrawled at the scene in blood, as Manson tried to blame the crime on blacks. On August 9, a Manson hit team raided the home of movie director Roman Polanski, butchering Polanski's wife—pregnant actress Sharon Tate—and four of her guests: Abigail Folger, Jay Sebring, Vojtek Frykowski, and Steven Parent. The following night, Manson's "creepy crawlers" killed and mutilated another couple, Leno and Rosemary LaBianca, in their Los Angeles home.

An atmosphere of general panic gripped affluent L.A., the grisly crimes demonstrating that no one was safe. On August 16, sheriff's deputies raided the Spahn ranch, arresting Manson and company on various drug-related charges, but Charles was back on the street by August 26. That night, he directed the torture-slaying of movie stuntman Donald "Shorty" Shea, a hanger-on who "knew too much" and was suspected of discussing "family" business with police.

Ironically, Manson's downfall came about through a relatively petty crime. On the night of September 18–19, 1969, members of his cult burned a piece of road-grading equipment that was "obstructing" one of their desert dune buggy trails. Arson investigators traced the evidence to Manson, and he was arrested again on October 12. A day later, Susan Atkins was picked up in Ontario, California, and she soon confided details of the Tate-LaBianca murders to cellmates in Los Angeles. Sweeping indictments followed, but even Manson's removal from circulation could not halt the carnage.

On November 5, 1969, "family" member John Haught— a.k.a. "Zero"—was shot and killed while "playing Russian roulette" in Venice, California. Eleven days later, another "Jane Doe"—tentatively identified as "family" associate Sherry Cooper—was found near the site where Marina Habe's body had been discovered in January. On November

21, Scientologists James Sharp, fifteen, and Doreen Gaul, nineteen, were found dead in a Los Angeles alley, stabbed more than fifty times each with a long-bladed knife. Detectives learned that Gaul had been a girlfriend of Bruce Davis, a "family" member subsequently convicted of first-degree murder in L.A.

And Manson's arm was long. Joel Pugh, husband of Mansonoid Sandra Good, flew to London in late 1968, accompanied by Bruce Davis. Their mission included the sale of some rare coins and the establishment of connections with satanic orders in Britain. Davis returned to the United States in April 1969, but Pugh lingered on, and his body was found in a London hotel room on December 1, his throat slit with razor blades, his blood used to inscribe "backwards writing" and "comic book drawings" on a nearby mirror. In the absence of suspects, police ruled the curious death a suicide, but Pugh's wife wasn't convinced. Good later told a friend, "I would not want what happened to Joel to happen to me."

In March 1970, Inyo County sheriff's officers received a tip that Mansonites were planning to murder prosecution witness Paul Watkins, once Charlie's number-two man in the "family." Three days later, Watkins narrowly escaped from a fire in his trailer, suffering burns on his face, arms, and neck. He told investigators that he was "unsure of the origin of the blaze."

Charged with the seven Tate-LaBianca murders, Manson and three of his female disciples—Susan Atkins, Patricia Krenwinkel, and Leslie Van Houten—went to trial in June 1970. The defense rested on November 19, and attorney Ronald Hughes disappeared eight days later, after he was driven to Sespe Hot Springs by two "family" associates called "James" and "Lauren." The lawyer's decomposing corpse was found in Sespe Creek five months later, around the time Manson's death sentence was announced, with positive identification confirmed through dental X-rays.

Prosecutor Vincent Bugliosi believes that he has traced the fate of "James" and "Lauren," suspected of guilty knowledge in Hughes's death. On November 8, 1972, hikers found the body of twenty-six-year-old James Willett, shotgunned and decapitated, in a shallow grave near Guerneville, California. Three days later, Willett's station wagon was spotted outside a house in Stockton, and police arrested two members of the Aryan Brotherhood inside, along with three Manson women.

Lauren Willett, wife of James, was buried in the basement, and an initial tale of "Russian roulette" was dropped when four of the suspects pleaded guilty to murder charges.

The Process Church of Final Judgment, meanwhile, was working overtime to distance itself from Manson. When Vincent Bugliosi asked Manson if he knew the cult's leader, Robert Moore—a.k.a. Robert DeGrimston—Manson replied, "You're looking at him. Moore and I are one and the same." In May 1971, Process spokesmen "Father John" and "Brother Matthew" flew into L.A. from Cambridge, Massachusetts, huddling with Bugliosi and local FBI agents, disavowing all links with the "family." A day later, they met with Manson in the county jail, after which Charlie's references to the Process "became evasive."

Meanwhile, the Manson trials continued in Los Angeles. Triggerman Charles "Tex" Watson was convicted and sentenced to die for the Tate-LaBianca murders in 1971. Robert Beausoleil, Susan Atkins, and Mary Brunner picked up death sentences for the murder of Gary Hinman, while Manson, Bruce Davis, and Steve Grogan were convicted in both the Hinman and Shea murders. Various death sentences were overturned by the U.S. Supreme Court in 1972, and all of the "family" hackers are now technically eligible for parole.

Manson's "Helter Skelter" motive in the August massacre has long puzzled students of the case, but evidence of another, more compelling motivation awaited discovery by authors Ed Sanders and Maury Terry, long after the fact. Several L.A. informants linked the Tate-LaBianca murders to narcotics traffic, describing Rosemary LaBianca as an established LSD dealer. FBI agents also described Vojtek Frykowski as a dealer, his operation bankrolled by coffee heiress Abigail Folger. Manson and Shorty Shea were seen lunching with Folger in September 1967, and Folger reportedly "shot Manson down" when he invited her to share his bed. Beyond the drug connection, Leno LaBianca owed $230,000 to L.A. bookies on the night he died; he also served on the board of directors of a Hollywood bank linked to organized crime.

Nor was Sharon Tate herself the innocent some headline articles portrayed. Initiated as a witch by British occultist Alex Sanders, before her marriage to Polanski, Tate had drifted into drugs and sordid sexual affairs around Los Angeles. As actor Dennis Hopper described the Tate-Polanski set, "They had fallen into sadism and masochism and bestiality—and they recorded it all on videotape, too. The L.A. police told me this. I know that three days before they were killed, twenty-five people were invited to that house for a mass whipping of a dealer from the Sunset Strip who'd given them bad dope." In 1987, Manson asked an interviewer: "Don't you think those people deserved to die? They were involved in kiddie porn."

Still, the primary motive comes back to Frykowski and drugs. As a "family" associate told Maury Terry: "Frykowski was the motive. He had stung his own suppliers for a fair amount of money, and that didn't go down well at all with the people at the top of the drug scene here. And to make it worse, he was upsetting the structure of the LSD marketplace by dealing independently, outside the established chain of supply. He was a renegade."

A decade after the slaughter, serial killer David Berkowitz provided independent confirmation of the story from New York's Attica prison. A cell block confidant of Berkowitz explains:

> When Manson had the Tate murders done, he was not just doing it out of some Helter Skelter fantasy. That was part of it, he believed in that shit. But there was a real motive, Berkowitz told me. He said Manson was working for somebody else when those crimes were committed. He said Manson volunteered to do the killings for somebody else. Manson was a puppet.

If so, then who pulled the strings?

According to Berkowitz, Manson—like Berkowitz himself—was a member of the lethal "Four P" cult, immersed in drugs, pornography, prostitution, and ritual murder. Confirmation comes from Ed Sanders, who heard "family" members refer to Manson as the "Grand Chingon"—a title used by the leader of the "Four P Movement"—during 1970. Considering his fraternization with blood-drinking Satanists around the Devil House and Spiral Staircase, such allusions clearly defy coincidence. Before the year was out, in May and December 1970, two of Sanders's informants were murdered by persons unknown, one in New York and the other in Florida.

In Manson's absence, Lynette "Squeaky" Fromme held the

"family" reins, corresponding with Charlie in prison and spreading his gospel on the streets, forging new alliances with sundry cults and racist groups. In September 1975, she tried to assassinate President Gerald Ford, but her pistol misfired, and Squeaky was sentenced to life imprisonment three months later. That same December, Mansonites Sandra Good and Susan Murphy were indicted for mailing death threats to corporate leaders across America; convicted in March 1976, both received long prison terms. Good has since been paroled, still proclaiming her loyalty to Manson, and "family" remnants survive to the present day, members reportedly linked to groups promoting child pornography and sexual abuse, as well as rumored human sacrifice. [See: Aryan Brotherhood; "Four P Movement"; Kellum, George; Order of the Rainbow; Process Church of Final Judgment; "Snuff" Films]

"MAXWELL'S SILVER HAMMER"

Keith Montgomery could have done without the Sunday shift, but holidays threw everything off schedule. If you let the good times roll, somebody had to clean up afterward, and it was his turn, pulling morning duty in the chemistry department of the University of California at Santa Barbara. Montgomery left his Isla Vista digs at half past eight, and fifteen minutes later he was trudging by himself along a bluff that overlooked the beach. No sweat, he still had time.

But he was going to be late.

At first, the figures huddled in their sleeping bags seemed perfectly natural. Hundreds of students and locals had thronged the beach last night—July 4, 1970—to watch the freebie fireworks show. Some joints and pills changed hands, and there was always lots of beer around. If anything, Montgomery was surprised that only three of those who turned out for the show had stayed behind to sleep it off.

It took a second, closer look to tell him there was something wrong about those figures on the sand. The sun was shining in their faces now, but only one of them was moving, more like twitching feebly in his sleeping bag than getting up to meet the day. Montgomery squinted, raised a hand to shade his eyes, and realized the dark smears on the camper's face were blood.

He ran back toward the campus, found a call box for security, and summoned the police. The first responding officer confirmed two dead and one in critical condition, barely hanging on. Before he radioed for help, he told Montgomery, "This is the most brutal thing I've ever seen."

Physicians at Goleta Valley Community Hospital agreed. Two of the victims, seventeen-year-old Thomas Dolan and twenty-year-old Larry Hess, were dead on arrival at emergency receiving. Dolan had been stabbed four times in the chest, with numerous lacerations and several compound fractures of the face suggesting a ferocious beating. Hess had suffered five stab wounds in the back and two in the chest, before or after someone pulped his face and split his skull.

The lone survivor, nineteen-year-old Thomas Hayes, clung to life after five hours of surgery to repair internal injuries. When he was fit for questioning, he told police that he was on his way to San Francisco with his friends, when they had camped out on the beach, within a hundred yards of the UCSB marine biology lab. His memories of the attack were vague, but they included waking up to find himself surrounded by a ring of chanting figures dressed in hooded, flowing robes.

Police, meanwhile, were at a loss to understand the savage crime. They had no suspects, and there was no evidence of robbery, with cash and watches left behind. No weapons were discovered at the scene, but measurement of wounds told homicide detectives they were looking for a cleaver or machete, plus at least one knife that had a twelve-inch blade.

Worse yet, the massacre on Independence Day was Santa Barbara's third beach killing of the year. On February 22, John Hood and his fiancée Sandra Garcia had been found, beaten and stabbed to death in similar fashion on East Beach, a short distance from Santa Barbara Cemetery. Three months later, on May 24, Erwin Faulmann was sleeping on the beach at Isla Vista when a pair of strangers tried to cut his throat. He managed to escape and call police, but no arrests were made.

One possible solution for the unsolved crimes emerged from the Charles Manson murder trial, then underway in Los Angeles. On July 27, author Ed Sanders was lunching with attorney Ron Hughes and Mansonite Catherine ("Gypsy") Share—herself jailed for robbery and attempted murder a year later—when he mentioned the Santa Barbara slayings and evoked an immediate, excited reaction. Gypsy Share was animated as she talked about the murders, crediting the series of attacks to a Satanic cult called "Maxwell's Silver Hammer," presumably after a popular Beatles song of the same name.

No members of the cult were ever publicly identified, and they presumably remain at large today. The beachfront crimes are still officially unsolved.

McCUISTIAN, DELL JAY

An Oklahoma ex-convict with prior convictions for burglary and grand larceny, Dell McCuistian decorated his body with tattoos of satanic symbols to highlight his scorn for authority. On February 5, 1988, he lured a three-year-old girl from a restaurant in the Koreatown district of Los Angeles, marching her to the laundry room of a nearby apartment house, where she was raped. Tenants heard her screams and interrupted the attack before McCuistian could strangle the child, putting the attacker to flight. Police combed the neighborhood for thirty minutes before they found their man hiding in some shrubbery, a block away. Suspected of molesting children in four other states, McCuistian was convicted in the L.A. case and sentenced to a long prison term.

McMARTIN PRESCHOOL—CHILD ABUSE

Manhattan Beach, California, is an upscale Los Angeles suburb, populated by attorneys, aerospace engineers, and two-income families working overtime to make their mortgage payments in the high-rent district. At a glance, the town seems to have no more in common with tiny Jordan, Minnesota, than it does with the dark side of the moon, but both communities would be divided, polarized, and traumatized by allegations of ritual child abuse in the summer of 1983. Despite judicial findings in both cases, the main issues remain essentially unresolved today.

Quality day care for children is in high demand around the L.A. basin, where married couples frequently hold down two "power" careers. Prior to August 1983, the leading child care institution in Manhattan Beach was the McMartin Preschool, founded by fifty-nine-year-old Virginia McMartin in 1956 and subdivided into two facilities a decade later. By 1983, some 5,330 children had passed through McMartin classrooms, and the waiting list was always full.

Like any quality preschool, McMartin had a strict code of conduct, though the rules applied more to parents than children. It was only later, in the wake of arrests and criminal charges, that stunned residents would look back on the list of rigid guidelines as potential warnings. No parental visits whatsoever were allowed within the first six weeks of any child's enrollment at the school; thereafter, visits were permitted by appointment only, with time reserved well in advance. If parents wished to pick a child up early, they were warned to call ahead, and nap time was never to be interrupted under any circumstances. If anyone stopped to consider the rules, they were blandly dismissed as sensible security precautions. Likewise some parents were too busy to ask questions when their children came home from school minus underpants, or wearing another child's clothing. As one father explained, too late: "It just blew by me."

Still, by the summer of 1983, several mothers were moved to complain about staff member Raymond Buckey, often seen at the school dressed in nothing but swim trunks, bouncing young girls on his lap. A college dropout, Buckey had no qualifications for teaching, but he did have excellent connections: he was Virginia McMartin's grandson, and his mother—Peggy McMartin Buckey—ran the school.

That August, Judy Johnson's two-year-old son came home from McMartin with blood leaking from his anus, complaining of abuse by "Mr. Ray." Johnson went directly to the Manhattan Beach Police Department, and from there to the UCLA Medical Center, where doctors confirmed that her son had been sodomized. With Johnson's complaint in hand, officers arrested Ray Buckey on September 7, and he routinely posted bond. He would later admit flushing most of his pornography collection down the toilet while free on bail, belatedly insisting that none of the photos depicted children.

Police in Manhattan Beach were wholly without experience in handling child abuse cases, and from the start their bumbling efforts undermined hopes for a successful prosecution. Another fourteen months would pass before the locals asked for outside help from experts; in the meantime, Chief Harry Kuhlmeyer dictated a form letter to all parents with children enrolled at the school, announcing Ray Buckey's arrest and asking parents to quiz their children about prior abuse. The appended plea for confidentiality was too little and too late, Kuhlmeyer's letter touching off a full-scale exodus from the McMartin school.

Almost at once, it was apparent that police had an unusual situation on their hands. Dozens of children described acts of sexual abuse, "naked games," and even more bizarre activities—including apparent satanic rituals, death threats, and the cruel slaughter of animals kept at the school as "pets." Nor was the specter of abuse a new phenomenon, apparently. As news of the investigation spread, police received calls from several McMartin alumni in their teens and early twenties, relating identical tales of terror.

By November 1983, Manhattan Beach police were sending alleged victims to the Children's Institute International, which specialized in cases of child sexual abuse. There, interviews were videotaped as the children demonstrated sexual acts with anatomically detailed dolls, some expanding on their tales of ritual abuse. A number of the victims spoke of being drugged or driven to other locations where they were molested by strangers. One four-year-old called himself the "son of Satan." A five-year-old's mother was trying to teach her daughter a prayer, when the girl announced, "I tried it your way. There is no God." Some students recalled being shut up in caskets with a rotting corpse; others spontaneously sketched demons, witches, and scenes of human sacrifice. All told, the children fingered most of the McMartin staff, plus thirty more suspects and a handful of unidentified "strangers." A total of 389 past and present students were interviewed, with some 350 reporting various forms of abuse; a full eighty percent displayed physical symptoms, including vaginal or rectal scarring, anal bleeding, painful bowel movements, and the "wick anal reflex" associated with violent penetration.

Police officially closed the McMartin school in January 1984, their investigation spreading to three other preschools nearby. The Manhattan Ranch School was closed after several McMartin students described being taken there for sex, and sheriff's officers reported "a substantial number" of children at each school who displayed physical symptoms of abuse. Another institution, the Learning Game Preschool, was also described by police as "clearly linked to McMartin."

Apparent confirmation of the satanic charges surfaced when police in Torrance arrested Robert Winkler, a thirty-five-year-old handyman, on unrelated child-molesting charges, linked to a baby-sitting service he ran with two other suspects. Several McMartin students saw Winkler's photo in the newspaper, picking him out as one of their assailants, previously known only as "the Wolf Man." A police search of Winkler's residence turned up a black robe and candles, occult literature, and a pair of severed rabbit ears, as described by the McMartin victims. Dead of a drug overdose on the eve of his trial in Torrance, Winkler was never officially charged in the McMartin case.

In March 1984, a county grand jury indicted seven defendants on 115 counts of felony child abuse, listing eighteen victims. The accused included: Virginia McMartin, then 78; Peggy McMartin Buckey, 58; Ray Buckey; Ray's sister Peggy Ann Buckey, 29; Betty Raidor, 66; Mary Jackson, 58; and Babette Spitler, 37. All were past or present members of the preschool staff. No outsiders were named in these or any subsequent indictments.

Unfortunately for the cause of justice, 1984 was an election year, with incumbent District Attorney Robert Philibosian locked in a bitter campaign against liberal contender Ira Reiner. Some observers of the case believe Philibosian was more concerned with publicity than common sense in May, when he filed an expanded complaint against the seven defendants, raising the ante to 354 felony counts with forty-one victims. A month later, when the McMartin preliminary hearing convened before Judge Aviva Bobb, Philibosian described the preschool as a front for child pornographers.

Preliminary hearings are normally short, if not necessarily sweet. In the McMartin case, proceedings dragged on for twenty grueling months, at a cost of $6 million, producing 540 volumes of testimony. Much of the delay was traceable to the battery of seven defense lawyers, billing L.A. County an average of $116 per hour, keeping each witness on the stand for weeks of repetitive, often nonsensical interrogation. Of the lot, attorney Daniel Davis set the record for most obnoxious performance in his defense of Ray Buckey, moving Judge Bobb at one point to denounce him as "childish." In May 1985, with the marathon hearing still in progress, California's legislature passed a new law permitting children to testify via closed circuit TV in sex abuse cases, but Judge

Bobb found the new law irrelevant to cases in progress, and twenty-seven children were promptly withdrawn from the list of witnesses, their parents dreading the consequences of an inquisition by Davis and company. Those who remained were predictably confused by the rapid-fire questions of multiple lawyers, often uncertain of names and dates, sometimes contradicting their previous statements. (Older victims, in their teens and twenties, were barred from giving testimony by California's six-year statute of limitation on child abuse.) Finally, on January 9, 1986, Judge Bobb ordered all seven defendants to face trial on a reduced slate of 135 molestation counts and one charge of conspiracy.

Two days later, new D.A. Ira Reiner dismissed prosecutors Glenn Stevens and Christine Johnson from the case, following one surprise move with another on January 17, when he summarily dropped all charges against five McMartin defendants. Despite Judge Bobb's opinion of the case, Reiner denounced much of the evidence as "incredibly weak." Peggy Buckey and her son would stand alone for trial, facing a total of ninety-nine molestation counts between them, with one shared count of conspiracy. Even so, Reiner could not resist a parting shot at Bob Philibosian for blowing the case "massively out of proportion." (A group of twenty-three outraged McMartin parents filed suit to have the other charges reinstated, but they lost their case.) Glenn Stevens, meanwhile, resigned from the D.A.'s office and went into real estate, but not before selling his story to TV producer Abby Mann. Overnight, Stevens had developed a new faith in Ray Buckey's innocence ... which, by the way, would help his "docu-drama" sell. "You want this stuff to generate a lot of controversy," Stevens told Mann. If the Buckeys were acquitted, he now believed, "We'll be sitting on top of the world."

In December 1986, Judy Johnson died of a liver disease linked to alcoholism. Rumors had already begun to circulate about her mental state, including charges that the D.A.'s office had deliberately suppressed proof of insanity, but prosecutor Roger Gunson strongly disagreed. As he told the press, "Everyone who has described [Johnson] prior to the preliminary hearing calls her lucid. By the end of 1985 she was a different person." And the charges were irrelevant in any case, since Johnson's state of mind had not induced her son to bleed or point to "Mr. Ray" as his abuser.

Jury selection finally began in April 1987, with the trial officially beginning on July 13. Prosecutor Lael Rubin's open-ing statement stressed the weight of medical evidence and parental observations, while Dan Davis set the tone for the defense, describing McMartin victims as having been "artifi-cially traumatized into believing they were molested when they weren't." Judge William Pounders did his best to run an orderly court, but it was often difficult, between the antics of attorneys and defendants. Several jurors were so prone to tar-diness or sleeping in court that Pounders threatened them with jail time for contempt. Elderly Virginia McMartin drew similar warnings for shouting at prosecutors and calling the judge's questions "dumb." (As for herself, the matriarch of clan McMartin could be mightily obtuse when it suited her purpose: "I'm not at all sure what any of you mean by 'molested.' Until this came up, I never heard of it.") Dan Davis was blasted by Pounder for "outrageous" and "total-ly improper" conduct, including a tedious six-day cross-examination that ended only when Judge Pounder ordered Davis to "sit down and shut up." By August 1988, four more children had withdrawn from the case to spare themselves further abuse, resulting in dismissal of another thirty-five fel-ony counts.

Still, there seemed to be ample evidence of guilt, ranging from bizarre entries in Virginia McMartin's private journal to the testimony of Ray Buckey's cell mate, one George Free-man, that Buckey had confessed to sodomizing Judy John-son's son. Dan Davis denounced Freeman as a "pathological liar"; Judge Pounder found his testimony "very detailed, ex-tensive, and damning." Even one of the McMartin family, a granddaughter of Virginia's, suspected that two of her own kids had suffered abuse at the school. A black robe and por-nographic photos confiscated from one defendant's home were introduced as evidence, while defense attorneys harped on the theme of a "witch-hunt" inspired by counselors who "brainwashed" children into imagining their injuries.

At last, on January 18, 1990, jurors returned not-guilty ver-dicts on fifty-two felony counts, reporting themselves hope-lessly deadlocked on twelve charges filed against Raymond Buckey. McMartin defenders claimed a sweeping victory, but it was hardly that. As juror John Brees told the press, the Buckeys "weren't proven innocent," rather "we just found them not guilty, based on the evidence." In fact, other jurors chimed in, they believed the children *were* abused, but slip-shod investigation techniques and poor presentation of evidence left them unsure of whom to blame. Ray Buckey's second trial produced another hung jury in July 1990, and charges were finally dismissed in the interest of economics. Meanwhile, countless questions surrounding the case remain unanswered, perhaps forever. [See: Child Abuse]

McNALLY, SALLY and STEWART, SHANE

The rebellious product of a broken home in San Angelo, Texas, teenage Sally McNally worried her mother by sneaking out a bedroom window at night to visit "friends," refusing to discuss the excursions when she was caught returning in the predawn hours. Her stock reply, before lapsing into silence: "You don't know anything about this, and you wouldn't understand."

Some private sleuthing on the part of Sally's mother soon revealed that Sally had been meeting with the youthful members of a small satanic cult. The group's "ritual parties" included black robes, burning candles, and invocations of "Father Satan" through a ouija board. Sally once invited a girlfriend to one of the gatherings, but the friend grew alarmed and bailed out when McNally "went into a trance."

In the autumn of 1987, Sally began dating Shane Stewart, introducing him to the local cult. Shane's parents noted changes in their son's behavior, but the boy was old enough to go his own way, and he soon set up housekeeping with Sally on a permanent basis. In March 1988, the couple spoke with deputies of the Tom Green County sheriff's office, explaining that recent cult activities had frightened them to the point of dropping out. Sally and Shane described drug use, group sex, and stockpiling of weapons. One pistol, given to detectives, had allegedly been used by cultists in a robbery and murder; a check of the serial number proved the gun was stolen, but no matching crime was discovered.

Sally and Shane left San Angelo a short time after talking to police, but they were back by early summer, living with their respective parents but still dating regularly. In late June, Sally told a friend that she believed some members of the local cult might try to kill her for defecting and reporting their activities, but she apparently took no steps to protect herself.

On the night of July 4, 1988, Shane and Sally drove to Lake Nasworthy, for a 9:00 P.M. fireworks show. Two hours later, they were seen at nearby O.C. Fisher Lake, spotted by fisherman Randall Littlefield from his boat offshore. Shane and Sally were sitting on the fender of Stewart's car when several young men arrived in a pickup truck, and a loud argument ensued. Littlefield could only pick up snatches of their conversation from a distance, but he recalls Shane telling the new arrivals, "We're not into that anymore."

It was the last time Shane or Sally would be seen alive.

Shane's car was found abandoned on July 5; another four months elapsed before two decomposed bodies were found in the desert outside town. Both victims had been killed by shotgun blasts, but wind and rain had scoured the scene of useful evidence. No arrests have been made in the case, but detectives consider local Satanists their prime suspects, stating for the record that cult activities led directly to the double murder. A $5,000 reward is offered for information leading to a solution of the case.

MENTZER, WILLIAM

Gunman David Berkowitz was working on his third year of confinement for the brutal "Son of Sam" murders when he began describing a satanic cult's involvement in the crimes. At first, his claims were thought to be another pipe dream, like his tale of ancient demons speaking through a neighbor's Labrador retriever, but detectives changed their minds as Berkowitz provided accurate, unpublished details from an unsolved California murder case, predicting other homicides before they happened in New York.

The eerie dialogue began in October 1979, when Berkowitz wrote to a friend in Manhattan, describing the 1974 ritual murder of Arlis Perry at California's Stanford University. According to Berkowitz, he learned the details of the crime from a direct participant, who had entertained New York Satanists with "a detailed soliloquy directed at the victim, describing her annihilation." A month later, trying to put his friend's mind at ease, Berkowitz wrote:

Don't worry, because I didn't commit this crime. Nor was I present when it was done. Back in October '74 I was busy and at work as a piss-poor paid security guard. I was here in N.Y. But (and I say BUT) in my travels with different people in this area, I met someone who was involved in her death and spoke freely of the slaying—bragging. He knew many details, and I know that this guy, Manson #2, doesn't bull. I know he killed often, him and his "crew." This is what this new investigation is going to rest on.

The reference to "Manson #2," as Berkowitz later told detectives from Santa Clara, California, meant that Perry's killer was affiliated with the Charles Manson "family" and other cults, including the sinister "Four P Movement," around Los Angeles in the late 1960s. A decade later, he was still active in satanic rituals from coast to coast, including human sacrifice and contract murders linked to cult activities and organized narcotics traffic. As Berkowitz informed a fellow prisoner:

When Manson had the Tate murders done, he was not just doing it out of some Helter Skelter fantasy. That was part of it, he believed in that shit. But there was a real motive, Berkowitz told me. He said Manson was working for somebody else when those crimes were committed. He said Manson "volunteered to do the killings" for somebody else.

The source of Berkowitz's inside information on the Manson massacre was named as "Manson #2." More to the point, where New York detectives were concerned, "Manson #2" was also named as a participant in the "Son of Sam" murders. A prison contact close to Berkowitz told newsman Maury Terry:

Manson #2 wasn't from North Dakota. He was from the L.A. area. That's where the Sam cult has its headquarters. The North Dakota branch wanted Arlis [Perry] dead, and they called California for help. Manson #2 went north to Stanford to arrange it. At least one, maybe two people from Dakota came out to help, but it was Manson #2's show to run. He was involved with the original Manson and the cult there in L.A. That's why Berkowitz used that name as a clue.

Terry's source further described the elusive killer as "an occult superstar" who remained on call for "special jobs" around the country. One such, in January 1977, was the murder of Christine Freund in New York City. Berkowitz described the Freund shooting as a "deliberate hit," perhaps warning her fiancé, John Diel, to terminate his acknowledged affair with a rich married woman in Queens. Police initially considered the murder another random "Sam" attack, but witnesses report a series of anonymous calls to Freund shortly before her death, and Diel recalls a yellow car following his in an "unusual" manner the night of the shooting. The driver of that yellow car, according to independent witnesses, closely resembled "Manson #2." In retrospect, Berkowitz was willing to reveal this much because he feared and hated the gunman, blaming "Manson #2" for his own imprisonment as a scapegoat "Son of Sam."

Maury Terry followed the elusive killer's trail for months, running into years, without discovering his name. Along the way, witnesses to a second "Sam" shooting described the same man, or his twin, and graduates of Stanford University provided similar descriptions of a man seen entering the church were Arlis Perry died. The case broke for Terry in June 1984, when Los Angeles police named William Mentzer as a suspect in the May 1983 kidnap-slaying of millionaire Roy Radin.

At once, the pieces started falling into place. Mentzer was identified as a frequent traveler to Miami and Houston, linked with Florida drug dealers and cultists in the Texas city (where Berkowitz purchased his .44 Bulldog eight years earlier). He was also involved in the drug and music scene around L.A., from 1968 to 1972, hanging out with the same rock musicians Charles Manson was courting before his arrest. A local source confirmed that "Mentzer knew Manson and all the cult people" around Los Angeles. He also knew coffee heiress Abigail Folger, and was seen lunching with her a few days before she died in the Tate massacre. By 1987, LAPD spokesmen frankly admitted Mentzer's membership in "some kind of hit squad." An FBI source, meanwhile, placed him in northern California at the time of Arlis Perry's murder. As Terry was told: "He and a couple of his friends liked to go up to Stanford and hang around the campus occasionally."

A Vietnam veteran and dedicated weight lifter, Mentzer was working as a bodyguard for crippled pornographer Larry

Flynt in 1983, when he met Karen Greenberger, wife of the number-two man in Colombian Carlos Lehder's drug cartel. One of Mentzer's closest friends at the time was Alex Marti, an Argentinian Jew-hater who filled his L.A. apartment with portraits of Adolf Hitler and books on the Third Reich (another fascination of the neo-Nazi "Four P" cult). Commissioned to murder Roy Radin in May 1983, Mentzer borrowed a limousine from a former employer and took his victim on a one-way ride into the desert. Mentzer and Marti later boasted of shooting Radin while the "fat Jew pig" begged for mercy.

A year later, in May 1984, Mentzer was linked to a double homicide in Los Angeles, gunning down James Pierce and June Mincher, a transvestite who had threatened Mentzer's latest client in the bodyguard business. That July, he was back in Miami, helping Karen Greenberger extort cash and personal property from attorney Frank Rubino—who, ironically, had once helped Mentzer beat a drug possession charge. Police were on his trail in California, but they had no solid evidence until April 1988, when one of Mentzer's associates turned over the pistol used on Pierce and Mincher. Three months later, detectives had Mentzer on tape, boasting about the Roy Radin contract, and a September conversation leaked details of impending drug murders in Florida.

"Manson #2" never got the chance to collect his commission on that job, however. Arrested on October 2, 1988, he was held without bond on charges of first-degree murder with special circumstances; Marti, Greenberger, and accomplice Robert Lowe were jailed on identical charges, making a clean sweep in the Radin case. On July 22, 1991, all four defendants were convicted of murder, with Mentzer and Marti facing the death penalty.

At this writing, police and private cult-watchers continue their investigation of Mentzer's link to other slayings and the drug-cult underground. "Manson #2," for his part, maintains judicious silence and refuses interviews. [See: Berkowitz, David; "Four P Movement"; Manson "Family"; Perry, Arlis]

MILLER, KATHLEEN ANN

On Sunday, February 1, 1987, an intruder entered the Antioch, California, home of Rev. Carol Knox, armed with a sawed-off .22-caliber rifle. Without a word of explanation, the stranger fired three shots and killed the forty-eight-year-old minister instantly, wounding housemate Dorothy Jo Dunning with two rounds, afterward fleeing in the dead woman's car. Dunning was able to call police, and officers noted her description of a prowler who appeared to be a woman dressed in men's clothing. The wounded witness's impression was apparently confirmed by a duffel bag found in the bushes outside, containing a woman's wig, sunglasses, and jewelry.

An all-points alert was broadcast for the missing car, and patrolmen soon spotted the vehicle, with a woman at the wheel. The high-speed pursuit ended when their quarry ducked low in her seat for a moment, afterward crashing into a parked tractor-trailer. Later identified as twenty-five-year-old Kathleen Miller, the woman was dead when police pulled her from the wreckage. She wore men's clothing with women's garb underneath, and autopsy results showed that she died from a self-inflicted bullet wound before the crash.

Inside the car, officers found the murder-suicide weapon, along with a bizarre letter that began: "I was Eva Braun, Hitler's mistress." The rambling note also made reference to "the Satan-lite [*sic*] inside of me," but no motive was revealed for the shooting of victims Knox and Dunning.

A former high school homecoming queen, Kathleen Miller was already familiar to police in Redding, California, where Detective David Mundy suspected her of a murder dating from May 1986. In that month, a prowler described as a woman wearing men's clothes had invaded the home of seventy-four-year-old Lilburn Pasley, beating and stabbing the old man to death, leaving his seventy-two-year-old wife battered but breathing. Pasley was the grandfather of Miller's ex-husband, and posthumous fingerprints linked Miller to the crime scene.

As in the Knox attack, police were left without a solid motive for the Redding homicide. Detective Mundy told the press that Miller was "fairly normal and had good work habits, but she was heavily into the occult stuff and from time to time she'd think she turned into someone else. One of the personalities she thought she could turn into was Hitler's mistress, Eva Braun." In recent months, Miller had also hallucinated visits by an unidentified woman, whom, police speculate, she may have confused with the well-known Reverend Knox.

MONTOYA, SIMON

A wealthy Peruvian businessman with homes in Yunguyo, Puno, Lima, and Tacna, Simon Montoya travels extensively along the Bolivian border in pursuit of various enterprises. A fringe benefit of his travels, according to police, is the opportunity for bagging victims used in human sacrifice-for-profit, commissioned by the area's richest miners, manufacturers, and drug runners. Suspected of a link to the Yunguyo sacrifice of victim Clemente Limachi, in February 1986, Montoya escaped prosecution through lack of concrete evidence. Authorities and local priests report that he intimidates his critics by threatening to steal their souls through sacrifice and thereby turn them into "serpent spirits." At this writing, Montoya is reportedly at large and still in business, hunting humans for their value on the open market.

MOTORCYCLE GANGS

Within a quarter century, they have passed from police blotters into American folklore. The wild ones—portrayed on screen by Marlon Brando, Lee Marvin, and Peter Fonda, elevated to classic rebel status in the "gonzo" prose of Hunter Thompson. They are the "one-percenters" who don't fit and don't care, reveling in their odious reputations, working overtime to outrage anyone and everyone they meet.

Motorcycle gangs are an American phenomenon, born in the wake of World War II, but they are no longer solely an American problem. With sixty-seven recognized chapters in thirteen countries, the Hell's Angels Motorcycle Club qualifies as an international corporation, dealing primarily in drugs and death. A number of competitors are striving hard to compete with the original hell-raisers, both in terms of income and sadistic violence.

Ironically, despite the later affiliation of several motorcycle gangs with known satanic cults, the pioneer Hell's Angels took their name from an Allied bomber squadron immortalized in a Howard Hughes movie of the same title. Notoriety bred competition from coast to coast, spreading into Canada and beyond, with the "clubs" graduating from pure nihilism to free enterprise by the early 1970s. A decade later, federal narcotics officers would describe outlaw bikers as the domi-

nant force in sales and manufacture of illegal methamphetamines, branching out into other drugs, commercial sex, and
large-scale theft of motor vehicles. Sometimes, the gangs
compete with established crime syndicates, waging brushfire
wars against the old-line mafiosi, but they are also known to
cooperate with the Mob where it suits their purpose. In many
locales, greasy leathers and denim have given way to custom-
tailored suits, switchblades replaced with Uzis and antitank
weapons stolen from military arsenals. When eleven Hell's
Angels were indicted in San Francisco during 1988, they
raised $3 million bond out of pocket and drove away from
the courthouse in a chauffeured limousine.

Along the road from raunch to riches, many of the gangs
developed ties with various occult fraternities, a link which
some authorities suggest has lingered to the present day. In
California, through the 1960s, leaders of the Process Church
of Final Judgment actively recruited from the ranks of Hell's
Angels and Gypsy Jokers, calling the bikers "agents of Satan." One Processean, known to the faithful as "Brother Ely,"
actively rode with the Jokers for two years, before a rumble
with Angels drove him out of San Francisco during 1969.

Charles Manson's "family" also fraternized with the Gypsy
Jokers in northern California, shifting allegiance to the
Straight Satans and Satan Slaves when the tribe moved south
in 1968. Manson envisioned the bike gangs as his personal
storm troop, holding the line against "Blackie" in the race
war known as "Helter Skelter," and he used his female disciples as sexual lures for ever-ready knights of the road. One
Straight Satan, Danny DeCarlo, actually moved into Manson's camp at the Spahn movie ranch, serving as the "family's" personal gunsmith until he turned state's evidence in
1970. Drugs were also a factor in the Manson–motorcycle
gang connection, with the traffic flowing both ways, and
members of the Straight Satans club were listed as suspects in
the Tate-LaBianca massacre before Susan Atkins spilled the
beans in jail and Charlie's angels were charged with the
crimes.

Elsewhere in California, outlaw bikers have associated
with the gore-sipping Kirke Order of Dog's Blood and the
homicidal "Four P Movement." A Harley-riding defector
from the latter group gave police their only recognizable
name of another member—Erickson—but the meager clue led
nowhere when they tried to run it down. On the East Coast,

meanwhile, bikers also hung around the mansion of million-aire mogul Roy Radin, himself the victim of a 1981 assassi-nation that mingled drugs with demonology. In January 1984, informant Terry Newsome—seized by Texas lawmen with a stash of drugs and several human fetuses—explained that he had lifted the remains from an Indiana "cult house," where bikers met for grim satanic rituals. Authorities in Lake County, Indiana, confirmed the existence of a local devil-worship cult, but ownership of the tiny corpses was never traced. A year later, in Hamilton, Ontario, two children of an outlaw biker were removed from home by the police after the children related tales of sexual abuse, bestiality, and satanic rites incorporating human sacrifice. Around Milwaukee, Sa-tan's Dragons drew their inspiration from a leader nicknamed "Pop Satan," scoring their first major headlines when four members were jailed for a mutilation-murder in May 1987.

Drugs and demonology are not the only interests of the outlaw motorcycle gangs. They also thrive on hard-core big-otry, as demonstrated by the turnout of Straight Satans for a 1968 Ku Klux Klan rally in Los Angeles County. Nine years later, when the Klan tried for a comeback in Illinois, most of the early recruits were drawn from another cycle gang, the Devil's Advocates.

Commercially, the reputed interests of satanic cults and outlaw bikers also overlap in the realm of prostitution, vic-timizing juveniles. Federal agents identify America's top four pimping gangs as the Hell's Angels (West Coast), the Banditos (Southwest), the Outlaws (in Dixie), and the Pagans (East Coast). Regardless of their chosen "colors," bikers treat their juvenile victims like community property, subject to bar-ter, sale, or purchase on a whim. The punishment for resist-ance includes sadistic beatings, gang rapes, imprisonment in fortified "clubhouses," and occasional murder. Escapees are tracked down through the national network of club chapters, with bounties of $100 or $200 per head. When the girls are properly conditioned and "turned out," after marathon rapes by twenty or thirty bikers, they are sent to work the streets or rented out to massage parlors where proprietors live in fear of offending their local gang. With the merger of gang mentality and occult philosophy seen in some areas, the national cult-vice network suggested by some investigators may be an es-tablished fact.

MULTIPLE PERSONALITY DISORDER

Widely popularized by dramatic films like *Sybil* and *The Three Faces of Eve*, multiple personality disorder (MPD) is a psychiatric condition in which alternate personalities—called "alters"—are generated by the mind to protect an individual from psychic trauma, trauma frequently associated with prolonged abuse in early childhood. In extreme cases, hundreds of alters may be identified, including personalities of both sexes and all races. (Even nonhuman alters, such as dogs and cats, have been recorded in rare instances.) Treatment of MPD typically involves long-term psychotherapy, with extensive use of hypnosis to "reintegrate" the several personalities as one cohesive whole.

MPD may be fairly described as the psychiatric "growth industry" of modern times. First recognized in the wake of World War II, an estimated five hundred cases had been diagnosed by 1979. Seven years later, at least five thousand bona fide MPD patients were recognized, with female victims outnumbering men by a 9-to-1 ratio. Regardless of sex or race, however, the root causes of MPD are remarkably consistent, as described by Dr. Frank Putnam in a 1989 survey of MPD cases.

> I am struck by the quality of extreme sadism that is frequently reported by most MPD victims. Many multiples have told me of being sexually abused by groups of people, of being forced into prostitution by family members, or of being offered as sexual enticement to their mothers' boyfriends. After one has worked with a number of MPD patients, it becomes obvious that severe, sustained, and repetitive child abuse is a major element in the creation of MPD.

Over the past decade, psychotherapists across America have also noted persistent, specific references to satanic ritual abuse from many of their MPD patients. In Kansas City, Dr. Al Sarno reports that thirty-five of his patients have been active in demonic cults, either as victims or abusers. From Huntington Beach, California, Dr. Timothy Maas describes two-thirds of those he counsels as victims of childhood sexual abuse, with "a fair percentage" specifying satanic rituals. At least two psychiatrists—Chicago's Bennett Braun and

Kathy Snowden, in Virginia—report death threats from cultists, linked to their treatment of MPD victims. Dr. Braun's own survey of 250 therapists active in MPD work reveals that some twenty-five percent—an estimated 63 psychiatrists nationwide—have at least one patient claiming abuse by demonic cults.

In his book *Satan's Children,* New York psychiatrist Robert Mayer relates the case histories of five MPD patients, two men and three women, who professed backgrounds of satanic ritual abuse in childhood. Their memories—including references to human sacrifice, blood drinking, child pornography, "magical surgery," and cult use of "breeders" to generate sacrificial infants—are remarkably consistent, not only with each other, but with tales related by dozens of children in recent sex abuse cases across the United States and Canada. Of Mayer's five patients, one committed suicide, and four were successfully "reintegrated" through therapy. One of the four survivors finally recanted her satanic memories, blaming them on exaggeration of sexual abuse inflicted by her father and several of his friends—an explanation which skeptics like criminologist Robert Hicks would apply to *all* MPD patients—but three others remained steadfast in their memories of ritual assault. Dr. Mayer, for the record, believes their memories are accurate.

The most alarming aspect of this strange phenomenon, reported by Dr. Mayer's patients and others, is the assertion that Satanists *deliberately* create "alters," employing specific forms of torture to produce desired personalities. Thus, one alter may present a "normal" face at school, while others are amenable to bestiality or murder, child pornography or prostitution. Sadly, work with adult victims of child abuse rarely yields much in the way of evidence suitable for criminal prosecutions. Parents die, evidence disappears, memories blur, and statutes of limitation expire, leaving detectives with nowhere to turn. Until such time as graves are found, remains identified and linked to a specific cause of death, the controversy over MPD's occult/satanic roots will be a topic for the academic lecture circuit, rather than a court of law. [See: Child Abuse]

MURDER: See HUMAN SACRIFICE; SERIAL MURDER

NATIONAL RENAISSANCE PARTY

A small neo-Nazi group founded by James Madole and based in New York City, the NRP actively recruited members of the Ku Klux Klan and the American Nazi Party. In July 1963, Madole and two of his followers served ten days in jail following a brawl with blacks at a New York restaurant; a search of their truck revealed weapons, including several knives, an ax, and a crossbow. The party was embarrassed in 1965, when members Dan Burros and Robert Burros (no relation) were identified as Jews; Dan Burros, then a leader of the KKK in New York state, committed suicide to purge his "shame." In July 1967, an NRP rally at the Newburgh, New York, courthouse touched off two days of black rioting, with seventy persons arrested. A year later, the *NRP Bulletin* headlined Madole's formal alliance with delegates from the Minutemen, the National Socialist White People's Party, and Roy Frankhouser's Pennsylvania Klan to form a so-called United Racist Front.

Thus far, there was little to distinguish Madole's party from any of a dozen other Nazi splinter groups across the country, but a new twist, in the early 1970s, was seen in the NRP's drift toward Satanism. Two Michigan-based cults, the Order of the Black Ram and the Shrine of the Little Mother, openly courted Madole, adopting his anti-Semitic doctrines as their own. Anton LaVey, from the Church of Satan, was also approached by Madole, but accounts of his reaction vary: LaVey asserts that he rejected any link with Nazism, while a rival Satanist—the Temple of Set's Michael Aquino—recalls LaVey's visiting NRP headquarters in New York and accepting a membership card from Madole. Madole, meanwhile, erected a large satanic altar in his New York apartment, offered LaVey's publications for sale through the NRP newsletter, and played selections from LaVey's "Satanic Mass" record at party gatherings. Occult transfusions failed to save the shrinking NRP, however, and it finally vanished in the late 1970s. [See: Nazism; Order of the Black Ram; Shrine of the Little Mother]

NAZISM

The public history and genocidal horror of Adolf Hitler's Germany are too well known for repetition here, but most students of the Third Reich ignore the significant—some say pivotal—links between Nazism and the occult. In fact, the bizarre merger of ritual and racism continues to the present day, and we ignore it at our peril.

The occult roots of German fascism are traceable to the mid–nineteenth century, when Guido von List began flavoring his worship of "Wotan" and other Nordic deities with heavy helpings of Teutonic racism. By 1875, von List and his disciples had found an emblem for their superstitious bigotry, adopting the swastika, which had previously served as an innocuous decoration from ancient Grecian pottery to Hindu texts and the rock paintings of Native American tribes. By 1908, members of the Guido von List Society had spread throughout western Europe, carrying the message of a Nordic master race spawned by ancient magicians.

A year earlier, German occultist Georg Lanz von Liebenfels had founded his own Ordo Novi Templi—the Order of New Templars—to put a racial twist on the old Knights Templar legend. A friend and fellow traveler of Guido von List, by 1909 von Liebenfels was advocating imprisonment and forced sterilization of "socially inferior elements" such as Jews, "mongrel" races, and mental defectives. One of von Liebenfels's early admirers was a young man of dubious ancestry named Adolf Hitler, who dropped by the ONT office in 1909 for a personal conference with his mentor. Only one meeting between Hitler and von Liebenfels has been documented, but there is reason to suspect a more enduring association. Years later, in 1932, von Liebenfels wrote to an ONT recruit that "Hitler is one of our pupils. You will one day experience that he, and through him we, will one day be victorious and develop a movement that will make the world tremble."

Other mystic skeletons in the Nazi closet include two secret fraternities known as the German Order and the Thule Society. Founded by Theodor Fritsch in 1912, the German Order offered a strain of "pure Nordic" occultism to counter the menace of "Jewish" Freemasonry, conducting rituals with its members dressed in white robes and Viking helmets, their leader brandishing the sacred "spear of Wotan." When Fritsch went to his reward in 1933, Nazi newspapers mourned the passing of "the old Teacher," but his beliefs went marching on, in lockstep—or goose step—with the racist drivel preached by von List and von Liebenfels.

The Thule Society, meanwhile, was created in 1917, with World War I still in progress. Its founder, Walter Nauhaus, was a wounded veteran and a member of the German Order who adopted a curved swastika with sword and wreath as his society's official emblem. Generally regarded as a front group or recruiting body for the German Order, the Thule Society created an activist Workers' Political Circle in November 1918. Two months later, Circle leaders organized the German Workers' Party—a right wing, anti-Semitic body which later added "National Socialist" to its title, thereby becoming the Nazi Party. Adolf Hitler joined the movement in mid-1919, while other early recruits included occultists and sexual deviates in roughly equal numbers. Another Thulist group, the German Socialist Party, officially merged with the Nazis in the summer of 1922, and Marthe Kuenzel—head of the German Ordo Templi Orientis and a confidante of Rudolf Hess—introduced Hitler to the writings of Aleister Crowley in 1927. Sadly for Kuenzel, her personal devotion to Hitler as the satanic messiah or "magical child" did not prevent der Führer from banning the OTO a few years later. As Hitler later described the relationship of his own cult to its competitors—

All the supposed abominations, the skeletons and death's heads, the coffins and the mysteries, are mere bogeys for children. But there is one dangerous element, and that is the element I have copied from them. They form a sort of priestly nobility. They have developed an esoteric doctrine not merely formulated, but imparted through the symbols and mysteries in degrees of initiation. The hierarchical organization and the initiation through symbolic rites, that is to say, without bothering the brain but by working on the imagination through magic and the symbols of a cult, all this is the dangerous element, and the element I have taken over. Don't you see that our party must be of this character? An Order, that is what it has to be—an Order, the hierarchical Order of a secular priesthood.

As a symbol of his new order, Hitler reversed von List's "right-handed" swastika in favor of the "left-handed" version, generally regarded by occultists as a signature of evil on a par with the inverted crucifix. The Nazi battle flag finally approved by Hitler was designed by Friedrich Krohn, a long-standing Thulist and member of the German Order since 1914.

Another early Nazi fascinated by the black arts was Heinrich Himmler, appointed to lead the dreaded SS in 1929. From that vantage point, Himmler sought to create his own pagan religion, adopting ancient runic lightning bolts as the official SS insignia, requiring all initiates to participate in special Wotan-worship ceremonies of his own design. The Wewelsburg castle in Westphalia was renovated by Himmler at a great cost in cash and human lives, serving as the spiritual headquarters of his own Black Order, while strains of occultism riddled the SS from top to bottom. Mystic "scholar" Hermann Wirth was named to head a branch of Himmler's "Ancestral Heritage" division in 1935, his search for Atlantis near the Arctic circle prompting heinous cold-weather experiments on human guinea pigs. Another branch of Himmler's death machine worked steadily researching ancient runes, until the Reich collapsed in 1945.

Philosophy aside, there is compelling evidence that Hitler's personal occult beliefs influenced—or perhaps determined—the outcome of World War II. Der Führer's reliance on astrologers for major policy decisions is well-known, but less attention has been paid to his acceptance of the bizarre "World Ice Theory," a revisionist view of human history promulgated by occultist Hans Horbiger. Scorned by reputable scientists across the board, Horbiger found a safe haven with the Nazis in 1937, when Himmler announced that he was "taking the World Ice Theory under his protection." Some historians believe that Hitler's personal interpretation of the crackpot theory influenced the timing of his Soviet invasion and the otherwise inexplicable delays in his advance on Moscow. In simple terms, it seems Hitler was convinced that strict adherence to a form of cultic mumbo jumbo would persuade the Russian winter to retreat before him, on command.

With such a background, it is no surprise that modern Satanists still find a soft spot in their hearts for Nazi Germany. In the 1960s, New York's neo-facist National Renaissance Party forged links with the Order of the Black Ram and the

Church of Satan, though reports vary on whether or not Anton LaVey accepted membership in the NRP. In any case, LaVey's *Satanic Rituals* incorporate Teutonic ceremonies, along with quotations from Hitler's friend and mentor, Dietrich Eckart. Across the continent, in California, Charles Manson told his followers that "Hitler had the best answer to everything," further describing Hitler as "a tuned-in guy who leveled the karma of the Jews." Michael Aquino, defecting from the Church of Satan to form his own Temple of Set in 1975, visited Himmler's Wewelsburg castle for a private ritual six years later, emerging to write editorials on the "certain unique quality in mankind" which the Nazis displayed. Missouri Satanist Pete Roland, sentenced to life imprisonment for a ritual murder near Joplin, told police: "I thought all the time about Auschwitz. That's what I wanted to do." In New York City, police reports confirm that "Son of Sam" triggerman David Berkowitz "possessed and wore Nazi insignia." According to Berkowitz, he was also a member of a satanic cult that adopted the SS lightning bolt as its insignia, dabbling in numerology with a code that numbered letters of the alphabet from A=100 to Z=125. In that system, numbers assigned to the letters of Adolf Hitler's last name add up to . . . 666. [See: Aquino, Michael; Aryan Brotherhood; Cowan, Frederick; Ku Klux Klan; National Renaissance Party]

NEWBERRY, STEVEN

At age nineteen, obese and careless with his hygiene, Steve Newberry would never be mistaken for a member of the "in-crowd" at his high school in the Joplin, Missouri, suburb of Carl Junction. Still, he aspired to winning friends by imitation, the sincerest form of flattery. When all else failed, he turned to cold, hard cash.

In 1987, the in-crowd at Carl Junction High revolved around seventeen-year-old Jim Hardy, the senior class president. With cronies Ron Clements and Theron ("Pete") Roland, Hardy ruled a clique some wags referred to as the Hardy Boys, but they were far removed from wide-eyed innocence. Behind the thin veneer of campus leadership, Jim Hardy's circle of disciples was immersed in heavy metal music, drugs, sadistic violence—and Satanism.

The religious angle came from Ron Clements, whose earnest readings from *The Satanic Bible* soon graduated into full-blown "hell parties." Death was a favorite topic of conversation in those days, on campus and around the campfire, but Hardy and Roland took the lead in cruel experiments, torturing and killing numerous pets in makeshift rituals contrived as offerings to Lucifer. Skeptics attribute those actions to the same youthful sadism displayed by other felons—serial killers included—but the chicken-egg debate is ultimately pointless. If Hardy and Roland *believed* they were killing in Satan's name, it is not for us to second-guess their motives after the fact. Around campus, meanwhile, the clique terrorized classmates with anonymous death threats, while administrators managed to ignore the facts.

In September 1987, the Hardy Boys began discussing human sacrifice in earnest, six or seven hard-core members earnestly debating candidates. One suggested Steve Newberry, but Jim Hardy rejected the choice, pointing out that Newberry held down a part-time job, spending most of his paycheck on drugs or other party favors for his would-be friends. "I had him in the palm of my hand," Hardy later said of Newberry. "Anything I told him to do, he would do. He practically worshiped me."

One report claims Newberry stole some drugs from the Hardy Boys, thus incurring their wrath, but Steven's adoration for Jim Hardy and company belies the story. According to Hardy himself, the final decision to kill Newberry was more prosaic, even frivolous. One afternoon in October 1987, Ron Clements nudged Hardy in the midst of a boring class and asked if Hardy ever *really* thought of killing someone. As Hardy recalls, "I said yeah, 'cause, you know, we talked about it a lot. And he said, 'Well, let's kill Steve.'"

Accomplishing the deed was something else, however. Targeting their sacrifice for Halloween, the teenage Satanists were foiled when Newberry's family left town for the weekend. On Thanksgiving eve, they invited Steve to help them catch some sacrificial dogs and he accepted, trailing the others into some nearby woods, where an old cistern lay hidden from prying eyes. At the last minute, the would-be killers lost their nerve and called the murder off, but Newberry was already suspicious. At home, his mother told friends that Steve was "obsessed" with the notion that his "friends" meant to do him in.

"Every time we failed," Jim Hardy told the press, "I don't

know what drove us, but we wanted that experience. Me and Pete from killing animals, I think, and Ron just from talking about it. We just had to have that experience. I know it had to spring from Satan."

On Sunday, December 6, Newberry returned to the cistern with Hardy, Roland, and Clements, watching his heroes beat a stray kitten to death before they turned their baseball bats on him. In the midst of the beating, Steven cried out, "Why me, guys?" Ron Clements answered, laughing, "Because it's fun, Steve."

Hardy claimed the honor of delivering the final blows, intoning "Sacrifice to Satan! Sacrifice to Satan!" while he finished off their victim. Newberry's body was dropped in the cistern, but Pete Roland began getting cold feet on the ride home. Suddenly frightened of demonic possession, he made a point of telling Hardy "I didn't kill Steve as a sacrifice to Satan; I did it for personal gratification."

Newberry was missing next day, but his sister overheard the three killers at school, joking about their weekend murder of "a fat guy." Police were on the case by sundown, grilling suspects, and Pete Roland was the first to confess. As the investigation spread, it turned up links between the Hardy Boys and other satanic groups in Missouri, including a gang called the Midnight Angels and a shadowy group of adults who simply dubbed themselves "The Crowd." Detectives were suddenly swamped with reports of mutilated pets, satanic graffiti, and chanting figures in the woods—none of it reported earlier because Carl Junction's residents dismissed the incidents as pranks or "someone else's business."

Nearly a year after the murder of Steve Newberry, all three defendants were convicted and sentenced to finish their natural lives behind bars. Closing the case was a different matter, though, with responsible adults working overtime to assess blame. As Principal Ray Dykens remarked from Carl Junction High, "It was right under a lot of people's noses, evidently, and nobody noticed it, or if they did, nobody took it seriously." [See: "Crowd, The"; Human Sacrifice]

NEWELL, PATRICK MICHAEL

At age twenty, Patrick Newell was considered "a trifle weird" by his friends in Vineland, New Jersey. Immersed in

ritual magic, he enjoyed "collecting ancient spells" and sometimes tried them out in gruesome ceremonies, placing hamsters in a nail-studded box and shaking them until their flesh
was shredded, chanting prayers to Satan all the while. Another form of sacrifice, described by a teenage eyewitness,
was reported in the local press.

> He had a triangular chart on a piece of paper that he put
> down on the floor inside a circle. In the corners of the tri-
> angle he placed fake animal skulls with candles burning in-
> side them. Then, from a small case, he took two hamsters.
> He held one in each hand and said an incantation. He
> screamed as loud as he could and squashed the hamsters
> with his hands. One moment they were squealing; the next
> they were dead. He rubbed the blood on his arms and gave
> a closing incantation.

Newell's occult studies convinced him that immortality lay
within his grasp if he was willing to make the ultimate sacrifice. By his calculations, any Satanist murdered by his own
friends was automatically reborn as a "captain of devils,"
commanding forty legions of fallen angels. In early July
1971, Newell approached two friends—star high school athletes Richard Williams, eighteen, and Wayne Sweikert,
seventeen—and asked them, "Why don't you kill me? Then
I can join the devil."

Some blamed drugs for what followed; others, including
attorneys for Williams and Sweikert, insist the boys never
took Newell's request seriously. In any case, they joined him
on a drive to Clear Pond, in southern New Jersey, where the
duo followed Newell's instructions to bind his hands and feet
with adhesive tape. On the command "Proceed, as friends,"
they pushed him in the pond—insisting, later, that they both
thought Newell would free himself and call the whole thing
off. Instead, he sank and drowned, three days elapsing before
his body was recovered.

Williams and Sweikert were held without bond on murder
charges, ministers affiliated with their defense claiming a local cult membership of fifty to one hundred teenage Satanists
in Vineland. Police fixed the number of hard-core cultists
closer to a dozen, with a larger group of curiosity seekers assembling to watch mystic rituals. In the woods near Clear
Pond, detectives found a lean-to Newell had built, marked

with the words "I'll be back." So far, the young Satanist has not made good on his boast.

NGOC VAN DANG

On July 21, 1987, police in Weldon, North Carolina, were approached by two drifters who spun a tale of gruesome homicide in Orlando, Florida, far to the south. Daniel Paul Bowen and Elizabeth Rebecca Towne claimed they were witnesses to the crime, held at gunpoint and threatened by the killers before they were finally freed with the gift of their lives. The murder was a day old, and authorities might have a chance to catch the killers if they hurried.

Urgent phone calls burned up the line between Weldon and Orlando, where no similar crimes were on file. Weldon detectives bought their informants a pair of bus tickets on July 22, but the Greyhound was short two passengers on arrival. By that time, though, investigators had a local address for the pair, and both were soon in custody, less thrilled about the prospect than they had been yesterday. Reluctantly, they led police into neighboring Volushia County, where a body was discovered. Victim Ngoc Van Dang, age twenty-five, lay with his mouth, wrists, and ankles taped. He had been shot seven times, and an inverted cross had been carved on his abdomen.

As seventeen-year-old Elizabeth Towne reconstructed the crime, she and Bowen had gone riding with two other friends, named Tony and Bunny, on July 20. Tony was driving a stolen car with pistols and knives on the front seat, Bunny toying with one of the guns and pointing it toward her backseat companions in a threatening manner. Once they were out in the country, Tony stopped the car and released an Oriental from the trunk, relieving him of cash and a bank card before Bunny carved the satanic cross on his stomach. Afterward, Tony and Bunny took turns shooting the man, one or the other keeping Towne and Bowen covered all the while. The killers then fled in their victim's car, with Towne and Bowen hitchhiking north.

Dan Bowen, twenty-three, told the same basic story, but police were skeptical. A round of "good cop/bad cop" quickly broke him down, and homicide investigators heard a rather different version of the crime. Triggerman Tony Hall, twenty-five, was an old cell mate of Bowen's from state prison, and they had lately renewed their friendship in Orlando. Bunny Nicole Dixon, seventeen, knew Elizabeth Towne from time spent in a juvenile detention home. All four had kidnapped Ngoc Van Dang, intending to steal his cash and car, but things got out of hand. Bunny, a Satanist, had dreamed up the plan with help from a Ouija board and tortured their victim by carving his stomach, after which he was riddled with bullets. Hall and Dixon took off in the car, planning to join a carnival, while Bowen and Towne were "pissed" at being left behind. Their anger drove them to police, and finally to jail.

On August 1, two boys in Salem, Arkansas, were stopped by police while joyriding in Ngoc Dang's car. They had obtained the vehicle from Bunny Dixon, who was staying with a relative, and they had also dropped Tony Hall on the nearest state highway, thumbing north toward Springfield, Missouri. While Salem police bagged Dixon, Missouri officers were alerted to Hall's itinerary, and he was captured late that night, in Howell County. A search of Ngoc Dang's car turned up ammunition, several knives, and Bunny Dixon's well-thumbed copy of *The Satanic Bible*. Acquaintances confirmed Dixon's reputation as a devil worshiper, reporting that she often spoke of having sex with Satan so that she could "bear the Antichrist."

Back in Volushia County, Florida, Hall was convicted of first-degree murder and sentenced to death on March 22, 1989. Danny Bowen was also convicted, on May 4, and sentenced to life. Bunny Dixon and Elizabeth Towne pleaded guilty to charges of second-degree murder; Dixon was sentenced to fifty years imprisonment, while Towne drew a term of seventeen years.

NOBLE, MICHELLE and DOVE, GAYLE STICKLER

Sexual abuse was the last thing on a young El Paso, Texas, mother's mind one afternoon in February 1985, when she put her three-year-old son to bed for his usual nap. The boy seemed nervous, telling his mother he wanted to talk about something, but his behavior suddenly shifted from anxious to downright bizarre. As described under oath by his mother, the boy pulled down his underwear and "started grabbing his penis and his testicles and squeezing them real hard. He was acting like he was in some kind of trance, like he didn't know I was there anymore. He started saying, 'This is what they did at school. This is what Miss Mickey and Miss Dove did.' And then he reached for his hiney. He got an erection and started hollering at me to get some pennies. He poked them very hard at the end of his penis."

"School" was a day-care facility at the nearby East Valley YMCA. "Miss Mickey" and "Miss Dove" were members of the staff, identified as thirty-four-year-old Michelle ("Mickey") Noble and forty-year-old Gayle Stickler Dove. In addition to the original display of genital fondling, the child also told his mother, "When I'm a bad boy, Miss Dove and Miss Mickey kiss my pee-pee." According to the boy, both women also "stuck their finger in my hiney, and it hurt." Later revelations included charges of child pornography, with the camera described as "a big one that Miss Mickey held on her shoulder."

As authorities pursued their investigation, they found a total of eight children—six girls and two boys—who described incidents of sexual abuse or other aberrant behavior, usually performed at Noble's house, where her class ended up after going for "walks to the park." The victims described as many as ten adults watching or participating in acts of abuse, some of them men dressed in werewolf costumes which were used specifically to terrorize the children. The young witnesses described being fondled, participating in oral sex and licking the breasts of "Miss Mickey" or "Miss Dove," bathing with adults or each other, and suffering through the insertion of fingers or foreign objects into their rectums and genitals. On more than one occasion, the children reported, they were forced to urinate or defecate before a camera, receiving swats from a plastic tennis racquet when they were unable to perform on command. Aside from werewolf costumes, occult paraphernalia reported by the children included skeletons, a cauldron, robes, and knives. (Despite these stories, police managed to "complete" their investigation without ever searching Noble's home for evidence.)

At a glance, it would seem that Noble and Dove were remarkably careless in selection of their victims. Parents of the eight children included an FBI agent, a U.S. Border Patrol officer, a retired El Paso policeman, and four past or present

YMCA staff members. Silence was reportedly insured by threats of death at the hands of "the Big Bad Wolf" or a sinister "chainsaw man." The threats seemed real enough, the children said, because they had also witnessed the sacrificial murders of an infant and an adult male.

Noble and Dove were indicted in October 1985, with "Miss Mickey" facing trial on twenty-two felony counts, while Dove was accused of six counts. Their cases were separated, and Noble went to trial first, in March 1986. New Texas statutes permitted adults to relate hearsay testimony from children under twelve years of age, and the young victims were also permitted to testify via videotape, without facing the sort of cross-examination that turned California's McMartin Preschool case into a three-ring circus. Convicted on eighteen counts of molestation, Michelle Noble was sentenced to life imprisonment plus 311 years, the longest term imposed for child abuse in Texas history. On October 29, 1986, Gail Dove was convicted on all six counts, drawing three life terms plus an additional 60 years.

Parents and prosecutors were jubilant, but the case was far from over. Granted a new trial on appeal, Gail Dove went back to court in March 1987. This time, jurors convicted her on a single count of aggravated battery against a child, the judge imposing a flat twenty-year sentence. That November, an appeals court also ordered a new trial for Michelle Noble, ruling that videotaped testimony from children was an unconstitutional violation of the defendant's right to "confront her accusers." Faced with sixteen felony counts at the start of her second trial, Noble saw five charges dismissed by the judge. On April 10, 1988, she was acquitted on the other eleven counts, emerging from court with a vow to work tirelessly for Gail Dove's freedom.

Following the verdict of acquittal, a spokesmen for the outraged parents told newsmen, "Each and every one of us believes as strongly in our children today as we did three years ago. It is important to understand that sometimes a verdict of not guilty does not imply innocence." That sentiment was apparently shared by the East Valley YMCA, which settled a parental lawsuit out of court, in the amount of $605,000. [See: Child Abuse]

ORDER OF THE BLACK RAM

A Michigan-based spin-off from the Church of Satan, created around 1973, this cult was founded by Satanist Michael Grumbowski, a.k.a. Seth-Klippoth. Strongly influenced by Nazi racial doctrines, Grumbowski borrowed his eclectic doctrines from Anton LaVey, early paganism, and Robert Heinlein's novel *Stranger in a Strange Land*. Affiliated groups have been identified as the satanic Shrine of the Little Mother and New York's neofascist National Renaissance Party. [See: National Renaissance Party; Nazism; Shrine of the Little Mother]

ORDER OF THE GOLDEN DAWN

Founded by a group of British Rosicrucians in 1888, the Order of the Golden Dawn was based on the manuscripts of psychic Fred Hockley and mystic elements borrowed from the declining Theosophical Society, once led by Madame Helena Blavatsky. A merger of the Hebrew Kabbalah and Eastern mysticism dubbed "Western magick," the OGD's philosophy appealed primarily to literary figures of the day, including poet William Butler Yeats and such authors of supernatural fiction as Algernon Blackwood, Bram Stoker, Arthur Machen, and Sax Rohmer. After putting down roots in London, the society soon expanded to include chapters in Paris, Edinburgh, Bradford, and Weston-super-Mare.

By 1897, the OGD was dominated by founding member Samuel MacGregor Mathers, pursuing a belief in the mysterious "Secret Chiefs" who supposedly control mankind's destiny from their stronghold in the Far East. A year later, the order attracted its most famous member in the person of Aleister Crowley, but Crowley's instant personality clash with Mathers led to a kind of civil war within the ranks, each man launching "psychic attacks" on the other over a period of years. Crowley's defection to the rival Ordo Templi Orientis failed to end the feud, and he publicly claimed credit for Mathers's death—allegedly produced by means of a magic curse—in 1918.

Some historians claim that the OGD "broke up" soon after Mathers died, but a New Reformed Orthodox Order of the Golden Dawn was organized in San Francisco during 1968.

New covens were propagated through the early 1970s, largely relying on rituals borrowed from Gardenerian Wicca. An off-shoot called The Foundation was reported active in Houston, Texas, in 1985. The group's "sacred texts" remain in print to-day, offered for sale by a publishing house that still bears the name of the Golden Dawn. [See: Crowley, Aleister]

ORDER OF OSIRUS

Founded by Edward Wharton, a British occultist, in the year 1572, the Osirian Order reached America a century later, when disciples Mary Austin and Anne Brintone settled in Boston. Charged with witchcraft in 1676, the women escaped trial by shelling out ten pounds sterling and vowing to leave the city. Ironically, they moved to Salem, and there organized the New World's first Osirian coven. By 1692, there were thirty-seven functioning covens around New England, but that year's witchcraft panic drove the cult underground for nearly two centuries.

Resurfacing in the 1970s, the "new" Osirian Order was led by Samuel Graves, who shifted cult headquarters to Kearney, Nebraska. Members described themselves as "white" witches, devoted to nature and Pan, the Horned God. Goat skulls were held as sacred objects, and Osirian rites were conducted within a traditional magic circle. Graves authored two books on Osirian ritual, but sparse publicity and a flat five-dollar membership fee failed to draw many recruits. In 1985, J. Gordon Melton's *Encyclopedia of American Religions* described the Osirian Order as defunct, and yet . . .

Two years later, Alabama state troopers arrested drifter William Schmidt on a warrant alleging federal firearms violations. At the time of his arrest, Schmidt was driving a pickup truck with a hose linking the exhaust pipe to a camper shell in back, thus creating an effective mobile gas chamber. The suspect's single piece of jewelry was an amulet forged in the shape of a pentagram, one side marked with astrological signs, while the flip side simply read: THE OSIRIAN OR-DER.

A dated relic, perhaps . . . or perhaps not. Authorities suspected Schmidt of running weapons for the neo-Nazi Posse Comitatus, which boasts a strong following in Nebraska. In 1984, posse member Arthur Kirk died in a shootout with police at Cairo, thirty miles northeast of Osirian headquarters in Kearney. Throughout the state, right wing "survivalists" have rallied to the posse banner, some mixing reactionary politics with bizarre occult doctrines. One such "patriotic" cult, raided by police at Rulo, Nebraska, in 1985, counted wife swapping, bestiality, and child murder among its rites.

In addition to gunrunning, William Schmidt was suspected of multiple murders, with victims including two of his wives. Arizona police suspected him of poisoning his latest spouse in 1990, but they lost their chance to file charges when Schmidt was found dead in a Phoenix motel room. As for the Osirian Order whose symbol he wore in life, there is at least a chance that it survives today.

ORDER OF THE RAINBOW

Striving to recapture control of his disintegrating "family," Charles Manson created this new "religion"—also dubbed "nuness"—in early 1974. Specific colors were assigned to past and present family disciples, coordinated with Manson's vision of "the spectrums of light in thought." Thus, Lynette "Squeaky" Fromme became red, Sandra Good was dubbed blue, Susan Atkins was violet, Leslie Van Houten green, Patricia Krenwinkle yellow, and so forth. (The latter trio publicly rejected Manson and his "church," prompting Squeaky to call them the "Suckatash Sisters"—Squash, Corn, and Bean.)

According to Manson, speaking from prison through Fromme, the new sect would have seven degrees of initiation, including witch, queen, goddess, alikeen, and three more to be christened at a later date, if anyone progressed that far. Manson also ordered Squeaky to "Make a new clock divided into four or six parts. Morning is red, noon is gold, afternoon is green, the evening is blue, and the night is sleep time." As Fromme elaborated the sect's ideals in May 1974, "One degree in nuness can be gotten by sleeping in an open grave at the graveyard. No violence. Only completion of the old Christian fears."

Despite some halfhearted recruiting efforts in northern California, membership in "nuness" was apparently restricted to Fromme and Sandy Good, sharing low-rent digs on P street, in Sacramento. A year later, both women were jailed—Good for extortion, Fromme for attempting to kill President Gerald Ford—and the last, pathetic gasp of Mansonism died away. [See: Manson "Family"]

ORDER OF THELEMA

Based in San Diego, California, this ritual magic "study group" rejects the Ordo Templi Orientis while revering Aleister Crowley and his "sacred" writings. Members believe that Crowley still operates close to the earthly plane of existence, keeping in touch with the Order of Thelema ("will") by psychic means. Rituals are lifted from Crowley's *Book of the Law,* and membership—presumed to be minute—is kept a secret. [See: Crowley, Aleister; Ordo Tempi Orientis]

ORDO TEMPLI ASTARTE

Based in Pasadena, California, this ritual magic society traces its history to Aleister Crowley through disciple Louis Culling, who claimed to possess Crowley's charter for an autonomous lodge. Now deceased, Culling allegedly passed the charter on to current OTA leaders, but it is not available for inspection.

Born of a rift in Crowley's parent organization, the modern OTA claims to preserve "the secret rituals of the Ordo Templi Orientis in Crowley's original holographs." Magic is defined by the group's leaders as a "system of ritual hypnotic induction (conjuration) that calls upon archetypal forms from the unconscious (evocation) and allows them to be visualized from the frankly psychotherapeutic to the more abstract system research and development."

Obtuse language has failed to swell the OTA ranks, however. A second lodge in Pittsburgh, Pennsylvania, failed to survive the 1970s, and California membership has not topped fifty in the past ten years.

ORDO TEMPLI ORIENTIS

Founded in 1902 by German occultist Karl Kellner, the OTO claims a direct spiritual link to the original Knights

Templar, with all of that order's mystical trappings intact. Never one for understatement, Kellner assured his followers that "Our Order possesses the KEY which opens up all Masonic and Hermetic secrets, namely, that teaching of sexual magic, and this teaching explains, without exception, all the secrets of Freemasonry and all systems of religion."

Be that as it may, the secret of longevity eluded Kellner, and he died three years after organizing the OTO, replaced by disciple Theodor Reuss. The order expanded under new management, planting chapters in Denmark, France, and England. Sexual magic was especially appealing to Aleister Crowley, who took over leadership of the British OTO in 1912, soon adding a homosexual "eleventh degree" to his branch of the order. Doctrinal differences led to a rift with the German home office in 1916, but Crowley later patched up the relationship, succeeding Reuss as international chief of the OTO in 1924.

Meanwhile, black magic had bridged the Atlantic, with OTO disciple C.S. Jones—a.k.a. "Frater Achad"—planting chapters in Los Angeles, Washington, D.C., and Vancouver, British Columbia. Crowley himself visited the Vancouver "lodge" in 1915, there meeting Winifred Smith—"Frater 132"—and giving him permission to start a new lodge of his own. Fired up with evangelical zeal, Smith took off for Hollywood, where he set in motion a chain of events that were bizarre, even by OTO standards.

Newly appointed by Crowley as Frater Achad's replacement to head the North American OTO, Smith got things rolling with a bang in Hollywood, luring celebrities to special invitation-only "Gnostic Masses," typically featuring Smith's heroic attempt to have sex with as many new women as possible. No one seemed to mind that Smith's Agape Lodge was little more than a front for group sex; if anything, that may have been the Hollywood OTO's main selling point. One of the women Smith seduced was the wife of disciple John Parsons, an explosives expert at the California Institute of Technology and Smith's ultimate successor as head of the lodge. Apparently untroubled by his wife's infidelity, Parson's took up with his sister-in-law, soon rising to dominance in the lodge and moving it to his Pasadena home, whereupon he renamed it the Church of Thelema. By March 1946, Parsons was involved in a series of sexual experiments with his lover and new recruit L. Ron Hubbard. As described by Aleister

Crowley: "Apparently Parsons or Hubbard or somebody is producing a moonchild. I get fairly frantic when I contemplate the idiocy of these louts."

The "moonchild" failed to materialize, but Hubbard made good all the same, skipping town with Parsons's mistress and some $10,000 in OTO funds, rolling on to found his own Church of Scientology a few years later. In 1947, Crowley's life of drug addiction and debauchery came to an end, with leadership of the OTO passing to Karl Johannes Germer, living in California since his 1941 expulsion from Germany. Parsons, meanwhile, busied himself with a "black pilgrimage," changing his name to "Belarian Armiluss Al Dajjaj Antichrist." As he wrote in his private journal: "I am pledged that the work of the Beast 666 [Crowley] shall be fulfilled, and the way for the coming of BABALON be made open and I shall not cease until these things are accomplished." In fact, Parsons ceased four years later, vaporized at age thirty-seven in the explosion of his basement laboratory, where he bootlegged nitroglycerine for private sale.

An American offshoot of the OTO, founded in Chicago during 1931, was the Choronzon Club, also dubbed the Great Brotherhood of God. Led by OTO veteran C.F. Russell, who once studied with Crowley at the Abbey of Thelema, the splinter group came full circle when defector Louis Culling rejoined the San Diego OTO, en route to formation of his own Ordo Templi Astarte. As recently as 1988, the "Choronzon" label was still being used by an authorized OTO lodge in Sydney, Australia.

Elderly Karl Germer went to his reward in 1962, creating a power vacuum that sharply divided the OTO. In Switzerland, Karl Metzger aspired to the throne, but his rule was disputed in England by Kenneth Grant, and in America by Californian Grady McMurtry, a member of the old Agape Lodge who possessed several letters from Crowley, supporting McMurtry's candidacy. The letters were enough for most of the OTO faithful, and McMurtry carried the day, though Grant persisted in his opposition from England, while a renegade chapter in Roanoke, Virginia, followed the leadership of Robert E.L. Shell. Under McMurtry's guidance, the OTO experienced dramatic growth, expanding throughout the United States and into several other countries. At McMurtry's retirement in 1982, a new—and anonymous—leader was elected by ranking disciples, with the OTO headquarters shifting from Berkeley, California, to New York City. By 1988, the order claimed forty-eight chapters in the United States, nine in Canada, two each in Australia, Norway, and West Germany, with one each in England, France, Guadaloupe, New Zealand, and Yugoslavia.

While the OTO officially denies any link with criminal activity, various lodges and individual members have been tied to crimes ranging from child abuse and drug running to ritual murder. One "renegade" faction, the so-called Solar Lodge, was organized in southern California during the mid-1960s by Richard Brayton, a professor of philosophy at USC, and his kooky wife Georgina. Devoted to the prospect of a coming race war between black and white, Georgina sent her disciples as far as Utah and New Mexico in search of desert hideouts, where the faithful could lie low and weather the storm. One such bastion, acquired by the cult in 1966, was a ranch near Blythe, California. The Solar Lodge derived its income from bookstores in Blythe and Los Angeles, a cult-owned service station in L.A., and sale of drugs allegedly procured from contacts inside the USC medical school. Within the cult, Georgina enforced discipline with an iron hand, commanding that one disciple slash his own arms each time he experienced sexual desire. Another member—a Palm Springs dentist—called in sick one morning and vanished without a trace, his fate unknown to this day. On their desert ranch, the cultists freely indulged in drugs, sacrificed animals, and drank the still-warm blood in mystic rituals.

It was finally Georgina Brayton's love of power that destroyed the Solar Lodge. On May 20, 1969, one of the ranch buildings burned down, with two goats trapped inside. Georgina fixed the blame on six-year-old Anthony Gibbons, first scorching his hands with matches in an effort to make him confess, afterward forcing him to bury the charred goats before he was "beaten all day" by cultists armed with bamboo poles. Still unrepentant, the boy was chained inside a packing crate, exposed to the broiling desert sun from May 23 to July 26, when some visitors noted his plight and called the county sheriff's office. The Braytons and three other cultists escaped before raiders arrived, but eleven OTO members—including Anthony's mother—were arrested at the ranch and later convicted of felony child abuse. The police search also turned up a corpse, apparently dead of an accidental drug overdose. FBI warrants were issued for the Braytons, but they remained at large for a year before surrendering to take their medicine. Months after the fact, multiple informants told author Ed Sanders of the Solar Lodge's ongoing contact with Charles Manson's homicidal "family" through much of 1968 and early 1969. Suspicion remains that Georgina's race-war theory may have inspired Manson's own obsession with apocalyptic "Helter Skelter."

A decade later, in December 1979, police in West Paterson, New Jersey, found the bodies of Howard Green and Carol Marron laid out beside a highway, drained of blood with some instrument resembling a veterinarian's syringe. Both victims were involved in the occult and had specifically informed acquaintances of their attempts to join the OTO. San Francisco police faced a similar riddle in June 1985, with the mutilation-slaying of "John Doe #60." The victim was never identified, but Satanist Clifford St. Joseph was finally convicted of the murder in March 1988. Correspondence with OTO members was found at St. Joseph's home, though no direct proof of his membership in the order was discovered. [See: Crowley, Aleister; Green, Howard; Manson "Family"; St. Joseph, Clifford]

ORDO TEMPLI SATANAS

A short-lived splinter of the Ohio-based Church of Satanic Brotherhood, this cult was organized in 1974 by Joseph Daniels, a.k.a. "Apollonius, priest of Hermopolis." Temples were established in Indianapolis and Louisville, Kentucky, with membership composed primarily of defectors from the parent church. The OTS faithful staged a "memorial service" for CSB founder John DeHaven, after the ex–high priest moved to Florida and announced his conversion to Christianity, but such high jinks cannot sustain a religion, and the movement soon faded away.

OSIRIAN ORDER: See ORDER OF OSIRUS

OUR LADY OF ENDOR COVEN, THE OPHITE CULTUS SATANUS

Predating Anton LaVey's Church of Satan by nearly two decades, this cult was founded in 1948 by Herbert Sloane, a Toledo, Ohio, barber turned fortune-teller. Basing his doctrine on traditional gnosticism, Sloane viewed Satan as a benevolent messenger from God—the earthbound "Demiurge"—sharing divine knowledge with mankind at large. No criminal behavior was ever traced to Sloane's coven, and the tiny group dissolved with his death in the 1980s.

PACEWITZ, MICHAEL

At 6:00 A.M. on March 4, 1990, police in Fullerton, California, received an anonymous call from a man who told them, "I just killed a baby." The caller blurted out an address, then broke the connection, leaving dispatchers to scramble field units in a rush. Patrolmen swarmed the Brentwood apartment building, found the specific apartment unlocked, and charged inside. A nine-month-old infant lay screaming in his crib, but his older sister was silent. Sprawled on a nearby bed, three-year-old Marcelline Onick had been raped before her assailant plunged a knife into her head, throat, and torso forty-four times.

No adults were present at the scene, and it took police several hours to locate Marcelline's mother. Horrified, the woman reported spending the night with friends, leaving her children in the care of an adult male acquaintance. The baby-sitter, meanwhile, told police he bailed out early to rest up for work the next day, after twenty-one-year-old Michael Pacewitz dropped in and agreed to take over the chore of child watching.

Pacewitz was a friend of Marcelline's mother, once her next-door neighbor before she moved to Brentwood. They met in a Bible-study group, Pacewitz hoping to kick his methamphetamine addiction through religion, and while she never thought him dangerous, Marcelline's mother admitted that Michael was odd. For one thing, he liked to drop his pants and "moon" total strangers at every opportunity—at football games, in crowded restaurants, even in church. The quirk had landed him in mental wards on two occasions that she knew of, but antipsychotic medication seemed to muffle the voices Pacewitz heard talking "about God and the devil." From time to time, he also mentioned his desire for a sex change, suspecting that a former girlfriend was trapped inside his body.

Curious indeed, but that was not the half of it. In recent months, religion had become the focal point of Pacewitz's aberration, moving from a brush with Pentecostal "holy rollers" into ardent Satanism. He was also turning violent. Two days prior to Marcelline's murder, he had invaded the home of a female relative, wounding the woman and her boyfriend with a long-bladed knife.

Detained for questioning, Pacewitz freely admitted raping and killing the child. "The devil wanted me to do it for him," he informed detectives. "I'm not sorry, because I wanted to do it. I molested her and killed her." Taking Pacewitz at his word, a jury convicted him of first-degree murder on October 3, 1990. Officially declared sane on October 24, he drew a prison term of twenty-six years to life.

PAINECUR, JOSE LUIS

A five-year-old Indian native of Chile, Jose Painecur was sacrificed to appease the water gods in 1960, after an earthquake and tidal wave ravaged the reservation at Lago Bundi. Two local tribesmen, Juan Panan and Jose Vargas, were charged with flinging Painecur into the sea at Cerro Mesa, and both men swiftly confessed, explaining that they acted under orders from a Mapuche tribal *machi*—sorceress—named Juana Namuncura. Convicted of murder, Panan and Vargas served two years in prison before their release, a new judge ruling that they acted without free will in the killing, "compelled by irresistible psychic force" of ancient beliefs. (Juana Namuncura was never charged in the case.) The curious doctrine remains established law in Chile, where courts have acquitted other confessed practitioners of human sacrifice in modern times. [See: Catrilaf, Juana]

PALO MAYOMBE

Often described as "the dark side of santeria," palo mayombe is actually a distinct and separate religion, traceable to Bantu tribesmen from the Congo region of central Africa. (Santeria, meanwhile, derives from the ju-ju religion practiced by members of the Yoruba tribe.) Both cults recognize a full pantheon of deities, called *orishas,* and both likewise found it expedient to camouflage the practice of their native religion during slavery days by renaming African gods and goddesses after Catholic saints. It is also true that some practitioners attempt to follow *both* religions, erecting separate altars in different parts of their homes, but superficial resemblance between the two cults should not confuse their different goals.

While santeria is frequently advertised as a "Christian" religion, practicing "white"—or, at worst, "gray"—witchcraft, palo mayombe concerns itself primarily with "black" magic, pursued through domination of the dead. There is occasional dissent within the cult, a minority of "white" practitioners describing themselves as "paleros Christianos," but the clear majority are "paleros Judios"—borrowing a bit of Western prejudice to equate their deliberate evil with Jews, who are not baptized in holy water.

In basic terms, paleros seek to manipulate spirits of the dead for their own advantage, believing the dead have power to control the living, either for protection and material advancement of the palero, or to effect the destruction of his enemies. The heart of a palero's presumed power lies in his *nganga,* a "magic" cauldron wherein the practitioner strives to create a miniature universe of death and corruption where souls are sucked in and trapped, compelled to do the palero's bidding. Typical contents of the *nganga* include blood, bones, spices, coins, remains of men and animals, poisonous insects, railroad spikes, and antlers from a deer. Twenty-eight "sacred" sticks protrude from the cauldron and are ritually manipulated to summon the captive spirits, also called *nkisi.* *Palo* is the Spanish word for "stick," hence the name palo mayombe, variously interpreted as "stick magic" or "stick witchcraft."

Before preparing his *nganga,* a palero must meditate, preferably while sitting under a ceiba tree or while wearing a crown of ceiba leaves. When contact has been made with the spirit world, a grave-robbing expedition is organized, with the palero selecting a fresh cadaver—called *kiyumba*—and opening the grave to steal its head, ribs, fingers, toes, and tibia. These items are the key ingredients of the *nganga*, but fresh materials are added over time, including blood, bones, and organs acquired through ritual human sacrifice. As in ju-ju and other Afro-Caribbean cults, death by torture is preferred for sacrificial animals and human beings, so that the spirits are "charged up" with pain and fear when they reach the "other side."

The earliest case of documented human sacrifice by paleros in this century involves the murder of a young Cuban girl in 1903. More recently, Adolfo Constanzo's palo mayombe cult was linked with more than twenty ritual murders around Mexico City and Matamoros between 1987 and 1989. Authorities in Florida, Texas, New Jersey, and California have recovered *ngangas* containing human blood and decomposed remains, but prosecution for murder is rare without a documented cause of death.

Since the late 1960s, palo mayombe has become a favorite religion of Latin American drug dealers, who sincerely believe that specific rituals will make them bulletproof, even invisible to their enemies. The Constanzo cult, in Mexico, was finally exposed when one member drove through a police roadblock without stopping, refusing to believe the officers could see him or his vehicle. There is no reliable census of paleros active in America today, but their number must be significant. Ernesto Pichardo, a priest of the santeria cult, estimated in 1990 that there were two thousand palero priests—called *tata nkisi*, or "father of the spirit"—practicing in Miami, Florida alone. [See: Constanzo, Adolfo; Human Sacrifice; Ju-Ju; Santeria]

PERRY, ARLIS

Saturday nights can be hectic on a college campus, and California's Stanford University is no exception. There are parties in the dorms, all-night keggers on Fraternity Row. For many students, alcohol replaces academics as the top priority on weekends, with a chance to lay the books aside and raise a little hell.

It didn't work that way with Bruce and Arlis Perry, though.

The nineteen-year-old newlyweds from Bismarck, North Dakota, marked their eight-week anniversary on Saturday, October 12, but they were not inclined to squander time on drunken merriment. For one thing, Bruce was barely getting settled in at Stanford's med school; for another, Arlis was a gung ho Christian of the fundamentalist persuasion, known to friends and family as a persistent missionary-type. Husband and wife were both involved with Stanford's Fellowship of Christian Athletes, and Arlis was also a member of Young Life, a student evangelical society. Weekdays, she worked as a receptionist for a Palo Alto law firm, helping cover Bruce's bills.

At half past eleven that night, Arlis told her husband she was stepping out to mail some letters home. Bruce went along to keep her company, but they began to argue on the way back from the mailbox, bickering about whose fault it was they had a flat tire on their car. A trivial dispute, but tempers flared, and they were passing Stanford Memorial Church, around 11:40 P.M., when Arlis told Bruce she wanted some time alone. Steaming, he walked the half mile back to their quarters in Quillen Hall, reserved for married students.

Late-night worshipers remember Arlis entering the chapel around 11:50 P.M., and she was still there when the stragglers left at midnight. Closing time. Ten minutes later, security guard Steve Crawford checked the sanctuary, warned an empty room that it was time to go, and locked the outer doors behind him as he left.

Back at Quillen Hall, Bruce Perry was getting nervous. He walked back to the chapel at 12:15 and found it locked, no sign of Arlis on the premises. Disgusted, with a headache coming on, he went back home to wait. So far, it had not crossed his mind that Stanford had no mail pickup on Sundays; any urgency that Arlis felt to stretch her legs that night had nothing to do with a note to her parents in Bismarck.

The doubts would surface later. Afterward.

At 3:00 A.M., Bruce phoned campus security to report his wife missing. Officers were sent to check the church and found it locked, but they declined to look inside. When Steve Crawford made his next scheduled stop, at 5:30, he found a side door forced open from within. Cautiously, he made his way inside the church ... and walked into a nightmare.

Arlis Perry lay beneath one of the pews, her head aimed toward the sanctuary's altar. She was nude from the waist down, her legs spread wide, blue jeans draped over her thighs upside down, to create a diamond pattern when viewed from above. Her blouse had been ripped open, and an altar candle was wedged between her breasts, held in place by folded arms. Another candle, thirty inches long, protruded from the lips of her vagina. Arlis had been choked and beaten, but the cause of death had been an ice pick buried in her skull behind the left ear.

Police initially suspected Bruce of murdering his wife, suspicion fading once he passed a polygraph exam. Back at the church, witnesses recalled a sandy-haired young man, midtwenties, casual dress, about to enter when the late-night worshipers came out. In Washington, FBI technicians found a perfect palmprint on the candle removed from Arlis's vagina, but it matched none of the prints on file. If nothing else, at least it finally cleared Bruce Perry—and one hundred other suspects culled from local sex-offender lists.

Church spokesmen described the murder as "ritualistic and satanic," but police clung fast to their "sex-nut" hypothesis. Meanwhile, Perry's coworkers at the law firm recalled a curious encounter from October 11. Around noon that Friday, a young man with blondish hair and "regular looks" turned up at the office, engaging Arlis Perry in a fifteen-minute conversation described by witnesses as "serious and intense." Employees had assumed the man was Perry's husband, but a glimpse of Bruce proved otherwise.

Questions had begun to multiply around the case, though local homicide investigators did their best to see and hear no evil. Who was Perry's visitor the day before she died? Could she have planned to meet him and continue their discussion when she left her apartment on Saturday, perhaps staging a fight to rid herself of Bruce when he tagged along unexpectedly?

· Two weeks later, on the eve of Halloween, the mystery moved east. In Bismarck, someone stole a temporary marker from Arlis's grave, no other trace of theft or vandalism in the cemetery. When detectives started asking questions, they ran into rumors of a devil-worship cult in nearby Mandan, with reports that Arlis once had visited the Satanists, endeavoring to save their souls.

And there matters rested for almost exactly four years, until convicted serial killer David Berkowitz smuggled a book on witchcraft out of his New York prison cell. Police lieutenant Terry Gardner, in Minot, North Dakota, received the book on October 23, 1978, as an anonymous package shipped from Manhattan. Thumbing through the pages, Gardner found underlined passages dealing with the Process Church of Final Judgment, a message written in the margin. It read: "Arliss [sic] Perry, Hunted, Stalked And Slain. Followed to California. Stanford Univ."

Around the same time, police in Santa Clara, California, received an anonymous envelope from New Orleans, containing news clips on Berkowitz and the recent death of John Carr, an unindicted suspect in New York's "Son of Sam" murders. If anyone had taken time to check—as newsman Maury Terry later did—they would have found that Arlis Perry died on John Carr's birthday ... which was also Aleister Crowley's birthday ... which was also the fifth anniversary of Charles Manson's arrest in southern California.

Kismet.

On October 25, Berkowitz penned a letter from prison, reading in part:

Look, there are people out there who are animals. There are people who are a fearless lot. They HATE God! I'm not talking about common criminals. You know who I'm talking about.

There are people who will follow a "Chosen Lamb" throughout the ends of the earth. If they feel that this person is the "next one"—well, they have money. They have brains and hate.

They will even kill in a church. Do you think I am joking? Do you think I'm just bending your ear? Well, do this—do this quickly (I'm serious):

Call the Santa Clara Sheriff's office (California). This is by Santa Clara University and close to Stanford University. Please ask one of the sheriffs who have been there since late '74 what happened to ARLISS [sic] PERRY. Remember this name: Arliss Perry!

Please don't let them give you the "Psychopathic Homicidal Maniac" line or something similar. They know *how* she was murdered. They cannot tell you who did it or why. It was NO sex crime, NO random murder.

Ask them *where* she was killed. Ask them how. Ask them how often she wandered into that building of gold, purple, and scarlet.

Please ask them for the autopsy report. Let the police provide you with everything—every little detail. Make them tell you what she went through. Don't let them skip one single perverted atrocity that was committed on her tiny, slender, little body. Let the Santa Clara police tell you all.

Oh, yeah, lastly (and this is important), make sure you ask them where she lived—I mean where she came from. Doing this will solve the whole case. Back in little, tiny B____. This is where the answer lies. The place (state) with the lowest crime rate of anywhere!

Two days later, another letter issued from Berkowitz's cell, hitting on the same theme. It included the following passage:

You know damn well that these Satanists cover their tracks pretty good. You are aware of their intelligence (businessmen, doctors, military personnel, professors, etc.). Cults, as you know, flourish around college campuses. They also flourish around military bases. Drugs flow all over these two places (universities and bases). Young servicemen and young college students are involved in sexual relations. So mix the two of them up. Put them near each other and what do you have? You've got a pretty wild, dedicated and nasty bunch of young, zealous, anti-establishment devil-worshipers. And what a deadly mixture it is. My, my. Didn't Miss Perry wander around the Stanford Campus frequently? Well, start adding, kid. What have we got here?

In fact, Arlis Perry *was* in the habit of roaming Stanford's grounds, though the fact was never publicized. Neither had Berkowitz gained his accurate knowledge of the chapel's color scheme or Perry's "tiny, slender, little body" from four-year-old news clippings. As Maury Terry pressed his investigation of the case, Berkowitz described a New York cult meeting in 1976 or 1977, where a satanic contract killer—later named as William Mentzer—allegedly passed around photos of Perry and delivered "a detailed soliloquy directed at the victim, describing her annihilation."

Terry's search for evidence in North Dakota turned up more than forty witnesses—including undercover policemen—who spoke of a satanic cult operating in Bismarck and

Mandan between 1971 and 1974. At one point, the black-garbed cultists had rented quarters across the street from Arlis Perry's grandmother, and friends were "almost certain" that Arlis attended at least one cult meeting. On the day before Arlis's funeral in Bismarck, some early passersby had spooked a black-caped stranger who seemed bent on breaking into the church.

Another aspect of the mystery, apparently confirming that the sacrifice was planned out in advance, dates back to late September 1974. On September 27, Arlis wrote to an old friend in Bismarck, trying to explain a recent breakdown in communications with the home front.

> I had to laugh about your call to Bruce Perry. Mrs. Perry [Bruce's mother] made the same mistake. She called them, too. But the strange part of it is that his name is not only Bruce Perry but it is Bruce D. Perry, and not only that but it is Bruce Duncan Perry and he attends Stanford University, and he just got married this summer. One thing, his wife's name is not Arlis. Anyway, next time you get the urge to call the number is ———. This time I guarantee you'll get the right Bruce Perry.

As it happened, there were *not* two Bruce Duncan Perrys at Stanford, or anywhere else in the state. Santa Clara police dismissed the event as meaningless, but others disagree. In 1980, Minot newsman Jack Graham was told by a local source that Arlis Perry's murder involved "someone registering at Stanford under a false name." At this writing, the case remains officially unsolved. [See: Berkowitz, David; Carr, John; Mentzer, William; Process Church of Final Judgment]

PORNOGRAPHY

When modern investigators discuss cult-related crime, the subject of illicit income is invariably raised, with reference made to drugs, prostitution, and pornography. In the latter area, police suspect certain satanic and Afro-Caribbean cults of particular involvement with child pornography—a "labor of love," as it were, combining business with pleasure—but skeptics point out that lawmen have had problems making their case in court. Still, a review of the "kiddie porn" scene reveals some compelling evidence of cult involvement, in apparent conjunction with established elements of organized crime.

The first federal statute on child pornography was passed in 1978, forbidding production and sale but ignoring private possession and free exchange. A new law, passed in 1984, prohibited trading of films or photos regardless of price, further lifting the requirement of explicit sexual acts to qualify material as obscene. In 1990, private possession of child pornography was still legal in forty-four states, but the source—at least theoretically—had been eliminated.

In fact, most child pornography found in America comes from Denmark, Sweden, or the Netherlands, where such material is either legal or authorities have chosen to ignore prevailing laws. At the same time, European police assert—and U.S. Customs officials agree—that most of the films and photographs published abroad are actually obtained from American pedophiles in the first place. Stateside distribution has been linked to traditional organized crime, with federal officers pointing fingers of blame at Mafia families in Chicago, New York, and New Jersey.

Where, exactly, do cults figure into the network? By early 1968, Charles Manson's "family" was camped out in the backyard of a wealthy Los Angeles voyeur in Topanga Canyon, allowing their host to film numerous orgies. Manson has privately boasted of his commercial links to a syndicate of underworld pornographers, described by Charlie as "an elite bunch that was worldwide." Investigators also link the Tate-LaBianca massacre to a combination of drugs and pornography, with actor Dennis Hopper noting of the victims: "They had fallen into sadism and masochism and bestiality—and they recorded it all on videotape, too." A police search of the Tate murder scene recovered sex tapes of Roman Polanski and wife Sharon Tate, while Manson himself asked an interviewer, in 1987: "Don't you think those people deserved to die? They were involved with kiddie porn."

Allegations of pornography are also routine in various cases involving alleged ritual child abuse, with similar charges reported from Canada and all across the United States. Prosecutors have yet to obtain the alleged incriminating tapes, but their failure seems more a matter of police negligence than blind wishful thinking. In Jordan, Minnesota, and Dade County, Florida, quantities of porn and videocassettes were observed at the homes of indicted suspects, but the evidence vanished while police delayed their requests for search warrants. Elsewhere, in Ontario and in El Paso, Texas, police—for reasons best known to themselves—never got around to searching suspect premises at all. Significantly, children from Los Angeles and Reno, Nevada—while never in contact with one another—have reported being photographed in a game their abusers called "Naked Movie Star," complete with identical rhyming songs. It is also worth noting that the allegations raised by four- and five-year-olds are replicated in the memories of adult cult survivors, with reports of cult-related child pornography dating back to the 1960s and beyond.

On the East Coast, "Son of Sam" triggerman David Berkowitz has told prison confidants that "the key" to his satanic cult in Queens, New York, "is through drug and porn connections." The 1985 New York rape-murder case of reputed Satanist John Kogut also involved allegations of pornography, but authorities were stymied when a key witness "committed suicide"—with a disappearing shotgun. Three years later, officers of the New Jersey Port Authority were investigating a child pornography ring in the Garden State when they uncovered a santeria altar, with prayers inscribed to secure divine protection for the illegal racket. A pot of human blood was also found, and while police suspect that it was drained from one of the small "movie stars"—still missing at this writing—no murder indictments were possible without more substantial proof. [See: Drugs; Prostitution; Slavery; "Snuff" Films]

PROCESS CHURCH OF FINAL JUDGMENT

No satanic cult in modern times has enjoyed a more sinister reputation or been linked with more sensational crimes than the Process, created by Robert and Mary Ann DeGrimston in 1963 and officially dissolved twelve years later. So powerful was the group's aura of evil, so pervasive its underworld contacts, that tales of resurgence, revival, and reconstitution still circulate, nearly two decades after the cult's disappearance from public view.

Shanghai-born in 1935, Robert DeGrimston Moore was the son of a British engineer, the grandson of a vicar. Returned to England in his first year of life, by 1963 he was an advanced student at London's Hubbard Institute of Scientology, when he met Mary Anne MacLean in one of his classes. Four years older than Robert, Mary Anne could boast of a colorful past that included a brief engagement to boxer Sugar Ray Robinson and a fling at prostitution, putting her on the fringes of the John Profumo–Christine Keeler affair. The two Scientologists hit it off at once, finding themselves so well attuned that they soon split from L. Ron Hubbard's cult, founding their own "therapy" group under the title of "Compulsion Analysis." By 1964, the original label had been discarded in favor of a new, suitably mystical name: "The Process."

As with Scientology, Process "therapy" cloaked itself in religious trappings, with new recruits surrendering a major portion of their worldly goods to Robert and Mary Anne DeGrimston. (Mary Anne had nixed the surname "Moore" as much too common for her taste.) In essence, followers were offered a choice of deities: Jehovah called for strict obedience and sexual abstinence, while Lucifer encouraged his followers to party at will. Ardent Jehovans resorted to self-flagellation at times, to expiate their real or imagined sins, and Mary Anne DeGrimston especially enjoyed the disciplinarian side of cult management, giving free rein to what sociologist William Bainbridge has charitably called her "control perspective." In fact, as described by other students of the cult, Process members were actively encouraged to grovel in fear before the DeGrimstons, addressing them as "God" and "Goddess."

By March 1966, the cult had sufficient funds to lease a mansion in London's Mayfair district, the DeGrimstons moving in with some twenty-five disciples and a pack of German shepherd dogs—each canine possessing its own cult title, pursuant to a special doggy oath. The digs were sumptuous, but England had begun to feel a trifle small to the DeGrimstons. Robert was already cultivating his hair and beard in a fair impersonation of Christ, while Mary Anne variously called herself "Hecate," "Circe," "the Oracle," or the reincarnation of Nazi propaganda minister Josef Goebbels.

That June, the DeGrimstons, their wolf pack, and a select team of disciples embarked for Nassau in the Bahamas. Six weeks later, they surfaced in Yucatan, Mexico, founding a commune near the coastal fishing village of Sisal. They called the place "Xtul," creating a whole nonsense lexicon of "magic" words starting with "X," taking their dogs for long walks on the beach between rituals. It was there, in Mexico, that Robert DeGrimston picked up a third deity in the person of Satan, meanwhile formally adopting the title of Christ for himself. The commune survived a hurricane in late September 1966, but British attorneys showed up on the scene two months later, hired by the families of Process recruits to liberate three brainwashed members.

Momentarily daunted by their latest clash with the "gray forces" ruling earthly society, the Processeans moved back to London. They spruced up the Mayfair mansion, opened a coffeehouse, and made determined efforts to convert members of such rock bands as the Beatles and the Rolling Stones. When that fell through, Robert and Mary Anne—now billing themselves as "The Omega"—launched a tour of Greece, Israel, and Turkey in April 1967. Somehow, they wound up in Miami, Florida, and by August they had put down roots in New Orleans, operating under cover of a three-month visitor's permit. In January 1968, the cult was formally incorporated on U.S. soil as the Process Church of Final Judgment. The New Orleans chapter officially closed its doors two months later, though Process outposts would survive in the Crescent City for at least six more years, and the cult struck off for California, riding the coattails of the hippie movement.

DeGrimston's personal entourage was new on the scene in San Francisco that spring, but their message had preceded them, with Process evangelists cropping up during 1967's "summer of love." One early Frisco member, leather craftsman Victor Wild—a.k.a. "Brother Ely"—rode with the Gypsy Jokers motorcycle gang when he wasn't turning out hand-tooled belts and wallets. Wild is generally credited with turning the DeGrimstons on to the idea of recruiting outlaw bikers—"agents of Satan" in Processese—as shock troops for the coming apocalypse. It is also worth noting that Wild's home-cum–Process chapel was located a mere two blocks from the crash pad occupied by yet another fledgling cult: the Charles Mason "family."

War—and specifically a kind of hodgepodge racial Armageddon—was much on the mind of Process members in 1968 and 1969. One member of the cult, questioned by LAPD on his link to a pair of biker homicides, described the "natural hate" Processeans reserved for blacks, but the cult was also willing to use minorities, where feasible, "to begin some kind of militant thing." Robert DeGrimston, meanwhile, did his talking in the guise of various deities. In *Satan on War*, he advised his disciples to "Release the fiend that lies dormant within you, for he is strong and his power is far beyond the bounds of human frailty." If anyone was curious how that power should be used, DeGrimston supplied the answer in a sequel called *Jehovah on War*. "My prophecy upon this wasted earth," he wrote, "and upon the corrupt creation that squats upon its ruined surface is: THOU SHALT KILL." Mary Anne, meanwhile, was engrossed by a concept of psychic terrorism dubbed "The Fear," which members of the cult apparently regarded as a beneficial growth experience. Satanist Mendez Castle, writing in the "Sex" issue of the Process newsletter, urged readers to sample necrophilia and grave robbing if it turned them on.

The U.S. Immigration Service, meanwhile, was less concerned with religious teachings than deadlines, issuing deportation orders for the British Processeans in May 1968. Some promptly went underground and disappeared, while the DeGrimstons found it convenient to visit Europe. In their native England, spokesmen for the Anglican Church were denouncing the Process as a group that showed "two faces to the world. One is that of a pious respectability and the other is that of self-indulgent depravity." Still, there is no such thing as bad publicity, and that summer saw short-lived Process chapters planted in Rome, Paris, Amsterdam, Munich, and Hamburg. By late 1968, the DeGrimstons were safely back in London, but their dragon's teeth had taken root in North America. Chapters of varying size were reported in New York City, Boston, Chicago, and Toronto, but the big news would continue to flow from California.

Research by journalists Ed Sanders and Maury Terry reveals that Charles Manson was exposed to Process teachings by the spring or early summer of 1967, when he rubbed shoulders with a group calling itself the Final Church of Judgment—a.k.a. the Companions of Life—at San Francisco's infamous "Devil House." He may also have dropped in for some of Robert DeGrimston's lectures at the Esalen Institute, near Big Sur. In any case, by the time he moved his tribe to southern California in 1968, Manson was referring to his "family" as the "Final Church," working overtime to recruit outlaw bikers and instill "The Fear" in his loyal disciples. Indeed, Manson's whole "Helter Skelter" rap on race war, Armageddon, and the Beatles was an obvious rip-off from Process dogma, with a dash of Manson mania added to spice up the brew. In the midst of his murder trial, Manson was asked by prosecutor Vincent Bugliosi if he, Manson, knew Robert Moore. Manson's reply: "You're looking at him; Moore and I are one and the same."

A short time later, in May 1971, Bugliosi was visited by Process members "Father John" and "Brother Matthew," who had flown from Cambridge, Massachusetts, to deny any links with Manson's cult. A day later, they visited Manson in jail, after which Bugliosi reports that Manson became suddenly evasive in his comments on the sect. The wandering Processeans also turned up at L.A. FBI headquarters on May 25, just in case the G-men were interested. As recorded in an FBI memo of that date: "They explained they were ministers of a religious cult and preached about Satan and that Charles Manson had been a follower of a similar cult." Later that year, when Ed Sanders published his book on the Manson family, including detailed analysis of Manson's link to the Process, cult members threatened his publisher with a libel suit. The American editors folded, deleting mention of the Process from future editions, but their counterparts stood firm in England—and won their case when it finally went to trial in March 1974.

By that time, the public Process was beginning to unravel. Bad vibrations from the Manson trial and the cult's rumored links to assassin Sirhan Sirhan prompted the DeGrimstons to clean up their image in 1971 and 1972. A "faith-healing" tour of Canada helped fatten up the ranks a bit, and the Process was claiming 100,000 members by mid-1972 . . . a doubtful figure, since the cult's largest chapter, in Chicago, had only 150 disciples. Already, splinter movements had begun to dot the countryside, from the homicidal "Four P Movement" in California—drawing its name from the swastikalike Process "power sign"—to the Luciferians in New Orleans, led by "Pope Satan I," with their "true holy trinity" of God, Satan, and the serpent. A major, ultimately fatal rift occurred in early 1974, but cult historians still disagree on the cause of the split and its final results.

Religious scholar J. Gordon Melton reports that Process members devoted to Christ or Jehovah were fed up with Robert DeGrimston's emphasis on Satan by March 1974, dumping their founder to pursue a path of high-minded morality. Other sources describe the rift as a marital spat between Robert and Mary Anne, with Robert either "ousted" by his wife or "running off" to try life on his own. In any case, the end result was a new cult, dubbed the Foundation Church of the Millennium, later renamed the Foundation Faith of the Millennium (in 1977) and the Foundation Faith of God (in 1980). Mary Anne apparently led the new church for a time before dropping from sight. Robert, meanwhile, tried to rally loyal Processeans from his base in New Orleans, with small chapters surviving in Boston, Toronto, Chicago, New York, San Francisco, and London. Various sources agree that he returned to England and obscurity by the end of the 1970s, but the movement he founded was far from dead.

In New York City, for instance, "Son of Sam" triggerman David Berkowitz was seen to consort with one "Father Lars," spokesman for a known Process splinter group. Berkowitz has since confessed his membership in a satanic cult, described as "an offshoot of Scientology," which hated blacks, idolized deceased Nazis, and practiced canine sacrifice on German shepherds. Journalist Maury Terry also theorizes a Process connection in the January 1978 New York murders of Robert and Mary Hirschmann, found a day apart in East Fishkill and Queens, respectively. Robert Hirschmann, shot six times, displayed a tattoo of a swastika on his arm, above the legend "Brother Tom"—a caption in keeping with the Process tradition of adopting cult names when members reached the middle rank of "messenger."

If Sanders and Terry are correct, as the evidence suggests, members of the Process and its offshoots may still be active in America, committing crimes that range from rape and the ritual slaughter of animals to human sacrifice. Significantly, members of the New York Police Department's Intelligence Division report that Robert DeGrimston was back in the United States by 1990, teaching at a college on Staten Island. His wife, the detectives say, is an attorney working for the city of New York. [See: Berkowitz, David; "Four P Movement"; Hubbard, Lafayette]

PROSTITUTION

Over the past decade, police active in cult-crime investigations have repeatedly warned that some "magical" groups—specifically satanic and Afro-Caribbean sects—were becoming involved in commercialized sex, including prostitution and pornography, frequently emphasizing the sexual exploitation of children. Cult apologists, meanwhile, flatly deny the charge, calling for "hard evidence" ... which, in fact, already exits.

As early as 1968, members and associates of the Charles Manson "family" reported Manson's links with a Hollywood prostitution syndicate, its patrons including affluent members of the entertainment industry. At the time of his arrest in 1969, Manson was preparing to place at least four of his female disciples on the street, to boost the "family" income and strengthen his ties with the network. Manson and other cultists were also active in recruiting members from the major outlaw motorcycle gangs, which today play a major (if not dominant) role in prostitution across America. According to police and FBI reports, four gangs—the Hell's Angels, Bandidos, Outlaws, and Pagans—are extremely active in organized prostitution, including abduction and virtual enslavement of female juveniles.

A decade after Manson's mass murder conviction, police in Fall River, Massachusetts, exposed the pimping activities of Satanist Carl Drew, who terrorized the women in his "stable" with occult rituals and the sacrificial murders of at least three victims. In 1982, ex-convict William Acree was jailed in Denver for operating a male prostitution ring, again employing satanic rites to intimidate and control the young boys he victimized. In New York, around the same time, convicted "Son of Sam" killer David Berkowitz was describing his own participation in a satanic cult, supplying attorneys and prison confidants with supporting details of unsolved crimes. According to Berkowitz, his group—affiliated with the lethal "Four P Movement"—recruited both its members and potential hookers from various college campuses, executing individuals who tried to interfere with cult activities. Journalist Maury Terry has confirmed two Manhattan slayings described by Berkowitz in 1981, but the actual killers remain unidentified.

More recently, in July 1991, a Los Angeles jury convicted forty-eight-year-old Mary Ellen Tracy—a.k.a. "Sabrina Asset"—on prostitution charges, the trial judge pronouncing a sentence of one year in prison. Tracy, in her role as high priestess for the Church of the Most High Goddess, freely admits having sex with more than twenty-seven hundred men, describing the acts as "sin-cleansing rituals." Male participants in the "ceremony" typically left a "sacrifice" of $100, toward support of the church. [See: Acree, William; Drew, Carl; Motorcycle Gangs; Pornography; Slavery]

RADIN, ROY ALEXANDER

Journalist Maury Terry was investigating the New York "Son of Sam" murders in 1979, when convicted triggerman David Berkowitz began describing his involvement with a homicidal satanic cult. Aside from ritual murders, Berkowitz claimed the cult was also involved in drugs and pornography, with leaders including prominent, wealthy residents of New York and Los Angeles. One such, described as a cult "fat cat" or "Mr. Big," was referred to in prison correspondence as "R.R.," "Roy Rogers," and "Rodan the Flying Monster." According to Berkowitz, "R.R." was heavily involved with drugs, collected "bizarre videos"—including a tape of one "Sam" shooting—and lived on Long Island, in a town whose name started with "S." On one occasion, prison confidants of Berkowitz reported, "this guy beat the shit out of some actress and took videotapes of it."

Terry's investigation led back to millionaire entertainment producer Roy Radin, a resident of Southampton, Long Island, whose addiction to cocaine and video pornography was a topic of frequent comment in the tabloid press. Drug dealers and outlaw bikers frequented Radin's palacial home—dubbed Ocean Castle—but most of his income derived from benefit programs he organized for police organizations across the country. In 1975, New York's attorney general filed suit against Radin, claiming that he pocketed seventy-five percent of the proceeds from his fund-raisers, but Radin escaped punishment with a promise to sever his ties with police in New York state. Five years later, in April 1980, he was accused of beating and sexually assaulting actress Melonie Haller in front of video cameras. Police confiscated LSD, cocaine, and an unlicensed pistol in that case, but Radin struck another plea bargain, escaping with payment of a $1,000 fine and probation on a reduced charge of unlawful firearms possession. That October, Radin was questioned regarding the murder of associate Ronald Sisman, a known cocaine dealer, but no charges were filed. On the night of his 1981 wedding—an event attended by art dealer Andrew Crispo, later tied to the Bernard LeGeros murder case—Radin was accused of sexually assaulting model Jacey Layton at the Ocean Castle. Police were called again, and while they could not document a rape charge, they confiscated more drugs and narcotics paraphernalia from Radin's home.

By 1982, with his business failing and his marriage on the rocks, Radin was spending an estimated $1,000 per week on cocaine, alternating the dosage with tranquilizers he called "horse pills." New sources of income were his top priority, and to that end he began negotiating with Hollywood producer Bob Evans—a friend of Roman Polanski—to help raise $35 million for a gangster musical called *The Cotton Club*. On the side, Radin was also dealing with Karen Greenberger, a Miami cocaine smuggler whose sponsors included members of the Colombian drug cartel.

In February 1983, prodded by Maury Terry, prison associates of David Berkowitz began briefing police on Radin's alleged links to Satanism and the "Son of Sam" murders. Two months later, Radin surprised his sister with the news that he "had to get away for awhile." On Friday, May 13, he flew into Los Angeles, climbed into a rented limousine with Karen Greenberger . . . and vanished.

Four weeks later, on June 10, beekeeper Glen Fischer found Radin's corpse—gnawed by predators and nearly decapitated by close-range shotgun blasts—in a desert canyon sixty miles north of L.A. Maury Terry planned a trip west to examine the death scene, and a prison informant advised him to "look for those [cult] signs we've discussed in the past." Terry took the inmate's advice and uncovered a King James Bible tucked under a bush and half-buried by sand, near the spot where Radin was killed. The Bible was open to Isaiah Chapter 22, including the verse: "Let us eat and drink, for tomorrow we shall die."

Terry's suspicion of cult involvement in the murder was strengthened in October 1988, when police arrested Karen Greenberger, Robert Lowe, Alex Marti, and William Mentzer on charges of murdering Radin. Mentzer had earlier been named by Berkowitz as a member of the same cult responsible for the "Son of Sam" slayings. In addition to alleged participation in those crimes, he was also named by police as a prior associate of Charles Manson and a possible suspect in the 1974 ritual murder of Arlis Perry at Stanford University.

All four defendants were convicted of Radin's murder on July 22, 1991, with Mentzer and Marti facing the death penalty. [See: LeGeros, Bernard; Mentzer, William; Perry, Arlis; Sisman, Ronald]

RAIS, GILLES DE

Born of French nobility in 1404, Gilles de Rais married a wealthy heiress at age sixteen, thus becoming the richest man in France—some say in all of Europe. He was known as Bluebeard, for the glossy blue-black color of his whiskers, and he moved among the highest circles in the land. As Marshal of France, he fought beside Joan of Arc at Orléans, fielding a personal army of two hundred knights against the English invaders. Following the coronation of Charles VII, at which he personally crowned the new king, Gilles retired from public life, dividing his time among five lavish country estates at Machecoul, Malemort, La Suze, Champtoce, and Triffauges.

In retirement, Gilles squandered his wealth in extravagant style, selling off some of his land to cover expenses before his heirs obtained a royal injunction barring further sales. On the side, he indulged a passion for sadistic pedophilia, molesting and murdering peasant children of both sexes to amuse himself. Gilles admittedly patterned his life after that of the Roman emperor Caligula, known for his debauchery and bloodlust in ancient times.

Still spending money by the cartload, Gilles de Rais turned to alchemy and black magic in hopes of producing gold from base metals. An aide, Gilles de Sille, conducted "scientific" experiments on the problem, without success, and his master soon fell in with charlatans promising lavish returns for a modest investment. Kidnapped children, once mere playthings in a game of life and death, now became sacrificial objects in the pursuit of boundless wealth. By 1439, Gilles de Rais was in league with Francisco Prelati, a defrocked Italian priest, who guided him through ghoulish rituals, employing children's blood in vain attempts to conjure gold from common iron and lead.

A year later, Gilles ran afoul of the law on a trivial point, selling off his estate at Malemort to the treasurer of Brittany, Geoffroi le Ferron, in violation of the royal injunction. More to the point, Gilles barred the new owner's brother—a priest—from entering the property, beating and caging Jean le Ferron when he demanded admission. Assaulting a priest left him open to trial by the church, which also filed charges of sorcery and sexual perversion with children. Torture was applied to Gilles de Rais, his servants, and four alleged accomplices in October 1440, producing a variety of confessions. Gilles himself confessed numerous murders, begging forgiveness from the parents of his victims. On October 26, Gilles and two of his associates were strangled to death, the nobleman's body partially burned.

In retrospect, some historians regard the trial of Gilles de Rais as an ecclesiastical frame-up, noting that some of his lands were seized and sold by the church before his trial even began. Critics of this view point out that Gilles refused to confess under torture, pleading guilty on murder counts only when threatened with excommunication from the church. Dismembered remains of some fifty children were also found in a tower at Machecoul, with similar finds reported from another of the defendant's estates. Published accounts of the case "credit" Gilles de Rais with at least two hundred murders, some reports quadrupling that figure, and he certainly qualifies as a major serial killer in any case.

RAMIREZ, RICHARD LEYVA

Los Angeles is the serial murder capital of the world. It takes a special "twist" to capture headlines in a city where, by autumn 1983, five random slayers were reportedly at large and acting independently of one another. In the summer months of 1985, reporters found their twist and filled front pages with accounts of the sinister "Night Stalker," a sadistic home invader with a preference for unlocked windows and a taste for savage mutilation. As the story broke, the Stalker had three weeks of freedom left, but he was bent on making every moment count, and he would claim a minimum of sixteen lives before the bitter end.

Unrecognized, the terror had begun a full year earlier, with the murder of a seventy-nine-year-old woman at her home in suburban Glassell Park, in June 1984. Police lifted fingerprints from a window screen at the site, but without a suspect the clue led them nowhere.

By February 1985, authorities had two more murders on their hands, but they were keeping details to themselves. They saw no link, at first, with the abduction of a six-year-old Montebello girl, snatched from a bus stop near her school and carried away in a laundry bag, sexually abused before she was dropped off in Silver Lake Park on February 25. Two weeks later, on March 11, a nine-year-old girl was kidnapped from her bedroom in Monterey Park, raped by her abductor, and dumped in Elysian Park.

The Stalker reverted from child molestation to murder on March 17, shooting thirty-four-year-old Dayle Okazaki to death in her Rosemead condominium, wounding roommate Maria Hernandez before he fled. Hernandez provided police with their first description of a long-faced intruder, notable for his curly hair, bulging eyes, and wide-spaced, rotting teeth.

Another victim on March 17 was thirty-year-old Tsa Lian Yu, ambushed near her home in Monterey Park, dragged from her car and shot several times by the attacker. She was pronounced dead the following day, and her killer celebrated his new score by abducting an Eagle Rock girl from her home on the night of March 20, sexually abusing her before he let her go.

The action moved to Whittier on March 27, with sixty-four-year-old Vincent Zazzara shot to death in his home. Zazzara's wife, forty-four-year-old Maxine, was fatally stabbed in the same attack, her eyes gouged out and carried from the house by her assailant. The Zazzaras had been dead two days before their bodies were discovered on March 29, and homicide detectives launched a futile search for clues.

On May 14, sixty-five-year-old William Doi was shot in the head by a man who invaded his home, in Monterey Park. Dying, he staggered to the telephone and dialed an emergency number before he collapsed, thus saving his wife from a lethal assault by the Stalker. Two weeks later, on May 29, eighty-four-year-old Mabel Bell and her invalid sister, eighty-one-year-old Florence Lang, were savagely beaten in their Monrovia home. The Stalker paused to draw satanic pentagrams on Bell's thigh and a bedroom wall before he fled. Found by a gardener on June 2, Lang would survive her injuries, but Mabel Bell was pronounced dead on July 15.

In the meantime, the Night Stalker seemed intent on running up his score. On June 27, thirty-two-year-old Patty

Higgins was killed in her home at Arcadia, her throat slashed, and seventy-seven-year-old Mary Cannon was slain in identical style, less than two miles away, on July 2. Five days later, sixty-one-year-old Joyce Nelson was beaten to death at her home, in Monterey Park. The killer struck twice on July 20, first invading a Sun Valley home where he killed thirty-two-year-old Chainarong Khovanath, forced Khovanath's wife to pronounce Satan's name while she was beaten and raped, sodomized the couple's eight-year-old son, and finally escaped with $30,000 worth of cash and jewelry. A short time later, Max Kneiding, sixty-nine, and his wife Lela, sixty-six, were shot to death in their home, in Glendale.

Police were maintaining silence on the subject of their latest maniac-at-large, but they began to feel the heat on August 6, after thirty-eight-year-old Christopher Peterson and his wife Virginia, twenty-seven, were critically wounded by gunshots in their Northridge home. Descriptions matched the Stalker, and he struck again on August 8, shooting thirty-five-year-old Elyas Abowath dead in his Diamond Bar home, raping and brutally beating the dead man's wife while he forced her to "swear upon Satan." That night, authorities announced their manhunt for a killer linked with half a dozen recent homicides, a toll that nearly tripled in the next three weeks, with fresh assaults and new evaluations of outstanding cases.

On August 17, the Stalker deserted his normal hunting ground, gunning down sixty-six-year-old Peter Pan at his home in San Francisco. Pan's wife was also shot and beaten, but she managed to survive her wounds, identifying suspect sketches of the homicidal prowler. At the murder scene, police found pentagrams and satanic graffiti written in lipstick on the bedroom walls, along with the signature "Jack the Knife." Ballistic tests from San Francisco matched bullets extracted from two of the Night Stalker's Los Angeles victims, thus completing the chain of evidence.

By August 22, police had credited the Stalker with a total of fourteen murders in California. Three days later, in Mission Viejo, he wounded twenty-nine-year-old Bill Carns with a shot in the head and raped his fiancée, ordering the woman to say she loved Satan before he left the house, stealing a car for his escape. The car was found on August 28, complete with a set of fingerprints belonging to Richard Ramirez, a twenty-five-year-old drifter from Texas whose L.A. rap sheet included numerous arrests for traffic and drug violations. Acquaintances described Ramirez as an ardent Satanist and longtime drug abuser, obsessed with the mock-satanic rock band AC/DC. According to reports, Ramirez had adopted one of the group's songs—"Night Prowler"—as his personal anthem, playing it repeatedly, sometimes for hours on end. Aside from inking pentagrams on his arms and stomach, Ramirez had also wangled a one-on-one meeting with head Satanist Anton LaVey in 1983. Shrugging off the rumored links between his teachings and the Stalker's crimes, LaVey described Ramirez as "the model of deportment, one of the nicest, most polite young men you'd ever want to meet."

An all-points bulletin was issued for Ramirez on August 30, his mug shots broadcast on television, and he was captured by civilians in East Los Angeles the following day, mobbed and beaten as he tried to steal a car. Police arrived in time to save his life, and by September 29, Ramirez was facing a total of sixty-eight felony charges, including fourteen counts of murder and twenty-two counts of sexual assault. Eight more felonies, including two more rapes and one attempted murder, were added to the list of charges in December 1985.

In custody, Ramirez first denied responsibility for his crimes, claiming the devil compelled him to murder and rape against his will. "You think I'm crazy," he groused at detectives, "but you don't know Satan." Passing time revised his tune, however, and a few weeks later Ramirez told Deputy Jim Ellis, "I love to kill people. I love to watch them die. I would shoot them in the head and they would wiggle and squirm all over the place, and then just stop. Or I would cut them with a knife and watch their faces turn all white. I love all that blood."

A sister of Ramirez told the press he wanted to plead guilty, a desire supposedly frustrated by his attorneys, but the suspect made no public display of repentance. Sporting a pentagram on the palm of one hand, Ramirez waved to photographers and shouted "Hail Satan!" during a preliminary court appearance. Similar disruptions were a regular feature of his fourteen-month trial, climaxing on September 20, 1989, with Ramirez convicted of thirteen murders and thirty other felonies.

Prior to sentencing, Ramirez told the crowded court: "You don't understand me. You are not expected to. You are not capable of it. I am beyond your experience. I am beyond good and evil. Legions of the night, night breed, repeat not the errors of the Night Prowler and show no mercy. I will be avenged. Lucifer dwells within us all. That's it."

Judge Michael Tynan pronounced the formal sentence of death, but Ramirez remained unimpressed. Exiting the courthouse through an underground garage, he grinned at reporters who asked his impression of the sentence, responding, "Big deal. Death always went with the territory. I'll see you in Disneyland."

RAPE

With "sex magick" playing such a prominent part in the rituals of groups like the Ordo Templi Orientis, certain "Wicca" covens and satanic cults, it comes as no surprise that violent rape has been alleged in several cult-related cases spanning the United States and Canada. Many of the allegations derive from cases of alleged ritual child abuse, discussed elsewhere, but others involve the more "traditional" rape of teenage girls or adult women, abducted specifically as the objects of occult ceremonies.

Mike Warnke, ex-Satanist and born-again "Christian comedian," describes the abduction and gang rape of young women as a common practice of a satanic cult he calls "The Brotherhood," reported active in California during the 1960s. According to Warnke, victims were typically procured with invitations to "a party," afterward given the choice of voluntary submission to group sex or punishment with torture, including broken fingers, if they refused to submit. Virgins were preferred, as a symbol of innocence, but the cultists would take what they could get. In any case, the rapes were accomplished with Warnke leading off as high priest, with silence insured by beatings and threats of death.

A decade later, "Son of Sam" triggerman David Berkowitz taunted New York police with letters including references to one "John Wheaties, rapist and suffocator of young girls." The man in question was identified as John Carr, a real-life neighbor of Berkowitz and known Satanist, spared from indictment on murder charges by his suspicious "suicide" in 1979. Posthumous investigation identified Carr as a drug dealer and addict, linked to violent cult activities in New York and North Dakota. Journalist Maury Terry further suspects Carr and fellow cultists of participation in a series of rapes around Westchester, New York, in the year prior to the "Sam" murders.

Rape was also an integral part of the serial murders committed by Satanist Robin Gecht and his three accomplices in Chicago during 1981 and 1982. At least six women were kidnapped, gang raped, strangled and cannibalized by the gang before a surviving victim fingered her attackers, and police say the final body count may be closer to twenty. Most of the crimes were committed at Gecht's home, in a makeshift satanic chapel, but the cultists were not above utilizing cheap motels for a change of scene.

In June 1983, Detroit policewoman Linda Greene and accomplice Arzell Jones were jailed in lieu of $25,000 bond, on charges of first-degree sexual assault, kidnapping, and firearms violations. According to the prosecution's case—resulting in a December 1983 conviction for both defendants—Greene and Jones abducted a woman from a Detroit nightclub, dragging her to a nearby motel where she was beaten, sexually assaulted, and forced to chant "Satan is my master. I denounce the words of Jesus Christ." Another female witness at the trial described Jones's attempt to recruit her for "some kind of ritualistic ceremony" involving black robes. Upon conviction, both defendants were sentenced to prison.

Two years later, reputed Satanist John Kogut was linked to a series of gang rapes on Long Island, New York, convicted with two accomplices in the murder of one teenage victim. According to police, at least two other slayings and "several" more rapes were committed over the span of a year, by a mobile gang including an estimated dozen members. Clothing of murdered victim Theresa Fusco was recovered from a kind of cult "clubhouse," decorated with satanic graffiti, near the spot where her body was found.

Authorities in San Francisco are still searching for an unidentified "satanic rapist," linked with one sexual assault and one murder during January 1987. The rapist's surviving victim described her assailant and his van, adorned with portraits of Satan and the body of a murdered woman, but the sex slayer remains at large today, presumably still on the prowl.

As recently as March 1991, a satanic rape case was reported from peaceful Sioux City, Iowa, where three cultists stand convicted and sentenced to prison for abducting a teenage girl on the spring equinox, driving her to a local cemetery, there subjecting her to rape and torture while they chanted incantations to their deity.

A more "legitimate" outlet for perverse sexual appetites is found in the SM Church, dedicated to "goddess worship" and the practice of sadomasochistic sex. Founded in Berkeley, California, during the 1970s, the SM Church is currently based in San Francisco, associated with an "educational" group called the Essemian Society, dedicated to the promotion of enlightened sadomasochism. An estimated one hundred members belonged to the "church" at last count, in 1985. [See: Bugh, Randolph; Carr, John; Child Abuse; Fusco, Theresa; Gecht, Robin; Ramirez, Richard; "Satanic Rapist"]

RED EAGLE, VICTOR LOUIS

At 1:46 A.M. on October 27, 1987, firefighters in Hominy, Oklahoma, responded to an alarm at the rural mansion occupied by Victor Red Eagle, an oil-rich member of the Osage Indian tribe. Inside the house, flammable liquid had been spilled and set afire in thirteen separate places, but the flames spread slowly and were quickly doused. As the smoke cleared, firemen found a body lying facedown on a love seat in the living room, blood seeping from a ragged scalp wound. Feeling for a pulse, they swiftly verified that the man was dead.

Police responded to the call and readily identified the corpse as thirty-eight-year-old Victor Red Eagle. At first, they thought he had been shot or bludgeoned, but autopsy results listed the cause of death as strangulation. Red Eagle's clothing had been doused with lighter fluid in an apparent effort to burn the body, but the fire had somehow failed to catch.

Aside from his position as a wealthy resident of Hominy and a descendant of historic Osage chiefs, Red Eagle was known to police as a homosexual and a "professional victim." In one recent case, he had been beaten and robbed by his gay chauffeur, then run over with his own car. All things considered, it seemed likely that his wealth and/or his sex life had contributed to Victor's death.

Red Eagle was famous for his parties, and detectives learned that he had thrown one on October 25, two nights before he died. The festivities were marred by Red Eagle's quarrel with a drunken Osage youth, seventeen-year-old Maurice Jerome Barnes III, who resented being barred from the party. Recently arrested with a stolen motorcycle and suspected in a string of local burglaries, Barnes had an unsavory reputation, but he staunchly denied killing Victor Red Eagle, insisting that friends would vouch for his whereabouts on the night in question.

Another suspect, twenty-one-year-old Prentice Crawford, was a gay Osage whose love affair with Red Eagle had ended bitterly after Victor caught him stealing money from the house. Crawford denied both the theft and the slaying, but police were hearing darker rumors on the street. Acquaintances of Crawford said he was an ardent Satanist—in fact, he thought he was the son of Lucifer, the product of a pact his mother made before his birth. A blood relation to the prince of darkness gave him special powers, Crawford thought, including the ability to curse his enemies. One recent target of a Crawford curse was Maurice Barnes III.

By that time, officers had questioned Barnes's friends and watched his alibi go up in smoke. Confronted with the truth, Barnes grudgingly admitted being present when Red Eagle died, but he insisted Prentice Crawford was the strangler. As Barnes explained the motive, Crawford had informed him that the only way to lift his curse was through a human sacrifice to Satan. Victor Red Eagle was the logical choice, since he had recently angered both young men, and so his fate was sealed.

On the night of the murder, Barnes said, they had walked from Crawford's farmhouse to the Red Eagle mansion, Crawford lecturing his teenage companion on the powers of Satan. "He told me I should pray to his father for power and strength," Barnes explained. Red Eagle let them in the house without misgivings, Barnes engaging him in conversation while Crawford clubbed him from behind with a wine bottle. It took fifteen minutes to strangle Red Eagle, Crawford finally slipping a plastic bag over his victim's head to speed up the process, solemnly chanting, "This is my gift to you, Father." In an attempt to cover up the crime, fires were set before they fled.

Both suspects were indicted for first-degree murder on February 3, 1988, Barnes quickly turning state's evidence in a bid to reduce his own sentence. Crawford's trial opened on May 28, with Barnes repeating his story of ritual murder, and

Crawford took the stand to deny killing Red Eagle, pointing the finger of guilt back at Barnes. Confused by the contradictory stories, perhaps skeptical of the satanic motive, jurors acquitted Crawford on June 3, 1988. He was promptly indicted on new charges of first-degree arson and accessory to Red Eagle's murder, with trial pending as this is written. Barnes, meanwhile, pleaded guilty to a reduced charge of second-degree murder and was sentenced to twelve years in prison.

RODRIGUEZ, JAIME, Jr.

In retrospect, it may have been the tattoo that got Jaime Rodriguez in trouble, or his resort to bizarre violence may simply have been inevitable. A dedicated Satanist since age sixteen, by the spring of 1990 Rodriguez had five years of demonology under his belt, and he was ready for the leap from theory to practice. When he met Stephanie Dubray, a fifteen-year-old runaway who sported a "666" tattoo on her chest, the die was cast. No turning back.

With some help from his cousin, fifteen-year-old Agustin Pena, Rodriguez persuaded Stephanie to hole up at the Clinton Township home Pena shared with his mother, Betty Stasiak. They made a happy threesome for several weeks, Rodriguez dropping by for frequent visits from his home in Saginaw, before Jaime felt a sudden urge to kill the girl in mid-July.

In fact, he was already over the edge, with kidnapping charges filed in Saginaw. On June 17, a sixteen-year-old high school student was driving Rodriguez home from a party when he commandeered her car, drove to Detroit, and there kicked her out of the vehicle before driving away.

At that, she was lucky.

On July 11, Rodriguez decided that Stephanie Dubray should die. As later reconstructed from his statements to police, Rodriguez held the girl while Pena stabbed her repeatedly with a kitchen knife. When she was dead, Rodriguez dismembered her body, cutting off her right index finger to wear as a charm around his neck. The victim's head was skinned, stuffed in a bag, and left in the freezer at Pena's home. As luck would have it, twenty-two-year-old Valerie Rapson found the grisly souvenir later that day, on a visit to the house, and delivered it to the police. Both suspects were held without bond on murder charges, the county prosecutor scheduling Pena for trial as an adult.

The murder charges interrupted jury selection in Jaime's kidnapping trial, and that case was postponed pending disposition of the more serious charge. At his murder trial, in July 1991, the defendant's Satanism was introduced as evidence of insanity, but prosecutor Carl Marlinga reminded jurors that "You can freely choose evil over good and it does not mean you're insane." In fact, Marlinga had nothing to say on the matter of Satanism, though a county medical examiner described the crime as "definitely ritualistic."

Jurors found their task made easier on July 18, when the judge dismissed Jaime's insanity plea. A mere thirty minutes of deliberation was required to convict Rodriguez of first-degree murder, conspiracy, and mutilating a corpse. On July 18, 1991, the defendant was sentenced to a double term of life imprisonment. Agustin Pena's trial is still pending at this writing.

ROSE, JASON WAYNE and JONES, JOHN RAY

On June 1, 1988, police were summoned to investigate a woman's body lying in a wooded area near a water filtration plant, outside of Springfield, Oregon. Young and seminude, the victim had been bludgeoned with a heavy object prior to strangulation, stripped of any jewelry she was wearing, with her handbag missing from the scene.

On Thursday morning, June 2, Springfield police received a phone call from Seattle, concerned parents worried that the girl might be their adopted daughter, nineteen-year-old Melissa Ann Meyer. Dental records confirmed the suspicion, and authorities began piecing the victim's life story together from scratch. Enrolled in a Seattle drug-rehab program before she moved to Eugene, Oregon, in February 1988, Meyer was unemployed as far as anyone could tell, but she had never been arrested. Acquaintances described her many visits to a downtown mall in Springfield, a mall frequented by addicts and their pushers. It was there, on May 30, that Melissa was last seen alive.

Police were still scrounging for leads on June 3, when they

received a new missing-person bulletin in Springfield. Candice Michelle Roy, age seventeen, had failed to come home overnight, and in light of the recent murder, detectives waived their standard twenty-four-hour rule for missing juveniles. On June 6, Roy's strangled body was discovered in a grove of trees four blocks from home—and barely five miles from the site where Melissa Meyer was killed. Assistant D.A. Brian Barnes referred to "certain similarities" between the murders, but he kept the details to himself.

Telephone tips were pouring in to police headquarters, meanwhile, and one led detectives to a pair of young women who fingered their boyfriends—twenty-year-old Jason Rose and seventeen-year-old John Jones—as the killers of Melissa Meyer. As outlined by the women, Meyer met her killers at the downtown mall, returning with them to a rural campsite, where the young men strangled her and stripped her jewelry as an extra prize. It was an easy charge to make, but certain information from the two young women jibed with details the police had not released to journalists.

It was enough to justify a warrant for the search of Rose's mobile home, where Jones was crashing as a live-in guest. Neither suspect was present when police arrived, but the search went ahead as planned, turning up various grimoires, rune stones, a "spell book" for communication with the dead ... and a videocassette depicting what police believe to be a "real, live" human sacrifice.

On June 13, manhunters traced Rose and Jones to the mountain hamlet of Show Low, Arizona, bordering the state's Papago Indian reservation. Springfield detectives flew into Phoenix and drove the rest of the way with local authorities, routing their men from a rundown motel at 8:00 P.M. and arresting both on suspicion of murder. Arraigned on extradition warrants the following day, Rose and Jones surrendered without a fight, returning to Oregon on Friday, June 17.

Ten days later, a county grand jury indicted Rose for aggravated murder and first-degree robbery, charging that he tortured and killed Melissa Meyer "while deliberately effecting a human sacrifice." John Jones had celebrated a birthday, meanwhile, and he would face trial as an adult on the same charges, though his age at the time of the murder ruled out a potential death sentence. Formal charges against Jones specified that he helped Rose strangle their victim to death, after cracking her skull with a machete. In jail, Rose whiled away the hours sketching pentagrams and goats' heads, answering the inner call of evil spirits only he could hear.

Rose went to trial in April 1989, Assistant D.A. Barnes recounting his confession to police that Meyer's fate had been decided by the rune stones, death conjured up with a flick of the wrist. Defense attorney Terry Gough dismissed the charge as "nothing but smoke and malarkey," relating Meyer's death to simple robbery or a drug deal gone sour, but jurors were impressed by the defendant's statements ... and the gruesome tape police had confiscated from his home. Convicted on April 20, Rose was formally sentenced to death on May 16, 1989.

Barely three weeks later, John Jones stood before Judge Gregory Foote in Springfield, waiving his right to a full jury trial. The evidence of guilt was overwhelming, and Jones was convicted of intentional murder, plus a collateral charge of third-degree robbery. On June 10, 1989, he was fined $5,000 and sentenced to life in prison, with a minimum twenty-five years before parole. At this writing, no charges have been filed in the "similar" slaying of Candice Roy. [See: "Snuff" Films]

ST. JOSEPH, CLIFFORD

On June 15, 1985, police were summoned to investigate reports of a body found on San Francisco's Sixth Street, at an auto-wrecking yard. Patrolmen answering the call found a nude male wrapped in a blanket and bound with guitar strings, the body wedged beneath a truck. Extensive injuries made homicide a probability, with Inspectors Napoleon Hendricks and Earl Sanders assigned to the case.

An autopsy confirmed the case as an especially repulsive murder. Abrasions on the victim's wrists and ankles indicated that he had been handcuffed, with a chain wrapped tightly around his legs. Bruises and whip marks mottled his back, buttocks, and thighs. He had been sodomized repeatedly, two three-inch gashes carved into his upper lip, with other cuts and burns appearing on his neck. A satanic pentagram, nine inches in diameter, was carved into the victim's chest, while residue of molten candle wax was found in his hair and right eye socket. Postmortem tests determined that the torture lasted several days before the killers gouged a slit between their victim's genitals and anus, deliberately draining most of the blood from his body.

No clothing or ID was discovered with the corpse, and the victim remains unidentified to this day, listed in police and medical records as "John Doe #60." Detectives knew they had a sacrificial murder on their hands, but at the moment they were short of suspects in the case.

Nine days later, in the early-morning hours of June 24, residents of Stillman Street phoned in complaints of loud music and screams emanating from a nearby apartment. Arriving at the scene, patrolmen followed the noise and found twenty-six-year-old Edward Spela passed out on the doorstep, apparently intoxicated. When they finally got an answer to their knocking, the police found three more men inside. Tenant Clifford St. Joseph, age forty-three, was dressed in a black hood and cloak, his face heavily made-up, a small leather whip in one hand. Companion Maurice Bork, twenty-six, was stripped to the waist, his face daubed with cosmetics, eyes glassy from the combined effects of alcohol and drugs. The guest of honor was a nineteen-year-old man who lay before them, handcuffed and surrounded by a ring of candles planted on the floor. Another candle stood atop a human skull on the mantel, and a copy of *The Satanic Bible* adorned St. Joseph's coffee table.

St. Joseph first identified himself as the "Dark Prince," yielding his true identity when the officers persisted. A brief interrogation of the handcuffed youth resulted in a call for paramedics, and he was rushed to a city rape clinic for examination and treatment of injuries caused by sexual assault. In custody, St. Joseph granted permission for a search of his apartment and vehicle, yielding handcuffs and chains, along with human bloodstains in the bedroom, living room, and in his station wagon. He described the "party" as an example of sex between consenting adults.

At the rape treatment center, St. Joseph's young victim described his ordeal, beginning with a June 21 pickup by St. Joseph and Ed Spela—the victim's former lover and a part-time prostitute—outside a gay bar in the city's "meat rack" district. Back at St. Joseph's apartment, the victim was offered a bowl of ice cream, apparently containing drugs. When he finally woke, the young man was naked and chained to a bed. Over the next three days he was allegedly raped and tortured by both men, with Maurice Bork and unidentified others dropping in to join the game. He was also forced to have sex with a dog and listened while St. Joseph lectured his friends on the pleasures of human sacrifice.

Police were putting two and two together, but their luck went sour when Maurice Bork made bail and promptly disappeared. Too late, they learned that Bork was a fugitive from Canada, where he had escaped from prison in the midst of a term for armed robbery. He would remain at large until January 1987, when another robbery arrest in San Francisco left him open to interrogation. This time, when confronted with the grisly photographs of John Doe #60, Bork broke down and told detectives everything he knew.

According to Bork, he first met St. Joseph in May 1985, soon moving into the Satanist's apartment. One evening in June, Bork came home to find St. Joseph and an unidentified companion celebrating a Black Mass, with a third man chained to the bed. Bork was a witness to the carnage that ensued, playing Black Sabbath records on the stereo while St. Joseph and his friend abused their victim, finally draining his blood into a golden chalice and drinking a toast to Satan. Bork denied any direct role in the murder, but admitted helping St. Joseph dispose of the body.

Charged with first-degree murder, sodomy, and false imprisonment, St. Joseph pleaded not guilty and was jailed in lieu of $1 million bond. An August 1987 preliminary hearing bound him over for trial, with the jury impaneled in late March 1988. Finally convicted on all counts, St. Joseph was sentenced on May 5 to a prison term of twenty-five years to life. His unnamed accomplice in the sacrificial homicide is still at large, and Inspector Sanders believes other persons are linked to the cult. Their chosen victims, he maintains, are homeless drifters like John Doe #60, "not necessarily confined to San Francisco." As Sanders told the press, "Some of those who participate are people of substantial means, members of the gay community. It is a gay satanic cult." No positive link with the local Church of Satan was established, but St. Joseph's correspondence reportedly yielded connections with the Ordo Templi Orientis, which includes a homosexual "11th degree" for members who are so inclined. [See: Ordo Templi Orientis]

SANDERS, ALEXANDER

Advertised since the late 1960s as England's "King of the Witches," Alex Sanders was only seven years old in 1933, when he surprised his grandmother in the midst of a nude magic ritual. Startled by the boy's arrival, she ordered him to strip and join her in the consecrated circle, nicking his scrotum with a razor blade and proclaiming, "Now you are one of us." Three years later, the old witch took Sanders to London and left him with a certain "Mr. Alexander"—later identified as Aleister Crowley—who instructed Sanders in the so-called "Rites of Horus."

With that kind of background, it is small wonder that Sanders felt himself drawn to black magic in general and "sex magick" in particular. In 1952, he wangled a free house and monthly allowance from total strangers, a middle-aged Manchester couple who took Sanders for the "exact double" of their late son, but he later repented of the fraud, admitting a "dreadful mistake in using black magic in an attempt to bring myself money and sexual success."

Newfound ethics aside, he was still inextricably bound to witchcraft, signing on with Gerald Gardner's "Wicca" religion in 1954, subsequently revising the basic texts to create his own "Alexandrian" style of magic. Nude rituals are preferred, as in the Gardnerian cult, and initiation into the "third degree" requires performance of a special "Grand Rite"—that is, public sexual intercourse.

With its nudity and sexual trappings, the Alexandrian cult was a godsend for sensational tabloid journalists. Sanders was helping out on a movie called *Eye of the Devil* in 1965, when he met—and supposedly initiated—actress Sharon Tate (murdered four years later by the Charles Manson "family"). By 1969, Sanders was a national celebrity, calling himself the "High Priest Verbius" and claiming two hundred loyal covens in England alone. Stateside, the Alexandrians have their headquarters in Boston, with active covens reported from coast to coast. The Canadian headquarters is located in Toronto. While most Alexandrian witches claim to practice "white" magic, their founder has never directly renounced his "black" roots or devotion to witchcraft as a sexual tool. [See: Crowley, Aleister; Gardner, Gerald; "Wicca"]

SANTERIA

Santeria—literally "the path of the saints"—is a hybrid religion combining the ju-ju cult of central Africa's Yoruba tribe with symbols drawn from the Roman Catholic church. The sect apparently evolved in Cuba during the late eighteenth or early nineteenth century, as African slaves sought to disguise the practice of their native religion, syncretizing the various ju-ju deities—*orishas*—with Catholic saints to avert suspicion. Despite the Christian trappings, however, santeria remains essentially a form of pagan witchcraft, incorporating blood sacrifice of animals ... and sometimes human beings.

Throughout the Western Hemisphere, African slaves and their offspring disguised their native religions with similar trappings and various names—as voodoo in Haiti; as santeria, abaqua, or palo mayombe in Cuba; as candomble, macumba, or umbanda in Brazil. From these centers of cult activity, immigration has spread various sects to the United States, with a virtual flood of Cuban refugees bringing santeria to Miami and environs as they fled from Castro's communist regime. (Ironically, rumors persist that Fidel, like Fulgencio Batista and other Cuban presidents before him, has been secretly ordained as a santeria priest—a *babalawo*.) In 1980, the surprise Mariel boatlift brought thousands of new practitioners to American shores, this time including large numbers of hard-core criminals among the so-called "political refugees."

No proper census is available for practicing santeros in America. Cuban spokesmen placed the Miami head count around ten thousand in 1981, a figure which had multiplied tenfold by 1990. *Babalawo* Ernesto Pichardo estimates that there are twenty thousand santeria priests in Miami alone, and local police agree that the cult is "very widespread." With the dispersion of Cuban immigrants in the past twelve years, reports of active santeria cults have been filed from coast to coast, with evidence of forays into Canada.

Like other "magic" cults, santeria is essentially an amoral religion, devoid of guidelines for individual behavior. Members of the cult look out for Number One above all else, with rituals and prayers that emphasize material rewards, destruction of their enemies, and private gain. Some practitioners openly advertise their criminal specialties with small tattoos on their hands, specific symbols identifying drug dealers, kidnappers, robbers, assassins, and so forth. When Panama's drug-dealing president, Manuel Noriega, was arrested by American troops in January 1990, army investigators found a santeria altar in his home, complete with effigies designed to curse President Ronald Reagan, Vice President George Bush, and other prominent enemies.

Santeros staunchly defend their ritual slaughter of animals ranging from poultry to goats and larger livestock, but there is also evidence of sacrifice involving human beings—dubbed "goats without horns" in cult terminology. The February 1981 murder of Leroy Carter, in San Francisco, bore clear evidence of santero involvement, and ritual murders are a fairly regular occurrence in Miami, where Detective Roberto Rodriguez told author Larry Kahaner: "We'll find dead bodies of dealers who were killed as part of a drug deal, and they were killed as part of a santeria sacrifice. All the indicators are there. Sometimes we find small animals, chickens, ducks, whatever, along with the deceased that were sacrificed first." At this writing, similar evidence of cult-related murder has been reported from Texas, Connecticut, New York, and New Jersey. [See: Abaqua; Animal Sacrifice; Carter, Leroy; Drugs; Fuster, Francisco; Human Sacrifice; Ju-Ju; Palo Mayombe; Pornography; Voodoo]

SATANIC ORGANIZATION OF CONNECTICUT

Described by self-styled spokesmen as a statewide cult, claiming a membership of some ten thousand disciples, the Satanic Organization of Connecticut (SOC) was first publicized through its link to criminal activities around the town of Ridgefield, between December 1978 and June 1979. The grandiose membership figure was doubtless inflated, and it remains unclear whether the group has survived to the present day.

The cult's first foray into crime occurred on Christmas Eve 1978, when a KKK-style cross was burned at the Ridgefield home of an interracial couple. Five men were arrested in that case, with one defendant—twenty-year-old Robert Bryant, admitting membership in the SOC. Bryant, described by police as the instigator of the cross burning, called it a form of "celebration," planned since he originally constructed the cross on Halloween. Another suspect in the case, eighteen-year-old Robert Stewart, had more prosaic motives, telling police that he simply hated blacks.

Following the Christmas incident, the SOC dropped out of local headlines until June 10, 1979, when Ridgefield policeman Michael Passaro was assaulted and beaten by persons unknown. As Passaro described the incident, he was patrolling Oscaleta Road at 2:30 A.M., when he stopped his car to investigate the sound of voices from some nearby woods, where local residents had earlier reported "strange" music and gunshots. Approaching on foot, he saw a group of black-robed figures chanting in some unknown language, four of them rushing toward him as he approached. Passaro was mauled by his assailants before he escaped to his car, scaring them off with a can of Mace and the sound of his siren. Minor head injuries and numerous bruises kept the patrolman off-duty for several days.

Passaro's attackers were never identified, but an admitted "lieutenant" from the SOC was quick to deny any role in the assault. As quoted in the press, the anonymous nineteen-year-old claimed to know the identity of those responsible, describing them as "bad eggs" expelled from the SOC for various infractions of cult rules. Said to draw its rituals and inspiration from Anton LaVey's *Satanic Bible*, the SOC claimed fifteen active members in Ridgefield, ranging in age from seventeen to twenty. The unidentified "bad eggs," meanwhile, were said to number around a hundred statewide. [See: Ku Klux Klan]

"SATANIC RAPIST"—SAN FRANCISCO

Around 10:00 A.M. on Monday, January 26, 1987, a twenty-two-year-old woman was walking in San Francisco's Mission District, when she was accosted by a knife-wielding stranger, forced to enter a black van parked at the curb. Inside the vehicle, her assailant bound the woman's hands behind her back and gagged her with a strip of red cloth, leaving her prostrate while he took the driver's seat and pulled into morning traffic.

The van's interior was decorated with red curtains and numerous pictures of Satan, but the real shock came when the young woman found herself sharing the rear deck with a corpse. Gray flesh and a putrescent odor told her that the slender girl with blond hair cut to shoulder length had been dead several hours, at the very least; deep stab wounds in her neck and naked chest revealed the cause of death, apparently inflicted with a bloody knife that lay between them on the floor.

Paralyzed with fear, the driver's latest victim lay silent for several hours, while her captor drove aimlessly around San Francisco. Finally stopping the van, he crawled back to join her, brandishing a knife as he threatened, "I'm going to kill you." Instead, he peeled off his pale-blue jumpsuit and donned surgical gloves before raping the young woman repeatedly. Despite her pain and terror, she memorized the description of a white man in his early thirties, with long, dirty brown hair and a burn scar extending from his right cheek to the adjacent shoulder. Underneath his jumpsuit, he wore a silver necklace with a satanic pentagram.

At some point in the midst of her ordeal, the woman's hands were untied, and she finally managed to fight her attacker off, escaping from the van around 5:00 P.M. Instead of giving chase, her rapist fled, leaving his battered victim to seek help and summon police. Detectives received some two hundred reports of black vans overnight, but none turned out to be the rapist's vehicle.

Inspector Kevin O'Connor, of SFPD's sex crimes division, told the press: "We have no reason to doubt the victim's story. We're continuing our investigation full-bore." In spite of good intentions, no results were forthcoming, and San Francisco's "Satanic rapist" remains unidentified at this writing. [See: Rape]

SATANISM

The initial problem with any discussion of Satanism is defining the term itself. Religious scholar J. Gordon Melton views Satanism as a doctrine "subsequent to Christianity," and author Art Lyons defines a Satanist as any "worshipper of the Christian Devil, whatever he perceives that to mean," but such attempts to bind Satanism with Christianity are clearly simplistic. The entity known as Satan or Lucifer made his first public appearance in the Old Testament Book of Genesis, predating Christ by some two thousand years, and his very name derives from the Hebrew word for "adversary."

Nor did the Biblical Satan spring full-blown from some Jewish patriarch's fertile imagination. Ancient Greeks celebrated bloody rites in honor of the goat-god Dionysus, while Tiamat was the primary devil in Babylon. Dog-headed Set was the evil god of Egypt, and a society devoted to his worship—Michael Aquino's Temple of Set—bills itself as the leading "satanic" religion in modern America.

It *may* be accurate to say that Satanism, as we recognize the term today, has roughly paralleled the spread of Christianity, embodied by the Roman Catholic church. An early heretical sect, the Gnostics, regarded life on earth as a season in Hell, condemning Jehovah as evil for creating man in the first place. From that perspective, it was a short step to revering Satan as the valiant adversary of "evil" Jehovah, denouncing Jesus as the wicked son of a corrupt god, and heralding Judas Iscariot for helping put Christ on the cross. Gnostic cults were suppressed after A.D. 392, when Christianity became the official religion of Rome, but "subversive" ideas have a way of clinging to life on their own.

Chief among the stewards of Gnostic beliefs were the Messalians of Armenia, moving westward in the fourth century, reaching the Balkans by the eleventh century; the Paulicians, active in Armenia and Asia Minor by the fifth century, deported to the Balkans in 872; and the derivative Bogomils, firmly entrenched in Bulgaria by the year 950. Of the three, the Bogomils proved themselves the most zealous evangelists, planting outposts in northern Italy and southern France by the twelfth century. In essence, the Bogomils regarded Satan as the Old Testament god of creation. Satan had two sons, Michael and Satanel, who were eternally at odds: Satanel rebelled and was exiled to earth, where he created Adam and Eve; Michael later put in an appearance as Jesus, trying to dominate mankind, but Satanel conspired to have him crucified.

In southern France, this altered gospel appealed to several sects, including the Albigenses (organized at Albi in the eleventh century), the Waldenses (followers of Peter Waldo, dating from A.D. 1170), and the Cathari—"pure ones"—who regarded life on earth as bondage to the devil, thus disdaining procreative sex as a device for generating future captives. Some Cathari lived their faith by staying celibate, while others followed the lead of certain Albigenses in practicing sodomy or bestiality—any type of sex, in fact, which would not lead to pregnancy. Enough Bogomils shared the jaundiced view of heterosexual intercourse that they would finally lend their name to the language as a root of "buggery."

The Roman church was ever vigilant to heretics, and Pope Innocent III launched a purge of the Cathari in 1208, with the sect finally crushed in 1244. Albigenses and Waldenses were targeted for slaughter around the same time, with a few members of the latter sect surviving to join the Protestant Reformation four hundred years later. In the meantime, France witnessed the first trial and execution for witchcraft, in 1275, as the Inquisition gathered momentum. In 1312, the crusading Knights Templar were condemned for worshiping Baphomet, their grand master burned outside Paris in 1314. Another satanic cult, the Brethren of the Cross, was annihilated at Thuringia in 1453, for preaching that Satan would one day expel Christ from heaven. Estimates vary widely on a final body count for the Inquisition, with scattered witch trials continuing into the eighteenth century, but it is clear that persecution merely drove the cult of devil worship underground, perhaps romanticizing it in places where it otherwise might have faded with time.

In France, King Henry III actively worshiped the devil in private ceremonies, while his enemies did likewise, scheming to kill him with black magic curses. (A lone fanatic finally did it for them, in 1589.) Around the same time, Catherine de Médicis was refining the Black Mass as a perverse entertainment for French aristocrats, spreading the seeds of evil throughout western Europe. In northern France, night-riding Satanists kidnapped peasant girls and performed vile rituals over their naked bodies before galloping off into darkness. In Germany, a cult called the Buxen went prowling in cloaks and death's-head masks, pausing on a whim to rape, rob, and kill. Similar reports were filed from Austria and Italy, but France remained the center of aristocratic Satanism. It was there, at Loudon, that Father Urbain Grandier was burned for sorcery in 1633, after signing a pact with Satan in his own blood. At least fifty more priests were executed between 1673 and 1680, while the royal court itself was scandalized by reports of Black Masses and human sacrifice in the "Chambre Ardente affair." By comparison, the British Hell-fire Clubs of the mid-eighteenth century were almost benign.

In our century, the practice of black magic—with or without the formal "satanic" label—has been perpetuated by groups like the Ordo Templi Orientis and the Aurum Solis, founded by Aleister Crowley. America's first overt satanic church was founded in Toledo, Ohio, in 1948, but the tabloids reserved their headlines for Anton LaVey's California-based Church of Satan, organized in 1966. Nine years later, a rift in the church created LaVey's principal competition in the Temple of Set. Our constitution forbids the proscription of any religion per se, and the nearest thing to a ban on Satanism, thus far, is a statute passed in Louisiana during 1989. While no specific reference to Satan or any religion appears in the law, it penalizes certain ritualistic acts traditionally linked to the occult, including animal sacrifice and the consumption of human blood or waste. Participants in an act of ritual murder or sexual abuse likewise face stiff penalties in addition to the usual punishment for murder or rape.

Meanwhile, debate continues over the culpability of "legitimate" satanic churches in violent crimes committed by unstable worshipers, with spokesmen like Aquino and LaVey publicly disowning "renegade" Satanists. Cult apologists also stress the difference between "real" Satanism and various hybrid cults known to practice human sacrifice, but the distinction blurs in areas like Peru, where peasant shamans draw their inspiration from the *Great Book of San Cipriano*— listing Lucifer, Belzebuth, and Astaroth as the ranking nobility in Hell—and Mexico, where priests of the palo mayombe cult advertise Black Masses for a price. In fact, considering the fluid mix-and-match philosophy of many practicing occultists, there may be no valid distinction at all. [See: Black Mass; "Chambre Ardente" Affair; Human Sacrifice; "Magick"; Witch Cults]

SCIENTOLOGY:
See HUBBARD, LAFAYETTE RONALD

SEEKERS OF MERCY

A satanic cult based in Switzerland, the Seekers of Mercy made international headlines in 1966, when police raided its headquarters in the small town of Helikon. Investigating the sudden death of a young female cultist, detectives found the "church" equipped with black candles, occult paraphernalia, and a well-stocked torture chamber. Further investigation revealed that the girl had died after being sexually assaulted, bound to an inverted cross, and brutally flogged with a whip. Several members of the cult were subsequently tried, convicted, and sentenced to prison for their roles in the sadistic "Black Mass."

SELLERS, SEAN

Born in 1969, Sellers was eighteen months old when his parents divorced. A year later, in 1972, he was left with relatives while his mother hit the road, seeking work. By 1976, she had remarried—to auto mechanic Paul Bellofatto—but they still traveled widely on jobs, and young Sean spent most of his time with aunts and uncles, developing a painful sense of rejection along the way. By age twelve, he was actively studying Satanism, immersed in the dark fantasy world of "Dungeons & Dragons." Frequent moves increased his sense of isolation, and a 1983 reunion with his mother and stepfather scarcely improved matters. Dumped with an aunt at Okmulgee, Oklahoma, in March 1984, Sellers plunged deeper into his occult studies, drinking the blood of fellow teenage cultists and using it to write his own personal "dedication to Satan."

Sean's family was reunited in the fall of 1984, in Oklahoma City, but the brooding fifteen-year-old was already over the edge. In February 1985, Sellers used his own blood to write: "I renounce God, I renounce Christ. I will serve only Satan . . . Hail Satan." Discovery of his occult interests led to angry scenes with Paul Bellofatto, Sean's stepfather telling the troubled boy, "You don't exist."

On September 8, 1985, Sellers and another teenage Satanist invaded a local convenience store, Sean fatally shooting a clerk—Richard Bower—who had once refused to sell them beer. In his own words, the murder "opened a new portal" for Sellers, and he "plunged into Satanism with everything I had."

A few months later, in the middle of the night, he crept into the master bedroom of his family home, executing his mother and Bellofatto with his stepfather's own pistol. Sellers contrived to "find" the bodies next day, but his friends were suspicious, and his accomplice in the Bower homicide eventually turned state's evidence to save himself. Convicted on three counts of murder in September 1986, Sellers was sentenced to die, becoming the youngest inmate on Oklahoma's death row.

SERIAL MURDER

In the past thirty years, the United States has suffered an onslaught of brutal, senseless homicides, frequently committed by repeat killers who choose their victims at random, claiming the lives of strangers selected on a whim. Sadistic predators like Ted Bundy, John Gacy, Gerald Stano, Jeffrey Dahmer, and Seattle's still-unidentified "Green River Killer" have scattered bodies from coast to coast, joining in what one federal investigator calls "an epidemic of homicidal mania."

Prior to 1960, American police were called upon to deal with fewer than two serial killers per year, nationwide. By the end of the sixties, a new homicidal maniac was surfacing every two months, and their number tripled in the 1970s. By 1989, serial killers were being arrested at a rate approaching three per month, and the 1990s threaten to set a new record for carnage, with fifty-two repeat killers identified in the first eighteen months of the decade.

Motives for serial murder are as diverse as the killers themselves, including racial prejudice and twisted sexuality, religious fanaticism and simple greed ... but a disturbing number of the modern cases have apparently been motivated by belief in Satanism or a similar occult philosophy. In fact, since 1969, an estimated eight percent of American serial killers have confessed or otherwise demonstrated occult motives for their crimes. Aside from cases covered elsewhere in this book, their ranks include:

Antone Costa—Imprisoned in 1970 for the mutilation-murders of four young women around Provincetown, Massachusetts, and suspected of four other killings, Costa stocked his cell with books on ritual magic, including a copy of Anton LaVey's *Satanic Bible*. After serving four years of a life sentence, Costa committed suicide by hanging himself with a belt.

Larry Eyler—A homosexual slasher linked to the

deaths of twenty-three young men and boys around the Midwest, Eyler stands convicted of two murders, facing a sentence of death in Illinois. Four of his victims were found buried together in Newton County, Indiana, near an abandoned barn marked with an inverted pentagram. Ritualistic mutilations also marked a number of Eyler's known victims.

Robert Berdella—The confessed torture-slayer of six men in Kansas City, Missouri, Berdella denies any link to the occult, although police confiscated books on witchcraft and a satanic ritual robe in a 1988 search of his home.

Thomas Creech—Captured by Idaho authorities in 1975 and reliably linked to nine murders in six Western states, Creech confessed a total of forty-two slayings since 1967. Many of the killings were described as human sacrifices by a cult of Satanists, while others represented "contract" murders financed by an outlaw motorcycle gang. As in the case of Henry Lucas and Ottis Toole, the cultists remain elusive, and some authorities doubt Creech's claims.

Vernon Butts—A professional magician who decorated his apartment with coffins and sometimes used a casket for sex with his girlfriend, herself a practicing witch, Butts was a participant in southern California's infamous "Freeway Murders" during 1979 and 1980. In custody, Butts confessed his role in six murders, committed with ringleader William Bonin, and described the experience as "a good little nightmare." On January 11, 1981, Butts committed suicide in the Los Angeles County Jail.

Leonard Lake—A repeat killer from northern California, Lake was arrested for shoplifting in 1985 and committed suicide in custody by swallowing a cyanide capsule. A search of his rural retreat in Calaveras County turned up skeletal remains of some twenty-five victims, along with videotapes of torture-slayings committed by Lake and accomplice Charles Ng. In the wake of those disclosures, Lake's ex-wife described his long-running affiliation with a coven of witches in San Francisco. Former neighbors of Lake's from that city also recalled his claims of membership in a "death cult" that practiced ritual murder.

Michael Swango—An Illinois physician with a genius-level IQ, Swango was convicted of assault in 1985, after poisoning several hospital paramedics without apparent motive. He is also suspected of killing several patients at an Ohio hospital where he served his internship, and his medical license has been revoked in that state. A search of Swango's home revealed numerous items of occult paraphernalia, along with stockpiles of acid, chemicals, and poisons.

Wayne Nance—A Montana truck driver whose devotion to Satan dated from his teens, Nance used a heated coat hanger to brand himself with satanic symbols while he was still in high school. In September 1986, at age thirty, he was shot and killed while attempting to murder a Missoula couple in their home. Subsequent investigation linked Nance to at least five unsolved slayings since 1974.

Donald Harvey—America's premier serial killer, with eighty-seven documented victims, Harvey stalked his prey in the quiet wards of hospitals where he worked as a nurse's aide. Finally captured, more by luck than good police work, Harvey confessed his crimes in detail, drawing multiple life sentences. In a 1987 televised interview, Harvey discussed his fascination with black magic, but pointedly refused to answer questions dealing with Satanism.

Vaughn Greenwood—The infamous "Skid Row Slasher" of Los Angeles, linked to eleven murders between 1964 and 1975, Greenwood killed his victims in ritual style, posing their bodies, filling cups with blood and leaving them nearby, sprinkling salt around the corpses, and surrounding various wounds with markings of unknown significance. Convicted of nine murder counts in 1976, he was sentenced to life.

Bobby Joe Maxwell—Following in Greenwood's footsteps as the "Skid Row Stabber," Maxwell claimed nine homeless victims in October and November 1978, scrawling Satan's names in blood near one of the corpses. An ex-con from Tennessee, where he regaled cell mates with his devotion to Satan—also dubbed "Luther," for no apparent reason—Maxwell was finally arrested in the act of trying to stab another derelict. In custody, awaiting his life sentence, he told other inmates that he murdered transients "to obtain souls for Satan."

William Schmidt—Suspected of at least four murders, with victims including two of his wives, Schmidt was wearing an amulet of the mystic Osirian Order when Alabama state troopers arrested him in 1987 on a federal firearms charge. At the time of his arrest, Schmidt was driving a pickup truck with a hose connecting the exhaust pipe to a camper shell in back, creating an effective gas chamber. In 1990, Arizona police were seeking Schmidt on murder charges, when he was found dead in a Phoenix motel room.

James and Susan Carson—Adding a new twist to occult serial murders, these self-styled Moslem "warriors of Allah" took their marching orders from a passage in the Koran: "Thou shalt not allow a witch to live." Their three known victims, slain in California between 1981 and 1983, were all suspected of witchcraft by the Carsons and summarily executed for their "crimes."

William Sarmento—Slayer of two young boys near Providence, Rhode Island, in 1987, Sarmento was captured after mailing a letter to police that read, in part: "I didn't want to do it. Satan ordered me to." The same note directed authorities to the body of one victim, where physical evidence was recovered leading to Sarmento's arrest.

Joseph Danks—L.A.'s "Koreatown Slasher," sentenced to life for the murders of five male transients in January 1987, Danks continues his reign of terror behind bars. In December 1990, he strangled his elderly cell mate to death for the hell of it, telling prison guards, "I figure well, if I ever get a chance to kill somebody, I'll just kill them, even if it was just an old man." Questioned about his state of mind, Danks replied: "My transgressions are not outlandish nor reprehensible. To me they are justified. The pagan I adhere to overwhelms the Christian morality." [See: Atlanta "Child Murders"; Baker, Stanley; Berkowitz, David; Gecht, Robin; "Hands of Death"; Ramirez, Richard; "Zodiac"]

SHERMAN, PAULETTE JUNE

A resident of southwestern Missouri, known for her devotion to fundamentalist Christianity, Paulette Sherman became yet another victim of ritual murder on June 4, 1987. A coroner's report described the grisly scene:

> Subject was found by her husband, Daniel Sherman, when he returned from work at 10:12 P.M. Subject was lying on her back, feet facing the bedroom, north. Subject had been stabbed numerous times about the body, with several areas of concentration. It appeared that the assailant had tried to remove the vulva by cutting; there was a cross cut into the victim's abdomen; the heart had been repeatedly stabbed and tried to be removed; several defense wounds about the hands; the throat had been severely cut; all vessels of the neck area had been severed, both carotid arteries, both jugular veins, esophagus, wind pipe, all cut down to the spine; stab wounds to the back of the trunk, approximately 87 stab wounds in all. A black plastic-handled steak knife was found near the victim's head. The knife had been bent in a curving angle, approximately 45 degrees, and had probably been bent by striking a bone while cutting.

The bloody cross and "areas of concentration"—heart and genitals—all smack of a satanic murder, but the case remains unsolved today. The killer or killers of Paulette Sherman are still at large.

SHOSTROM, RONALD LEE

On Halloween night, 1986, teenagers Stephen Martin and Danny Machado were walking toward Martin's home, in the Los Angeles suburb of Bellflower, when a car rolled past them in the narrow alleyway. They just had time to register the driver's face—Ron Shostrom, a classmate from Sommerset High School—when Martin noticed something hanging on the fence behind his house. It was the mutilated body of a cat, rope tied around its broken neck. Nearby, fresh blood had been employed to mark Martin's garage door with the number "666" and graffiti reading "Burn in hell Steve Martin."

Sheriff's deputies were summoned to the scene, provided

with Shostrom's name, address, and description. Martin and Shostrom had once been friends, until Ronald drifted into devil worship and became obsessed with the occult. Around the time they parted company, he put a "curse" on Martin, and the latest incident appeared to fit his style.

Background investigation, including an interview with Shostrom's mother, confirmed his involvement with Satanism spanning several months. A group of friends reported seeing Shostrom with a cat that matched the slaughtered animal's description on October 31, and they recalled his threat to sacrifice the cat and drink its blood. Arrested for cruelty to animals on November 2, 1986, Shostrom was processed through the L.A. courts as a juvenile offender, his record permanently sealed when he reached age eighteen. [See: Animal Sacrifice]

SHRINE OF THE LITTLE MOTHER

A Detroit spin-off from Anton LaVey's Church of Satan, this cult was founded around 1973 by defector John Amend, also known to his disciples as Seth-Typhon. Diverging from LaVey's doctrine, Amend practiced chicken sacrifice at ceremonies and espoused a neo-Nazi stance that led him to affiliate his cult with groups like the Order of the Black Ram, the National Renaissance Party, and Canada's far-right Odinist Movement. The group faded from sight by the end of the 1970s. [See: Nazism; National Renaissance Party; Order of the Black Ram]

SIMMONS, THERESA

The van with Georgia plates was cruising slowly through downtown Gonzales, Louisiana, when patrolmen spotted it in the early hours of January 26, 1988. Suspicious of the driver's motives, the police hung back and watched until he ran a stop sign, seizing the excuse to pull him over for a chat.

Terry Belcher, age sixteen, was at the wheel; his passengers were Robert McIntyre, sixteen, and seventeen-year-old Malisa Earnest. All three hailed from Douglasville, in Georgia, and while Belcher told the officer that he was on vacation, heading for New Orleans, a computer trace revealed that the van had been reported stolen by McIntyre's parents. All three juveniles were jailed, pending investigation and determination of charges.

Later that morning, a female inmate was being released on a loitering charge when she took her jailer aside and poured out a bizarre story. Young Malisa Earnest was her cell mate, and the girl had come in babbling a mile a minute, all about a gruesome murder back in Douglasville. According to Malisa's story, she was thumbing rides with another, unnamed teenage girl when McIntyre and Belcher picked them up, proceeding to a rural farmhouse where they smoked some grass, got down with heavy metal music, and the boys began to pray in Satan's name. From there, the party had degenerated into violence, with Malisa's girlfriend sacrificed and buried in the nearby woods.

Detectives in Gonzales phoned the Douglasville police on January 27, hoping to resolve the mystery. By that time, they had freed Malisa Earnest, lacking any charge on which to hold her, but the boys remained in jail. Authorities in Douglasville reported that Malisa had been recently committed to a home for troubled juveniles, from which she fled a few days earlier with three other runaways. Two of the girls had since returned, but Earnest and another girl—seventeen-year-old Theresa Simmons—were still at large. A friend of Simmons had received a call on January 22, Theresa saying that she didn't trust the two boys who had picked her up, and she was planning to return within a day or two.

She never made it.

Belcher and McIntyre were flown back to Atlanta, where Georgia detectives took over the grilling. Terry Belcher admitted picking Earnest and Simmons up along the highway, but he insisted Theresa was alive and well when they parted company. Trying a different tack, investigators asked if Belcher knew anything about Satanism ... and their subject seemed to come alive.

In fact, said Belcher, he had joined a devil-worship cult about twelve months ago, nine members regularly sacrificing animals and guzzling the blood, sometimes consuming eyes and other organs for dessert. In time, Belcher went on to form his own coven, recruiting McIntyre and Earnest as two of his disciples. "It was neat. It gave me power," Belcher said.

And, having gone that far, he grudgingly admitted that Theresa Simmons had been killed. Malisa Earnest was the culprit, Belcher said. The four of them had spent an evening sharing drugs, invoking Lucifer, and dancing to the heavy metal beat, but things got out of hand. At one point, Belcher left the room with McIntyre, and they returned to find Malisa strangling her girlfriend in a frenzy. Simmons had been killed before the boys could pull Malisa off.

That afternoon, patrolmen found Malisa Earnest at the Atlanta bus depot, and they brought her in for questioning. The news of her arrival rattled Terry Belcher, and he soon revised his story to conform more closely with the truth. It seemed that he and McIntyre were hot to graduate from snuffing helpless animals. They wanted larger game, a human sacrifice, and Earnest had agreed to put her girlfriend on the spot. With drugs to give them courage and appropriate quotations from LaVey's *Satanic Bible* hanging in the air, they took turns strangling Theresa Simmons with a leather shoelace, later planting her behind the vacant house.

All three cultists were charged with first-degree murder, and Terry Belcher went to trial in May 1988. Unrepentant on the witness stand, Belcher regaled jurors with his descriptions of animal sacrifice: "We ate their eyeballs and innards and drank their blood. We toasted the devil by drinking the blood. The rituals were performed for power, the taste of blood. I got money, power, sex, drugs, anything I wanted. It was easy to get. It was like Satan helped you get them."

Belcher was duly convicted of murder, returning to court a month later as the state's chief witness against Robert McIntyre. Both killers were sentenced to life, while Malisa Earnest—convicted as an accomplice—got off with a three-year prison term.

SISMAN, RONALD

Maury Terry's investigation of the New York "Son of Sam" murders produced much disturbing evidence of satanic crime in America, but none more persuasive than triggerman David Berkowitz's ability to predict ongoing crimes from behind prison walls. In mid-October 1981, Berkowitz informed a jailhouse confidant that his cult had a ritual murder planned for Halloween, described as "an inside, housecleaning thing" that would combine human sacrifice with the elimination of a perceived weak link.

As described by the informant, quoting Berkowitz, the

murder would take place in or near Greenwich Village. "On October 31, look for a kinky or bizarre assassination," the informant wrote to Terry. "Male(s) and female(s). Their heads shot off. And they'll remove the evidence just like they ransacked Berkowitz's place."

Shortly after midnight, on the morning of October 31, 1981, unknown gunmen invaded the Manhattan brownstone occupied by Ronald Sisman on West 22nd Street, adjoining Greenwich Village. Before they left, Sisman and his companion—twenty-year-old Elizabeth Plotzman, from Long Island—were executed by close-range shots to the head. As predicted two weeks in advance, the dwelling was ransacked in an apparent search for concealed valuables.

Police identified Sisman as a thirty-five-year-old Canadian photographer, suspected of pimping and dealing in drugs. The double murder was officially listed as a drug burn, but Berkowitz offered another motive. In his version, Sisman possessed "snuff" tapes taken at the scene of one "Sam" shooting, and he planned to trade them for immunity on pending cocaine charges. Thus, the elimination of a "weak link" in the cult, while his execution also provided the desired Halloween bloodletting. Berkowitz also furnished an accurate description of Sisman's apartment, complete with ornate chandelier.

Further investigation by Terry and others revealed that Sisman was a close associate of millionaire Roy Radin, himself described by Berkowitz as a "fat cat" or "Mr. Big" of the cult in New York. Police questioned Radin about Sisman's death, but he claimed total ignorance. Other questions were pending, about his drug and cult connections, when Radin was kidnapped and murdered in May 1983. At this writing, the Sisman-Plotzman homicides remain officially unsolved. [See: Berkowitz, David; Radin, Roy; "Snuff" Films]

SLAVERY

Dating from the early 1970s, persistent tales have surfaced linking devil-worship cults in the United States and elsewhere to illegal trafficking in captive human beings. Such reports of modern slavery are often linked to prostitution or pornography, especially where teens and children are concerned. Skeptics point to a lack of convictions to buttress such claims, but their blanket dismissal of the notion seems ill-founded.

In April 1978, for instance, the *New York Times* reported that growing numbers of European girls and women were being abducted for sale as prostitutes in the Middle East. A Swiss police official described most of the victims as runaways or adventure seekers, targeted by roving "talent scouts." "At some point," he explained, "an organization takes over and channels them into enforced prostitution." A Turkish policeman confirmed the report, but said police in Europe and the Middle East "are too busy with terrorists to be bothered with more runaways."

Closer to home, Dr. Judianne Densen-Gerber, founder of Odyssey House for abused children, estimates that between eight hundred and one thousand American children are stolen each year, for sale or "lease" to foreign pedophiles. "We understand they are sold to cultures which have a tremendous interest in children," she says, "such as the Arab cultures. And, of course, in their world, blond, fair-haired children would get a higher price."

Author Robin Lloyd, an expert on child prostitution rings, told the U.S. House Select Committee on Education and Labor of an eleven-year-old Texas boy who was kidnapped in the late 1970s by agents of a pornographer who offered $25,000 per head for blond Anglo children delivered to Mexico City. "I don't believe the figure for one moment," Lloyd told the committee, "but both the Texas Rangers and the FBI have told me on the phone that the operation is very much active and that children are being taken into Mexico for that purpose." Around the same time, spokesmen for the Texas House Select Committee on Child Pornography announced that investigators were following leads to organized rings in Dallas, Houston, and other large Texas cities, suspected of holding slave auctions for teenage Mexican boys smuggled into the United States. The committee was also pursuing rumors of "snuff" films produced in Texas, featuring murders of children, but the films remain elusive. Five years later, serial killer Henry Lucas described his membership in a satanic cult, with paid duties including the transportation of kidnapped American children to Mexico, but subsequent retraction of the charges has largely discredited Lucas, and the FBI shows no interest in pursuing his claims.

Lucas aside, if legislators and detectives are correct in their description of a modern, organized flesh trade, it would go far toward solving America's persistent problem of missing children. In 1984, the U.S. Department of Health and Human Resources estimated that 1.8 million children vanish from home every year. Ninety-five percent are listed as runaways, and ninety percent of those return home within two weeks, leaving a "mere" 171,000 children at large on the streets. Five percent of the missing—some 90,000 children—are tagged as abductees, with 72,000 reportedly kidnapped by parents involved in bitter custody disputes. The other 18,000 children are simply gone.

FBI spokesmen, meanwhile, have changed their tune in the face of implied criticism, reporting that the Bureau investigated only 150 "stranger abductions" of children between 1984 and 1986, but what does this disclaimer really prove? Federal agents normally remain aloof from kidnap cases in the absence of ransom demands or concrete evidence of interstate flight, and they take no notice whatsoever of runaways. In practice, this means that no one is looking for potential victims of modern slave traders, satanic or otherwise. As FBI "cult expert" Ken Lanning explains, for the record: "There's nothing to it, so we don't waste time investigating." [See: "Cole, Toby"; "Hands of Death"; Pornography; Prostitution; "Snuff" Films]

SMITH, HAROLD GLENN

At seventeen, Harold Smith was best described as odd. A year had passed since he dropped out of high school in his native Houston, Texas, and informed his mother: "Mom, I've called up Satan and I've given him my soul." Since then, he had been working part-time with his brother, trimming trees, but mostly he smoked grass or gobbled pills and wandered the apartment complex, "casting spells." Friends called him Jack, but Smith preferred to call himself "The Wizard," and he wore a pointed hat to match his nickname, painting dark mascara circles underneath his eyes.

By July 1985, Smith's reliance on drugs was so flagrant that his mother kicked him out of the apartment. Joined by sixteen-year-old Martin Wayne Tosh, Smith moved in with another friend, one Dennis Keith Medler, but their rowdy ways soon wore on Medler's nerves and they were shown the door. Yet another crony, John-Michael Alexander Trimmer, offered the pair a place to stay, but their luck ran out when Trimmer himself was evicted, and Smith was forced to go home, begging his mother for a second chance.

She gave him one, but her son had no intention of turning over a new leaf. By that time, Tosh and Trimmer had joined him in organizing a small satanic cult, whose other members were eighteen-year-old Michael Gene Cravey, sixteen-year-old Shannon Rivera, and Shannon's roommate Bridgette Stowe. The group experimented with drugs and sacrificed animals to Satan, but something was missing. What they needed to spice things up, The Wizard decreed in early August, was a human sacrifice. And who better to serve the cause than Dennis Medler, who had already wronged the cult by kicking Smith and Tosh out of his home?

On the night of August 6, Cravey lured Medler to a field in northern Harris County, behind Rest Haven Cemetery, on the pretense of hunting psychedelic mushrooms. Smith and company were waiting when the two of them arrived, five cultists falling on Medler, binding his hands and feet before they launched their ceremony. Told that he was marked for death, Medler asked his captors to knock him unconscious, but repeated blows to the head and face with a length of pipe failed to do the job. As the ordeal went on, Medler was strangled, beaten, and stabbed; Shannon Rivera tried to set his hair on fire with a cigarette lighter, but fresh blood quenched the flames, spoiling her fun. After each of the five took turns slashing Medler's throat, Trimmer told the corpse: "Hey, Keith, it was nothing personal. We just wanted to see someone die."

Medler's mutilated, decomposing body was found on August 14 by a rancher tending cattle in the field. Sheriff's officers were still searching for evidence on September 3, when twenty-five-year-old Donald Dull was hospitalized in Houston, suffering from knife wounds to the throat and arm. Dull's assailant was a teenage hitchhiker who had also stolen his car, and the description led police to John-Michael Trimmer. In custody, Trimmer swiftly confessed the attack on Dull, then surprised detectives with a recitation of his role in the Medler attack, naming names.

The roundup began on September 10 and was finished the following day. Smith, Tosh, and Rivera were captured in Houston, while Cravey was run to earth and arrested near

New Orleans. In addition to the Medler slaying, Michael Cravey was also charged with murder in the case of twenty-five-year-old Ronald Monahan, found stabbed to death in his Houston apartment on September 7. As with Medler's case, the Monahan murder was described by police as a brutal, apparently motiveless crime.

While Trimmer was content to take his chances with a guilty plea on murder and attempted murder charges, he refused to testify against his fellow Satanists. Prosecutors found their witness in the person of Bridgette Stowe, who had waited at home while the others went off to kill Medler, afterward listening in horror as they returned to boast of their deed. By late November, with Tosh and Rivera certified to stand trial as adults, the D.A.'s office was ready to proceed.

Harold Smith was the first to face trial, in August 1986, with Bridgette Stowe describing how Medler's death was planned for weeks before the fact, his killers scheming to make the ordeal as slow and painful as possible. An hour after the killing, Smith had bragged of beating Medler with a metal pipe, gouging out one of his eyes, and slashing the teenager's throat. The murder, Smith had said, was "like a sacrifice." Smith, for his part, testified that discussions of Medler's impending death were "a joke." He was "surprised" when his companions sprang upon their victim, and while he admitted binding Medler's legs—supposedly fearing for his own life if he refused—The Wizard denied ever striking or stabbing the victim. Jurors believed Stowe's account, convicting Smith of first-degree murder on August 13. A day later, he was sentenced to life imprisonment, plus an uncollectable $10,000 fine.

Seven weeks later, on October 2, John-Michael Trimmer entered formal guilty pleas to murder and attempted murder (in the case of Donald Dull), receiving two concurrent sixty-year prison terms. Michael Cravey was sentenced to life imprisonment on April 6, 1987. A month later, on May 8, Shannon Rivera was sentenced to fifteen years for her part in the crime, a jury's decision that she used no "deadly weapon" permitting parole after less than two years. Martin Tosh was the last of the cult to face trial, pleading guilty to murder and drawing a twenty-year sentence on May 13, 1987. The cultists were also suspected of two other slayings—those of sixteen-year-old Wayne Schubert and a teenage "Jane Doe"—

but in the absence of confessions or compelling evidence, no further charges were filed.

SMITH, MICHELLE

The first publicized survivor of satanic ritual child abuse, Canadian Michelle Smith was twenty-three years old in 1973, when she first consulted psychiatrist Lawrence Pazder for treatment of depression in Victoria, British Columbia. Three years later, following her third miscarriage, Smith returned to Pazder's office for further therapy, haunted by nightmares of spiders erupting from the skin of her hand. By that time, Dr. Pazder was familiar with Michelle's background—including the loss of her mother to cancer when Michelle was fourteen, followed by her alcoholic father's disappearance, Michelle's placement with her maternal grandparents, and her enrollment at a convent school. Still, something more than the evident trauma of adolescence seemed to be dogging his patient's dreams.

Pazder used hypnosis to unlock Michelle's past, resulting in a twenty-five-minute bout of nonstop screaming followed by fourteen months of sessions in which she recalled grim satanic rituals from early childhood. As remembered by Michelle in therapy, her mother was a member of the cult led by a sadist named Malachi. Michelle's hypnotic memories—eerily similar to reports from numerous child abuse victims in the 1980s—included candlelit ceremonies conducted by black-robed adults, graveyard visits in the dead of night, mutilation of cats, plus the sacrifice and cremation of human infants. On one occasion, Michelle says, she witnessed the beating death of an adult woman, after which she and the lifeless victim were placed in a car and deliberately run off the road in a staged "accident." Medical reports confirm Michelle's injury in an auto crash at age five, but surviving files contain no reference to a fatality in the case.

Michelle's credibility suffered when she began to describe a climactic ritual called the "Feast of the Beast," performed at intervals of twenty-seven years. In 1955, she was reportedly selected as the cult's sacrifice to Satan . . . who appeared in the scaly flesh, complete with barbed tail and a penchant for third-rate poetry. Michelle was finally rescued, she says, by the personal intervention of the Virgin Mary and Jesus

Christ, whereupon Satan departed in a huff, scolding his disciples with a last bit of verse: "It's your mistake, you'll have to pay. I give her back. You can't give her away."

How much credence should be given to Michelle's report or Pazder's personal endorsement of her memories as accurate? Skeptics suggest that Smith's memories are simply hysterical fantasy, rooted in "normal" childhood abuse, which Dr. Pazder—a Roman Catholic—has willfully misinterpreted to create a religious crusade. The hundreds of adults and children who corroborate her statements with their own reports are dismissed as pathological liars, unbalanced mental cases, or publicity seekers. More to the point, psychiatrists in England, Canada, and the United States are charged with reading Smith's 1980 biography—*Michelle Remembers*—and casting their education aside to pursue a medieval witch-hunt, blindly jeopardizing their lucrative careers to promote fundamentalist superstition and slander innocent persons with false charges of child abuse. On balance, while some of Smith's "memories" are clearly implausible, it is easier to believe in localized satanic cult activity than in a global plot by self-destructive mental health professionals. [See: Child Abuse; "Feast of the Beast"]

"SNUFF" FILMS

An enduring subject of controversy in the media and law-enforcement community, "snuff" films—that is, a cinematic record of actual murders—represent the ultimate obscenity, combining homicide and pornography for a select, perverted audience. Reports of such movies or videotapes have circulated throughout America since the late 1960s, with cult-crime investigators claiming that Satanists and other "black" magicians sometimes turn a profit by recording gruesome deaths. Cult apologists deny that such films exist, but persuasive evidence points to an affluent, sadistic clientele for whom "ordinary" pornography lacks the desired "kick."

As far back as June 1977, Sgt. Lloyd Martin, chief investigator for LAPD's sexually abused children's unit, described a network of kidnappers who smuggle Mexican boys into the United States for sale to violent pedophiles. As outlined by Martin, specially designed vehicles were used to carry human prey across the border. "They bring them in eight at a time under the floorboards," Martin told newsmen. "Then they take them to a motel and clean them up. It's getting more violent. It's as if the kids aren't enough. Now there's the need for blood."

Dr. Judianne Densen-Gerber, founder of Odyssey House for abused children, agrees that foreign children are being smuggled into the U.S. and sold "primarily for the purpose of killing. An American youngster has a school record and a family. But if a child has been taken off the streets of Guadalajara or Acapulco, it's much easier. There are thousands of these nameless, faceless children whose parents may have been told that the child is going for adoption, and whose parents may agree simply because they want to afford that child a better life than they had. So here is a man in a Cadillac who looks nice. And they never hear from that child again."

If reports from occult survivors are correct, at least some of the smuggled children wind up on sacrificial altars, thereby answering the skeptic's question: "Where do these alleged victims come from if we don't have any missing children in the neighborhood?" One of Dr. Robert Mayer's psychiatric patients, describing satanic rituals as the root of her own multiple personality disorder, has described the bloody sacrifice of children "illegally imported, mostly from South America," and similar tales are told by scores of other children and adults alike. In Bakersfield, California, for instance, children who complained of satanic ritual abuse lost credibility when they described the murders of "brown babies" whose bodies were never found.

In 1980, New York police reported persistent rumors of 8mm "snuff" films selling for $1,500 each or screening for $200 a head at private showings. No movies were ever seized, but around the same time, Associated Press reports noted the mutilation-murders of several prostitutes in Argentina, local police suggesting that the crimes may have been captured on film. Detective Joseph Horman, of NYPD's Organized Crime Control Bureau, suggested that some of the films may only simulate murder, while others depict the real thing. Reports are on file of such films being shot in New York, Los Angeles, Miami, New Orleans, and Houston, but hard evidence remained elusive through the 1970s.

In terms of border crossings, evidence suggests the highway runs both ways. Serial killers Henry Lucas and Ottis Toole, professed members of a satanic cult that dealt in drugs and snuff, have each described their trips carrying Anglo children kidnapped in America to a ranch in Mexico. A map drawn by Lucas placed the ranch close to Matamoros, in the same vicinity where Adolfo Constanzo's cultists sacrificed fifteen victims in 1988 and 1989. At the same time, ex–FBI agent Ted Gunderson, former Los Angeles bureau chief, told reporters, "I've received information from numerous sources about a ranch in Mexico where the children and some of these women are taken." The Texas House Committee on Child Pornography reports that "slave" auctions of sixteen- and seventeen-year-old boys are a routine fact of life in Mexico, with at least some of the victims murdered on camera.

Do snuff films exist? And if so, *is* there a cult connection?

In 1970, Charles Manson, Bobby Beausoleil, and other members of the Manson "family" freely admitted that films were made of various cult activities around southern California. During the "family" murder trials, loops of Manson porn were selling for a quarter of a million dollars in New York, and associate Vern Plumlee has also described films of Mansonites "dancing with knives" and "pretending to cut each other up." Another informant, speaking to author Ed Sanders, professed personal knowledge of Manson films depicting both animal and human sacrifice. One reel portrayed the slaughter of a dog, he said, while another featured a cat blown apart with powerful "M80" firecrackers. The final reel depicts a nude, decapitated woman lying on a beach while black-robed, hooded figures circle the corpse, "throwing blood all over."

A decade later, in 1981, convicted "Son of Sam" gunman David Berkowitz told prison confidants that at least one "Sam" attack—the shooting of Robert Violante and Stacy Moskowitz—was recorded on videotape for the private collection of a Satanist "Mr. Big," later identified as millionaire Roy Radin. In October 1981, Berkowitz predicted the Halloween murder of photographer and suspected drug dealer Ronald Sisman, allegedly committed because Sisman planned to trade the Moskowitz tape for leniency on a pending cocaine charge. The tape has not been found, and Radin was himself assassinated before he could be questioned by police.

In 1985, in Hamilton, Ontario, the daughters of Gordon and Sharon Wells accused their parents of satanic ritual abuse, including human sacrifices that were filmed and photographed. The girls directed police to a local television studio, describing its interior from memory, but skeptical authorities refused to search the studio or question members of the staff. No evidence of homicide was found, but a judge was sufficiently impressed with the girls' testimony to remove them permanently from the custody of their parents.

Following the June 1985 suicide of serial killer Leonard Lake, police found pits filled with human remains at his rural home in northern California. Also found were videocassettes depicting the humiliation, torture, rape, and death of several female victims—that is, "snuff" tapes by definition. Unproven rumors suggest that Lake may have financed his paramilitary arsenal by selling off copies of the tapes. However that may be, Lake's ex-wife recalls his enduring fascination with witchcraft, and neighbors in San Francisco report Lake describing himself as a member of a "death cult."

Three years later, in June 1988, Satanists Jason Rose and John Jones were charged with the murder of victim Melissa Meyer in Springfield, Oregon. Both killers were convicted and sentenced to prison, thanks in large part to the videotape they preserved of their "sacrifice," a crucial piece of evidence found when police searched Rose's home.

Still, cult-watchers insist that "snuff" films are as much a matter of business as pleasure. In August 1989, U.S. Attorney Henry Hudson announced the arrest of two men in Alexandria, Virginia, held without bail on charges of plotting to kidnap, molest, and murder a boy between the ages of eight and thirteen. As described in the indictment, thirty-four-year-old Dean Lambey and twenty-eight-year-old Daniel Depew plotted to abduct or purchase a boy between the ages of eight and thirteen, then videotape his suffering during two weeks of torture. According to Hudson, the defendants planned to kill their victim, erase all signs of torture in an acid bath, and dump the body in a swamp outside Washington, D.C. The plot fell through when Lambey and Depew tried to strike a bargain with an undercover policeman, who in turn reported their intentions to the FBI.

"SON OF SAM": See BERKOWITZ, DAVID

SONS OF SATAN

In early 1974, a student at Kilgore (Texas) Junior College submitted a term paper detailing the bloody rites of a cult calling itself "The Sons of Satan." The paper described nocturnal raids on ranches where the cultists killed and mutilated cattle, timing the event to catch dawn's early light filtering down through the branches of surrounding trees. So essential were the limbs, in fact, that members of the sect took spares along on every hunt, in case they were compelled to kill on open ground, without a tree nearby.

The paper raised some skeptical eyebrows at Kilgore J.C., and the student was forced to start from scratch with a new topic after he named his source as a friend acquainted with several cult members. Meanwhile, an English professor from Pennsylvania claimed knowledge of the same group, telling Texas newsmen that he knew "some [cult] girls who cut off their fingers and pieces of their ears and things like that." A sure road to advancement in the Sons of Satan allegedly called for members to demonstrate courage by eating their own flesh. At this writing, no members of the group have been identified, but speculation persists on a possible link to unsolved cattle mutilations in Texas and elsewhere. [See: Livestock Mutilations]

SPREITZER, EDWARD: See GECHT, ROBIN

"STONERS"

A generic term for loose-knit adolescent gangs that mix drug abuse with Satanism and sporadic criminal activity, "stoners"—so called for their chronic drug use—have emerged since the late 1970s as a unique problem for American law enforcement. More inclined to purchase drugs than sell them—though the evidence of trafficking has grown in recent years—teenage stoners live on heavy metal music and defiance of authority in any form. Across the country, they are linked with incidents of vandalism, random violence, grave robbing, self-mutilation, and animal sacrifice.

Stoner rituals are typically a hodgepodge lifted from LaVey's *Satanic Bible* and the drugged imaginations of the

various participants. While animals are often slaughtered and
their blood or flesh consumed by celebrants, authorities agree
that stoners are more interested in shocking the adult community than conjuring Lord Satan and his minions in the flesh.
Around Los Angeles, Detective Pat Metoyer calls the stoners
a "subculture within the subculture" of local gangs, moving
from one turf to another with relative impunity. An LAPD
staff report described the stoner rituals, but it was "eighty-
sixed," according to Metoyer, to avoid potential claims of in-
terference with religious freedom. In Las Vegas, juvenile
authorities are more succinct. White youths try Satanism, the
police maintain, "because they get their ass kicked going up
against the black and Latin gangs."

SULLIVAN, THOMAS, Jr.

A fourteen-year-old Boy Scout and student at a Catholic
parochial school in Jefferson Township, New Jersey, Tom
Sullivan was described as an "all-American boy" before December 1987. Around that time, one of his teachers assigned
students to research unfamiliar religions, and while Sullivan
wrote his paper on Hinduism, he appeared more interested in
the reports of several classmates dealing with a different
topic: Satanism.

Over the next two weeks, friends and family reported a
change "like night and day" in Sullivan, as he immersed himself in books on the occult and "heavy metal" music, making
a rapid slide into angry rebellion and defiance. For a solid
week in January 1988, Sullivan's father recalls the boy singing a morbid song "about blood and killing your mother."

On Saturday, January 11, a family argument drove Sullivan
from lyrics to action. That night, he killed his mother, stabbing her at least twelve times with his Boy Scout knife, then
set fire to the house, apparently trying to kill his father and
ten-year-old brother while they slept. Trudging through the
snow to a neighbor's backyard, Sullivan finished the rampage
by slashing his own wrists and throat, slumping dead on the
spot. His father and brother escaped the burning house without injury, but Jefferson Township would never be the same.

In the wake of the grim murder-suicide, rumors of rampant
teenage cultism spread through town like wildfire. "I'm willing to bet there's got to be more involved," Mayor Fran

Slayton declared. "There's just something that's bothering me about this situation. It bothers me that a good kid like that can go in two weeks." At this writing, no evidence of wider cult activity has been uncovered in the area, but fears and doubts remain.

TEMPLE OF NEPTHYS

An offshoot of Michael Aquino's Temple of Set, the Temple of Nepthys (female counterpart to Set in Egyptian mythology) was founded in 1986 by Lynn Johnson, a recent defector from Aquino's sect and fiancée—later wife—of Aquino's brother-in-law. Disenchanted with what she perceived as the Temple of Set's authoritarian leadership, antifeminist slant, and growing preoccupation with Nazi ritual, Johnson sought a more comfortable setting for mystic expression, persuading fiancé William Butch to join her in foundation of a new, custom-tailored cult.

Incorporated as a nonprofit organization, the Temple of Nepthys is based in Mill Valley, California, near San Francisco. From nine founding members, the cult soon expanded to an estimated ninety followers, most of them females ranging in age from their late teens to midthirties. While most of the Temple's doctrines are similar to those of the parent body, a strong feminist flavor appeals primarily to young women—hence the selection of Nepthys as the cult's titular deity. Disciples of Nepthys practice the "red arts"—as opposed to black or white—aiming for a state in which "the psychecentric consciousness can evolve toward its own divinity." By 1988, financial difficulties led to discussion of a loose merger with Anton LaVey's Church of Satan, thus bringing the Aquino exodus full circle. [See: Aquino, Michael; Nazism; Temple of Set]

TEMPLE OF SET

Organized in June 1975, the Temple of Set developed from a philosophical rift in Anton LaVey's Church of Satan. Defector Michael Aquino, formerly in charge of the church's *Clo-*

ven Hoof newsletter, couched his move in terms of a divine—or demonic—revelation from Set, the ancient Egyptian counterpart of Satan, as spelled out by Aquino (presumably speaking for Set) in *The Book of Coming Forth by Night.* According to Aquino/Set: "Upon the ninth solstice, I destroyed my pact with Anton LaVey. Thus all may understand that he is dearly held by me, and that the Church of Satan is not a shame to him. But a new Aeon is now to begin, and the work of Anton Szandor LaVey is done."

Behind the scenes, Aquino was admittedly put off by LaVey's theatrical corruption of "ethical" Satanism, including sale of priesthoods to the highest bidder without regard to magical qualifications. The Temple of Set was designed as a rallying point for disaffected Satanists, and the new group's ruling Council of Nine drew its membership from ex-priests in the Church of Satan. The Temple copied its overall structure from LaVey's church, calling its local chapters "pylons" instead of "grottoes." In terms of doctrine, however, Aquino's "Setians" regarded Set—or Satan—as a literal deity, while LaVey denied the existence of any supreme being. The Temple of Set promotes evolution into "higher men" through a process dubbed "xeper" (pronounced "keffer"), and new recruits are supplied with a lengthy reading list, various novels and nonfiction volumes rated by Aquino as "essential," "highly-specialized," or "dangerous." (Curiously, the "dangerous" titles include three novels in the fictional *Omen* series, based on screenplays for popular horror films produced between 1976 and 1980. No explanation of their "danger" is supplied, but Aquino was reportedly obsessed with the films, to the extent that he had the number "666" tattooed on his scalp.)

Aquino's exodus marked the nadir of LaVey's satanic church, but it was not the genesis of a new mass movement. By the end of the decade, recognized "pylons" were active in San Francisco, San Jose, Los Angeles, Detroit, New York, and Washington, D.C. Author Art Lyons estimates the total membership at 100 "Setians," but other estimates credit the Temple with two or three times that number, including a dominant group of U.S. military officers. Aquino, himself a lieutenant colonel in the army, stepped down as High Priest in 1979, but the "dictatorial" tactics of his unnamed successor sparked protests in the ranks, and the Council of Nine lured Aquino from retirement in 1982. By that time, however, the

Temple was already plagued with dissension, its membership slipping beyond recall.

Aquino described the great rift of 1985 as a kind of demonic coup, with disloyal members striving to undermine his "ethical" Satanism. For their part, the defectors—led by Aquino's sister-in-law, Lynn Butch—tell a very different story. In their version, it was Aquino's authoritarian attitude, male chauvinism, and preoccupation with Nazi Germany which drove ex-Setians to create the new Temple of Nepthys, a "kinder, gentler" cult dedicated to the female counterpart of Set. Aquino's image was further damaged in November 1987, when police raided his home in connection with a child-molesting scandal at the San Francisco Presidio. No charges were ever filed against Aquino or any other member of the cult, but the adverse publicity was hard to overcome.

Perhaps the most telling commentary on the Temple of Set is provided by sociologist Gini Graham Scott, who studied the sect in the early 1980s and published her findings in a 1983 book titled *The Magicians*. Calling Aquino's group the "Church of Hu," with its members dubbed "Hutians," Scott described the average gathering as a session where initiates sit around and complain of the "everyday frustrations which led them to want power—such as problems with jobs and relationships." In this respect, the Temple might be therapeutic, but Scott ended her survey on a more ominous note, concluding that the Setians "represent a potentially growing threat to society," their specific philosophy contributing to a "growing climate of fear and hatred" in America. [See: Aquino, Michael; Nazism; Temple of Nepthys]

TERRORISM

At first glance, any link between occult practitioners and a political agenda may appear unlikely—even ludicrous—but a review of history suggests that self-styled witches, "black" magicians, and the like are often drawn to the extremes of politics and social activism, their peculiar view of man, morality, and "magick" predisposing some of them toward violence on behalf of this or that selected cause. For others, no apparent cause is necessary. As with the political extremists who have left their bloody mark from the United States to

Europe and the Middle East, sometimes the urge to terrorize society becomes an end unto itself.

Medieval witch cults are a prime example, shifting from idyllic paganism into peasant revolution as the Inquisition gathered steam, with members setting off by night to trample crops, tear down barns and bridges, or slaughter livestock. By the sixteenth century, coven meetings featured regular "show-and-tell" sessions, with individual witches reciting their acts of mischief, and satanic groups like Germany's Buxen enjoyed nocturnal forays of rape, robbery, and murder. Even New York's Dr. Leo Martello, founder of the short-lived Witch's Antidefamation League, admits that early pacts with Satan included pledges to "kill men with poison," "sink ships," "bewitch men's corn," "kill men's cattle," and "create terror in humans." In that respect, European witch cults—and, by extension, their covens in the American colonies—were as much anarchic terrorist societies as they were embodiments of any pre-Christian religion.

The Bavarian Illuminati, founded on occult Masonic principles in 1776, was openly dedicated to the violent overthrow of royal families throughout Europe, and scholars still debate its role in the French Revolution and subsequent Reign of Terror. Ninety years later, in the American South, occultist Albert Pike incorporated Masonic ritual and the teachings of magician Eliphas Levi when he composed the constitution of the original Ku Klux Klan. Thousands of innocent persons were killed or maimed by the night-riding KKK before federal troops restored order in 1872, and cult links with the resurgent Klan have endured to the present day.

No modern government has been more firmly linked to terrorism—or more steeped in the occult—than Nazi Germany. Adolf Hitler's National Socialist Party was conceived and organized by German occultists after World War I, and the ultimate course of the next global conflict—including significant aspects of the Holocaust and some of Hitler's more peculiar military strategies—were determined by the mystical beliefs of Der Führer and his closest associates. Today, many Satanists are still obsessed with the Third Reich's "magical achievements," a fascination that includes acceptance of repugnant Nazi racial theories.

Some occult societies practice terrorist violence within their own ranks, as demonstrated by the American Ordo Templi Orientis after World War II. In California, a personal feud between OTO members Jack Parsons and L. Ron Hubbard climaxed in the supposed bombing of Hubbard's new yacht, purchased with stolen cult funds; six years later, Parsons was killed while manufacturing illegal explosives in the basement of his Pasadena home. Nor was Hubbard prone to turn the other cheek. Defectors from his spin-off cult, the Church of Scientology, have for years accused Hubbard and other "church" leaders of terrorist activities including death threats, late-night anonymous phone calls, and ruinous harassment lawsuits.

In Haiti, birthplace and Mecca of the voodoo religion, dictator "Papa Doc" Duvalier and his successor son—dubbed "Baby Doc"—took full advantage of local superstition to strengthen their totalitarian regime. The elder Duvalier went so far as to pose as Baron Samedi, voodoo's lord of the dead, and kept an effigy of Baron Samedi in his office at the presidential palace. Duvalier's secret police, the dreaded Tonton Macoutes, also invoked the trappings of voodoo to terrorize peasants when bullets and torture failed. Outside official circles, Haitian voodoo priests have intimidated their neighbors for generations with the threat of being turned into "zombies," a process that medical science has only begun to understand in recent years.

The late 1960s brought a new rash of occult-related terrorism to America, spawned by the London-based Process Church of Final Judgment. Cofounder Mary Anne DeGrimston preached about "The Fear," recruiting members of California outlaw motorcycle gangs as "Satan's agents" for the coming war to end all wars. Charles Manson was a student (and perhaps an active member) of the Process, borrowing the "fear" rap when he urged the drugged-out members of his cult to "terrorize society" and launch a black-white race war christened "Helter Skelter." At least eight persons died in the pursuit of Charlie's dream, but his conviction and imprisonment did not prevent surviving members of his "family" from wreaking havoc on society. In the summer of 1975, Mansonites Lynette "Squeaky" Fromme and Sandra Good began mailing death threats to corporate executives they accused of polluting the earth. That September, Fromme was arrested for threatening President Gerald Ford with a pistol in Sacramento, California, and conviction earned her a life sentence. In March 1976, Sandra Good was convicted for her role in the letter-writing campaign; she drew a sentence of fifteen years and served nearly ten before she was finally paroled, still professing her undying loyalty to Manson.

Elsewhere in America, satanic cults like the Order of the Black Ram and the Shrine of the Little Mother have openly joined ranks with neo-Nazi groups and factions of the modern Ku Klux Klan. In June 1969, a group called WITCH—the Women's International Terrorist Corps from Hell—surfaced at the University of Chicago, staging demonstrations to protest the lack of occult studies on campus. In Atlanta, Georgia, private investigators hired by the Congress of Racial Equality have linked a series of brutal children's murders to a drug-dealing cult and fringe elements of the KKK, apparently desirous of provoking riots in the black community.

Indeed, from coast to coast, sporadic acts of violence and vandalism indicate a sick trend toward terror for its own sake. Cemeteries and houses of worship are desecrated, vandalized with satanic graffiti and worse. Pets are tortured and killed, their mutilated remains left on doorsteps, in driveways, or draped across fences. In 1982, a satanic cult calling itself the Reign of Terror—ROT for short—harassed investigators working on a string of arson fires. Four years later, in Las Vegas, a teenage Satanist blew his own foot off while constructing pipe bombs at home. Public schools are often the scene of cult-related incidents, from Collins, Colorado (where teacher Audrey Marshall reports that forty percent of her special education students have been beaten or harassed by teenage Satanists) to Nashville, Indiana (where threats from the heavy metal "Wrath Child" gang left one student injured with stab wounds and another in jail). [See: Animal Sacrifice; Atlanta "Child Murders"; Hubbard, Lafayette; Human Sacrifice; Illuminati; Livestock Mutilations; Manson "Family"; Nazism; Ordo Templi Orientis; Process Church of Final Judgment; Shostrom, Ronald; "Stoners"; Witch Cults; Zombies]

THEE ORTHODOX SATANIC CHURCH OF NETHILIUM RITE

Organized in Chicago during 1971, this cult was founded by Terry Taylor, owner of the Occult Book Shop, as an alternative to Anton LaVey's Church of Satan. In Taylor's philosophy, God the Creator was responsible for Satan's existence, with Satan in turn serving man as the source of all knowledge. Weekly meetings were held at the book shop until 1974, when Taylor's ex-wife filed suit to prevent him from bringing their daughter into the cult. According to documents filed with the court, Taylor not only drove the girl to his store in a hearse, but also habitually slept in a coffin. Public embarrassment shattered Taylor's group, which had claimed 538 members in 1973. A splinter group, Thee Satanic Church, struggled to survive under the leadership of Dr. Evelyn Paglini, but its days in Chicago were numbered.

THIRD TEMPLE OF BAAL

A paper organization conceived and advertised by a Minneapolis accountant, this one-man "cult" is described in magazine ads as a "spiritual organization dedicated to dominance, conquest, murder, and slavery." Based on investigation by journalist Arthur Lyons, the "group" has a mailing list of two hundred correspondents, but no membership per se. [See: Warlords of Satan]

TOOLE, OTTIS ELWOOD:
See "HANDS OF DEATH"

UNDERWAGER, RALPH

A Lutheran minister turned Ph.D., Minnesota's Ralph Underwager spent two decades dabbling in sex therapy and psychology before striking gold in the 1980s as a professional defense witness for accused child molesters. Operating from his home in Minneapolis, Underwager was Johnny-on-the-spot when charges of ritual abuse rocked Jordan, Minnesota, in neighboring Scott County, during 1983 and 1984. Despite a total lack of formal training or certification in the fields of child psychology and child development, he charged into the fray as a self-styled "expert," insisting that none of the children in Jordan were really abused. Rather, he proposed, they had been "brainwashed" by a pack of therapists and social workers predisposed to search for nonexistent evidence of sex and Satanism, whipping up a superstitious frenzy reminiscent of the Salem witch trials.

Underwager was impressive on the witness stand at six-foot-six, complete with snow white beard, comparing the techniques of local child psychologists with those of Red Chinese interrogators. His performance was assisted by the inexperience of prosecutor Kathleen Morris, who declined to cross-examine Underwager on his striking lack of expertise. When two defendants were acquitted, and charges were dropped against several others, Underwager claimed the credit for himself, already shopping for a national audience.

His timing was propitious. In a decade marked by widespread claims of ritual abuse, Underwager had the answer, assuring defendants that "no one knows how to tell accurately whether a child's been abused." Furthermore, he was prepared to testify that no known method of interrogation could yield credible results, since children were "suggestible," incapable of differentiating fact from fantasy. In Underwager's world, preschoolers never hide abuse from their parents, since "children do not yet have the cognitive ability at this age to do the abstract thinking necessary to have emotions, like embarrassment or shame." The thought of children being terrorized by threats was also laughable, since threats "lose their hold, they won't control the child" beyond a perpetrator's line of sight. (He saw no contradiction, though, in children who allegedly recalled elaborate lies, repeating them verbatim, months after the fact.) In Underwager's view, unless children produced accusations through free recall, without adult prompting, "it should not be prosecuted, case closed." Even simple repetition of a child's statement was enough to invalidate the charge, in Underwager's view. Thus, if a child told his mother "Joe hit me," and the mother responded "Joe hit you?" Underwager felt obliged to disregard the claim as false.

Underwager emerged from Jordan as the hero of a new group called VOCAL—Victims of Child Abuse Laws—and his motto gave heart to embattled pedophiles from coast to coast. "It is more desirable," he told the press, "that a thousand children in abuse situations are not discovered than for one innocent person to be convicted."

Following his courtroom triumph with a guest spot on "Donahue," Underwager warned the nation that modern techniques of interviewing child abuse victims "conform precisely, exactly, and in detail" to the methods used by Asian communists "and all tyrants who've sought to control and dominate people throughout the centuries." Worse yet, any member of the television audience might be accused tomorrow if the witch-hunts were allowed to spread.

Overnight, Underwager had become a celebrity. Granted, he was not a diplomate of the American Board of Psychologists—"I made the judgment that it really was meaningless"—nor had he ever published in a professional journal, but at least he claimed to have a manuscript in progress. He began to spend sixty percent of his time on the road, traveling as an "expert" witness in child abuse cases, demanding a minimum fee of $1,000 a day plus expenses. By 1987, Underwager had testified in thirty-five states and two foreign countries—some two hundred trials and hearings, including thirty cases of reputed ritual abuse in day-care centers—with each new case strengthening his facade of expertise.

At that, some outings were less triumphant than others. In Eatonton, Georgia, Underwager spoke in defense of an elderly pedophile, assuring the court that his client was impotent and, more to the point, he did not fit the "profile" of a child-molester. Jurors in that case chose to believe the young victim, returning a verdict of guilty on all counts.

A few weeks later, retained on behalf of ritual abuser Frank Fuster, Underwager was subpoenaed by the state of Florida for a deposition to confirm his vaunted expertise. His performance on that occasion, under questioning by prosecutor John Hogan, left much to be desired.

Q: What is the average number of words a three-year-old child would be expected to understand, Dr. Underwager?

A: I don't know the average number a three-year-old would be expected to understand.

Q: When I say "three-year-old," I mean a child of the developmental age of three.

A: I don't know.

Q: How about to speak?

A: They understand so much more than they can speak, but I don't know how you would assess that.

Q: Do you know of any study that has been done in this area?

A: Not offhand.

Q: What is expressive language?

A: Expressive? Anything that has to do with the expression of the emotion more than description.

Q: What is receptive language?

A: I don't know.

Q: Could you explain the changes that take place in cognitive development in children between three years of age and four years of age?

A: Not right now.

Q: Could you explain the changes that take place in social development in children between four and five years old?

A: Between four and five years of social development?

Q: Uh-huh.

A: Not right now.

Q: Could you explain what changes take place in language development in children between the ages of two and three?

A: Not right now.

Q: How about changes in motor development between children two and three?

A: Not right now.

Q: Is there a difference in your mind between the age in which a child distinguishes between truth and falsehood and when they begin to realize the impropriety of telling falsehoods?

A: Approximately puberty they begin to recognize impropriety. Some may a bit before that.

Q: Do you feel that children whose tapes you saw in this case have been brainwashed?

A: I feel that the children whose tapes I have seen have been influenced to produce statements that were desired by their interrogators.

Q: Would you classify that as being brainwashed?

A: I don't like to use the term "brainwashed."

Q: Would you compare the techniques used by [Doctors Joseph and Laurie Braga] in this case with those used by the Chinese or Red Chinese or North Koreans or North Vietnamese?

A: There, certainly a comparison can be made.

Q: Tell me how the Red Chinese program someone.

A: I can't.

Q: How about the North Koreans? What specific techniques did they use?

A: Much the same. And the best report on North Koreans is from Bernette Scheim.

Q: What is your understanding of how they brainwashed or forced people to conform?

A: Used a lot of subtle pressure, repeated interviews, repeated interrogations.

Q: What type of subtle pressures? We're talking about the North Koreans.

A: Things like saying, "You will help," "We need you to tell us these things, and if you do, things will, you know, get better—improve." Right now, I can't recall anything more specific.

Q: How about the North Vietnamese?

A: They use many of the same techniques.

Q: So you would compare anyone that says "Things will get better" to another human being, is similar to the Red Chinese, North Koreans, North Vietnamese? You compare the techniques used, to "conform precisely and—"

A: Right.

Q: The techniques used for the Chinese, Red Chinese, North Koreans, North Vietnamese, and all other tyrants, too? All other tyrants? Is that a correct summary of your statements?

A: Yes.

Q: So which techniques of the Red Chinese, North Koreans, North Vietnamese, and other tyrants were used by the Bragas?

A: I can't say right now.

Q: Can't you tell me any?

A: Not right now.

Following his deposition, Underwager withdrew—or was dropped—from the Fuster defense team without explanation. In parting, he retained Fuster's attorney, Jeffrey Samek, to defend against perjury charges that Underwager seemed to anticipate from Dade County in the wake of his appearance. (No such charges were filed by the state.)

In 1986, Underwager was sought as a witness in the Canadian child custody case of Gordon and Sharon Wells, with its charges of satanic ritual abuse, but his busy schedule precluded a trip north. Never one to let a forum slip away, however, Underwager sat for interviews, repeating his stock description of how "simply touching" could be magnified over time to include charges of fondling, intercourse, oral sex, even animal and human sacrifice. "So you get police officers digging in backyards for bodies," he explained, "looking for pornography, cultic objects. They have never been found. No empirical data for any of this material has ever been discovered." (Seemingly, the expert witness had forgotten—if he ever knew—about the evidence recovered in the Fuster case and elsewhere.)

A year later, Underwager turned up in New Jersey, repeating his "it-never-happened" litany on behalf of child molester Margaret Kelly Michaels. Once again, this time under cross-examination by prosecutor Glenn Goldberg, he appeared less than expert on the witness stand.

Q: Did you interview the investigators involved in this case?

A: No.

Q: Did you ever talk to [Investigator] George McGrath?

A: No.

Q: Did you ever attempt to talk to the parents?

A: No.

Q: Did you ever interview Kelly Michael's co-teachers at Wee Care?

A: No.

Q: Did you read transcripts?

A: Some of Lou's [Investigator Lou Fonolleras], cross-examination of [psychologist] Eileen Treacy, George McGrath's testimony.

Q: Would it be correct to say then that you did not read the testimony of the parents?

A: That is correct.

Q: You did not read the testimony of any of the children?

A: That is correct.

Q: You did not view the videotapes of the children as they testified in judge's chambers?

A: That's correct. I believe, though, that they have another expert coming in to do that.

Q: So, as you sit there now, you do not know what the children said before this jury?

A: That's correct.

Q: Do you still feel you have all relevant data for your testimony?

A: For my testimony? Yes.

Q: You consider yourself an expert on suggestibility?

A: I don't know if I would say that.

Q: So you're not an expert.

A: I wouldn't say that.

Q: Then you are.

A: The American Psychological Association says—

Q: No. I want to know what you think, not someone else. Are you an expert on suggestibility?

A: I have some special knowledge of suggestibility.

Q: But you're in court, testifying as an expert witness.

A: For the purposes of this court, I'd say I was.

Q: Oh, so for the purposes of this court you're an expert, but outside this court you're not?

A: The difficulty is that our profession discourages calling yourself an expert.

Despite his ignorance of virtually all recorded testimony in the case, Underwager was ready to state under oath that the young New Jersey victims had been "brainwashed" by prosecution investigators.

A: The behavior of the parents, investigators, and prosecutors in this case can be likened to the behavior of the adults in the Salem witch trials.

Q: Did you ever hear any tapes of their interviews?

A: No.

Early in the cross-examination, Underwager complained to Judge William Harth that Goldberg was trying to ruin him professionally, part of a nationwide plot by malicious district attorneys who allegedly regarded Underwager as their prime enemy among defense witnesses. Glen Goldberg had to smile at that, evoking laughter when he answered, "Certainly not any more; not after testifying in this court." In his final summation, Goldberg blasted Underwager as "a disgrace to the science of psychology" who "knows what he's doing is wrong" when he "picks figures out of the air." Jurors seemingly agreed, convicting defendant Michaels on more than 120 separate counts of child abuse.

Disgrace or not, Underwager was well paid for his trip to New Jersey, pocketing $54,518 of the taxpayer's money for eleven days on the witness stand. More trials lay ahead, and if defendants were convicted, it did not affect the flow of cash to "expert" witnesses. Questioned afterward on the defense team's choice of Underwager, attorney Bob Clark could only answer with a shrug and query of his own: "Who else does suggestibility?"

UNITED SATANIC EVIL DESIGN

In March 1989, leaflets stamped with the name of this reputed cult were distributed at schools, markets, and government offices in Zamboanga City, a metropolis of 500,000 residents in the southern Philippines. Including a list of the sect's holy days and "secret signs" that would identify cult members, the pamphlets sparked widespread rumors of kidnapping and human sacrifice in the neighborhood. The present status of the cult remains unclear, as police investigation failed to uncover any such group, and Capt. Nonito Gader dismissed the publication as a hoax by "drug addicts or pranksters."

UNIVERSAL CHURCH OF MAN

A spin-off from Anton LaVey's Church of Satan, this cult was created around 1972, from the ruins of Detroit's "Babylon Grotto." LaVey's chief spokesman in Motown was Wayne West, a defrocked Catholic priest from England, whose personal preference for bondage and homosexuality came to intrude on church rituals, prompting complaints from some of the members to LaVey's San Francisco headquarters. West was formally excommunicated by LaVey, but he retained enough loyal disciples to found his own Universal Church of Man, described for the record as "Satanism without Satan." In practice, the idea was as lame as it sounded on paper, with

West and his congregation fading into obscurity by mid-decade.

URIARTI, JUAN DE DIOS

Identified as the richest beer distributor in Puno, Peru, Juan Uriarti reportedly safeguards his profit margin by means of periodic human sacrifice. Police report that he employed two men to sacrifice a young woman on Mt. Incahuasi in 1982, shortly after Uriarti moved his base of operations from Pomata to the Yunguyo district, and one informed source told journalist Patrick Tierney that human sacrifice is a long-standing "family tradition" in the Uriarti clan. "They've always kept too many young servant girls around," the source explains, "and then one or two disappear from time to time. These girls are brought in from out of town, so no one really knows them or misses them. All their wealth comes from those human sacrifices, but they say that he has to keep doing them, or else he'll have bad luck, or an automobile accident." The flexible nature of Uriarti business interests is suggested by the conviction of Juan's brother for smuggling cocaine, a case the family resolved by bribing prison guards to set him free. On one occasion, running short of servant girls, Juan drove his wife to Mt. Santa Barbara for a sacrificial outing, but Mrs. Uriarti talked her way out of the ritual and was allowed to live. At this writing, Uriarti remains at large, still bribing officials and "paying the devil" for his continued success.

VOODOO

Yet another Western derivative of the Yoruban ju-ju cult, voodoo—or *voudon*, in the original French—evolved in the West Indies, principally Haiti, during the early seventeen century. As in ju-ju, the supreme deity is represented by a serpent, called Damballah, and practitioners also worship a wide range of subordinate gods and spirits dubbed *loas*. Unlike most of the other Afro-Caribbean cults, however, voodoo makes no attempt to hide its deities behind the skirts of Christian saints. This significant difference, and the prominence of Haitian voodoo priests, is rooted in the peculiar history of Haiti itself.

In 1804, while African slaves in America and the Caribbean were closely guarded by their European captors, Toussaint-Louverture liberated Haitian blacks from French domination in the world's only successful slave revolt. With white rule and Catholicism overthrown, voodoo was established as the island's official religion, maintaining its grip when Haiti became a republic in 1820. Brief opposition was mustered in 1863, after eight voodoo practitioners were convicted and executed for kidnapping two women, sacrificing one and cannibalizing her body. An outraged President Geffrard—himself a Roman Catholic—tried to banish the religion, but voodoo leaders struck back with a vengeance, ambushing Geffrard's daughter and shooting her dead as she knelt in a church at Port-au-Prince.

With Geffrard's example in mind, most Haitian leaders have found it expedient to live and let live, with some—like Presidents Salnave and Soulouque—actively participating in voodoo rituals. President Antoine Simon's daughter was herself a voodoo priestess, known to practice rituals (including alleged human sacrifice) on the grounds of the presidential palace. More recently, President-for-life François ("Papa Doc") Duvalier used voodoo in conjunction with his dreaded secret police, the Tonton Macoutes, to rule Haiti with an iron hand from 1957 until his death in 1971. Duvalier was known to pose as a spokesman or physical manifestation of Baron Samedi, voodoo's lord of the dead, a practice continued with variations by his son Jean Claude—a.k.a. "Baby Doc"—from 1971 until his forcible ouster in February 1986.

Politics aside, voodoo remains a potent fact of life for many Haitians, and for numerous practitioners in the United States. Long confined to the Southern states where blacks were historically more numerous, voodoo rituals have spread nationwide in the years since World War II, with cults reported in Los Angeles, Chicago, New York, and other urban areas. New Orleans, with its historic French influence, still ranks as a major hotbed of voodoo in America, but recent immigration waves have placed Miami's "Little Haiti" district on a par with the Crescent City.

There is no such thing as a "typical" voodoo ceremony, each local cult selecting its own favorite deities and devising rituals to satisfy their needs. Blood sacrifice appears to be a universal theme, with the *loas* demanding earthly food, and mutilation of the chosen animals is generally carried out in an atmosphere of frenetic celebration, complete with drums and cymbals, wild dancing, and liberal consumption of rum. Voodoo celebrants are frequently "possessed" as the exhausting ritual proceeds, hallucinating or collapsing on the spot from the combined effects of their exertion, alcohol, and drugs. In some areas, as with New York's Asmodeus Society, Satanism and voodoo appear to merge in the worship of "Christian" demons with a display of voodoo paraphernalia. Likewise, white practitioners have been drawn to the cult in sizable numbers, accounting for an estimated one-third of all New Orleans voodoo worshipers by 1970.

Voodoo priests pride themselves on their ability to curse selected enemies, some performing the dark rites for profit, and there are numerous cases on record of deaths resulting from such "magic." Some victims doubtless fall prey to their own superstition, growing deathly ill when they refuse to eat or sleep, while others have been killed by herbal poisons slipped into a meal or beverage. In either case, black magic gets the credit for a victim's death or disability, thereby enhancing the priest's reputation as a man of great power. As recently as the early 1960s, an Arizona housewife told detectives she was forced to kill her husband "under the spell of a voodoo doctor."

Ironically, the curses sometimes backfire, placing the voodoo practitioner in more danger than his or her intended victim. In April 1940, Salvadore Laurie was shot and killed in New Orleans, police tracing the crime to a brother-in-law who admitted the shooting, insisting that Laurie had cursed him with voodoo. Haitian immigrant Claude Morreiset also believed himself cursed in January 1966, when he visited "priestess" Mary Dutchalellier in New York City. For reasons best known to herself, Dutchalellier refused to help lift the curse, whereupon Morreiset stabbed her to death. In September 1981, four persons were killed and two others wounded when frightened believers went gunning for a voodoo "root doctor" in Columbia, South Carolina.

Blood sacrifice of animals aside, most voodoo cults in the United States insist that they obey prevailing laws, but their secretive nature lends itself to suspicion and rumor, compounded when defectors speak of sacrificial rites involving human beings—the "goat without horns." Practitioners from

Harlem tried to found a private "voodoo kingdom" in Beaufort County, South Carolina, during 1973, but their commitment to Yoruban practices, including polygamy, left them open to criticism and eventual prosecution. No statistics are available on the extent of voodoo worship in America, but recent immigrants from Haiti and Jamaica share beliefs and rituals with Afro-Americans who trace their religious observation to the seventeenth or eighteenth century. [See: Ju-Ju; Palo Mayombe; Santeria; Zombies]

WARLORDS OF SATAN

Another paper "cult," created by the same Minneapolis accountant who devised the Third Temple of Baal, the Warlords of Satan describes its primary goal as "nothing less than to turn human beings into prey." Sharing a mailing list of some two hundred correspondents with its sister "temple," this "group" appears to be a one-man operation, with no active membership. [See: Third Temple of Baal]

WATERHOUSE, SCOTT

The fear invaded Sanford, Maine, in 1983. A quaint New England town of eighteen thousand residents, Sanford was rocked that summer by grim, persistent rumors of a devil-worship cult recruiting scores of local youths. Some fifty Satanists were said to hold their midnight meetings in an old mill near the heart of town, and while police could find no solid evidence to back the stories up, dread lingered on.

By autumn, many citizens of Sanford were convinced that the elusive cultists planned to sacrifice blond, blue-eyed virgins on the night of Halloween. Authorities heard confident reports of a Satanic "death list" as the holiday approached. Police Chief Arthur Kelly publicly dismissed the tales as "harmless pranks," but two detectives were assigned to double-check when several schoolgirls and adults received threatening notes signed "The Cult." Two hundred interviews led to fifteen juvenile arrests, on charges ranging from criminal mischief to issuing death threats, and Halloween passed without further incident ... but still the fear remained, some parents refusing to let their children leave home except for school.

"We're treating it very seriously," said Chief Kelly. "People are upset and concerned, but when you get right to the bottom of many rumors, we're talking about kids. We have just not found any organized group behind all the rumors that a cult exists."

Time passes. Fear subsides.

At half past five on Sunday afternoon, April 29, 1984, Gycelle Cote left her home on Jackson Street to join some friends on Pike's Hill, near the Mousam River, in the woods behind her home. A bright, outgoing twelve-year-old, Gycelle was looking forward to promotion from the sixth grade in a month or so, with junior high school in the fall, but April Sundays were a time for putting books away and playing in the woods.

Her friends were late that afternoon, and by the time they reached Pike's Hill, Gycelle was nowhere to be seen. She did not make it home by suppertime, and no one seemed to know where she had gone. The sun was setting by the time a search was organized, but friends and relatives forged on, supported by a team of city officers and sheriff's deputies, a state policeman and his tracking dog. Reluctantly, they called it quits at midnight and agreed to start again at dawn.

The new day yielded up immediate results, as two policemen found Gycelle Cote's body floating in the Mousam, several blocks from downtown Sanford. She was fully dressed, with the exception of a missing belt. An autopsy pegged strangulation as the cause of death.

More days of scouring the woods produced no evidence to link a suspect with the crime. A public plea for help produced four witnesses who placed Scott Waterhouse, an eighteen-year-old high school junior, near Pike's Hill on Sunday afternoon. At least one caller saw the suspect with a girl who matched Gycelle's description, walking through the woods, his hand upon her shoulder, guiding her along the riverbank.

The suspect had a history of problems that were largely medical in nature. Born without a proper hip joint, he had had one surgically constructed at an early age. More operations were required to mend a knee, two hernias, a ruptured spinal disc. He also had a record with the juvenile authorities, six months probation after helping two friends break into a car and swipe some fruit.

Police found Waterhouse at home on Thursday afternoon, May 3, and drove him to the jail at Alfred, Maine, for some extended questioning. They also brought a warrant granting officers the right to search his home for evidence. Another warrant was delivered to the high school, where the contents of the suspect's locker were examined, tagged, and bagged.

The afternoon Gycelle was murdered, Waterhouse was playing snare drum with the Sanford High School band at Scarborough Downs, a nearby race track, but he had returned to Sanford around five o'clock. His home was barely one block from Gycelle's, and the police decided Scott had ample time to shed his uniform, put on the army-surplus jacket witnesses recalled, and reach the woods by half past five or six o'clock.

Waterhouse denied seeing Gycelle, much less killing her, but he seemed more interested in discussing his religion. As Trooper Maurice Oullette recalled the interrogation, "several references were made to the religion of Satanism, which Mr. Waterhouse stated was his religion. He further advised me that one of the beliefs of his religion was that when someone wrongs you, you wrong them. He spoke of ritual."

As pieced together from the suspect, family, and friends, it seems that Waterhouse's involvement with Satanism dated from early 1983, when he happened on a copy of Anton LaVey's *Satanic Bible* in a local bookstore. Over several months, he became deeply immersed in "black" rituals, heightening his experience with marijuana and doses of LSD. As Waterhouse explained his conversation, "I just started questioning things. I see certain things and I say, 'If there's a God, why are these things happening?'"

Above all else, he appreciated Satanism's devotion to personal license. "Whatever floats your boat," he told police. "Whatever turns your crank."

One thing that turned Scott's crank was threatening to murder adolescent females. School authorities turned over several confiscated letters Waterhouse had written to a fifteen-year-old schoolmate, threatening her life if she persisted in attempting to regain a pair of shoes that he had stolen. In his last note, dated four days prior to Gycelle Cote's death, Waterhouse advised the girl to "Make the best of your every waking moment from now on, because your days are numbered."

From the suspect's home and locker, homicide investigators seized a notebook with a list of "Satan rules," a separate page of handwritten "questions about Satan," a "letter written to Scott from Christ," and another self-addressed letter "about Satan/Christian beliefs." Still missing were the victim's belt and Waterhouse's copy of *The Satanic Bible*, described by acquaintances as his inseparable companion, but authorities believed they had enough hard evidence to go to trial.

Arraigned on felony murder charges, Waterhouse pleaded innocent and was held without bail. His trial convened in November, with jurors accepting Assistant Attorney General Michael Westcott's contention that Waterhouse strangled Gycelle Cote "for the heck of it," as a demonstration of his commitment to evil. Convicted of first-degree murder, Waterhouse stood before Judge William Broderick for sentencing on December 20, 1984.

"The evidence indicates that you enjoyed killing," said Broderick, "and there is reason to believe you could do it again if given the chance. Thrill killing deserves the maximum penalty of life imprisonment."

In Maine, a term of life for Murder One has no provision for parole.

WELLS, GORDON and SHARON

The Hamilton, Ontario, marriage of Gordon and Sharon Wells was a traumatic affair from the beginning. A victim of sexual abuse in childhood, Sharon had a young daughter from a previous marriage when she met her future husband, and the birth of a second girl did nothing to cement their bizarre relationship. Gordon was a tattooed, hard-drinking ruffian who carried a machete and a sawed-off shotgun in his car, battered his wife and reportedly abused the children as well. When the marriage broke up, he continued to terrorize Sharon, escalating his campaign with racist overtones after she moved in with black boyfriend Gary Evans. By late 1984, both young girls were displaying precocious sexual activity in preschool, but physical examinations for symptoms of molestation were inconclusive. Finally, in February 1985, the children were placed in temporary foster care after Sharon attempted suicide and social workers from the Toronto Children's Aid Society deemed her apartment "a disaster area."

Two weeks into their new life, the girls began relating tales of sexual abuse. Gary Evans was named as the initial culprit, with charges quickly expanding to include both Gordon and Sharon Wells, plus assorted nameless strangers. Social workers from the Children's Aid Society began investigating on March 1, and the girls were officially taken into CAS protective custody five days later. Over the next two months, the allegations spread beyond "normal" molestation to include charges of pornography, graveyard rituals, animal and human sacrifice, cannibalism, consumption of human feces, and other behavior consistent with similar cases filed in the United States and England. Several murders were described, including the sacrifice of a woman named Elizabeth. When the girls were casually asked to describe a normal Halloween, they lapsed into tales of kidnapping, mutilation, and murder.

The police response to such charges was sluggish, at best. Sharon Wells was first questioned on March 2, but officers waited another six days before searching her home for evidence; even then, they never bothered to ask her about video equipment or pornographic tapes. Between March and July 1985, police "closed" the case five times, forced to resume their desultory search for evidence each time new allegations surfaced from the children. At that, detectives made no effort to trace several children described by the girls as murder victims, likewise refusing to visit or question the staff at a local television station where pornographic films were allegedly made. No effort was made to find suspect Gary Evans until August 1985, six months after the charges against him first aired. Detectives publicly dismissed some of the charges as "beyond belief," a May 1985 report noting for the record: "It is apparent that if there was any evidence that could assist in this investigation, it has long since been disposed of." In short, why bother?

Gordon and Sharon Wells dismissed foster mother Catherine McInnis as "a nut case" who brainwashed their children with fantastic stories, but the allegations continued after the girls were moved to a new foster home in mid-May. Meanwhile, a team of psychiatrists from Toronto's prestigious Hospital for Sick Children unanimously pronounced the girls rational and truthful. Dr. Paul Steinhauer, senior staff psychiatrist at the hospital, declared: "There is no way these kids were not involved in rituals along the lines of those described. I am convinced people were being killed, that they were forced to stick knives in victims. As to whether the flesh they ate was human or not, there is a possibility for error. We found nothing that allowed me to draw any conclusion other than the fact that what the children described was actually experienced."

Dr. William Wehrspan based his agreement on visible symptoms of stress. "There is no way to coach this," he said. "In cases proven to be fictitious, they are not present. We're talking real primitive stuff here. These kids literally had the crap scared out of them. Nobody's setting this up. They go to a funeral and ask if someone's been killed. They've got killing on the brain." Psychologist Alice Oliveira agreed that "Something happened. These children believe they saw their father kill children. No explanation at all has been offered which helps the children make sense of their reality. He would have to explain why the children would think such things. Either it happened, or something happened, which I could understand that the children could interpret as those events."

The child welfare hearing which began in October 1985, before District Court Judge Thomas Beckett, was scheduled to last ten days; instead, it consumed eighteen months and set a new Canadian record, producing 142 exhibits and fifteen thousand pages of recorded testimony. Sharon Wells gave birth to another child during the course of the trial, but this daughter—fathered by Gary Evans—was removed from her custody within days. Her older daughters "testified" on videotape, but the accused were on hand to speak for themselves. Sharon Wells denied any criminal acts of her own, but pointed an accusing finger at her ex-husband, reciting various death threats and referring under oath to his "satanic friends." Gordon Wells, meanwhile, dismissed his tattoo of Satan as "a little cartoon character"; he admitted threatening various people with knives and punching out his wife "by accident," but the other charges were "all B.S." Gary Evans, for his part, painted a portrait of Sharon Wells as an ideal mother and homemaker, veering so far from established fact that Judge Beckett pronounced his testimony "unacceptable" and "totally unsupported by any evidence."

The final 106-page decision from Judge Beckett opened with a statement of his own initial skepticism in the case. "In fact," he wrote, "I wanted very much to believe that none of the allegations made by Janis and Linda could be true." On balance, though, he was impressed by the "rich detail" and apparent sincerity of both girls. In regard to the satanic charges, Beckett noted:

I am left with the question of where the "florid" allegations originated. Was it fantasy? Were the children lying? If the children were fantasizing or lying, the question arises as to where the children got the material to produce their so-called lies or fantasies. I cannot accept that two little children this age could possibly describe the matters I have described above without some knowledge or some experience in order to create the lies or the fantasies. Such matters surely cannot come out of the minds of young children as native or original thought. But is not the fact that they said such things, that such horrors were in their minds, evidence of a very bizarrely disturbed relationship with their caretakers? Was this not evidence of brutal trauma to their psyche, just as would bruises and broken bones be evidence of physical abuse to their bodies?

The world of small children is a narrow one: it is mother, it is father and their families, their school and their playmates. It is in this milieu that a child's mental constructs are molded. What experiences did these children have, while in the care of the adults involved, that would cause them to say what they said and to say it with such fear and terror? To say that they "lied" or that it was "fantasy" falls far short of explaining how such things could have been in their minds. It also should not be forgotten that statements by small children must always be viewed from the perspectives of a child—what a child says may not be truth but that does not mean it is a lie or fantasy. What may not, in reality, be truth, may be interpreted as truth by a child. For example, a child told to eat meat, which is in reality raw chicken, but is represented to the child by his caretaker as human flesh, would not be "lying" if he said that he had eaten human flesh: he would just be mistaken.

But does it really matter, for the purposes of this case, whether the children saw murder or something that they interpreted as being murder? Whether they ate human flesh or ate something they thought was human flesh, whether they were in Channel 11

Telecenter, or whether they were in some place they
believed to be the Telecenter? It is really unimportant
in reality as to which it was.

Judge Beckett's order permanently removed both children
from the custody of their parents. In the face of police skepticism and passage of time, with physical evidence long since
vanished or destroyed, no criminal charges were filed. [See:
Child Abuse]

WICCA

Coined by British occultist Gerald Gardner as an alternative name for witchcraft, the term "wicca" is variously defined as a synonym for "wisdom" or a reference to the "wise
ones" who practice certain forms of ritual magic. When cap-
italized, it also serves as the formal name for any one of several cults that trace their roots to ancient witchcraft based in
Europe or the British Isles. As usual with "magic" cults, a
tendency to borrow deities and rituals has blurred dividing
lines between the several factions to a point where many of
their differences are more semantic than material.

While followers of Wicca universally attempt to date their
system of belief from prehistoric—or, at least, pre-
Christian—times, the birth of modern witchcraft can be
traced with fair precision to the early 1950s. Satanist Aleister
Crowley collaborated with Gardner on the early rituals prior
to Crowley's death in 1947, but practice was limited to a
small circle of Gardner's friends before 1951, when British
witchcraft statutes were repealed. Thereafter, Gardner spoke
and published widely on the joys of "wicca," but his magic
owed little to traditional European witchcraft. An ardent nud-
ist with eccentric sexual tastes and a fascination for Asian
mysticism, Gardner incorporated the Egyptian ankh and ritual
scourging practiced by Far Eastern cults, crafting ceremonies
to suit his own peculiar tastes. Disciples were advised to
work their magic in the nude, and lascivious rites like the
"fivefold kiss" owed more to Crowley and Gardner than any
historic tradition.

Gardnerian Wicca remains one of the dominant strains, but
Gardner's success as a guru was bound to inspire competition. Another student of Aleister Crowley's, one Alex San-

ders, broke ranks in the early 1960s to create his own Alexandrian Wicca, incorporating public sexual intercourse as a requirement for initiation to the cult's prestigious "third degree." An effort to reunite the two factions surfaced as "Algard" Wicca in 1972, spreading from its New York City roots to claim forty-eight American covens within a year, with others noted in Canada, England, and Greece. Atlantion Wicca, organized in the 1960s, claims to follow the teachings of one Elizabeth Sawyer, hanged as a witch by British authorities in April 1621. Cymry Wicca—founded in Washington, D.C., in 1967 and moved to Smyrna, Georgia, six years later—claims to follow Celtic traditions, but its deities bear a close resemblance to the Egyptian Isis, Osiris, and Horus. Dianic Wicca, born of Texas roots in 1972, is a feminist version of witchcraft, with the male goat-god deemphasized. The New Orleans–based Religious Order of Witchcraft, meanwhile, openly follows the teachings of Aleister Crowley and reveres its own "God of the Witches," otherwise known as the satanic Goat of Mendes. In New York, Leo Martello's Witches International Craft Associates loosely follows the Sicilian *strege* tradition, employing spells and prayers that threaten various gods to ensure a response. Seax-Wicca, organized by Gardnerian defector Raymond Buckland, claims a Saxon history and no link to competing groups; members still meet in the nude, but rituals include no sexual contact.

At that, Buckland's sect deviates from the rule of modern witch cults. Disclaimers notwithstanding, the majority of "wicca" groups incorporate some form of semipublic sexual activity which is at once a major selling point for new recruits and a release for the initiated members. Without engaging in a long debate on whether group and public sex is "natural" or "healthy," it is fair to say that some of the activities pursued by modern witches violate prevailing laws pertaining to adultery and statutory rape.

A case in point is the Church of Wicca, founded in North Carolina—and frequently advertised in supermarket tabloids—by Gavin and Yvonne Frost. In *The Witch's Bible*, first published in 1974, the Frosts strive to deemphasize sex as a part of witchcraft, but the main thrust of their scripture remains frankly carnal. Sexual "rest periods" are prescribed after ritual esbat dancing (p. 75), with the Frosts noting that "If an even number are present, but two are sex paired, the youngest members share their partners during the sexual inter-

lude." The Church of Wicca also aims at having "the first full
sexual experience take place in the pleasant surroundings of
the coven," and to that end "the physical attributes of male
and female virginity are destroyed at the youngest possible
age, either by the mother or by a doctor" (pp. 83–84).

Indeed, for the Frosts and their disciples, sex is an integral
part of cult initiation, with new prospects sitting for nude interviews, during which they are cautioned that cult rituals
"require sex with assigned partners" (p. 189). Females who
make the cut must spend the next two weeks practicing with
dildos to prepare themselves, "regardless of their sexual experience" (p. 200). On the big night, initiates copulate with a
"sponsor" of the opposite sex, followed by a "whipping" session said to symbolize obedience. Beyond initiation, the
Frosts have a formula for binding the coven "with love and
understanding": "Our rule is that twice a year every male and
female in the coven will live with a female or male other than
the spouse for one full lunar month" (p. 205). If some of the
women burn out in the stretch, there is even a spell for "re-
newal of female desire," requiring the weary witch to have
sex and experience climax in front of the coven at large. "Occasionally," the Frosts note, "it is necessary for more than
one male to assist," but they grant that the process is "very
tricky," since "the woman can easily be turned into a nym-
phomaniac" (pp. 145–146).

The Church of Wicca anticipates legal problems by having
all single females sign a release from liability in the event of
unplanned pregnancy, and since females are eligible to join
the cult at age sixteen—well below the legal age of consent
in some states—coven leaders are warned to obtain releases
from all *men* in the cult, generously absolving each other of
guilt in cases of statutory rape. Needless to say, such notes of
"permission" to commit a felony have no legal standing
whatever; they are, quite literally, worth less than the paper
on which they are written.

While the Frosts' Church of Wicca stands firm against homosexuality and other "unnatural" acts, covens drawing their
inspiration from Crowley and Gardner remain more flexible.
In May 1985, police in Des Moines, Iowa, charged "high
priest" and schoolteacher David Graham with sexually molesting a fifteen-year-old boy who attended several coven
meetings. Four other men were eventually charged in the

case, and all were convicted on various charges. [See: Gardner, Gerald; Sanders, Alexander; Witch Cults]

"WICCA LETTERS"

Allegedly intercepted by police after a 1981 meeting of the Witches International Coven Council in Mexico, the so-called "WICCA letters" are a bizarre outline for national domination by dedicated cultists. Widely published—and presumably believed—by fundamentalists, the document is dubious at best. To date, no such organization as the WICC has been found, in America or elsewhere, and enumeration of subversive goals in this manner would seem to be a risky proposition at the best of times. The "letters," as normally presented, read:

1. To bring about the covens, both black and white magic, into one and have the arctress to govern all—ACCOMPLISHED;

2. To bring about personal debts causing discord and disharmony within families—ACCOMPLISHED;

3. To remove or educate the "new age youth" by:

a. infiltrating boys/girls clubs and big sister/brother programs

b. infiltrating schools, having prayers removed, having teachers teach about drugs, sex, freedoms

c. instigating and promoting rebellion against parents and all authority

d. promoting equal rights for youth—ACCOMPLISHED;

4. To gain access to all people's backgrounds and vital information by:

a. use of computers

b. convenience

c. infiltration—ACCOMPLISHED;

5. To have laws changed to benefit our ways, such as:

a. removing children from the home environment and placing them in our foster homes

b. mandatory placement of children in our daycare centers

c. increased taxes

    d. open drug and pornography market to everyone—
NOT YET ACCOMPLISHED;
   6. To destroy government agencies by:
    a. overspending
    b. public opinion
    c. being on the offensive always, opposing, demon-
strating, demoralizing—NOT YET ACCOMPLISHED;
   7. Not to be revealed until all else has been accomplished. Target date for revelation—June 21, 1986—the
beginning of the Summer Solstice and great feast on the
Satanic calendar.

Author Art Lyons has reportedly traced "discovery" of this
document to a police "cult expert" in San Diego, California,
but there the trail ends. (There is—or was—an organization
dubbed the Witches International Craft Associates, led by
New Yorker Leo Martello, but no apparent connection exists
with the suspect document.) By all appearances, the "WICCA
letters" seem more like a clumsy hoax than any object of legitimate concern. [See: Wicca]

WILKINS, ROBERT S.
and BARTZ, LORI ELIZABETH

Lori Bartz loved children. When she had a chance, she
liked to spend her time in the vicinity of playgrounds, skating
rinks, and elementary schools, making young friends, inviting
them back to her home for games or snacks. In 1985, before
her marriage fell apart, it reached the point where Lori's husband had to tack a sign up on the door of their apartment,
reading: "No kids allowed after 4 P.M."
Divorced at twenty-two, no job to tie her down, Bartz devoted herself to the children full-time. Wherever she moved
in California's San Diego County—to La Mesa, Spring
Valley, Lakeside, or Santee—there were always more kids
waiting to be entertained. Lori's new boyfriend, thirty-
eight-year-old Robert Wilkins, didn't seem to mind at all. In
fact, the one-time manager of local pizza restaurants appeared
to love the children just as much as Lori did. It didn't even
matter whether they were girls or boys.
Lurid tales of Lori Bartz's special fondness for the younger

set began to reach the San Diego County sheriff's office in September 1986. Detectives from the child abuse unit interviewed four girls who claimed that Lori's attentions went well beyond friendship, lapsing into the obscene and terrifying. Graphic acts of sexual perversion were described, spelled out in sufficient detail to convince authorities that they were listening to facts, not fantasy.

As Sgt. Ron Cottingham told the press, "We know through talking with the kids that the mind games she played with them were incredible." Bartz sometimes used the surname Cappeletti, posing as a wealthy Italian national, and even tried to convince some of her victims that she was a man. Silence was ensured by threats against her victims' families, backed up with a display of firearms and satanic symbols said to represent a deadly cult. One of Lori's favorite tricks was a bit of demonic ventriloquism, gnawing on a black plastic ram before she summoned up the raspy voice of Satan, telling frightened children: "This is the devil. Do as I say!"

On October 10, 1986, sheriff's deputies arrested Lori Bartz at her apartment, jailing her on charges that included sixty counts of child molesting, fifteen counts of forcible lewd and lascivious action with a child, fourteen counts of oral sex with a person under sixteen, and one count of oral sex with a person under eighteen. The alleged crimes dated back to July 1984, with the victims described as girls between the ages of ten and fifteen. Held in lieu of $450,000 bond, Bartz pleaded not guilty on October 16. Judge Charles Hayes continued her high bail, noting "serious doubts as to her mental stability."

By this time, detectives knew they were looking for a second suspect in the case, and their investigation led them to Robert Wilkins on November 7. Four days later, Wilkins pleaded innocent on three child molestation counts, remaining in custody when he could not raise $250,000 bond. Lori Bartz, meanwhile, entered a not-guilty plea on ten new counts of felony child molestation, involving a mixed group of five boys and girls; she also faced three more counts of sexual activity with an eighteen-year-old girl.

As the satanic allegations surfaced, knee-jerk doubters raised the specter of "another Salem witch-hunt" in the making, but their propaganda line did not persuade a San Diego jury. Convicted on eight counts of sexual abuse in July 1987, Wilkins and Bartz were each sentenced to long prison terms.

Still, the question remains: Were the two defendants *really* Satanists? Or does it matter? Their convictions, with the documented use of occult icons and rituals to intimidate young victims, undermine the arguments of those who would dismiss such cases as the stuff of "urban myth." [See: Child Abuse]

WITCH CULTS—MEDIEVAL

Once regarded by "liberal" historians as a peasant myth or the product of Christian religious hysteria, medieval witch cults have gained credibility over time. Researchers like anthropologist Margaret Murray, Richard Cavendish, Arthur Lyons, and others now agree—and cite supporting evidence for their belief—that such cults did, in fact, exist. Beyond the fact of mere existence, though, it also seems that they were dedicated to an early form of Satanism, rather than the simple "nature worship" claimed by witches in the present day.

Unfortunately, most of our accumulated evidence on early witch cults is derived from testimony gathered by the Inquisition, that medieval version of the Holocaust which tortured, maimed, and executed thousands in the pursuit of "heresy." Pope Lucius III first called for an investigation of heretical religions in A.D. 1184, another half century elapsing before his program was formalized as the Inquisition in 1233. Witch-hunters got their own guidebook in 1486, with publication of *Malleus Maleficarum (The Hammer of Witches)*, and some 200,000 suspects were finally executed throughout Europe and the New World. Germany led the pack, with at least 100,000 "witches" put to death; France boasted 30,000 executions, while Scotland eliminated 10,000 suspects, and other nations were somewhat less zealous. Many victims were apparently framed, based on personal malice, political jealousy, or the church's desire to seize valuable land. Europe's witchcraft hysteria faded after the seventeenth century, with a corresponding decrease in trials. Holland executed its last witch in 1610, England in 1684, America in 1692, Scotland in 1727, and France in 1745; even the Germans had called it quits by 1775.

Despite the Inquisition's brutal reputation, the professional witch-hunters were also methodical bookkeepers, and we know that numerous suspects confessed their occultism freely, without torture and with no hope of clemency. Further evidence for the witch cult's existence is found in ancient rock carvings of the witches' "horned god," reported from Spain to the Soviet Union, with some of the art work more than 30,000 years old. And in A.D. 668, some 565 years before the Inquisition, the Archbishop of Canterbury had already decreed three years penance for heretics who ate or drank in heathen temples, donning animal heads in the course of their rituals.

An impartial review of the evidence clearly suggests the existence of a widespread, loosely knit occult religion that predated Christian times and lasted, despite all the risks, through the end of the European witch trials. Starting as a primitive fertility cult, the group—or *groups*—became distinctly anti-Christian over time, perhaps in understandable response to persecution from the church. Another view suggests that European peasants leaned toward witchcraft, merging into rustic Satanism, as a gesture of rebellion in the days when wealthy noblemen controlled the Catholic church and absolution too often came with a price tag attached.

In any case, it now seems well established that the witch cults *did* exist in Europe and America (where the mystic Osirian Order colonized Boston in 1676, moving on to Salem and other parts of New England in time for the later Massachusetts witch trials). Local groups were organized with secrecy in mind, practicing magic which—at least by the fifteenth century—had taken a decidedly malicious turn. An English witch named Isobel Gowdie first used the term "coven," in 1662, describing the normal membership as one leader and twelve disciples (presumably mocking Christ and the apostles).

Local coven meetings, or "esbats," convened weekly or even more often, without set times or schedules. Such gatherings concerned themselves with coven business and the practice of magic, either for pure mischief—as in blighting crops and cursing livestock—or to benefit some paying customer from the community. A farmer jealous of his neighbor's herd might thus take out a "contract" on his enemy, the coven pledged to do their worst in terms of magical afflictions—or, perhaps, some poison in the feed, if hexes failed. Esbats were held in close proximity to the members' village, and no costumes were worn. Witnesses agree, however, that feasting was typical, accompanied by dancing and sexual activity (still practiced by "traditional" witches today).

An altogether different kind of gathering were the quarterly sabbats, faithfully held on Candlemas (February 2) Walpurgisnacht (April 30), Lammas Day (August 1), and All Hallows' Eve (October 31). First described by two French witches in 1335, the sabbats drew a much larger turnout— some cultists, probably exaggerating, mentioned thousands of participants—and so the meeting grounds were necessarily remote, the gathering convened by night for reasons of security. A regional commander of the cult presided on Satan's behalf, dressed all in black, complete with goat's-head mask and cloven boots (quite popular with wealthy Europeans in the sixteenth century). Some "devils" embellished their animal masks with a ceremonial candle planted between the horns, and others apparently donned full-body suits of leather or metal, explaining why "Satan" was frequently cold to the touch.

Descriptions of the stand-in "Lucifer" were remarkably consistent from one country to the next, spanning centuries. Digna Robert, a Belgian witch, reported in 1565 that her devil was "cold in all his parts." From France, in 1578, we have accounts of a "huge man dressed in black and booted." The English devil, as described in 1646, was "a large man in blackish clothing, but with cloven feet." And from Salem, Massachusetts, come descriptions of "a black man in a high-crowned hat," reported during 1692. The wearing of animal masks also accounts for reports from England and Germany, describing the devil's "hollow, shrill voice."

Based on eyewitness descriptions, the sabbat began with "Satan" on his black throne, calling roll from a book of the faithful. If too many witches were present, coven masters answered on behalf of their disciples. As each name was called, the witches related their various sins, responding to variants of a standard question: "What harm hast thou done to date?" An energetic witch might claim destruction of crops or livestock, desecration of Christian graves, perhaps a bit of arson or the cursing of a neighbor. Evidence suggests, however, that most of their achievements owed more to muscle than magic. For example, after curses failed to drop a bridge at Forfar, Scotland, during 1661, witch Helen Guthrie and the other members of her coven tore it down by hand. Results were all that counted in the long run, and the devil got the credit, either way.

Following the roll call, it was time for Satan to initiate new members. All prospective witches were assumed to join the cult by choice, and many were raised in the faith from one generation to the next. Others were recruited, as today, with promises of sex, wealth, and power. When all else failed, a coveted recruit was sometimes helped to see the light with threats or blackmail, beatings, or curses that resulted in the burning of a house or barn. At sabbat ceremonies, new initiates were baptized by the devil after first renouncing Jesus, sometimes trampling on a crucifix or Bible to confirm their break with Christianity. Pacts with the devil were also required in some districts, usually written and signed in the new recruit's blood. That done, each fledgling member of the cult received a "witch's mark," in the form of a hidden tattoo or brand, which simultaneously identified the faithful, weeded out infiltrators, and served as a potential blackmail tool against defectors. As the Inquisition gathered steam, zealous witch-hunters often pointed to innocent scars and moles as "witches' marks," but the fact remains that tattoos and branding are not uncommon in secret societies, down to the present day.

With the initiation of new members completed, the cultists began their ceremony in earnest. Consistent descriptions include the sacrifice of a black goat or hen, followed by celebrants lining up to display their adoration of the devil. Many groups required the "kiss of shame," applied to "Satan's" genitals or buttocks, but some leaders were satisfied with a kiss on the feet or a simple bow. (Self-abasement is another common theme with secret societies, and while some historians dismiss the "kiss of shame" as fantasy, it pales by comparison to rituals of the Kenyan Mau Mau or the Ku Klux Klan.)

Beginning sometime in the sixteenth century, witch cults began including parodies of Christian masses in their sabbat ceremonies. Probably a form of protest against the Inquisition, more than any hard-core loyalty to Satan, this forerunner of the Black Mass included substitution of goat's urine for sacramental wine, consumption of black-stained turnips as the host, and alterations in the Roman Catholic liturgy to reflect Satan's dominance: "Our Father who *wert* in Heaven ..."

The twisted mass was not a universal constant, though witch-hunters later insisted on its inclusion in forced confessions.

Magic ceremonies at the sabbat were invariably followed by a feast, described by witches as including both abundant and delicious food, much of it stolen from surrounding farms. (Inquisitors, attempting to deemphasize the pleasures of the cult, ignored such testimony and described vile, noxious offerings.) Once everyone was fed, the witches danced around a bonfire to the music of fife, fiddle, and flute, stripping off their clothes and working themselves into a frenzy for the sabbat's predictable climax.

Rooted firmly in ancient fertility cults, the "new" witches apparently viewed public sex as a combination of homage to nature and titillating rejection of Christianity's moral constraints. The sabbat orgy began with female witches lining up to service Satan. He invariably chose the youngest, most attractive prospects first, and they described the coupling in ecstatic terms. (At least one cult, in France, supplied a female "devil" for the male practitioners.) As time went on and older, plainer witches took their turn, complaints arose of harsh and painful intercourse. Isobel Gowdie described Satan's penis as "great and long," its touch and spurt of semen "cold as ice," but he was "abler for them sexually than any man could be." Such reports were heard throughout Europe, and their evidence—coupled with common sense—suggest that Satan's stand-ins weren't above employing homemade dildos when their strength or interest failed. Once all the women present had been satisfied by Satan, more or less, the rank and file fell out for general debauchery in couples, threesomes, any combination they preferred. With heavy emphasis upon performance, aphrodisiacs and potions for endurance were a staple product of the early witch's cauldron, as today.

A major obstacle to the acceptance of a real-life witch cult by historians is found in numerous reports of witches flying to their sabbats, but a closer look explains the strange phenomenon without resort to magic. Witches who reported winging through the night invariably got their start with "flying potions" that included such ingredients as hemlock, belladonna, and ergot—a principal source of LSD, well known to early midwives as a muscle relaxant. When psychedelic mixtures are applied to naked skin—often massaged into genital tissue—the resultant descriptions of flight become comprehensible as hallucinations. A typical nightflyer, French witch

Antoine Rose, described how "Satan" once presented her with an eighteen-inch stick, smeared with ointment, probing her vagina with the shaft until she suddenly took wing. (In return for such favors, she not only swore obedience to Lucifer, but also paid him by the month, in cash.)

Another "fantastic" aspect of the witch cults, rejected by many scholars, is the consistent reference to child sacrifice and cannibalism. In 1438, a French cultist described the donation of his own infant daughter as a sacrifice to Lucifer, followed by a meal of human flesh, and similar reports were heard across the continent. In retrospect, such tales are no more unbelievable than identical cases, documented with convictions, from Los Angeles in 1970, Chicago in 1982, and Matamoros, Mexico, in 1989.

Despite cruel persecution, many witches were faithful to the death. Jeanne Dibasson, from Lorraine, described the cult's sabbat celebrations as "the true paradise, where there was more pleasure than it was possible to describe." A young French witch, on her way to the stake in the fifteenth century, told her executioners, "I will not be other than I am. I find too much content in my condition. I am always caressed." In England, witches Rebecca West and Rose Hollybread "died very stubborn and refractory, without any remorse or seeming terror of consequence for their abominable witchcraft." Two of their cohorts, Elinor Shaw and Mary Phillips, spent their last moments "calling to the devil to come and help them in such a blasphemous manner as is not fit to mention, and as they lived the devil's true factors, so they resolutely died in his service." [See: Black Mass; Wicca]

WORLOCK, CARL

On June 28, 1983, tenants of the Linden Grove Apartments in Jackson Township, New Jersey, were startled by a burst of gunfire, the sight of one young man pursued by another with a rifle, sprawling as bullets ripped into his flesh. Police arrived with sirens wailing, and they found two victims at the scene. Shawn Marchyshyn, eighteen, was dead on the lawn, while twenty-year-old Gaetano Abrahamson lay in a nearby apartment, staining the rug with his blood. Both men had died from gunshots to the lungs.

A search of the crime scene turned up several .22-caliber

shell casings from a semiautomatic rifle. It also revealed a curious photograph in Abrahamson's pocket, depicting a scrawny young man in a black leather mask and costume reminiscent of sadomasochistic bondage gear. Neither victim matched the photograph, and while the mask ruled out a positive ID, witnesses thought the snapshot bore a passing resemblance to the missing gunman.

Investigation of the victims traced their recent movements to a nearby beach resort, where they were remembered as traveling with a third young man. Police finally identified their shy companion as Carl Worlock, twenty-two, another resident of Jackson Township. Twice committed to the state hospital in recent years, Worlock was once diagnosed as psychotic, the second time as a schizophrenic. He was also a known drug abuser, Satanist, and self-styled "warlock," proud to bear a name that coincided with his faith.

Picked up for questioning, Worlock quickly confessed the murders and led police to the weapon, a live round still in its chamber. He had planned the shootings, Worlock told detectives, after his two "friends" stole a snapshot of him in his homemade "Satan costume," threatening to show the photograph around and publicly embarrass him. It was a point of pride for Worlock, resisting a challenge to his "masculinity." An insanity plea failed to impress the court, and Worlock was convicted of murder on October 19, 1984. Four months later, he was sentenced to life in prison, required to serve a minimum of sixty years before parole.

"WORSHIPPERS OF SATAN"

In February 1987, two members of this obscure Polish cult were indicted on charges of desecrating human remains and torturing an animal. Charges stemmed from an August 1, 1986, satanic mass attended by twenty celebrants at Jarocin, in southwestern Poland. According to police, the black mass followed a local rock music festival and was held in a Roman Catholic cemetery, with the two indicted Satanists serving as "masters of ceremony." The official Polish news agency, PAP, stated that "A casket removed from a tomb served the two as an altar during the ceremony." The ringleaders—left anonymous in media reports—also captured a stray dog, tortured it to death, and placed it in the casket as a part of their ritual celebrating Lammas Day. Little more was known about the cult, since it had failed to register with the Polish Ministry of Religion, as required by law.

"ZODIAC" KILLER—CALIFORNIA

California's most elusive serial killer claimed his first known victim on October 30, 1966, in Riverside. That evening, Cheri Jo Bates, an eighteen-year-old freshman at Riverside City College, emerged from the campus library to find her car disabled, the distributor coil disconnected. Police theorize that her killer approached with an offer of help, then dragged her behind some nearby shrubbery, where a furious struggle ended with Cheri stabbed in the chest and back, her throat slashed so deeply that she was nearly decapitated.

In November 1966, a letter to the local press declared that Cheri "is not the first and she will not be the last." Following publication of an article about the case, on April 30, 1967, identical letters were posted to the newspaper, police, and to the victim's father. They read: "Bates had to die. There will be more."

On December 20, 1968, seventeen-year-old David Faraday was parked with his date, sixteen-year-old Betty Lou Jensen, on a rural road east of the Vallejo city limits in northern California. A night-stalking gunman found them there and killed both teenagers, shooting Faraday in the head as he sat behind the wheel of his car. Betty Lou ran thirty feet before she was cut down by a tight group of five shots in the back, fired from a .22-caliber automatic pistol.

July 4, 1969. Michael Mageau, nineteen, picked up his date, twenty-two-year-old Darlene Ferrin, for a night on the town. At one point, Mageau believed they were being followed, but Darlene seemed to recognize the other motorist, telling Mageau, "Don't worry about it." By midnight, they were parked at Blue Rock Springs Park, when a familiar vehicle pulled alongside and the driver shined a bright light in their eyes, opening fire with a 9mm pistol. Hit four times, Mageau survived; Darlene, with nine wounds, was dead on arrival at a local hospital.

Forty minutes after the shooting, Vallejo police received an anonymous call, directing officers to the murder scene. Before hanging up, the male caller declared, "I also killed those kids last year."

In retrospect, friends and relatives recalled that Darlene Ferrin had been suffering harassment through anonymous phone calls and intimidating visits by a heavyset stranger in the weeks before her death. She called the strange man "Paul," and told one girlfriend that he wished to silence her because she had seen him commit a murder. Police searched for "Paul" in the wake of Darlene's slaying, but he was never located or identified.

On July 31, 1969, the killer mailed letters to three Bay Area newspapers, each containing one-third of a cryptic cipher. Ultimately broken by a local high school teacher, the message began: "I like killing people because it is so much fun." The author explained that he was killing in an effort to "collect slaves," who would serve him in the afterlife. Another correspondence, mailed on August 7, introduced the "Zodiac" trade name and provided details of the latest murder, leaving police in no doubt that its author was the killer.

On September 27, twenty-year-old Bryan Hartnell and Cecilia Shepherd, twenty-two, were enjoying a picnic at Lake Berryessa, near Vallejo, when they were accosted by a hooded gunman. Covering them with a pistol, the stranger described himself as an escaped convict who needed their car "to go to Mexico." Producing a coil of clothesline, he bound both victims before drawing a long knife, stabbing Hartnell five times in the back. Cecilia Shepherd was stabbed fourteen times, including four in the chest as she twisted away from the plunging blade.

Departing the scene, their assailant paused at Hartnell's car to scribble on the door with a felt-tipped pen. He wrote:

> Vallejo
> 12–20–68
> 7–4–69
> Sept 27–69–6:30
> by knife

A phone call to police reported the crime, but by that time a fisherman had already discovered the victims. Brian Hartnell would survive his wounds, but Cecilia Shepherd was doomed, another victim for the man who called himself the Zodiac.

On October 11, San Francisco cab driver Paul Stine was shot in the head and killed with a 9mm automatic pistol. Witnesses saw the gunman escape on foot, toward the Presidio, and police descended on the neighborhood in force. At one point in the search, two patrolmen stopped a heavyset pedestrian and were directed in pursuit of their elusive prey, not realizing that the "tip" had been provided by the man they sought.

In the wake of Stine's murder, the Zodiac launched a new barrage of letters, some containing swatches of the cabbie's bloodstained shirt. Successive messages claimed seven victims, instead of the established five, as the killer threatened to "wipe out a school bus some morning." He also vowed to change his method of "collecting souls": "They shall look like routine robberies, killings of anger, & a few fake suicides, etc." Five days before Christmas, he wrote to prominent attorney Melvin Belli, pleading for help, with the chilling remark that "I cannot remain in control for much longer."

On March 22, 1970, Kathleen Johns was driving with her infant daughter, near Modesto, California, when another motorist pulled her over, flashing his headlights and beeping his horn. The man informed her that a rear tire on her car seemed dangerously loose; he worked on it briefly, with a lug wrench, but when she tried to drive away, the wheel fell off. Her benefactor offered a lift to the nearest garage, then took Kathleen on an aimless drive through the countryside, threatening her life and that of her child before she managed to escape from the car, hiding in a roadside ditch. Reporting the abduction at a local police station, Johns noticed a wanted poster bearing sketches of the Zodiac, and she identified the man as her attacker.

Nine more letters were received from Zodiac between April 1970 and March 1971, but police were unable to trace further crimes in the series. On January 30, 1974, a San Francisco newspaper received the first authentic Zodiac letter in nearly three years, signing off with the notation: "Me–37; SFPD–0."

One officer who took the estimated body count seriously was Sheriff Don Striepke, of Sonoma County. In a 1975 report, Striepke referred to a series of forty unsolved murders in four western states, which seemed to form a giant "Z" when plotted on the map. While tantalizing, Striepke's theory seemed to fall apart with the identification of serial killer Theodore Bundy as a prime suspect in several of the homicides.

On April 24, 1978, the Zodiac mailed his twenty-first letter, chilling Bay Area residents with the news that "I am back with you." No traceable crimes were committed, however, and Homicide Inspector Dave Toschi was later removed from the Zodiac detail on suspicion of writing the letter himself. In fact, while Toschi confessed writing several anonymous letters to the press, praising his own performance in the case, expert analysts agree that the April note was written by the killer.

Theories abound in the Zodiac case. One was aired by author "George Oakes" (a pseudonym) in the November 1981 issue of *California* magazine, based on a presumption of the killer's obsession with water, clocks, binary mathematics, and the writings of Lewis Carroll. Oakes claims to know the Zodiac's identity and says the killer phoned him several times at home. He blames the Zodiac for an arson fire that ravaged twenty-five thousand acres near Lake Berryessa in June 1981, but *California* editors confessed that FBI agents "weren't very impressed" with the theory. Spokesmen for the California State Attorney General's office went further, describing the tale as "a lot of bull."

Author Robert Graysmith also claims to know the Zodiac by name, calling his suspect "Robert Hall Starr" in a book published in 1986. A resident of Vallejo, "Starr" is described as a gun buff and suspected child molester, confirmed as a prime Zodiac suspect by several detectives (and flatly rejected by others). Graysmith credits Zodiac with a total of forty-nine "possible" victims between October 1966 and May 1981, three of whom survived his attacks. In addition to the six known dead and three confirmed survivors, Graysmith includes fifteen "occult" murders linked to one unidentified slayer in northern California, and fifteen other victims killed in close proximity to a solstice or equinox—nine confirmed by police as the work of a single, unidentified man. Of forty "possible" victims, thirty-nine were female, variously shot, stabbed, beaten, strangled, drowned, and poisoned ... perhaps in accordance with Zodiac's promise to alter his method of "collecting slaves." [See: "Zodiac" Killer—New York]

"ZODIAC" KILLER—NEW YORK

On June 6, 1990, identical handwritten letters were mailed in New York City to the *New York Post* and the production office of the CBS news program "60 Minutes." The letters read:

This is the *Zodiac* the twelve sign
will die when the belts in the heaven
are seen

the *first sign* is dead on march 8 1990 1:45 AM
white man with cane shoot on the back in the street

the *second sign* is dead on march 29 1990 2:57 AM
white man with black coat shoot in the side in front of house

the *third sign* is dead on May 31 1990 2:04 AM·
white old man with can shoot   *Faust*
in front of house

no more games pigs

all shoot in *Brooklyn* with .380 RNL or 9mm
no grooves on bullet

In addition to the chilling message, each letter was decorated with two cryptic symbols. One was a circle with three pie-shaped wedges, each marked with the astrological signs for Gemini, Taurus, and Scorpio. The other was a cross and circle, variously interpreted as an ancient Celtic cross or the cross hairs of a telescopic gunsight. Police "studied" the letters for two weeks before going public with the announcement that their correspondent—"Zodiac" or "Faust"—was wanted in connection with three unsolved shootings from the dates in question. There were certain obvious discrepancies, including the fact that one victim had been shot in Queens and all three were still alive, but the description of events was otherwise strikingly accurate. Even the ballistics reference to caliber and "RNL"—for round-nosed lead projectiles—was precise. A similar note, including mention of the "Zodiac" and "belts of heaven" had been found beside the third victim, with a positive handwriting match completing the chain of evidence.

Target number one was forty-nine-year-old Mario Orozco, shot in the back near the intersection of Atlantic and Sheridan Avenues. Orozco told police that his assailant, wearing a brown ski mask and gloves, had crossed the street to intercept him, pressed a gun against his back, and fired one shot, then stood above his prostrate body for a moment or two, aiming the pistol at his victim's face before he fled the scene. Number two, thirty-three-year-old Jermaine Montenesdro, was staggering home from a late party in the Bronx when he was gunned down near a subway station, six blocks from the scene of the first attack. Shot in the back and seriously wounded, Montenesdro never got a look at his attacker. The third victim, seventy-eight-year-old Joseph Proce, was standing on 87th Road in Woodhaven, Queens, when a bearded black man approached him and asked for a dollar. Proce refused and was moving away when a shot from behind knocked him sprawling.

Initially, the gunman's pattern seemed to consist of close-range attacks on "elderly" white males (two walking with canes, while Montenesdro's boozy stagger indicated physical infirmity). The shocker came when a review of background information on the victims showed that each was born within the astrological sign noted by their attacker—Gemini, Taurus, and Scorpio, respectively. None of the wounded men had recognized his assailant, but the gunman obviously knew them well enough to pick his targets by their birth signs.

In short, the attacks were not random, but planned in advance.

While the gunman signed his letters "Faust"—a character from German literature who sold his soul to Satan—the "Zodiac" reference prompted speculation on a possible link with California's unidentified serial stalker from the 1960s. NYPD's new "Zodiac" task force requisitioned dusty files from San Francisco, poring over twenty-year-old leads in hopes of finding something, anything, to help them crack the case. Newsmen were quick to jump on the "Zodiac" bandwagon, noting "similarities" between the New York letters and some of the earlier California correspondence. Aside from the opening lines—"This is the Zodiac"—reporters noted duplication of the original "Zodiac's" cross hairs symbol, "similar" handwriting patterns, detailed ballistic descriptions, and reference to the police as "pigs." On the downside, the original "Zodiac's" letters had been widely published since 1969, and the California killer was known to be a white man. Barring some unknown personal relationship, New York's case seemed to be the work of a demented copycat.

Detectives noted that the gunman's three attacks had taken place at twenty-one- and sixty-three-day intervals, suggesting variations on a compulsive three-week cycle. Manhunters were ready on June 21, first day of the astrological month for Cancer, but the gunman outsmarted them, shifting his target zone miles away to Central Park. This time the victim was a homeless black man sleeping in the park. He would survive his wound, and police were mystified by the fact that his birth sign—Cancer—matched the note that his assailant left behind to mark the crime scene.

On June 22, angered by public debate over his link to the original "Zodiac" killer, New York's gunman sent another letter to the *Post*. Marked with the satanic number "666," it read in part, "The is the *Zodiac* I have seen the Post and you say the note sent to the Post not similar to any of the San Francisco Zodiac letters you are wrong the hand writing look different it is one of the same *Zodiac one Zodiac.*"

The charge became murder on June 24, when Joseph Proce finally died from his wound. Police continued their alerts at three-week intervals through August, but there were no more shootings, no more notes from the elusive gunman. In mid-July, members of the Zodiac task force announced that they were correlating passages from the killer's last letter with Aleister Crowley's *Book of the Law,* including a statement that "Nature's way is to weed out the weak." It was a tantalizing lead, but ultimately it proved fruitless and the task force was disbanded in October 1990. At this writing the case remains unsolved, the gunman still at large. [See: "Zodiac" Killer—California]

ZOMBIES

Best known to American moviegoers as rotting, reanimated corpses, slow on their feet and hungry for human flesh, zombies occupy a rather different place in their native Haitian culture. To the worshipers of voodoo, any person may be subject to a curse which kills and then allows the victim's enemy to resurrect his prey, the undead zombie forced to work forever as a mindless slave. Of course, enlightened men and women understand that no such creatures actually exist ... or do they?

Consider the case of forty-year-old Clairvius Narcisse, pronounced dead by physicians at Haiti's Albert Schweitzer Hospital on May 2, 1962, and buried the following day. Eighteen years later, a man claiming to be Clairvius Narcisse appeared in Narcisse's native village, introducing himself to the dead man's sister with a familiar childhood nickname. The man correctly answered intimate family questions, and experts from Scotland Yard finally confirmed his identity by matching fingerprints with those on Narcisse's death certificate. According to Narcisse's tale, his wicked brother hired a voodoo priest to curse him back in 1962, as part of a dispute involving real estate. Unearthed hours after his burial, he was taken to a plantation in northern Haiti, where he spent the next two years performing slave labor with other zombies. The "undead" farmhands finally rebelled and killed their master, but Narcisse spent another sixteen years in hiding, afraid for his life, returning only when he learned of his brother's death in 1980. The physicians who had pronounced Narcisse dead in 1962—including one American—had no explanation for his "resurrection."

A land dispute also led to the death of sixty-year-old Natagette Joseph in 1966. Thirteen years later, she was found walking near her village by the same man who pronounced her dead and supervised her burial. While no physicians were involved in this case, all concerned agreed that Natagette seemed reasonably dead when she was buried back in 1966.

In February, 1968, a Mexican gunboat commanded by Captain Domingo Coseguena was patrolling the Yucatan Channel when lookouts spotted a suspicious-looking cabin cruiser, *Le Roukur,* registered in Port-au-Prince, Haiti. The boat was stopped on suspicion of carrying contraband, and its solitary crewman identified himself as Emanuel Dessilies, stating that he was on his way to sell the boat at Key West. Searchers who opened the cabin below decks were met by "a terrible stench like decaying bodies." Inside, they found sixteen men squatting in cramped, filthy quarters, each with a blank expression on his face. None would respond to verbal questions, and the boat was escorted to Vera Cruz, where Dessilies abruptly changed his story. Instead of selling the cruiser in Flor-

ida, he planned to sell his zombie passengers to Haitian
exiles, all part of a bizarre plan to overthrown "Papa Doc"
Duvalier's regime with undead troops. Mexican doctors confirmed that the sixteen men were in "a deep catatonic trance
which could either have been induced by hypnosis or drugs
indigenous to Haiti," but breaking the trance was beyond
their power. Duvalier's government was duly notified, with
the boat and its occupants returned to Haitian custody. Two
weeks later, American news reports noted an FBI raid on a
Haitian exile compound in the Everglades . . . but no mention
was made of zombies or voodoo.

Back in Haiti, thirty-year-old Francina Illeus was pronounced dead on February 23, 1976, several days after her release from a hospital where she was treated for digestive
problems. A local magistrate verified her death and she was
duly buried. Three years later, in April 1979, the "dead"
woman was found at Ennery, mute and malnourished, wandering around the village marketplace. Her mother confirmed
identification from a childhood scar, and when the woman's
grave was opened, only rocks were found inside her casket.
Family members blamed Francina's jealous husband for the
curse that placed her in the undead zombie state.

Indeed, Haitian legislators take the zombie problem seriously enough that such curses may be legally punished under
Article 249 of the Federal Criminal Code. The relevant passage reads: "Also shall be qualified as attempted murder
under the employment which may be made against any person of a substance which, without causing death, produce a
lethargic coma more or less prolonged. If, after the adminis-
tering of such substances, the person has been buried, the act
shall be considered murder no matter what result follows."
The law's closing phrase is a clear reference to the standard
voodoo practice of resurrecting zombies as slaves, while allusions to chemical substances strike at the heart of the long-
running mystery.

In 1982, Harvard botany student Wade Davis launched a
three-year series of expeditions to Haiti, tracing the zombie
legend back to its native roots. He emerged from the investigation with malaria, hepatitis, and enough material for two
nonfiction books which document the fact that zombies can,
in fact, be made to order by proficient voodoo priests. The
"curse" involves application of various "zombie poisons," all
of which contain human remains, elements designed to irri-

tate the skin, and ingredients from various toxic plants or animals. Davis personally observed voodoo grave-robbing forays, in which bits of viscera and bone shavings were obtained for addition to the "magic" formula. Toxins were obtained primarily from poisonous fish and plants of the genus *Datura*, known for their narcotic properties. Abrasive ingredients, ranging from ground glass to caustic plant resins, permit the "zombie poison" to enter a victim's body through simple contact with the skin, as when walking barefoot over treated soil.

As described by victims of the "zombie poison," such concoctions apparently simulate symptoms of death without inducing unconsciousness. Thus, the chosen zombie is aware of having "died" and been buried. Traditional faith in voodoo provides the only explanation necessary when victims are later unearthed and revived with chemical antidotes—sometimes including drugs to promote amnesia or reduce physical resistance. Even so, as in the case of Clairvius Narcisse, zombies are not always safe for their masters and handlers. Like Frankenstein's monster, some apparently turn on their keepers, exacting a lethal revenge. [See: Voodoo]

Glossary

Adept/Adeptus—Skilled practitioner of magic, ready for formal initiation to a coven.

All Hallows' Eve—Occult holiday falling on October 31, also known as Halloween or Samhain, that marked the beginning of a new Celtic year. In Catholicism, November 1 is labeled All Saints' Day.

Amulet—Passive, protective charm worn on the person.

Ankh—Egyptian hieroglyphic sign for life.

Athame—Ceremonial dagger, one of the nine tools of magic.

Axogum—Macumba initiate in charge of animal sacrifices.

Babalao—Priest of macumba and variant Brazilian voodoo cults.

Babalorixa—Macumba priestess.

Baculum—Wand, staff.

Balefire—Ritual coven fire.

Baphomet—See entry in main text.

Baron Samedi—Voodoo lord and guardian of cemeteries.

Batuque—Name for macumba in Brazilian state of Rio Grande do Sul.

Bell—Rung at various points during occult ceremonies, one of the nine tools of magic.

Beltane—Occult festival celebrated on May 1, also called May Day or Walpurgis Day. Designated as a time for planting crops, Beltane was celebrated by various ancient cults with fertility rites and/or human sacrifice. In Catholic ritual, May 1 is designated Apostles' Day.

Beltine—Wiccan sabbat held on the first full moon closest to May 1.

Bizango—Voodoo secret society in Haiti, worshipers of Baron Samedi.

"Blessed Be"—Phrase used by witches as a greeting and farewell.

Bokor—Professional black magician in voodoo.

Book of Shadows—Occult diary of an individual or coven, recording "recipes" for spells and notations of rituals performed; one of the nine tools of magic.

Botanica—Store selling herbs, ingredients, and paraphernalia for *santeros*.

Candlemas—Occult festival held on February 2, also called Ormelc. Celebrating spring's arrival, in Catholicism this holiday is called the Festival of the Blessed Virgin Mary.

Candles of Illumination—Two tall candles used to light the altar, considered together as one of the nine tools of magic.

Candomble—Afro-Brazilian cult similar to voodoo, native to the state of Bahia.

Canzo—Ordeal by fire in voodoo initiation rites.

Catimbo—Name for the umbanda cult used in northeast Brazil.

Censer—Incense burner, one of the nine tools of magic.

Cephalomancy—Divination using the head or skull.

Chalice—Cup used in ritual ceremonies, one of the nine tools of magic.

Cingulum—Cord worn by some witches as a belt for ceremonial garb.

Coven—Group of occult practitioners. Any number may belong, but thirteen is a number widely preferred.

Covendom—A coven's theoretical sphere of influence, thought by believers to cover a three-mile radius.

Covenstead—Location where a coven meets.

Culto de Nacao—"Cult of the Nations." Afro-Brazilian cult in the state of Rio Grande do Sul.

Demon—Evil spirit, less powerful than Satan but generally considered his ally.

Despacho—Macumba offering, usually an animal sacrifice.

Enochian—Occult "language" named for an Old Testament character (Enoch), first published in 1629, later used in rituals by the Order of the Golden Dawn, the Church of Satan, and other cults.

Eshbat (or Esbat)—Monthly coven meetings, timed to coincide with the full moon.

Fire-Candle—Fat, red, slow-burning candle; one of the nine tools of magic.

Flamen—Male leader of a wicca coven.

Flamenca—Female leader of a wicca coven.

Frater—Literally "brother," a common rank for male members of the Ordo Templi Orientis.

Grimoire—Occult "cookbook," containing spells and rituals.

Halloween—See All Hallows' Eve.

Hand of Glory—See entry in main text.

Hoodoo—Variant form of voodoo, commonly used in the southern United States.

Hounfor—Voodoo temple.

Houngan—Voodoo priest.

Hunsi—Voodoo initiate who helps the houngan during ceremonies.

Imbolc—Wiccan sabbat held on the full moon closest to February 1.

Initiate—New member of a coven.

Lammas—Occult festival on August 1, beginning the harvest season.

Lithomancy—Magic using stones and semiprecious gems in various rituals, depending on their color.

Loas—Voodoo deities.

Lugnasad—Wiccan sabbat held on the full moon closest to August 1.

Macumba—Variant form of voodoo practiced in Brazil.

Macumbeiro—Follower of macumba.

Magic Circle—Drawn by practitioners to exclude or contain evil forces. Sizes vary, but "proper" circles usually measure nine feet in diameter.

"Magick"—See main entry in text.

Magister—Male leader of a coven.

Mambo—Voodoo priestess.

Midsummer's Eve—An occult holiday, also called St. John's Eve, celebrated on June 23.

Necromancy—Means of conjuring power from dead spirits, often by ritual use of bones, ash, or other human remains.

New Year's Day—Druid feast day celebrated by covens on January 1.

Nganga—Cauldron of blood (and other ingredients) used in rituals of palo mayombe.

Obeah—Traditional religion of Jamaica, similar to voodoo in its operation and West African roots.

Orishas—Gods of ju-ju, voodoo, santeria, and affiliated religions, syncretized with Catholic saints in the New World. Individual names and sacrificial requirements vary from one cult to another.

Pagan—Worshiper of pre-Christian nature deities.

Pajelanca—Afro-Brazilian cult native to the Amazon basin.

Pentacle—Flat plate inscribed with a five-pointed star and sprinkled with salt during ceremonies; one of the nine tools of magic. May also refer to the star itself, contained within a circle.

Pentagram—Five-pointed star, sometimes inscribed within magic circles. "Upright" pentagrams are understood to denote "white" magic, while inverted stars—with one point downward—signify black magic or Satanism.

Periapt—Amulet in the form of a pendant.

Quimbanda—Black magic in macumba and related cults.

Quimbandeira—Priestess of quimbanda.

Sabbat—"Great eshbats," held quarterly by witchcraft practitioners.

St. Agnes' Eve—Occult holiday celebrated on January 20.

St. Bartholomew's Day—Sabbat celebrated on August 24.

St. James's Day—Occult holiday celebrated on July 25.

St. John's Eve—See Midsummer's Eve.

St. Mark's Eve—Occult holiday celebrated on April 24.

St. Thomas's Day—Sabbat celebrated on December 21.

Samain—Wiccan sabbat held on the full moon closest to November 1.

Samhain—See All Hallows' Eve.

Shaman—Witch or medicine man in the American Indian and some other religions.

Shrovetide—Sabbat falling three days before Ash Wednesday.

Skyclad—Nude. The preferred mode of dress for many occult rituals.

"So Mote It Be"—Phrase used by witches at the end of a ceremony or conjuration, similar to use of "amen" at the end of Christian prayers.

Tabard—Ceremonial robe worn by witches.

Talisman—Occult power object, considered active rather than passive (as with amulets).

Umbanda—Alternate name for macumba, particularly used in Rio de Janeiro.

Vernal Equinox—Occult holiday falling on March 21, when day and night are the same length.

Walpurgisnacht—Sabbat celebrated on April 30.

Wand—One of the nine tools of magic.

Wanga—Evil voodoo charm.

Warlock—Misnomer for a male practitioner of witchcraft, used by those who fail to recognize that "witch" is the proper term for both sexes.

Witch—One who practices magic.

Working—A magic ritual.

Yule—Occult holiday falling on December 21, celebrating the winter solstice (shortest day of the year).

Zobop—Member of a secret society of voodoo sorcerers.

Bibliography

Adler, Margot. *DRAWING DOWN THE MOON*. New York: Viking, 1979.

Albers, Michael. *THE TERROR*. New York: Manor Books, 1979.

Aquino, Michael. *THE CRYSTAL TABLET OF SET*. San Francisco: Temple of Set, 1986.

Bainbridge, William. *SATAN'S POWER*. Berkeley, CA: University of California Press, 1978.

Bugliosi, Vincent, and Curt Gentry. *HELTER SKELTER*. New York: W.W. Norton, 1974.

Cavendish, Richard. *THE BLACK ARTS*. New York: Capricorn, 1968.

Crewdson, John. *BY SILENCE BETRAYED*. Boston: Little, Brown, 1988.

Davis, Wade. *PASSAGE OF DARKNESS*. Chapel Hill, NC: University of North Carolina Press, 1988.

———. *THE SERPENT AND THE RAINBOW*. New York: Simon & Schuster, 1985.

Ebon, Martin. *THE SATAN TRAP*. New York: Doubleday, 1976.

———. *THE WORLD'S WEIRDEST CULTS*. New York: New American Library, 1979.

Eddy, Paul. *THE COCAINE WARS*. New York: Bantam, 1988.

Finkelhor, David, and Linda Williams. *NURSERY CRIMES*. Newbury Park, CA: Sage Publications, 1988.

Freedland, Nat. *THE OCCULT EXPLOSION*. New York: G.P. Putnam's Sons, 1972.

Frost, Gavin and Yvonne. *THE WITCH'S BIBLE*. New York: Berkley, 1972.

Garvin, Richard, and Robert Burger. *THE WORLD OF THE TWILIGHT BELIEVERS*. Los Angeles: Sherbourne Press, 1970.

Godwin, John. *OCCULT AMERICA*. New York: Doubleday, 1972.

Grammary, Ann. *THE WITCH'S WORKBOOK*. New York: Pocket Books, 1973.

Haining, Peter (ed). *THE SATANISTS*. New York: Taplinger, 1969.

Hall, Angus. *STRANGE CULTS*. New York: Doubleday, 1976.

Hill, Douglas, and Pat Williams. *THE SUPERNATURAL*. New York: Hawthorn, 1965.

Hogg, Gary. *CANNIBALISM AND HUMAN SACRIFICE*. Secaucus, NJ: Citadel, 1966.

Hollingsworth, Jan. *UNSPEAKABLE ACTS*. New York: Congdon & Weed, 1986.

Holzer, Hans. *THE NEW PAGANS*. New York: Doubleday, 1972.

Humes, Edward. *BURIED SECRETS*. New York: Dutton, 1991.

Kagan, Daniel, and Ian Summers. *MUTE EVIDENCE*. New York: Bantam, 1984.

Kahaner, Larry. *CULTS THAT KILL*. New York: Warner Books, 1988.

King, Francis. *SATAN AND SWASTIKA*. Frogmore, England: Mayflower, 1976.

———. *SEXUALITY, MAGIC AND PERVERSION*. Secaucus, NJ: Citadel, 1972.

Larsen, Egon. *STRANGE SECTS AND CULTS*. New York: Hart Publishing Co., 1971.

LaVey, Anton. *THE COMPLEAT WITCH*. New York: Dodd, Mead, 1971.

———. *THE SATANIC BIBLE*. New York: Avon, 1969.

———. *THE SATANIC RITUALS*. New York: Avon, 1972.

Linedecker, Clifford. *CHILDREN IN CHAINS*. New York: Everest House, 1981.

————. *HELL RANCH*. Austin, TX: Diamond Books, 1989.

————. *NIGHT STALKER*. New York: St. Martin's, 1991.

Logan, Daniel. *AMERICA BEWITCHED*. New York: Morrow, 1974.

Lyons, Arthur. *SATAN WANTS YOU*. New York: Mysterious Press, 1988.

————. *THE SECOND COMING*. New York: Dodd, Mead, 1970.

Mandelsberg, Rose (ed). *CULT KILLERS*. New York: Zebra, 1991.

————. *TORTURE KILLERS*. New York: Zebra, 1991.

Manshel, Lisa. *NAP TIME*. New York: William Morrow, 1990.

Masters, Anthony. *THE DEVIL'S DOMINION*. New York: G.P. Putnam's Sons, 1978.

Mayer, Robert. *SATAN'S CHILDREN*. New York: G.P. Putnam's Sons, 1991.

Melton, J. Gordon. *THE ENCYCLOPEDIA OF AMERICAN RELIGIONS*. New York: McGrath, 1989.

————. *THE ENCYCLOPEDIC HANDBOOK OF CULTS*. New York: Garland, 1986.

Metraux, Alfred. *VOODOO IN HAITI*. New York: Schocken Books, 1972.

Newton, Michael. *HUNTING HUMANS*. Port Townsend, WA: Loompanics, 1990.

————. *MASS MURDER*. New York: Garland, 1988.

————, and Judy Newton. *THE KU KLUX KLAN*. New York: Garland, 1991.

Oke, Isaiah. *BLOOD SECRETS*. Buffalo, NY: Prometheus Books, 1989.

Provost, Gary. *ACROSS THE BORDER*. New York: Pocket Books, 1989.

Rachleff, Owen. *THE OCCULT CONCEIT*. New York: Bell Publishing Co., 1971.

Raschke, Carl. *PAINTED BLACK*. New York: Bell Publishing Co., 1971.

Reynolds, Richard. *CRY FOR WAR*. San Francisco: Squibob Press, 1987.

Roberts, Susan. *THE MAGICIAN OF THE GOLDEN DAWN*. Chicago: Contemporary Books, 1978.

St. Clair, David. *THE PSYCHIC WORLD OF CALIFORNIA*. New York: Doubleday, 1972.

————. *SAY YOU LOVE SATAN*. New York: Dell, 1987.

Sanders, Ed. *THE FAMILY*. New York: Signet, 1989.

Scammel, Henry. *MORTAL REMAINS*. New York: Edward Burlingame Books, 1991.

Schumacher, Emile. *WITCHCRAFT IN AMERICA TODAY*. New York: Paperback Library, 1970.

Schutze, Jim. *CAULDRON OF BLOOD*. New York: Avon, 1989.

Sheed, F.J. (ed.) *SOUNDINGS IN SATANISM*. New York: Sheed & Ward, 1972.

"Simon." *THE NECRONOMICON*. New York: Avon, 1977.

Smith, Michelle, and Lawrence Pazder. *MICHELLE REMEMBERS*. New York: Pocket Books, 1981.

Somerlott, Robert. *"HERE MR. SPLITFOOT."* New York: Viking, 1971.

Sparks, Beatrice. *JAY'S JOURNAL*. New York: Times Books, 1979.

Symonds, John. *THE GREAT BEAST*. New York: Rider & Co., 1951.

Terry, Maury. *THE ULTIMATE EVIL*. New York: Doubleday, 1987.

Tierney, Patrick. *THE HIGHEST ALTAR*. New York: Viking, 1989.

Valiente, Doreen. *AN ABC OF WITCHCRAFT PAST AND PRESENT*. New York: St. Martin's, 1973.

Warnke, Mike. *THE SATAN-SELLER*. Plainfield, NJ: Logos, 1972.

Wilson, Colin, and Robin Odell. *JACK THE RIPPER: SUMMING UP THE VERDICT*. Longon: Corgi, 1987.

Wolfe, Burton. *THE DEVIL'S AVENGER*. New York: Pyramid, 1974.

Index